CHARLES DARWIN: A COMPANION

Charles Darwin aged 59. Reproduction of a photograph by Julia Margaret Cameron, original 13 × 10 inches, taken at Dumbola Lodge, Freshwater, Isle of Wight in July 1869. The original print is signed and authenticated by Mrs Cameron and also signed by Darwin. It bears Colnaghi's blind embossed registration.

CHARLES DARWIN

A Companion

by

R. B. FREEMAN

Department of Zoology
University College London

DAWSON
ARCHON

First published in 1978

Wm Dawson & Sons Ltd, Cannon House

Folkestone, Kent, England

Archon Books, The Shoe String Press, Inc
995 Sherman Avenue, Hamden, Connecticut 06514 USA

British Library Cataloguing in Publication Data

Freeman, Richard Broke .
　Charles Darwin.
　1. Darwin, Charles – Dictionaries, indexes, etc.
　575'. 0092'4　　　QH31. D2
　ISBN 0–7129–0901–X
　Archon ISBN 0–208–01739–9
　LC 78–40928

Filmset in 11/12 pt Bembo
Printed and bound in Great Britain
by W & J Mackay Limited, Chatham

CONTENTS

LIST OF ILLUSTRATIONS

INTRODUCTION

THIS Companion is about Charles Darwin the man: it is not about evolution by natural selection, nor is it about any other of his theoretical or experimental work. A glance will show what it contains, and only a brief introduction is needed. It is intended to make easily available the facts of Darwin's life, his ancestry, collaterals and descendants, his friends and a few enemies, and his scientific correspondents. It covers what he wrote, and where he went, when and why. It also includes some more personal things, such as his appearance, including details of pictures of him, his day to day habits, and a little of his political and social views.

Darwin's name occurs in every relevant work of reference from about the time of his election to the Royal Society in 1839 until his death, and in superabundance from then onwards. In the British Museum's *General catalogue of printed books*, (1959–1966), the appendix of titles relative to Darwin contains more than 400 entries, whilst that for Galileo has about 150 and that for Newton less than 130. This excess is exacerbated because his name also occurs in every work on evolution and in every student textbook of biology as well as in many works about the religious and social implications of evolutionary theory. It is however ameliorated because the number of works which contain facts about him is small. Basically, there are seven volumes, three of *Life and letters*, and two each of *More letters* and *Emma Darwin*. To these may be added a handful of later books and papers which contain many new facts, and a larger number, mostly biographies of other people and works containing previously unpublished letters, which contain some information.

The basic three works were all edited by two of his children and published within the lifetimes of many people who knew him. Biographies by children of their subject have the advantage that the facts are probably right, but the disadvantage that the children are too close to see what will be of interest to later readers. *Life and letters* also has the disadvantage of being published within five years of Darwin's death, so that parts which might have been libellous or caused offence to the living had to be omitted. His autobiography, which is first printed there, has omissions for his widow's sake and its full text did not become available until seventy years later.

All the entries here are degressive. There are two reasons for this. Firstly, the further the subject is from Darwin himself, the less need there is for a comprehensive entry. Gladstone, Tennyson and Ruskin met Darwin, and all could have had long entries, but their contact was slight and their entries are therefore brief; his butler, Parslow, and his secretary-servant, Covington, deserve and get longer entries. Similarly, Paris, Dublin and Belfast, each of which he visited once, briefly, get little notice, but Tierra del Fuego, the Galápagos Islands and Glen Roy were much more important to him. The second reason for degression is ignorance. I have used a large number of reference sources and have sought the help of many friends, but there remains information which I would like to have entered which has escaped me. Much of this is about people that Darwin saw almost every day of his life, sometimes for years, such as the domestic staff at Down House, but if Francis Darwin or his sister merely mention Mary or Maryann, it is impossible to go further. There are also a number of villagers in Downe who are in a similar position. Amongst relatives, there are some, particularly women, whose dates of birth are available because these are given in the pedigrees made by people who knew them, but apparently they never die, because they did nothing to rate an entry in standard works of reference. The scientists are usually easy, although there are a few, such as 'old Jones' on page 177, who elude me. The two other main groups of entries, places and Darwin's works, present no difficulties.

About forty per cent of the entries are about people. These I have tried to keep uniform and I have used two conventions: women will be found under their maiden sur-names, when these are known to me; even Emma Darwin will be found under Wedgwood: titles, whether of honour or plain *Mr*, *Mrs* or *Miss*, are always given in italic. A full entry for a person starts with forenames followed by dates of birth and death, occupation in general, titles of honour and membership of important learned societies, marriage, children, blood relationship to Darwin if any. This is followed by a brief note of the post or posts which they held, and relevant dated quotations to show Darwin's connection with the subject of the entry. Finally, I have mentioned their more important published works, particularly those which relate to Darwin, and have listed a few biographies for the more important people, although in most cases I have made a reference to the *Dictionary of national biography* or *Who was who* suffice. Many of the entries for people are, intentionally, not nearly as full as this.

Darwin's books have been entered under short titles and all editions are listed, although mere reprints are ignored; first editions printed in America and in foreign languages are also listed. Foreign language editions are also entered under the language, so that a complete list is available of those of his works which have been translated into any given language; there is a similar list for English Braille. Almost all his books have appeared in facsimile in recent years and the dates of these are entered. Papers published in periodicals are entered by short title; these are widely scattered and some were not easily accessible until the most useful publication of a complete set by Paul H. Barrett in 1977; the page numbers of Barrett's reprints are given in each case. Much of the material which was left in manuscript by Darwin has also been published; most of it was never intended for publication, being notebooks or rough drafts. The titles of these have been consolidated under the heading 'Darwin, Charles Robert, Manuscripts', but their editors have been entered in the main list.

This work is a compilation, with almost nothing in it that has not appeared in print before. I have tried to stick to facts, although matters of opinion have crept in here and there. Darwin himself, in a letter to Huxley in 1859, said 'The inaccuracy of the blessed band (of which I am one) of compilers passes all bounds, The difficulty is to know what to trust.' I know that there are many omissions here and I am sure that there are errors, but hope that most of the facts are correct.

ACKNOWLEDGEMENTS

MY indebtedness to works of reference is large. Many of these are listed below, under Abbreviations, but others are, as usual, taken for granted. I give my thanks to the editors and compilers of hundreds of such works. More personally, I should like to thank the three great Cambridge darwinians, Nora *Lady* Barlow, *Dr* Sydney Smith and P. J. Gautrey: all three have answered my questions over the years with unfailing patience, as they have those of so many others. Peter Gautrey, sitting as he does on the Darwin archive in the University Library, has had to bear the brunt. I am indebted to many Librarians in National and University libraries, but especially to Joseph Scott, Librarian of University College London, whose library has been my daily haunt. The excellence of his reference rooms and the learning of his staff has saved me much journeying and letter writing. I would like to thank three of his staff by name: Joan Nash, who has looked after the Biological Sciences Library for many years; Susan Gove, in charge of the Thane Medical Library, who enjoys chasing obscure physicians and surgeons; and John Spiers, in charge of information, who regards chasing people as light relief from on-line reference retrieval.

R. B. Freeman

ABBREVIATIONS

Allan   Mea Allan, *Darwin and his flowers: the key to natural selection*, London, Faber and Faber, 1977.

Ashworth   J. H. Ashworth, Charles Darwin as a student in Edinburgh, 1825–1827: (An address delivered on October 28, 1935), *Proc.Roy.Soc.Edinb.*, 55:97–113, 1935

Atkins   *Sir* Hedley Atkins, *Down, the home of the Darwins: the story of a house and the people who lived there*, London, Phillimore for the Royal College of Surgeons of England, 1974; revised edition 1976 used.

B   Paul E. Barrett, editor, *The collected papers of Charles Darwin*, 2 vols, Chicago, University Press, 1977. Barrett volume and page numbers are given for all Darwin's papers published in serials.

Baehni   Charles Baehni, Correspondance de Charles Darwin et d'Alphonse de Candolle, *Gesnerus*, 12:109–156, 1955.

b   Brother.

Barlow   Nora Barlow, *Charles Darwin and the voyage of the Beagle*, London, Pilot Press, 1945.

Barlow—Autobiography   Nora Barlow, editor, *The autobiography of Charles Darwin 1809–1882, with the original omissions restored: edited with appendix and notes by his grand-daughter Nora Barlow*, London, Collins, 1958.

Basalla   George Basalla, The voyage of the Beagle without Darwin, *Mariner's Mirror*, 49:42–48, 1963.

BM (NH) Memorials   British Museum (Natural History), *Memorials of Charles Darwin: a collection of manuscripts, portraits, medals, books and natural history specimens* etc., London, British Museum (Natural History), 1909. Special Guides No. 4.

Britten & Boulger   James Britten & G. S. Boulger, *A biographical index of British and Irish botanists*, London, West Newman, 1893; 2nd edition, 1931, revised and completed by A. B. Rendle. For 3rd edition see Ray Desmond.

Burke   H. Farnham Burke, compiler, *Pedigree of the family of Darwin,* [?London], privately printed, 1888.

c   *Circa* (used with dates); child.

Carroll   P. Thomas Carroll, *An annotated calendar of the letters of Charles Darwin in the Library of the American Philosophical Society*, Wilmington, Scholarly Resources Inc., 1976. Numbers given refer to the numbers of the letters and not to pages.

CD   Charles Robert Darwin.

Christ's College Centenary Exhibition   A.E.S. & J.C.S. [Arthur Everett Shipley & James Crawford Simpson], editors, *Darwin centenary: the portraits, prints and writings of Charles Robert Darwin, exhibited at Christ's College, Cambridge 1909*, [Cambridge, University Press], 1909.

Climbing plants   Charles Darwin, On the movements and habits of climbing plants, *J.Proc.Linn.Soc.Lond.*, 9:1–118; as a book with same title, London, Longman and Williams & Norgate, 1865; 2nd edition, London, John Murray, 1875.

Cross and self fertilisation   Charles Darwin, *The effects of cross and self fertilisation in the vegetable kingdom*, London, John Murray, 1876.

d   Daughter.

d.s.p.   *Decessit sine prole*, died without issue.

Darwin-Bates   Robert M. Stecher, editor, The Darwin-Bates letters: correspondence between two nineteenth century travellers and naturalists, Part I, *Ann.Sci.*, 25:1–47: Part II, *ibid.*, 25:95–125, 1969.

Darwin-Gray   *Calendar of the letters of Charles Robert Darwin to Asa Gray*, Boston, Mass., Historical Records Survey, 1939, reprint 1973, introduction by Bert James Loewenberg.

Darwin-Henslow   Nora Barlow, editor, *Darwin and Henslow, the growth of an idea: letters 1831–1860*, London, John Murray, Bentham-Moxon Trust, 1967.

Darwin-Innes   Robert M. Stecher, editor, The Darwin-Innes letters: the correspondence of an evolutionist with his vicar, 1848–1884, *Ann.Sci.*, 17:201–258, 1961.

Darwin-Wallace   James Marchant, editor, *Alfred Russel Wallace, letters and reminiscences*, 2 vols, London, Cassell, 1916.

Darwin and modern science   Albert C. Seward, editor, *Darwin and modern science*, Cambridge, University Press, 1909.

Darwin, Francis   Some letters from Charles Darwin to Alfred Russel Wallace, *Christ's College Mag.*, 23:214–231, 1909.

de Beer, G. R., editor,   The Darwin letters at Shrewsbury School, *Notes & Records Roy.Soc.*, 23:68–85, 1968.

Descent   Charles Darwin, *The descent of man, and selection in relation to sex*, London, John Murray, 1871.

Desmond, Ray   *Dictionary of British and Irish botanists and horticulturalists, including plant collectors and botanical artists*, London, Taylor and Francis, 1977. This is a 3rd edition of Britten & Boulger, q.v.

Diary   Nora Barlow, editor, *Charles Darwin's diary of the voyage of H.M.S. Beagle*, Cambridge, University Press, 1933.

DNB   *Dictionary of national biography*, 63 vols & 3 vols *supplements*, London, Smith Elder, 1885–1901. 10 year *supplements* to 1960, Oxford University Press.

EB   *Encyclopaedia Britannica*, London. The 11th–12th edition, 32 vols, 1910–1911, 1922, has been referred to in a few places.

[ED]   H. E. Litchfield, editor, *Emma Darwin, wife of Charles Darwin: a century of family letters*, Cambridge, University Press, privately printed, 1904. This edition has not been quoted from.

ED   Used for Emma Darwin, wife of Charles Robert Darwin throughout. Also used, with volume and page reference, for Henrietta E. Litchfield, editor, *Emma Darwin, a century of family letters, 1792–1896*, London, John Murray, 1915. This, the published edition, is the one quoted from throughout.

Eiseley   Loren Eiseley, *Darwin's century: evolution and the men who discovered it*, Garden City N.Y., Doubleday Anchor Books, 1958.

Ellegård   Alvar Ellegård, Darwin and the general reader: the reception of Darwin's theory of evolution in the British periodical press, 1859–1872, *Götesborgs Universitets Arsskrift*, 64:1–394; *Göthenburg Studies in English*, 8.

Expression   Charles Darwin, *The expression of the emotions in man and animals*, London, John Murray, 1872.

F   R. B. Freeman, *The works of Charles Darwin: an annotated bibliographical handlist*, 2nd edition, Folkestone, Wm Dawson, Hamden, Conn., Archon Books, 1977. Freeman numbers are entered, just with the prefix F, for all Darwin's books and publications in serials. In the latter they follow the B of Barrett reprint numbers.

f   Father.

Feuer   Lewis F. Feuer, Is the 'Darwin-Marx' correspondence authentic?, *Ann.Sci.*, 32:1–12, 1975.

Freeman, R. B.   Charles Darwin on the routes of male

humble bees, *Bull.Brit.Mus.(nat.Hist.)*, hist. Ser., 3:177–189, 1968.

Freeman, R. B. & Gautrey, P. J.   Charles Darwin's *Questions about the breeding of animals*, with a note on *Queries about expression, J. Soc. Biblphy nat. Hist.*, 5:220–225, 1969.

Freeman, R. B. & Gautrey, P.J.   Charles Darwin's *Queries about expression, Bull.Brit.Mus.(nat.Hist.)*, hist. Ser., 4:205–219, 1972.

Freeman, R. B. & Gautrey, P. J.   Charles Darwin's *Queries about expression. J.Soc.Biblphy nat.Hist.*, 7:259–263, 1975.

FUL   G. R. de Beer, editor, Further unpublished letters of Charles Darwin, *Ann.Sci.*, 14:83–115, 1960 (for 1958). See also N&R which is the first part of this collection.

Gruber, Jacob W.   Who was the Beagle's naturalist?, *Brit.J.Hist.Sci.*, 4:266–282, 1969.

Huxley, Julian S. & Kettlewell, H. B. D.   *Charles Darwin and his world*, London, Thames and Hudson, 1965.

Insectivorous plants   Charles Darwin, *Insectivorous plants*, London, John Murray, 1875.

J. Researches 1839   Charles Darwin, *Journal of researches into the geology and natural history of the various countries visited by H.M.S. Beagle*, etc., Second edition, London, Henry Colburn, 1839.

J. Researches 1845   Charles Darwin, *Journal of researches into the natural history and geology of the various countries visited by H.M.S. Beagle*, etc., Second edition, London, John Murray, 1845.

Jensen, J. Vernon   The X Club: fraternity of Victorian scientists, *Brit.J.Hist.Sci.*, 5:63–72, 1970.

Jensen, J. Vernon   Interrelationships within the Victorian 'X Club', *Dalhousie Rev.*, 51:539–552, 1971.

Jesperson, P. Helveg   Charles Darwin and Dr. Grant, *Lychnos*, 1948–1949: 159–167, 1949.

Jordan, David Starr   *The days of a man*, 2 vols, Yonkers N.Y., World Book Co., 1922.

Journal   G. R. de Beer, editor, Darwin's journal, *Bull.Brit.Mus.(nat.Hist)*, hist. Ser., 2:1–21, 1959.

Keith, *Sir* Arthur   *Darwin revalued*, London, Watts, 1955.

LL   Francis Darwin, editor, *The life and letters of Charles Darwin, including an autobiographical chapter*, 3 vols, London, John Murray, 1887. Edition used is 7th thousand 1888, the definitive text.

m   Married.

Mellersh, M. E. L.   *Fitzroy of the Beagle*, London, Rupert Hart Davis, 1968.

ML   Francis Darwin & A. C. Seward, editors, *More letters of Charles Darwin: a record of his work in a series of hitherto unpublished letters*, 2 vols, London, John Murray, 1903.

Moorhead, Alan   *Darwin and the Beagle*, London, Hamish Hamilton, 1969.

Movement in plants   Charles Darwin, *The power of movement in plants*, London, John Murray, 1880.

N&R   G. R. de Beer, editor, Some unpublished letters of Charles Darwin, *Notes & Records Roy. Soc.*, 14:12–66, 1959. See also FUL, which is the 2nd part of this collection.

Narrative   Robert Fitz-Roy, editor, *Narrative of the surveying voyages of His Majesty's Ships Adventure and Beagle*, etc., 3 vols & appendix vol. to Vol. II, London, Henry Colburn, 1839. Vol. II is Charles Darwin, Journal and remarks, the first printing of *Journal of researches*, 1839.

Nash, Louisa Ann   Some memories of Charles Darwin, *Overland Monthly*, San Francisco, Oct.: 404–408, 1890.

Nash, Wallis   *A lawyer's life on two continents*, Boston, R. G. Badger, [1919].

OED   *Sir* James Murray and others, editors, *A new English dictionary on historical principles*, 10 vols in 13, 1888–1928, supplement 1933; new supplement, 2 vols [of 4], 1972, 1976, Oxford, Clarendon Press.

Orchids   Charles Darwin, *On the various contrivances by which British and foreign orchids are fertilised by insects, and on the good effects of intercrossing*, London, John Murray, 1862.

Origin   Charles Darwin, *On the origin of species by means of natural selection, or the preservation of favoured races in the struggle for life*, London, John Murray, 1859. Quotations from later editions are specified in the text.

Period piece   Gwen[dolen] Raverat, *Period piece: a Cambridge childhood*, London, Faber and Faber, 1952.

q.v.   *Quod vide*, which see.

Rogers, James Allen   The reception of Darwin's *Origin of species* by Russian scientists, *Isis*, 64:489–508, 1973.

s   Sister.

sc   *Scillicet*, namely.

Short life   Francis Darwin, editor, *Charles Darwin: his life told in an autobiographical chapter, and in a selected series of his published letters*, London, John Murray, 1892. A reduced version of LL, but with some alterations. Later editions are specified in the text.

Slevin, Joseph Richard   The Galápagos Islands: a history of their exploration, *Occ.Pap.Calif.Acad.Sci.*, No. 25:1–150, 1959.

Smith, Kenneth G. V. & Dimick, R. E.   Darwin's 'American' neighbour, *J.Soc.Biblphy nat.Hist.*, 8:78–82, 1976.

s.p.   *Sine prole*, without issue.

Stauffer, Robert C.   Haeckel, Darwin, and ecology, *Quart.Rev.Biol.*, 32:138–144, 1957.

Stauffer, Robert C., editor, *Charles Darwin's Natural selection: being the second part of his big species book written from 1856 to 1858*, Cambridge, University Press, 1975.

Thomson, Keith Steward   H.M.S. *Beagle*, 1820–1870, *Amer.Sci.*, 63:664–672, 1975.

Venn   J. A. Venn, *Alumnus Cantabrigienses 1752—1900*, 6 vols, Cambridge, University Press, 1922–1954.

Wells, Kentwood D.   Charles Wells and the races of man, *Isis*, 64:215–225, 1973.

WH   *Who's who*, London, Adam & Charles Black, 1971–1978. Used only for the unconsolidated volumes.

Winslow, John H.   Mr. Lumb and Masters Megatherium: an unpublished letter by Charles Darwin from the Falklands, *J.hist.Geogr.*, 1:347–360, 1975.

Worms   Charles Darwin, *The formation of vegetable mould through the action of worms, with observations on their habits*, London, John Murray, 1881.

WWH   *Who was who*, London, Adam & Charles Black, 6 vols, 1920–1972. Covering the years 1897–1970; issued every 10 years from standing type of WH.

A

Abbety 1879 A nickname used, with 'Boo', 'Mim', 'Lenny' (Leonard D) and 'Dadda' (CD), by Richard Meirion D for members of the family. None of them is ED.

Abbott, Dr F. E. Editor of *Index*, of Cambridge, Mass. 1871 CD letters to on religion—LLi 305.

Abinger Hall W of Dorking, Surrey. House of *Sir* Thomas H. Farrer. 1873 Aug. CD first visited, and often later, which he much enjoyed.

Abraham, Mr Resident at Downe—Darwin-Innes letters 227.

Abrolhos, Arquipélagodos dos Brazilian coastal islands S of Salvador, 1832 Mar.19 *Beagle* visited and CD landed. 1835 misspelt 'Abrothos' in *Letters on geology*, 4–5.

Academia Caesarea Leopoldino-Carolina Germanica Naturae Curiosorum 1857 CD Member under cognomen Forster. 'Accipe . . . ex antiqua nostra consuetudine cognomen Forster'. Either the father Johann Reinhold F (1729–1798), or the son Johann Georg Adam F (1754–1794), both of whom went on Cook's second voyage.

Academia Nacional de Ciencias de las República Argentina, Cordova. 1878 CD Honorary Member.

Academia Scientiarum Imperialis Petropolitana (Imperatorskaye Akademiya Nauk) 1867 CD Corresponding Member.

Académie des Sciences de l'Institut de France 1872 CD proposed for *Zoologie* section, but not elected. 1878 elected in *Botanique*. CD to Gray 'It is rather a good joke that I should be elected to the botanical section, as the extent of my knowledge is little more than that a daisy is a compositous plant, and a pea a leguminous one'—LLiii 224. 1899 'He was in fact guilty of evolution but with extenuating botanical circumstances'—Francis D, *Ann.Bot.*, 12:xi.

Académie Royale des Sciences, des Lettres et des Beaux-Arts de Belgique 1870 CD Associate.

Academy of Natural Sciences, Philadelphia 1860 CD Correspondent.

Acton, Mr 1855 Postmaster at Bromley.

Adventure [1] HMS Command vessel, under *Captain* P. P. King, of first voyage of HMS *Beagle*, 1827–1830.

Adventure [2] 1833 Mar. Schooner bought by Fitz-Roy on 2nd voyage of *Beagle*, from William Law, a sealer, at Port Louis, Falkland Islands, for £1300 & £403 for new equipment; 170 tons, then named *Unicorn*; originally built at Rochester as a yacht. J. C. Wickham in command. 1834 Oct. Admiralty refused to reimburse Fitz-Roy, so sold at Valparaiso for £1400.

Agassiz, Alexander Emanuel 1835–1910 Marine biologist. s of J.L.R.A. Converted to belief in evolution by reading and corresponding with Fritz Müller. 1869 Dec. 1 visited Down House with wife. Fairly frequent correspondent with CD. EB.

Agassiz, Jean Louis Rodolphe, known as Louis 1807–1873 Ichthyologist & geologist. For. Mem. R.S. 1838. Prof. Natural History Neuchâtel 1832–1847. Prof. Zoology & Geology Harvard 1847–1873. 1841 CD sent *J.Researches*, 1854 CD sent *Living Barnacles*, 1859 CD sent *Origin*. 1849 CD met at British Association, Southampton. 1860 Jan. Gray to CD 'He says it is poor—very poor!! (*entre nous*). The fact is he is very much annoyed by it'—LLii 268. 1860 Jul. 'I shall therefore consider the transmutation theory as a scientific mistake, untrue in its facts, unscientific in its method, and mischievious in its tendency'—*Silliman's J.*, 143—LLii 184. 1863 CD to Gray 'I enjoy anything that riles Agassiz. He seems to grow bigoted with increasing years. I once saw him years ago and was charmed with him'—Darwin-Gray letters 52. 1866 CD to Gray about an Amazonian glacier 'We [CD & Lyell] were both astonished at the nonsense which Agassiz writes . . . his predetermined wish partly explains what he fancied he observed'—Darwin-Gray letters 56. A continued against CD for the rest of his life and ML contains a number of other examples of his attitude and his absurdity. Biography: 1886 Elizabeth Cabot Agassiz (2nd wife), 2 vols, Boston; 1893 Holder, New York; EB.

Ainstie, Mr Resident at Downe. 1860 Innes was looking for a vicarage. A was perhaps selling his house and wanted £4000—Darwin-Innes letters 205, 207.

Ainsworth, William Francis 1807–1896 Physician, Wernerian geologist & middle-east traveller. CD 'Knew a little about many subjects, but was superficial and very glib with his tongue'—Barlow, Autobiography 48. DNB.

Airy, Dr Hubert s of *Sir* George Biddell A, Astronomer Royal.

1873 CD corresponded with on phyllotaxis, *Proc.Roy.Soc.*, 176. One of the people who pointed out the error in *Descent* i 19 that the platysmus myoides cannot be brought into action voluntarily.

Albury nr Guildford, Surrey. 1871 Jul.28–Aug.24 CD had a family holiday in a rented house. It belonged to George Drummond, the Irvingite.

Alderson, Lady Georgiana [I] *see* Drewe.

Alderson, Georgiana [II] d of *Sir* Edward H.A. m Marquis of Salisbury. 1882 A was on 'Personal Friends invited' list for CD's funeral.

Alderson, Sir Edward Hall 1787–1857 Judge, Baron of the Exchequer. m 1823 Georgiana Drewe. Had issue, amongst others, Georgiana [II]. 1827 lived Great Russell St, London. 'A most temperate man'.

Allen, Mrs Resident at Downe. *Mr* Robinson, Curate at Downe, had been having a relationship with one of her maids —Darwin-Innes letters 226.

Allen, Bertha *see* Eaton.

Allen, Baugh [I] *see* Lancelot Baugh A.

Allen, Baugh [II] *see* George Baugh A.

Allen, Bessy *see* Elizabeth A.

Allen, Bob *see* Seymour Phillips A.

Allen, Caroline [I] 1768–1835. 3c of John Bartlett A. m 1793 Edward Drewe. ED's aunt.

Allen, Caroline [II] *see* Romilly

Allen, Catherine [I] 1765–1830 May 6. 2c of John Bartlett A. m 1798 *Sir* James Mackintosh. Known as Kitty. ED's great aunt. 'She could neither make herself or others happy'.

Allen, Catherine [II] *see* Fellowes.

Allen, Charles 1842–? died young. 3c of Lancelot Baugh A & Georgiana Sarah A. ED's second cousin.

Allen, Charles Grant Blairfindie, known as Grant A. 1848–1899 Naturalist and general writer. Chronically sick and often in financial difficulty. 1877 CD to A, thanks for his book *Physiological aesthetics*, London. 1879 CD to Romanes, A was in some financial difficulty, CD subscribed £25, will send more if needed—Carroll 567, 569. 1881 CD to Romanes relates to A's trouble, acknowledging cheque for £12.10s in 50% repayment of loan, and about giving a present of a microscope to—Carroll 603. 1882 CD to Romanes, CD prefers to give the microscope now, rather than wait for the repayment of the other half of the loan—Carroll 612, 613. 1885 ED 'I do not like Grant Allen's book about your father. It is prancing and wants simplicity'. Biography: E. Clodd 1900. A was not related to the other Allens. WWH.

Allen, Clement Frederick Romilly 1844–? 1c of Lancelot Baugh Allen & Georgina Sarah. m 1877 Edith Louisa Wedgwood and had offspring. ED's second cousin.

Allen, Dorothea Hannah *see* Eaton.

Allen, Edith Louisa *see* Wedgwood

Allen, Edmund Eaton 1824–1898 2c of Lancelot Baugh A & Caroline. m 1848 Bertha Eaton and had offspring. ED's 2nd cousin.

Allen, Elizabeth [I] 1764–1846 Mar.31 1c of John Bartlett A. m 1792 Josiah Wedgwood [II]. Known as Bessy. CD's mother-in-law. 1833 early this year had a stroke, damaging a foot, and never walked again.

Allen, Elizabeth [II] *see* Hensleigh.

Allen, Elizabeth Jessie Jane c1846–? 2c of Lancelot Baugh A & Georgina Sarah. ED's 1st cousin.

Allen, Emma 1780–1866 Jun.4. 10c of John Bartlett A. unm. ED's aunt. ED named after her. 1843 moved from Creselly to Heywood Lodge, Heywood Lane, Tenby, on death of her brother John Hensleigh A. 1864 returned to Cresselly with sister Frances after death of brother John's wife.

Allen, Fanny *see* Frances A.

Allen, Frances 1781–1875 May 6. 11c of John Bartlett A. unm. Known as Fanny. ED's aunt. 1843 moved to Heywood Lodge, Heywood Lane, Tenby on death of her brother John Hensleigh A. 'A little low white house . . . the sleek spaniel Crab, and the well cared for garden'. 1864 returned to Cresselly, with sister Emma, on death of brother John's wife. F. A. was last surviving member of her generation.

Allen, George Baugh 1821–1898 Barrister. 1c of Lancelot Baugh A & Caroline. m 1846 Dorothea Hannah Eaton and had offspring. ED's 1st cousin.

Allen, Georgina Sarah *see* Bayly.

Allen, Gertrude *see* Seymour.

Allen, Gertrude Elizabeth ?–1824. 5c of John Hensleigh A. unm. ED's 1st cousin.

Allen, Grant *see* Charles Grant Blairfindie A.

Allen, Harriet 1776–1845 Nov.5. 7c of John Bartlett A. m 1799 Matthew Surtees. Known as Sad. ED's aunt. 1827, after death of husband, lived with sisters Emma & Frances at Tenby.

Allen, Harry *see* Henry George A.

Allen, Henry George 1815–1908. 2c of John Hensleigh A. unm. ED's 1st cousin.

Allen, Isabella Georgina 1818–1914. 4c of John Hensleigh A. m 1840 George Lort Phillips.

Allen, Jane *see* Louisa Jane A.

Allen, Jenny *see* Louisa Jane A.

Allen, Jessie 1777–1853 Mar.3. 8c of John Bartlett A. m 1819 J. C. Simonde de Sismondi. ED's favourite aunt. 1837 was already deaf by. 1842, after death of husband, lived with her sisters, Emma, Frances & Harriet, at Tenby. After 1842 she burnt Sismondi's journals and her own.

Allen, John 1810–1886 School Commissioner 1836–1846. Archdeacon of Salop 1847–1883. Friend of Edward Fitzgerald and of Alfred Tennyson. 1847 visited, with Jessie Sismondi and her sister Emma, the school at Caldy Island, which was paid for by Sarah Elizabeth Wedgwood [II]—EDii 107.

Allen, John Bartlett 1733–1803. m1 Elizabeth Hensleigh, 2s 9d, 1. Elizabeth; 2. Catherine; 3. Caroline; 4. John Hensleigh; 5. Louisa Jane; 6. Lancelot Baugh; 7. Harriet; 8. Jessie; 9. Octavia; 10. Emma; 11. Frances. m2 the daughter of a coalminer, 3d who all died young. CD's maternal great grandfather.

Allen, John Hensleigh [I] 1769–1843 Apr. 4c of John Bartlett A. m 1812 Gertrude Seymour 3s 2d, 1. Seymour Phillips; 2. Henry George; 3. John Hensleigh [II]; 4. Isabella Georgina; 5. Gertrude Elizabeth. ED's uncle. Master of Dulwich College after Lancelot Baugh A's marriage 1820.

Allen, John Hensleigh [II] 1818–1868. 3c of John Hensleigh A [I]. Known as Johnny as a child. m Margaretta Snelgar. Colonial Office. Worked much amongst the London poor. ED's 1st cousin.

Allen, Kitty *see* Katherine A.

Allen, Lancelot Baugh 1774–1845 Oct. 7c of John Hensleigh A [I]. m1 Caroline Romilly 2s, 1. George Baugh; 2. Edmund Edward. m2 Georgina Sarah Bayly 2s 1d, 1. Clement Frederick; 2. Elizabeth Jessie Jane; 5. Charles. ED's uncle. Master of Dulwich College.

Allen, Louisa Jane 1771–1836 5c of John Bartlett A. m 1794 John Wedgwood. Known as Jane or Jenny. ED's aunt. Died suddenly at Shrewsbury when consulting *Dr* R. W. Darwin.

Allen, Margaretta *see* Snelgar

Allen, Octavia 1779–1800 9c (8d) of John Bartlett A. unm. ED's aunt.

Allen, Sad *see* Harriet A.

Allen, Seymour Phillips 1814–1861. 1c of John Hensleigh A [I]. m 1843 Catherine Fellowes and had offspring. ED's 1st cousin.

Allfrey, Charles Henry 1838/39–1912. Physician of St Mary Cray & Chislehurst. 1882 A attended CD in his terminal illness. A was on 'Personal Friends invited' list for CD's funeral.

Alvey, Elizabeth d of Matthew A. m John Hill. CD's great great grandmother. Erasmus D's grandmother. Origin of forename Alvey in family.

Alvey, Frances *see* Wymondsold.

Alvey, Matthew s of William A. CD's ancestor in 5th generation.

Alvey, William ?–1649 m Frances Wymondsold. f of Matthew A. CD's ancestor in 6th generation.

Alwyne, Mrs 1871 played organ in Downe church.

Amazon valley fauna 1863 Contributions to an insect fauna of the Amazon valley, *Trans.Linn.Soc.Lond.*, 23:495–566, 2 col. plates, by H. W. Bates. Review of [unsigned] by CD, *Nat.Hist.Rev.*, 3:219–224 (Bii 87, F1725). One of CD's 2 reviews. *see also Naturalist on the river Amazons.*

American Academy of Arts and Sciences Boston. 1873 CD Foreign Honorary Member.

American Philosophical Society Philadelphia. 1870 CD Honorary Member. For their holdings in CD letters etc., *see* P. T. Carroll.

Ammonium carbonate 1882 The action of carbonate of ammonia on the roots of certain plants, *J.Linn.Soc.Lond.*, (*Bot.*), 19:239–261 (Bii 236, F1800); The action of carbonate of ammonia on chlorophyll bodies, *ibid.*, 19:262–284 (Bii 256, F1801). Abstract of these two papers by Francis D, *Nature*, Lond., 25:489–490.

Ampthill Park 1826 home of *Sir* James Mackintosh, lent to him by H. R. V. F. Holland, *Baron* Holland.

Anderson, John Parker 1887 in G. T. Bettany, *Life of Charles Darwin*, bibliography of CD and Darwiniana is the earliest source and still important. A was at Department of Printed Books, British Museum.

Andersson, Nils Johan 1821–1880. Swedish botanist who visited Galápagos Islands in the frigate *Eugenie*. CD perhaps sent him first edition of *Origin*—LLii 172.

Angro do Heroisma Capital of Terceira, Azores. 1836 Sep. 19–24 *Beagle* anchored off; CD visited.

Angulus Woolneri The infolded point of the human ear, also called A. Woolnerianus and Darwin's peak—LLiii 140; *Nature*, Lond., Apr. 6, 1871. *see also* Woolner.

Animal intelligence 1882 George J. Romanes, *Animal intelligence*, London, International Scientific Series XLI. Extracts from CD's notes throughout (F1416). First foreign editions: USA 1883 (F1419); French 1887 (F1429). *see also* Stauffer 1975.

Anne Domestic servant at Down House ?1865–1879.

Ansted, David Thomas 1814–1880. Geologist. FRS 1844. Prof. Geology King's College London. 1860 CD to about *Origin* and about *Geological gossip*, 1860, by A.—MLi 175.

Anthropologische Gesellschafte Vienna. 1872 CD Honorary Member.

Ants 1873 [letter] Habits of ants, *Nature*, Lond. 8:244 (Bii 177, F1761); introducing a letter from James D. Hague.

Ape cartoonist *see* Carlo Pellegrini.

Appleman, Philip 1970 *Darwin*, New York; extracts from CD's works selected by A (F1624).

Appleton, Mary American spiritualist, known as Molly. Sister of Thomas Gold A and Frances Elizabeth A (*Mrs* H. W. Longfellow). m Robert Mackintosh.

Appleton, Thomas Gold 1812–1884. Spiritualist & poet. Brother of Mary A and Frances Elizabeth A (*Mrs* H. W. Longfellow). 1868 A called on CD at Freshwater, I.O.W.

Arding, Willoughby 1805–1879. Physician. Ashworth identifies CD's Edinburgh naturalist friend 'Hardie' as A, but CD says that Hardie died early in India. A was at Bombay and then Wallingford, Berkshire.

Argyll, 8th Duke of *see* George Douglas Campbell.

Armenian First editions in: *Journal of researches* 1949 (F168); *Origin of species* 1936 (F630); *Biographical sketch of an infant* 1877 (F1310); *Vegetable mould and worms* 1896 (F1402): *Autobiography* 1959 (F1510).

Armstrong, Robert Physician at Royal Naval Hospital Plymouth & Inspector of Fleets. 1833 CD sent a large box of fossils to A for forwarding to Henslow—Darwin-Henslow 81.

Artizans' Dwelling Company 1871 CD took 10 shares at £100 each from John Royle Martin—Carroll 403. 1881 CD did not then own them—Atkins 96.

Ascension Island Atlantic Ocean. 1836 Jul.19 *Beagle* arrived. Jul.20 CD ashore.

Ash, Edward John 1799–1851 Bursar of Christ's College Cambridge—Darwin-Henslow 120. 1831 Nov.15 A failed to subtract furniture value from CD's final account with the College—LLi 215. Rector of Brisely and Vicar of Gateley, Yorkshire.

Ashburner, Misses 1871 George D and Francis D stayed with them in USA. Aunts of Sara Sedgwick. Their father was 'the youth beloved' of *Mrs* John Opie's (née Amelia Alderson) poem 'Forget me not'.

Ashworth, Emily m 1848 Edward Forbes.

Ashworth, James Hartley 1874–1936 Zoologist. FRS 1917. Prof. Zoology Edinburgh. 1935 Charles Darwin as a student at Edinburgh, *Proc.Roy.Soc.Edinb.*, 55:97–113, esp. 103–104. *see also* Plinian Society. WWH.

Asiatic Society of Bengal Calcutta. 1871 CD Honorary Member.

Athenaeum Club Pall Mall, London. 1838, before Aug. CD elected member; one of 40 new members called the 40 thieves; proposed by Marquis of Landsdowne. CD used the Club a lot before marriage. *see* Barlow *Autobiography* 35.

Auditory-Sac 1863 On the so-called 'auditory-sac' of cirripedes, *Nat.Hist.Rev.*, 3:115–116 (Bii 85, F1722).

Audubon, John James 1780–1851. American ornithologist. FRS 1830. CD met and heard him lecture at Edinburgh. 'Sneering somewhat unjustly at Waterton'—Barlow *Autobiography* 51.

Australia 1836 Jan.12–Mar.16 *Beagle* was at. 1839 'Farewell Australia! you are a rising infant and doubtless some day will reign a great princess in the south, but you are too great and ambitious for affection, yet not great enough for respect. I leave your shores without sorrow or regret'—*J.Researches* 538.

Autobiographical Fragment 1838 this autobiography of CD's early years was written in this year, but printed first in 1903 MLi 1–5. Foreign editions: USA 1903 in stereo edition of ML; Russian, fragment alone 1959.

Autobiography 1876 written between late May and Aug.3 with later additions. Ms title 'Recollections of the development of my mind and character'. Ms at Cambridge. 1887 first printed in LLi 26–160, with omissions which might possibly have caused offence to ED. 1892 abbreviated version printed in *Charles Darwin: his life*, 5–54. 1958 Nora Barlow, editor, *The autobiography of Charles Darwin 1809—1882. With the original omissions restored*, London (F1497): a retranscription of the original mss, which lists, 244–245, the more important omissions. *See also* Russian edition 1957 below. English braille edition based on Barlow 1958 (F1509). First foreign editions: Polish 1891 (F1538); Russian 1896 (F1533); Spanish 1902 (F1544); USA 1908 (F1478); Danish 1909 (F1512); Italian 1919 (F1522); Serbian 1937 (F1542); Hebrew 1948 (F1520); Ukrainian 1949 (F1547); Latvian 1953 (F1526); Hungarian 1955 (F1521); Armenian (F1510), Bulgarian (F1511), German (F1519), Lithuanian (F1527), Slovene (F1534) 1959; Romanian 1962 (F1532); Korean 1965 (F1525). Russian 1957 (F1540) is an independent transcription from the ms and precedes Barlow 1958. *See also* 1908 *The education of Darwin*, Old South Works Leaflets, 8:194 (F1478); A. C. Seward, editor, *Darwin and modern science; autobiographical fragment*, 1903 (F1479).

Avebury, Baron *see Sir* John Lubbock *Bart.*

Avebury, Lady *see* Alice A. L. L. Fox Pitt.

Aveling, Dr Edward Bibbins 1851–1898 Medical practitioner, freethinker & crook, took as common law wife, Eleanor Marx d of Karl Marx. 1881 A visited Down House—LLi 317. 1881 *The student's Darwin*; 1882 *Darwinism and small families*; 1883 *The religious views of Charles Darwin. see also* H. K. Marx.

Azores Atlantic ocean. 1836 Sep.19 *Beagle* anchored off Angra do Heroisma, capital of Terceira; CD visited Praya (Praia de Victoria). Sep.25 *Beagle* called at St Michael (São Miguel) for letters and left for England.

B

Babba Bernard Richard Meirion D's infant name for CD.

Babbage, Charles 1792–1871. Mathematician. FRS 1816. Lucasian Prof. Mathematics Cambridge 1828–1839. CD regularly attended his 'famous evening parties' in London—Barlow *Autobiography* 108. 'A man who did not seem to like his fellow men'—FUL 84. DNB.

Babington, Charles Cardale 1808–1895. Botanist. FRS 1851. Prof. Botany Cambridge 1861, succeeding Henslow. 1863 founded Cambridge Ray Club as a successor to Henslow's evenings. DNB.

Backgammon CD and ED played 2 games every evening when they were at Down House for many years. He won most games, she most gammons. 1876 Jan.28 CD to Gray 'she poor creature has won only 2490 games, whilst I have won, hurrah, hurrah, 2795 games!'—EDii 221.

Bacon Tobacconist of Cambridge. 1828 CD lodged over his shop in Sidney St, 'for a term or two'—LLi 163. The shop is now in the Market.

Baer, Karl Ernst, Ritter von, Edler von Huthorn 1792–1876. Embryologist. Born in Estonia of German parents who were Russian subjects. Copley Medal of Royal Society 1867. Librarian Academy of Sciences St Petersburg 1834– . 1860 Aug. B wrote to Huxley generally pro-*Origin*, although he never fully accepted CD's views—LLii 329. 1861 CD refers to B in Historical sketch. *see* J. A. Rogers, *Isis*, 64:488–493, 1972.

Bagshaw's Directory [? for Kent]. 1847 described CD as 'farmer'—Keith 44.

Bahia *see* Salvador.

Bahia Blanca Argentine, a military outpost, known as Fort Antonio, separating the Pampas from Patagonia. 1832 Sep.7–28 *Beagle* at. 1833 Aug.25–Sep.6 CD passed through on his journey from Rio Negro to Buenos Aires.

Bain, Alexander 1818–1903. Philosopher. Prof. Logic Aberdeen. 1873 CD to about B's theory of spontaneity. They had met at Moor Park Hydro—LLiii 172.

Baily 'Baily the poulterer'—MLi 139. A seller of fancy pigeons, poultry, rabbits in London. c1851 mentioned several times in LLii. CD arranged tickets for him to attend a lecture by Huxley—MLi 139. He was trying to get a half-lop rabbit for CD—Mli 181.

Baird, Spencer Fullerton 1823–1887. American ornithologist. Assistant Secretary Smithsonian Institution Washington 1850–1878, Secretary 1878– . 1867 B showed *Queries about expression* to George Gibbs.

Baker 1836 Dec. A missionary at Bay of Islands, New Zealand. CD was shown round by him. *see also* Thomas Kendall & John King.

Baker A dealer in the fancy, London. B was trying to get a half-lop rabbit for CD—MLi 181.

Baker, Nathaniel Civil Servant. 1875 Secretary to Vivisection Commission, to which CD gave evidence—LLiii 201.

Balfour, Sir Arthur James, *Earl* of Balfour. 1848–1930. Statesman. 1st *Earl* 1922 OM 1916 KG 1922 FRS 1888. Prime Minister 1902–1905. Cambridge friend of CD's sons. 1882 was on 'Personal Friends invited' list for CD's funeral, with *Miss* Balfour his sister. DNB.

Balfour, Francis Maitland 1851–1882. Embryologist. FRS 1878. Prof. Animal Morphology Cambridge 1882. Strong personal friend of CD's sons at Cambridge. Killed climbing on the Aiguille Blanche Jul. 1880 Jul. CD lunched with at Cambridge. 1881 Oct. B took tea with CD & ED at Cambridge. 'He has a fair fortune of his own. He is very modest, and very pleasant, and often visits here [Down House] and we like him very much'—LLiii 251. B told George D that he had never seen an experiment carried out except under anaesthesia—LLiii 203. 1882 B was on 'Personal Friends invited' list for CD's funeral. *A treatise on comparative embryology*, 2 vols, 1881.

Bangor Caernarvonshire. 1831 Aug. CD visited on geological trip with Sedgwick. 1843 Jun. CD visited.

Bar of sandstone off Pernambuco 1841 On a remarkable bar of sandstone off Pernambuco, on the coast of Brazil, *Phil.Mag.*, 19:257–260 (Bi 139, F266). Foreign editions: French [not traced]; Portuguese 1904 (F268); Russian 1936 (F270); Portuguese, English, French, as a pamphlet, 1959 (F269).

Barberio A large house bug (*Triatoma infestans*, Reduviidae) of South America; vector of Chagas' disease q.v., also lives in burrows of armadilloes. Also called benchuca.

Barbier, Edmond Translator of CD's works into French. 1880 Summer B visited Down House for lunch.

Barellien, Mlle 1865 B taught Elizabeth D French at Down House.

Barlaston Shropshire. Home of Francis Wedgwood. 1852 CD & ED visited on journey to Rugby, Betley & Shrewsbury. 1878 Jun. CD & ED visited.

Barlow, Mrs 'My father used to quote an unanswerable argument by which an old lady, a Mrs Barlow, who suspected him of unorthodoxy, hoped to convert him:—"Doctor, I know that sugar is sweet in my mouth, and I know that my Redeemer liveth"'—Barlow *Autobiography* 96.

Barlow, Lady [Emma Nora] *see* Emma Nora Darwin.

Barlow, Sir [James] Alan Noel, Bart 1881–1966. Civil Servant. GCB 1947 2nd *Bart* 1948. m Emma Nora Darwin 4s 1d. WWH.

Barmouth Caernarvonshire. 1828 Summer CD went on a coaching holiday under G. A. Butterton. 1829 Jun. CD visited with F. W. Hope to collect beetles, but CD had to return home after 2 days owing to illness. 1831 CD visited alone after geological tour with Sedgwick. 1869 Jun.10–Jul.30 family holiday at Caerdeon, 2 miles E of, on N side of estuary.

Barnacles 'Then where does he do his barnacles?'. This story of a child's misunderstanding is Lubbock's—MLi 38. For CD's work on barnacles see Cirripedia.

Barnard, Anne *see* Henslow.

Barrande, Joachim 1799–1883. Invertebrate palaeontologist. 1855 CD to Huxley, CD to Lyell, CD had proposed him for Foreign Member of Roy.Soc. He was not elected—MLi 81, MLii 231.

Barrett, Paul E. 1977 editor of *The collected papers of Charles Darwin*, 2 vols, Chicago. References to entries in this most useful work are given for each paper entered here as B, followed by volume and page number. *see also* Howard E. Gruber, *Darwin's notebooks*.

Barrow, Sir John, Bart 1764–1848. Civil Servant. 1st *Bart* 1835 FRS 1805. 1836 B communicated Fitz-Roy's paper on *Beagle* voyage to *J.R.geogr.Soc.*, 6:311–343. ?1850 CD to E. Cresy, CD considered that naval expeditions, especially those in search of missing vessels, were a waste of money. Barrow was much in favour of them. 'That old sinner'—MLi 68. DNB.

Bartlett, Abraham Dee 1812–1897. Superintendent, Zoological Society's Gardens, Regent's Park, London 1859–1897. Frequently helped CD by answering queries and sending material.

Basket, Fuegia ?1821–?1883. Woman of the Yahgan tribe from Tierra del Fuego. 1830 B was taken to England by Fitz-Roy, then aged about 9. 1833 Jan.23 B returned in *Beagle* and m York Minster. q.v. 1839 Fitz-Roy gives her name in Alikhoolip language (i.e. Yahgan) as Yokcushlu. ?1843 'Captain Sulivan . . . heard from a sealer, that . . . he was astonished by a native woman coming on board who could talk some English. Without doubt this was Fuegia Basket. She lived (I fear the term bears a double interpretation) some days on board'—*J.Researches*, 1845, 229. c1872 T. Bridges saw her, and again in 1883 when she was old and 'nearing her end'.

Bassett North Stoneham, Southampton. Ridgmount, home of William Erasmus D 1862–1902, sold on death of his wife Sarah.

Bassoon FD of CD 'Finding the cotyledons of Biophytum to be highly sensitive to vibrations of the table, he fancied that they might perceive the vibrations of sound, and therefore made me play my bassoon to it'—LLi 149.

Bateman, James 1811–1897 Botanist and plant breeder especially of orchids. Sent CD plants of *Anagraecum sesquipedale*, a native of Madagascar, which is now known to be fertilized by a sphingid moth, *Xanthopan morgani*, with proboscis c25 cm. long.

Bates, Henry Walter 1825–1892. Traveller & naturalist. FRS 1881. m 1861 Sarah Ann Mason 3s 2d. Assistant Secretary to Geographical Society 1864–1892. 1863 CD was most impressed by *Naturalist on the river Amazons*, 'the best work on natural travels ever published in England'—LLii 381. 1863 CD reviewed B's paper on insect fauna of the Amazon valley, which discusses Batesian mimicry, *Trans.Linn.Soc.Lond.*, 23:495–566, in *Nat.Hist.Rev.*, 3:219–224; the review is anonymous and one of only 2 which CD ever wrote. 1863 review of Amazons book, in *Nat.Hist.Rev.*, 3:385–389, is almost certainly not by CD; it is attributed to CD in early printings of Everyman edition of the book and from there by British Museum printed catalogue. 1861 CD sent B 3rd edition of *Origin*—MLi 176. Darwin-Bates correspondence published in R. M. Stecher, *Ann. Sci.*, 25:1–47, 95–125, 1969. Biography: G. Woodcock 1969; H. P. Moon 1977; DNB.

Bates, Marston & Humphrey, Philip S. 1956 *The Darwin reader*, New York, (F1613), selections from CD's works by.

Bathurst New South Wales, Australia. 1836 Jan.20 CD visited from Sydney.

Baxter, Mr Resident in Downe—Darwin-Innes 205.

Bayly, Georgina Sarah ?–1859. m 1841 as 2nd wife Lancelot Baugh Allen.

Beagle [I] His Majesty's Ship, sometimes called by Fitz-Roy His Majesty's Surveying Vessel. 3rd of the name. Sloop brig rigged as a brig. Built at Woolwich on the Thames and launched 1820 May 11; rerigged as a barque 1825. Displacement 235 tons; length of gundeck 90'; extreme breadth 24'6"; keel for tonnage 73'7$^7/_8$"; light draught 7'7" forward, 9'5" aft. No. 41 of a class of 107 ten-gun brigs which were nicknamed coffins, or half-tide rocks, from their ability to go down in severe weather. On second voyage carried 2 9lb guns & 4 carronades; special fittings included upper deck raised 8–12", Lihon's rudder, Harris's conductors on all masts, 24 chronometers. Complement 74; 16 are listed by name in *Narrative* ii, and without names Acting Boatswain, Sergeant of Marines & 7 privates, 34 seamen & 6 boys. There were 4 supernumeraries who are named, including CD, 3 Fuegians, Fitz-Roy's steward and CD's servant Syms Covington, who started as one of the boys. Much error has appeared in descriptions of *Beagle*. Revell scale model (x cl/110) 1972. Best contemporary illustrations can be found together in A. Moorehead, *Darwin and the Beagle*, 1969. *see* N&R 62, much in error; J. R. Slevin, *Occ.Pap.Calif.Acad.Sci.*, 25:75–88, 1959; K. S. Thomson, *Amer.Sci.*, 63:664–672, 1975.

FIRST SURVEYING VOYAGE To South America 1826–1830, in company with HMS *Adventure, Captain* P. P. King who commanded the expedition. *Beagle* commanded by *Lieut.* Pringle Stokes who committed suicide 1828 Aug.12, thereafter by Fitz-Roy.

SECOND SURVEYING VOYAGE To South America and round the world 1832 Jan.7 to 1836 Oct.2. Total time away from England 1737 days (1835 Nov.15 crossed date line, one day lost). Commanded by *Commander* Fitz-Roy, *Captain* 1835 Dec. CD on board as supernumerary, a guest of Fitz-Roy, throughout

voyage, but often on shore when *Beagle* was surveying.
Details of day-to-day positions and ports of call are given in
Narrative, Vol. II appendix. The following is only a summary:
1831 Nov.5 CD & Fitz-Roy boarded; 16 sailed, but returned to
Barn Pool below Mount Edgecombe; Dec.21 sailed, but again
put back; Dec.27 sailed. 1832 Jan.7 Santa Cruz, Tenerife;
Jan.7–Feb.8 Porto Praya, Cape Verde Islands; Feb.16–17 St
Paul's Rocks; Feb.20 Fernando de Noronha; Feb.28–Mar.18
Salvador; Mar.29 Abrolhos; Apr.5–May 10 Rio de Janeiro;
Apr.16–23 Salvador; Jun.4–Jul.5 Rio de Janeiro; Jul.26–31
Monte Video; Aug.3–19 Monte Video; Sep.7–28 Blanco Bay;
Oct.6–17 Blanco Bay; Oct.25–30 Monte Video; Nov.2–10
Buenos Aires; Nov.14–27 Monte Video; Dec.18–19 Good
Success Bay; Dec.24–30 San Martin Cove.
1833 Jan.15–Feb.8 Tierra del Fuego waters; Mar.1–Apr.6 Ber-
keley Sound; Apr.26–Jul.24 Monte Video & Maldonado;
Aug.25–Sep.6 Blanco Bay; Aug.16–23 Monte Video & Mal-
donado; Oct.4–Dec.5 Monte Video & Maldonado; Oct.24–
[1834 Jan.4] Port Desire.
1834 [1833 Oct.24]–Jan.4 Port Desire; Jan.10–18 Port Julian;
Feb.2–10 Port Famine; Feb.12–Mar.12 Tierra del Fuego waters; Mar.13–Apr.5 Port Louis, Falkland Islands; Apr.13–May
11 Santa Cruz River; Jun.1–8 Port Famine; Jun.9–12 Tierra del
Fuego waters; Jun.29–Jul.14 Chiloe; Jul.23–Nov.11 Valparaiso; Nov.22–[1835 Feb.7] Chiloe & Chonos Archipelago.
1835 [1834 Nov.22]–Feb.7 Chiloe & Chonos Archipelago;
Feb.9–21 Valdivia; Mar.4–7 Concepcion; Mar.12–17 Val-
paraiso; May 4–Jun.6 Herradura; May 14–29 Valparaiso;
Jul.3–6 Copiapó; Jul.13–14 Iquique; Jul.20–Sep.7 Callao;
Sept.16–Oct.20 Galápagos Islands; Nov.15–26 Tahiti;
Dec.21–30 Bay of Islands, New Zealand.
1836 Jan.12–30 Sydney Cove; Feb.4–17 Storm Bay & Hobart;
Mar.6–16 King George Sound; Apr.2–12 Cocos Keeling
Islands; Apr.29–May 9 Port Louis, Mauritius; Jun.1–17 Simon
Bay, Cape Colony; Jul.8–14 St Helena; Jul.20–23 Ascension;
Aug.1–6 Salvador; Aug.13–17 Pernambuco; Aug.31–Sep.
Porto Praya, Cape Verde Islands; Sep.19–21 Angro, Azores;
Sep.24 St Michael, Azores; Oct.2 Falmouth, CD disembarked;
Oct.5–17 Plymouth; Oct.28–Nov.6 Greenwich; Nov.6–9
Woolwich and paid off. During the S American part of the
voyage, Fitz-Roy used 4 schooners for inshore surveying
work, *Adventure [II]*, *La Liebre*, *La Paz* qq.v., and one, of 35

tons, whose name is not given, which was at first, 1835 Jun. loaned by Antonio José Vascunan of Coquimbo, when B. J. Sullivan surveyed parts of Chile coast. It was later bought, and A. B. Usborne surveyed the whole coast of Peru after Beagle left for Galápagos Is; finally sold at Paita, Peru—Fitz-Roy, *J.R.geogr.Soc.*, 6: 311–343, 1836.

THIRD SURVEYING VOYAGE To New Zealand & Australia 1837–1843, under command of *Captain* J. C. Wickham 1837–1841 when he retired through ill-health. 1841–1843 *Captain* J. L. Stokes. 1843 Oct.20 paid off for the last time.

Later history 1845–1870 Coastguard Watch Vessel on river Roach, nr Pagglesham, Essex, with masts and all gear removed. 1863 name removed and numbered W.V.7. 1870 May 13 sold to Murray & Trainer for scrap and towed to Thames estuary. 1888 *Beagle* stated in *Nature*, Lond., 37:443 to have been sold to Japan was not CD's *Beagle*, but the 4th of the name, a paddle steamer which had seen service in the Crimean war 1854. It is confused with *Beagle*, 3rd of the name, in de Beer, *Notes & Records* 62, 1959, and by H. E. L. Mellersh, *Fitzroy of the Beagle*, 1968.

Beagle [II] Research vessel of Darwin Research Station, Indefatigable Island, Galápagos Islands, 1964.

Beagle Channel Chile/Argentine. Tierra del Fuego, divides Isla Grande to the North from I. Hoste & I. Navarino to the South. Surveyed and named on 1st voyage of *Beagle*.

Beagle, Geology of *see Geology of the voyage* etc.

Beagle Islands Small islands in Galápagos group between James and Indefatigable Is. Offical Ecuadorian name 1892.

Beagle, Voyage of *see Narrative of the surveying voyages* etc., and *Journal of researches* etc.

Beagle, Zoology of *see Zoology of the Beagle*.

Beans 1857 Bees and the fertilisation of kidney beans, *Gdnr's Chronicle*, No. 43: 725 (Bi 275, F1697). 1858 On the agency of bees in the fertilisation of papilionaceous flowers and on the crossing of kidney beans, *Ann.Mag.nat.Hist.*, 2:459–465 (Bii 19), *Gdnr's Chronicle*, No. 46:828–829 (F1701).

Bear-Whale Story *see* Whale-Bear story.

Beaton, Donald 1802–1863. Plant breeder. 1861 CD 'I can plainly see that he is not to be trusted'—MLi 268. *see* Britten & Boulger.

Beaufort, Sir Francis 1774–1857. Naval Officer. KCB 1848 FRS 1814. *Rear Admiral*, Hydrographer to the Navy.

Originator of the Beaufort Scale of wind speeds. 1832 B offered CD post on *Beagle* through G. Peacock. 1832–1836 was a personal friend of Fitz-Roy. F's letters to B, during 2nd voyage of *Beagle*, contain many comments on CD; extracts in Francis D, *Nature*, Lond., 88:547–548, 1912; Barlow, *Cornhill*, 72:493–510, 1932. DNB.

Bees 1857 Bees and the fertilisation of kidney beans, *Gdnr's Chronicle*, No. 43:725 (Bi 275, F1697). 1858 On the agency of bees in the fertilisation of papilionaceous flowers and on the crossing of kidney beans, *Ann.Mag.nat.Hist.*, 2:459–465 (Bii 19), *Gdnr's Chronicle*, No. 46:828–829. 1874 Recent researches on termites and honey bees, *Nature*, Lond., 9:308–309 (Bii 182, F1768), introducing letter from Fritz Müller. *see also* Humble bees.

Beesby Lincolnshire. 1845 CD bought a farm for £13,592 borrowed from his father; rent 1845 £377, 1877 £555 16s. 1845 Sep. CD visited 'to see a farm I have purchased'—LLi 342, Keith 222. 1881 CD still owned it—Atkins 100.

Beetles CD collected avidly when at Cambridge, encouraged by W. D. Fox. His early collecting records are published in J. F. Stephens, *Illustrations of British entomology*, 1828–1835, *suppl.*, 1846, about thirty records in first 5 vols of Mandibulata. 1829 Feb.20 F. W. Hope gave CD specimens of c160 species of British beetles in London—LLi 174. 1829 CD went on beetle collecting tour with Hope to Barmouth, but CD was ill and had to return to Shrewsbury after 2 days. 1859 [Records of beetles at Downe], *Ent.weekly Intelligencer*, 6:99 (Bii 292, F1703), a note signed by Francis, Leonard & Horace D, who were 10, 8 & 7 years old, clearly written by CD—LLii 240.

Behrens, Wilhelm Julius 1854–1903. 1878 CD to on fertilisation of plants by insects, praising C. K. Sprengel, and thanking B for sending his Geschichte der Bestaubungs-Theorie, *Progr.K.Gewerbschule zu Elberfeld*, 1877–1878—LLiii 282.

Belfast 1827 CD visited on a spring tour.

Bell Mountain Chile. *see* Campana.

Bell, Lady Caroline 1836 'Lady Caroline Bell, at whose house I dined at the C. of Good Hope, admired Herschel much, but said that he always came into a room as if he knew that his hands were dirty, and that he knew that his wife knew that they were dirty'—Barlow *Autobiography* 107.

Bell, Sir Charles 1774–1842. Physician & surgeon. Kt 1830 FRS 1826. Probably the greatest human anatomist of 19c. Surgeon to Middlesex Hospital 1812–1836. Prof. Surgery Edinburgh 1836–1842. CD had high admiration of his *Anatomy and philosophy of expression*, 1806, quoting in *Expression* from 3rd edition 1844 which has B's latest corrections. 'Admirable work on expression'—Barlow *Autobiography* 138. DNB.

Bell, Thomas 1792–1880. Physician, dental surgeon & zoologist. He was the first dental surgeon to be registered. FRS 1828. Prof. Zoology King's College London. Often at Down House in the early years. 1861 CD dined with at Linnean Club, 'Bell has a real good heart'—MLi 185. Retired to The Wakes, Selbourne, Hampshire, Gilbert White's house. B wrote *Reptiles* for *Zoology of the Beagle*, and delayed completion for nearly 2 years through procrastination and ill-health. DNB.

Belloc, Anne-Louise Swanton 1796–1881. Translator from English into French. 1859 Dec. CD to ?Quatrefages, B considered translating *Origin*, but found it technically too difficult—Carroll 183, 192.

Belt, Thomas 1832–1878. Engineer, geologist & naturalist. 1874 CD to Hooker, refers to *Naturalist in Nicaragua* 1874, about glacial period—LLii 361. ?1878 CD to Hooker, 'It appears to me the best of all natural history journals which have ever been published', 'untimely death may well be deplored by naturalists'—MLiii 188.

Bemmelen, Prof. J. A. van 1877 B sent album of 217 photographs of Dutch distinguished men for CD's 68th birthday.

Benchuca Bug A large house bug of S. America (*Triatoma infestans*, Reduviidae). Vector of Chagas' disease q.v. Also lives in burrows of armadilloes. Another name for Barberio.

Bennett, Alfred William 1833–1902. Botanist. 1874 CD to B, when B had ceased to be assistant editor of *Nature*, asking for return of wood blocks for first edition of *Climbing plants*, 1865—Carroll 438.

Bennett, James Coxswain of *Beagle* on first voyage; remained with Fitz-Roy and looked after the four, later after the death of Boat Memory, three, Fuegians when they were in England, 1830–1831.

Bentham, Mr of Holwood, Downe. 1865 Sep. called at Down House. Apparently a new neighbour; ED liked him.

Bentham, George 1800–1884. Botanist, s of *Sir* Samuel B, nephew of Jeremy B. FRS 1862. 1844 CD discussed flora of Sandwich Islands with. 1854 B presented his books and herbarium to Kew and worked there daily. 1858 Jul.28 CD 'I have ordered Bentham, for, as—says, it will be very curious to see a Flora written by a man who knows nothing of British plants'—LLii 131. Jul.30 'I have got Bentham and am charmed with it'. These two quotations refer to *Handbook to the British flora*, 1858, which remained in print for more than 100 years. 1859 B accepted evolution. 1862 B approved of *Orchids* in his Presidential address to Linnean Society. 1882 B was on 'Personal Friends invited' list for CD's funeral. Biography: Jackson 1906, DNB.

Beob, Miss 1865 Governess at Down House for 6 months.

Berkeley Sound East Falkland Island. 1833 Mar.1–Apr.6, 1834 Mar.10–Apr.7 *Beagle* anchored at. CD there only in 1834.

Berkeley, Rev. Miles Joseph 1803–1889. Mycologist. FRS 1879. Vicar of Sibbertoft, Northants. 1862 Jun.14 B reviewed *Orchids* in *London.Rev.* 1868 CD thanks B for sending a copy of his Presidential address to Section D of British Association at Norwich—MLi 309 Dyer described B as 'the virtual founder of British mycology'. *see* Edible fungus from Tierra del Fuego. DNB.

Berliner Gesellschaft für Anthropologie CD Corresponding Member 1877.

Bessy *see* **Harding.**

Betley Staffordshire, nr Maer. Betley Hall, home of G. Tollet; CD & ED often visited in childhood. 1852 Apr. CD & ED visited on journey to Rugby, Barlaston & Shrewsbury.

Betsey ?1865–1879. Domestic servant at Down House.

Bettany, George Thomas 1850–1892. Botanist. 1887 *Life of Charles Darwin,* London, Great Writers Series, is the earliest biography of CD other than obituaries and Miall's lecture. Chiefly useful for J. P. Anderson's bibliography pp. i–xxxi.

Biographical Sketch of an Infant 1877 A biographical sketch of an infant, *Mind,* 2:285–294 (Bii 191, F1305). Observations made by CD 1839–1841 on his first born child William Erasmus D, written as a result of a paper on the same subject by Hippolyte Taine, a translation of which appeared in the previous number of *Mind* 252. First foreign editions; French (F1311), German (F1312), Russian (F1314) 1877; Armenian (F1310) 1914; USA (F1309) 1956. 1880 [On the bodily and mental development of infants], *Nature,* Lond., 74: 565 (Bii 732, F1797), report of a letter from CD to a social science meeting at Saratoga, N.Y.

Biological Society of Washington 1882 May 12 held a Darwin Memorial meeting, the first such. Proceedings published in *Smithson.Misc.Coll.*, 25.

Bird Talisman A fairy story by Henry Allen Wedgwood. 1. 1852 *The Family Tutor*, 3: 49–52, 89–92, 108–111, 143–146, 168–171, 208–212, 234–237. 2. 1887 Printed privately as a book, at Cambridge University Press, for CD's grandchildren, at the instigation of and with a 4 line preface by ED. 3, 1939 Only published edition as a book, illustrated by Gwen Raverat, W's great-niece and ED's grand-daughter. No. 2 is the second of ED's only printed works.

Bird, Mr 1831 B sent a fly to CD through Henslow—Darwin & Henslow 27.

Birmingham Warwickshire. 1829 CD visited with Wedgwoods for music meeting. 1839 Aug.26–Sep.11 CD visited for British Association meeting. 1849 Sep.11–21 CD visited for British Association meeting.

Bishop's Castle Shropshire. 1882 Jul. CD had a holiday at with sister Susan Elizabeth.

Bismarck *see* Elephant tree.

Blair, Rev. Robert Hugh Head of Worcester College for the Blind. 1872 B helped CD with observations on expression in the blind—MLii 109.

Blair, Rueben A. of Sedalia, Missouri. 1877 CD to about damaged goose wing and inheritance of similar damage by offspring—Carroll 529 seq. 1881 CD to B about *Mastodon* remains and B's daughter's love of natural history, 'I hope that the study of natural history may give your daughter a large share of the satisfaction which the study has given me'—Carroll 593.

Blane, Robert 1809–1871. Officer in 2nd Life Guards. Cambridge friend of CD. Assistant Adjutant General & Military Secretary 1854–1855. Colonel 1860.

Blomefield, Leonard *see* Jenyns

Bloom 1886 Francis Darwin. On the relation between the 'bloom' on leaves and distribution of the stomata, *J.Linn.Soc.Bot.*, 22:99–116 (F1805). Contains results obtained by Francis D working as research assistant to CD in 1878.

Blyth, Edward 1810–1873. Zoologist. Neglected his druggist business at Tooting in favour of natural history and got into financial difficulties—LLii 315. Zoological Curator of Museum of Asiatic Society of Bengal, Calcutta 1844–1862. 1855 B drew CD's attention to Wallace's species paper of that year. 1860 May, B wrote to CD in favour of *Origin*. CD to

Hooker, praising B's knowledge of Indian zoology, 'He is a very clever, odd, wild fellow, who will never do what he could do, from not sticking to any one subject'—MLi 63. Helped greatly with *Variation*. Biographical note on—MLi 62. Wrote under pseudonyms Zoophilus and Z. DNB.

Blytt, Axel Gudbrand 1834–1898. Botanist. Prof. Botany Christiania. 1876 B sent CD his work on Norwegian flora, *Essay on the immigration of the Norwegian flora*; CD much approved of it—LLiii 215, 248, MLii 11.

Boat Memory Man from Tierra del Fuego taken to England by Fitz-Roy in 1830, aged c20. 1830 Nov. died of smallpox in Plymouth Naval Hospital. 'A great favourite with all who knew him . . . a pleasing intelligent appearance . . . quite an exception to the general character of the Fuegians, having good features and a well-proportioned frame'—Fitz-Roy, Narrative 10.

Bobby, Bob A large half-bred black and white dog at Down House 1870. *see Expression* 64.

Boehm, Sir Joseph Edgar Bart 1834–1890. Sculptor. 1st *Bart*. RA 1882. 1883 B made statue of CD at British Museum (Natural History); life-size stone, seated in stylized chair. 1885 Jun.9 unveiled by Huxley in presence of Prince of Wales. Admiral Sulivan and Parslow were also present. There is also a half-size copy by the artist. 1887 B carved the deep medallion in Westminster Abbey. B was paid £2,100 for the statue and £150 for the medallion.

Bolton, Thomas Commercial aquarist of 146 High Holborn, London, and of Birmingham. Supplied CD with artificial sea salt for experiments on the longevity of seeds—Allan 152.

Bonn, University of 1868 CD Honorary Doctor of Medicine & Surgery.

Boo 1879 with 'Abbety', 'Mim', 'Lenny' (Leonard D) and 'Dadda' (CD) were Bernard Richard Meirion D's nicknames for the family at Down House. None is ED.

Boole, Mrs 1866 B writes to CD about his views on God and receives a characteristic answer—LLiii 63.

Boott, Dr Francis 1792–1863. American physician & botanist working in England. 1838 Aug. CD dined with at Athenaeum. 1856 Aug.20 Gray to CD 'Boott lately sent me your photograph which (though not a very perfect one) I am well pleased to have'—MLi 428. 1860 Mar.8 CD to Gray, CD has had a long letter from B 'full of the most noble love of truth and candour. He goes far with me but cannot swallow all. No one could until he had enlarged his gullet by years of practice, as in my own case'—Darwin-Gray 76.

Bosquet, Joseph Augustin Hubert de 1813–1880. Belgian carcinologist of Maestricht. 1854 CD sent him copy of *Living Cirripedia*—MLi 75. 1856 B named *Chthamalus darwini,* a fossil barnacle from the Chalk, for CD and sent him specimen—MLi 97. 1856 CD to B who was apparently also interested in carrier pigeons—Carroll 138.

Boston Society of Natural History 1873 CD Honorary Member.

Bosworthick, John Petty Officer, ropemaker, on *Beagle* second voyage.

Botanic Garden Cambridge. New Botanic Garden, Trumpington Rd, opened 1846. Holds CD's set of *Gardener's Chronicle.*

Boucher de Crèvecoeur de Perthes, Jacques 1788–1868. French geologist. 1863 CD complains to Lyell that L had not done B justice in *Antiquity of man*, B, in *Antiquité Celtiques,* 1847, had described flint artefacts with bones of rhinoceros and hyaena at Abbeville. 'Must be a very amiable man'—LLiii 13,15–16.

Bournemouth Hampshire. 1862 Sep.1–27 CD on family holiday after visit to William Erasmus D at Southampton.

Bowcher, Frank ?–1938. Sculptor & engraver. 1908 B designed Darwin-Wallace medal for Linnean Society. WWH.

Bowen, Francis 1811–1890. American theologian. Prof. Natural Religion, Moral Philosophy and Civil Polity, Harvard 1853–1889. 1860 anti-*Origin* reviews in *Mem.Amer. Acad.Arts Sci.* and *N.Amer. Rev.* (of which he was editor).

Bowman, Sir William, Bart 1816–1892. Ophthalmic surgeon. 1st *Bart* 1884 FRS 1841. Provided much information for *Expression*—LLiii 134, MLii 98, *Expression* 160, 192. 1868 CD had called on him in London, but he was away. He had done some kindness to one of CD's sons—MLii 98, Carroll 301. 1882 B was on 'Personal Friends invited' list for CD's funeral. DNB.

Brace, Rev. Charles Loring 1826–1890. American philanthropist & practical christian. 1872 summer, visited Down House—LLiii 165.

Bradley, George Granville 1821–1903. Dean of Westminster Abbey 1881–1902. B's name is on admission cards for CD's funeral. He was abroad at the time and sent his consent by telegram 'Oui sans aucune hésitation regrette mon absence'.

Braille English Braille editions of CD's works: *Journal of researches* (F168) 1916; *Origin of species* (F629) 1934; *Autobiography* (F1509) 1962.

Brass Close Darwin family estate at Marton, Lincolnshire. Ann D. née Waring, bequeathed in her will, dated 1722 May 18, 'the rents from Brass Close for four poor widows' who were to be provided with '4 grey coats' with a badge of red cloth 'cut in the shape of Two Great Roman Letters A.D.'. 1879 Leonard D visited Kirton when the piece of land was known as Darwin's Charity.

Braun, Alexander Carl Heinrich 1805–1877. German botanist. 1864 B was an early convert to CD's views on species. 1864 CD to D. B. Walsh—MLi 259.

Brayley, Edward William 1802–1870. Geologist. FRS 1854. A free-lance lecturer. *see Brayley testimonials.*

Brayley Testimonials 1845 *Additional testimonials submitted to the Council of University College, London, By Edward William Brayley . . . a candidate for the Professorship of Geology*, London, Richard & John E. Taylor printed (F324). CD's testimonial p.[7]. CD did not contribute to the earlier testimonials, for the same chair, of 1841. The chair was not filled because the College could not find the salary.

Brazil, Emperor of Pedro, II. 1825–1891. 1878 Jun. expressed a wish, whilst in England, to meet CD, but CD was away from home.

Bree, Charles Robert 1811–1886. Naturalist & anti-Darwinian. 1860 *Species not transmutable, nor the result of secondary causes*, London. CD's comments on—LLii 358. 1860 CD to Hooker, 'You need not attempt Bree', 'He in fact doubts my deliberate word, and that is the act of a man who has not the soul of a gentleman in him'—MLi 174. 1872 *An exposition of the fallacies in the hypothesis of Mr. Darwin*, London. *see* Bree on Darwinism, *Nature*, Lond.,6:279 (F1756).

Brehm, Alfred Edmund 1829–1884. German ornithologist & writer on popular natural history. [1863–]1864–1869 *Illustriertes Theirleben*, 6 vols, Hildburghausen. 1868 CD to the publishers about an English translation, not recommending it; one never appeared. CD used fourteen illustrations from it in *Descent*—Carroll 351.

Brent, Mr 1855 or 1856 a member of the Columbarian Society q.v.

Breslau, University of 1862 CD Honorary Doctor in Medicine & Surgery.

Bressa Prize 1879 awarded to CD by Reale Accademia della Scienze. Turin. 12,000 francs. CD gave £100 from it to the Zoologische Station at Naples.

Bridge, Sir [John] Frederick 1844–1924. Organist & composer. Kt 1897. Organist at Westminster Abbey 1875–1918. 1882 B composed and played anthem for CD's funeral, 'Happy is the man that findeth wisdom, and the man that getteth understanding . . .'—*Proverbs* iii 13–17.

Bridges, Esteban Lucas, christened Stephen 1874–1949. Farmer in Tierra del Fuego. 2nd s of Thomas B. Born at Ushuaia and spent most of his life at Harberton. 1947 *Uttermost part of the earth,* New York, contains later information on the 3 Fuegians who returned home on 2nd voyage of *Beagle.* Chapter 1 is about *Beagle* voyages; also detailed information on Indian tribes, especially Yahgan.

Bridges, Thomas 1841–1898. Missionary & later farmer in Tierra del Fuego. 1856 B arrived at Keppel Island Mission Station. West Falkland Islands. 1860 CD sent some preliminary queries about expression to—information from Admiral Sulivan about—LLiii 127. 1871 Oct. set up home at Stirling House, Ushaia. 1887 built farm at Harberton. *see* E. L. Bridges above, & Freeman & Gautrey, *J.Soc.Biblphy nat.Hist.,* 7:259–263, 1975.

Brighton Sussex. 1853 Jul. CD visited on day trip from Eastbourne.

Brinton, William 1823–1867. Physician. FRS 1864. Specialist on the stomach at St Thomas's Hospital, London. 1863 Oct. & Dec. CD saw, on the recommendation of George Busk, during his 6 months illness.

Brisbane, Matthew ?–1833. 1st British Resident at Falkland Islands. Murdered in an uprising of imported S. American labour at Port Louis. 1834 CD, from Port Louis, to C. Lumb, 'Such scenes of fierce revenge, cold-blooded treachery, & villany in every form, have been here transacted as few can equal it'—J. H. Winslow, *J.hist.Geogr.,*1:347–360, 1975.

Bristowe, Mrs ?–1829. Sister of W. Darwin Fox. 1827 CD to F mentions F's 2 charming sisters—Carroll 2. 1829 CD to F condoling on her early death—LLi 177.

British Association for the Advancement of Science Founded 1831 and first met at York in that year. CD went to meetings at Birmingham 1839; Southampton 1846; Oxford 1847; Birmingham 1849 (at which he was a Vice-President); Glasgow 1855 (his last). Carroll 32 seems to indicate that he was at Cork in 1843, but there is no other evidence that CD was ever in Ireland except for a brief visit to Belfast & Dublin 1838.

1860 Oxford; details of the Huxley/Wilberforce controversy at this meeting in LLii 320–323, MLi 156. There are many other versions of what was said, none of them verbatim. An excellent one in *Life of Newton*, 118–121. 1860 'When Professors lose their tempers and solemnly avow they would rather be descended from apes than Bishops; and when pretentious sciolists seriously enunciate follies and platitudes of the most wonderful absurdity and draw upon their heads crushing refutations from the truly learned'—*Guardian*, Jul.4:593. 1892 *Short life of CD*, 236–242 gives an extended version. 1900 Tuckwell, *Reminiscences of Oxford*, 50. 1923 Huxley 'There was inextinguishable laughter among the people, and they listened to the rest of my argument with great attention'—*Nature*, Lond.,920.

1958 'The Bishop . . . had turned to Huxley and mockingly asked him whether he reckoned his descent from an ape on his grandfather's or on his grandmother's side?—to which Huxley retorted 'If the question is put to me, would I rather have a miserable ape for a grandfather or a man highly endowed by nature and possessing great means and influence, and yet who employs those faculties and that influence for the mere purpose of introducing ridicule into a grave scientific discussion—I unhesitatingly affirm my preference for the ape'—Ellegård, *Darwin and the general reader*, 68. 1891 Huxley to Francis D 'When he turned to me with his insolent question, I said to Sir Benjamin [Brodie] in an undertone, "The Lord hath delivered him into my hands," '—*Short life*, 240. Many Presidential Addresses and addresses by Presidents of Section D, after 1860, give an excellent summary of the progress of evolutionary thought.

British Museum, Trustees 1848 *Enquiry by the Trustees of the British Museum*, (F345), contains letter from CD to R. I. Murchison—MLi 109.

British Museum (Natural History) 1866 *Memorial to the Chancellor of the Exchequer* [on transfer of natural history collections from British Museum, Bloomsbury, to South Kensington], signed by CD & 24 others (F869), 1873 [Letter from P. L. Sclater containing text of 1866 *Memorial*], *Nature*, Lond., 9:41 (F870). 1875 British Museum (Natural History) established in Cromwell Rd, S. Kensington.

Broderip, William John 1789–1859. Barrister & conchologist. FRS 1828. B assisted Philip Parker King in description of molluses & cirripedes from 2nd voyage of *Beagle*, printed in *Zool.J.*, 1839 and Vol.III of *Narrative*, 545–556, 1839. DNB.

Brodie ?–1873. Scottish nurse at Down House 1842–1851. Came from previous service with the Thackerays and Anne Thackeray (*Mrs* Richmond Ritchie). Left after death of Anne Elizabeth D in 1851 and returned to family home at Portsoy, Scotland. Continued to visit. ED wrote to her often, but she had a monomania that she was forgotten—EDii 214.

Brodie, Sir Benjamin Collins, Bart 1783–1862. Physician. FRS 1810. 1853 ED consulted. 1860 Apr. CD went to reception at his house. 1860 Jun. B sat next to Huxley during Wilberforce's speech at Oxford British Association. DNB.

Bronn, Heinrich Georg 1800–1862. German palaeontologist & zoologist. Prof. Natural History Heidelberg. 1860 B translated *Origin,* adding his own notes at CD's suggestion and slightly altering the text. CD was not pleased with the result—MLi 139, 172.

Brooke, Rajah Sir Charles Anthony Johnson (né Johnson) 1829–?. 2nd British Rajah of Sarawak GCMG 1888. 1868 B succeeded his uncle, *Sir* James B (1803–1868). 1870 Nov.30 B answered CD's *Queries about expression* from Sarawak.

Broom, Common *see Cytisus scoparius*.

Brown, Jane 1746–1835. d of Joseph Brown of Swineshead, Lincolnshire. m 1772 William Alvey D [I]. CD's great aunt in law.

Brown, Robert 1773–1858. Botanist. FRS 1811. First Keeper of Botany at British Museum. Von Humboldt called him 'Facile Princeps botanicorum'. Dilatory in describing plants of first voyage of Beagle—MLi 39. 1858 CD to Hooker, 'I am glad to hear that old Brown is dying so easily'—MLi 109. CD 'I saw a good deal of'—Barlow, *Autobiography* 103. 1858 The Darwin/Wallace paper was read at Linnean Society meeting at which B's death was announced, the fact perhaps overshadowing the importance of the paper. DNB.

Browne, Sir George Buckston 1850–1945. Surgeon. Kt. FRCS 1926. 1922 bought Down House for British Association. Brief amusing life of B in Atkins, *Down*, ch.13, 1974. Portrait by *Sir* Robin Darwin at Down House.

Browne, Sir James Crichton 1840–1938. Physician. Kt 1886 FRSE 1870 FRS 1883. Director of West Riding Pauper Lunatic Asylum, Wakefield. Visitor in Lunacy 1875–1922. Gave CD information for *Expression*. Sent CD *Annual Reports* of the Asylum, the run now being at Cambridge—Carroll 451.

Browne, William Alexander Francis Browne 1805–1873. Physician of Stirling. 1857 First Commissioner in Lunacy for Scotland. Naturalist friend of CD at Edinburgh.

Brullé, Gaspard Auguste 1809–1873. Zoologist. Prof. Zoology & Comparative Anatomy Dijon 1840–. 1864 H. Falconer to CD 'He told me in despair that he could not get his pupils to listen to anything from him except à la Darwin'—MLi 257.

Brummidge, Mrs c1890 Cook at Down House—Atkins, *Down*.

Brunton, Sir Thomas Lauder, Bart 1844–1916. Physician. 1st *Bart* 1908 FRS 1874. Consultant at St. Bartholomew's Hospital, London. B helped CD with experiments for *Insectivorous plants*. 1881 Nov.19 CD to B about prosecution of *Dr* D. Ferrier under the Vivisection act. CD wanted to be an early subscriber if a subscription was got up to pay F's costs. CD had met F at B's house, 50 Welbeck St.—MLii 437.

Bryanston Square, London No.4 R. B. Lichfield's house. *Sir* Thomas Farrer also lived in the square.

Bucket Ropes for Wells 1852 Bucket ropes for wells, *Gdnr's Chronicle*, No.2:22 (Bi 252,F1680).

Buckland, Francis Trevelyan 1826–1880. Physician & naturalist. s of William B. Known as Frank. Government Inspector of Fisheries 1867– . DNB.

Buckland, Rev. William 1784–1856. Geologist. FRS 1818. Prof. Mineralogy Oxford 1812– . Dean of Westminster 1845–1856. f of Francis Trevelyan B. 'Though very good-humoured and good-natured seemed to me a vulgar and almost a coarse man'—Barlow, *Autobiography* 102. DNB.

Buckle, Henry Thomas 1821–1856. Self-educated historian. c1842 CD met at Hensleigh Wedgwood's and discussed organization of facts. 1858 CD to Hooker 'I was not much struck with the great Buckle'. CD was reading B's *History of civilization* at the time—LLii 110. 'I doubt whether his generalisations are worth anything'—Barlow, *Autobiography* 109–110. DNB.

Buckley, Arabella Burton 1840–1929. Natural historian & author. Later, before 1875, *Mrs* Fisher. Secretary to Lyell. 1871 Mar. visited Down House with the Lyell's—LLiii 137. 1876 Feb.11 CD to B saying that he had enjoyed B's *A short history of natural science*, London 1871—LLiii 229. 1882 B was on 'Personal Friends invited' list for CD's funeral.

Buckman, James 1816–1884. Agriculturist & geologist. Professor of Botany & Geology Royal Agricultural College Cirencester 1848–1863. 1857 CD to B on varieties of domestic pigeon. 1859 CD sent 1st edition of *Origin* to B—unpublished letter.

Buenos Aires Capital of Argentine. 1832 Jul.26—1833 Dec.6 *Beagle* used mouth of La Plata river as a base for surveying trips. CD used Buenos Aires, Monte Video & Maldonado as bases for inland expeditions.

Bulgarian First editions in: *Journal of researches* (F170) 1967; *Origin of species* (F632) 1946; *Descent of man* (F1047) 1927; *Autobiography* (F1511) 1959.

Bull, Mr. A pigeon fancier in the Borough, London. 1859 B had crossed pouters with runts to gain size—LLii 281.

Bulwer, Sir Edward George Earle Lytton, Bart, *Baron* Lytton. 1803–1873. Novelist & parliamentarian, 1st *Baron* Lytton 1866 1st *Bart* 1838. A remote cousin of CD through Erasmus Earle. Added Lytton to his surname in 1843. In 'one of his novels a Professor Long, who had written two huge volumes on limpets' was CD—Autobiography, 81. The novel was *What will he do with it?*, 4 vols, 1858, under pseudonym Pisistratus Caxton. 'Lecture on conchology to the Gatesboro' Athenaeum', for which he was paid £5.5.0—Vol.1:284–296. The work was '*Researches into the natural history of limpets*, 2 vols, Post octavo'. DNB.

Bulwer, William Earle Gascoyne Lytton 1829–1910. *Brigadier-General*, late Scots Guards, of Haydon Hall, Norfolk. A remote cousin of CD through Erasmus Earle; nephew of *Lord* Lytton. 1890 Oct. William Erasmus D & George Howard D went on a visit to 'a beautiful place in Norfolk, to see the picture of Erasmus Earle, an ancestor'.

Bunbury, Sir Charles James Fox Bart 1809–1886. Palaeobotanist. 8th *Bart* 1860 FRS 1851. Of Mildenhall, Suffolk. m 1844 Frances Joanna Horner, 2nd d of Leonard H; brother-in-law of Lyell. Encouraged CD in persevering on species problem. Biography: [1894] by wife.

Bunbury, Frances Joanna *see* Horner.

Bunsen, Baroness *see* Frances Waddington.

Bunnett, Templeton An Australian who in 1867 answered *Queries about expression.*

Burchell, William, John ?1782–1863. Explorer & naturalist.

Burke, Sir Henry Farnham 1859–1924. Genealogist. Somerset Herald 1887–1911. 1888 *Pedigree of the family of Darwin*, privately printed, sixty copies. The most reliable pedigree, also contains illustrations of the arms of Darwin.

Burnham Beeches Fine woodland on Dunstable Downs. 1847 Jun. CD visited on a day trip from British Association meeting at Oxford.

Busby, James 1801–1871. First British Resident in New Zealand. 1835 Dec. CD met—*S.Afr.Christian Recorder*, 2:235, 1836, *J.Researches*, 1845, 421 (spelt Bushby).

Busk, George 1807–1886. Surgeon & man of science. FRS 1850. CD to Huxley, 'I have heard that Busk is on our side in regard to species'—MLi 130. 1863 B recommended *Dr* William Brinton to CD. 1871 CD to B, thanking him for pointing out an error about the supra-condyliod foramen in 1st issue of *Descent*—Carroll 387.

Butler, Miss 1859 Sep. CD invites to stay with him at Ilkley in Oct. since he might not be able to take his family; 'but if you were there I should feel safe and home-like'. In the end he took his family.

Butler, Rev. Samuel [I] 1774–1839. Schoolmaster & priest. Headmaster of Shrewsbury School 1798–1836, including the time when CD was there. Bishop of Lichfield & Coventry 1836– . f of Thomas B, gf of Samuel B [II].

Butler, Samuel [II] 1835–1902. Author & controversialist. s of Thomas B, gs Samuel B [I]. 1859 CD sent 1st edition *Origin* to. 1880 B had a one-sided quarrel with CD over Krause's biography of Erasmus D in its English version. For B's printed contributions *see Athenaeum*, Jan.31, *St James's Gaz.*, Dec.8. Also Festing Jones 1911 *Charles Darwin and Samuel Butler*. 1880 Dec.14 Romanes to CD, '[Butler] is a lunatic beneath all contempt—an object of pity were it not for his vein of malice'—*Life of Romanes*, 104. 1881 Jan. CD to Romanes on R's review of *Unconscious memory*, *Nature*, Lond., 23:285–287. B 'will smart under your stricture', R is right to attribute B's conduct to 'the disappointment of his inordinate vanity'; CD thanks R for saving him from, B's 'malignant revenge'—

Carroll 581. 1881 Feb. CD to T. R. R. Stebbing thanking S for his letter to *Nature*, Lond., 23:336 on the controversy. 1881 Apr. CD to Romanes, 'I am extremely glad that you seem to have silenced Butler and his reviewers. But Mr. Butler will turn up again, if I know the man'—Carroll 588. 1881 Krause wrote a strictly accurate letter on the subject, *Nature*, Lond., 23:288. Barlow, *Autobiography* gives references and reprints Jones' pamphlet in full. B's copy of *Erasmus Darwin*, with his mss notes, is in the British Library, B's books on evolution, a subject on which his knowledge was entirely theoretical, were 1879 *Evolution old and new*, 1880 *Unconscious memory*, 1887 *Luck or cunning*. Biography: Jones 1919, DNB.

Butler, Rev. Thomas 1806–1886. s of Samuel B [I], f of Samuel B [II]. Rector of Langar with Bamston, Notts, 1834–1876. Canon of Lincoln 1868. At St John's College, Cambridge, when CD was up. 1828 B was at Barmouth with a reading party in autumn with CD, under G. A. Butterton; B and CD collected beetles together. 1839 B and CD travelled together in a stage coach from Birmingham to Shrewsbury, at end of British Association meeting—Jones, *Life of Samuel Butler*, i:13; J says that this is the last time that they met. 1872 CD to J. M. Herbert, B has become 'a very unpleasant old man'—Carroll 425.

Butterflies 1880 The sexual colours of certain butterflies, *Nature*, Lond., 21:237 (Bii 220, F1787).

Butterton, George Ash 1805–1891. DD 1843. Fellow of St John's College, Cambridge 1828–1837. Headmaster Uppingham 1839–1845, Giggleswick 1847–1859. CD's tutor for classics and mathematics. 1828 B took a reading party to Barmouth in autumn. CD 'A very dull man'.

Butterton 1878 A stray minute female black and tan collie at Bassett, later thought to be a 'special breed of dog from Thibet'—EDii 287, Atkins, *Down*, 80.

Button, James, Jemmy Boy from Tierra del Fuego, taken to England by Fitz-Roy in 1830, aged about 14. 1833 Jan.23 returned. Fitz-Roy, *Narrative*, gives his name in Tekeenica (i.e. Yahgan) as Orundellico. Fitz-Roy says that he was bought for one mother-of-pearl button. E. L. Bridges calls him Jimmy. He was alive in 1863 and remained a bad lot; not mentioned later. A son visited England in 1866. Bridges says that the story about the button could not be true.

Byerley, Thomas ?–1810. Josiah Wedgwood's [I] partner at

Etruria Works and his cousin, s of Josiah's father's sister Margaret.

Bynoe, Benjamin c1804–1865 Assistant Surgeon on 1st & 2nd voyages of *Beagle*. Acting Surgeon from 1832 Apr. 1839 CD 'Thanks . . . for his very kind attention to me when I was ill at Valparaiso'—*J. Researches*, 1845, vii. Surgeon 1836. Later M.O. in charge of convicts.

C

Caddis-Flies 1879 Fritz Müller on a frog having eggs on its back—on the abortion of hairs on the legs of certain caddis-flies, etc., *Nature*, Lond., 19:462–463 (Bii 216, F1784); introducing a letter from M, *ibid*, 463–464.

Caerdeon 2m east of Barmouth, N. Wales, on N side of Barmouth estuary. 1869 Jun.10–Jul.29 CD had family holiday there.

Caernarvon N. Wales. 1842 Jun. CD visited.

Caird, Sir James 1816–1892. Agriculturalist. KCB 1882 FRS 1865. MP for Stirling 1859–1865. 1878 C subscribed, with CD & Farrer to keep Torbitt's experiments on potato disease going—LLiii 350. DNB.

Caldclough, Alexander ?–1858. Private Secretary to British Ambassador to Chile, later merchant. FRS 1831. 1834 CD stayed with at Valparaiso. 1835 CD to sister Susan D 'the author of some bad travels in S. America . . . took an infinite degree of trouble for me'—Barlow, *Charles Darwin and the voyage of the Beagle*, 118. *Travels in South America*, London 1835.

Caldwell, Mrs Anne Marsh 1791–1874. Novelist. A friend of the Wedgwoods from childhood. 1866 CD to C about her blind friend *Mr* Corbet—Carroll 323.

Californian Academy of Sciences 1872 CD Honorary Member.

Californian State Geological Society 1877 CD Corresponding Member.

Callao Seaport of Lima, Peru. 1835 Jul.20–Sep.7 *Beagle* at. Jul.20 CD landed.

Cambridge Apart from his residence as an undergraduate, for which *see* Cambridge University, CD was in Cambridge on the following occasions: 1831 Sep.2–4, 19, staying with Henslow when preparing for *Beagle* voyage; 1836 Dec.13–1837 Mar.6, staying with Henslow and in Fitzwilliam St, sorting *Beagle* material; he had 2 short trips to London during this period; 1838 May 10–12 to visit Henslow. 1870 May 20–24, to visit his sons, Francis, George & Horace, stayed at Bull Hotel; 1877 Nov.16–18 CD visited with ED for award of Honorary LL.D. 1880 Aug.14–18 CD & ED stayed with Horace D in St Botolph's Lane. 1881 Oct.20–27 CD & ED stayed with Horace D. 1883, after CD's death, ED moved to The Grove, Huntingdon Road for the winters. Cambridge life for the Ds is brilliantly depicted in Gwen Ravert's *Period Piece*, 1952.

Cambridge Philosophical Society Founded 1819, Henslow & Sedgwick being the leading instigators. 1835 issued for private circulation CD's *Letters on geology*, reprinted by them 1960. 1879 The members commissioned portrait of CD by W. B. Richmond, which still hangs in their rooms. CD was never a member.

Cambridge Ray Club Founded in 1837 when Henslow stopped his Friday evenings open house. *see* Babington, *The Cambridge Ray Club*, 1887, published on its fiftieth anniversary.

Cambridge University CD entered at Christ's College 1827 Oct.15, but did not come into residence until Lent term; left 1831 Jun. 1830 Dec. CD took degree examinations and kept two terms, leaving at end of May term. 10th in list of candidates who did not seek honours. 1831 Apr.26 CD admitted BA—*Cambridge Chronicle* Apr.29; he was 'Baccalaureus ad Baptistam' and therefore included in 1832 list—LLi 163. 1837 MA. 1877 Nov.17 Hon.LL.D. Public Orator, J. E. Sandys, ended 'Tu vero, qui leges naturae tam docte illustraveris, legum Doctor nobis esto'—LLiii 222. 1877 Nov.17 ED to William Erasmus D gives description of the scene with a monkey and a missing link lowered from the gallery by undergraduates—EDii 230.

Cambridge, Rev. Octavius Pickard 1835–1917. Arachnologist. Rector of Bloxworth, Dorset 1868–1917. 1874 CD to C on natural selection and on spiders—Carroll 437 (but not identified).

Cameron, Rev. Jonathan Henry Lovett 1807–1888. Cambridge friend of CD, Trinity College; member of Gourmet Club. 1830 C was gulfed [to be in the gulf is said of an honours candidate who fails, but is allowed an ordinary degree]. Rector of Shoreham, Kent 1860–1888.

Cameron, Julia Margaret (née Pattle) 1815–1879. Photographer. Sister of *Mrs* Prinsep & *Lady* Somers. m Charles Hay Cameron (1795–1880). 1868 CD with ED, Erasmus Alvey D

& Horace D, visited C at Freshwater, Isle of Wight. C photographed CD, EAD & HD, but not ED. 'She came to see us off and loaded us with presents of photographs, and Erasmus called after her "Mrs Cameron, there are six people in this house all in love with you"'—LLiii 102. CD 'I like this photograph very much better than any other which has been taken of me'—LLiii 92. There are 2 versions: *a*: Profile facing right, which has often been reproduced; *b*: Half-face facing left, which does not seem to have ever been reproduced. Authentic originals bear *Mrs* Cameron's signature and Colnaghi's blind authentication stamp. DNB.

Camp Hill House on Maer Heath, Staffs. Home of Sarah Elizabeth Wedgwood [I] 1823–1847, when she moved to Petley's, Downe.

Campana A peak in Chile, 6,400 ft. 1834 Aug.16–17 CD climbed to summit, which now bears a plaque—*J. Researches*, 1845, 255–257.

Campbell, George John Douglas, Duke of Argyll 1830–1900. Statesman & geologist. 8th Duke 1847 FRS 1851. 1862 C reviewed *Orchids* in *Edinb.Rev.*—LLiii 274. 1864 C addressed Royal Society of Edinburgh anti-*Origin*. 1867 CD to Huxley about *Reign of law*, 'or Dukelet's? how can you speak so of a living real Duke?'—MLi 277. 1867 CD to Kingsley about *Reign of law*, 'Very well written, very interesting, honest & clever & very arrogant'. 1881 C 'I wish Mr. Darwin's disciples would imitate a little of the dignified reticence of their master. He walks with a patient and a stately step along the paths of conscientious observation'—MLi 396. 1881 Feb. CD called at Argyll House, London. 1882 C was pall-bearer at CD's funeral. Main works relating to evolution: 1867 *The reign of law*, London; 1884 *The unity of nature*, London, DNB.

Canary Islands 1831 CD planned a trip there with Kirby & Ramsay, perhaps also Dawes, before *Beagle* invitation came. *see also* Tenerife.

Canby, Dr William Marriott 1831–1904. Botanist of Wilmington, Delaware, USA. C provided information on *Dionaea* for *Insectivorous plants*.

Candolle, Alphonse Louis Pierre Pyrame de 1806–1893. Botanist. Prof. Natural History Geneva 1841–1850, succeeding his father. 1840 C dined at 12 Upper Gower St to meet the Sismondis—LLii 216. 1859 CD sent 1st edition of *Origin* to. 1880 C used the same portfolio method of reference as CD, independently evolved—LLiii 333. 1880 C visited Down House in autumn. 1855 C's *Géographie botanique raissonée*, Paris, was very important to CD in his study of cultivated plants. Letters to & from CD, *Gesnerus*, 12:109–156, 1955. 1873 *Histoire des sciences et des savants depuis deux siècles*, Geneva. 1882 *Darwin considéré au point de vue des causes de son succès*, Geneva.

Canestrini, Giovanni 1835–1900. Acarologist. C translated nine of CD's works into Italian. 1877 *La teoria dell'evoluzione*, Turin.

Canning Fishmonger at Downe. C went to Billingsgate three times a week. His mother was unqualified midwife at Downe—Atkins, *Down* 104.

Cape Verde Islands 1832 Jan.17–Feb.8 *Beagle* at Porto Praya, Santo Jago. CD landed. 1836 Aug.31–Sep.5 *Beagle* again at. CD landed. These islands, known as Ilhas do Cabo Verde in Portuguese, derive their name from Cape Verde on the mainland of Africa c300 miles away. It is one of the few differences between 6th edition *Origin* 1872, 11th thousand, and the altered 6th edition 1876, 18th thousand, that the name is changed from Cape de Verde to Cape Verde.

Capel Curig Caernarvonshire. 1831 Aug. CD visited with Sedgwick for geology. 1842 Jun. CD visited.

Cape Town Cape Colony, S. Africa. 1836 Jun.1–7 *Beagle* at. CD landed and made short excursion inland Jun.4–7. CD met *Sir* John Herschel there. CD's first published work, with Fitz-Roy, A letter containing remarks on the moral state of Tahiti, New Zealand &c., *S.Afr.Christian Recorder*, 2:221–238, 1836 Sep. was published there.

Cardwell, Edward *Viscount* 1813–1886. Statesman. 1st *Viscount* 1874 FRS 1873. 1875 C was Chairman of Vivisection Commission, to which CD gave evidence.

Caricatures *see* CD Iconography.

Carlisle Cumberland. 1855 Sep.19 CD visited on return from British Association meeting at Glasgow.

Carlisle, Bishop of *see* Harvey Goodwin.

Carlisle, Sir Anthony 1768–1840. Surgeon. Kt 1820 FRS 1804. 1847 May CD 'Old Sir Anthony Carlisle once said to me gravely that he supposed Megatherium and such cattle were just sent down from heaven to see whether the earth would support them'—MLii 219. DNB.

Carlyle, Jane Baillie *see* Welsh

Carlyle, Thomas 1795–1881. Essayist & historian. m 1836 Jane Baillie Welsh dsp. CD met several times at Erasmus Alvey D's and at C's in London. DNB.

Carpenter, William Benjamin 1813–1885. Physician & naturalist. FRS 1844. Prof. Physiology London. Registrar London University 1856–1879. 1859 CD sent 1st edition of *Origin*. 1860 Jan. C reviewed *Origin* in *Nat.Rev.*, Apr. in *Med.Chirurg.Rev.* 1861 or later visited Down House.

Carr, Anne Jane *see* Wedgwood.

Carr, Ralph Edward 1833–1892. Colonel. m 1870 Ann Jane Wedgwood. 1872 lost 1st child.

Carroll, P. Thomas 1976 editor of *An annotated calendar of the letters of Charles Darwin in the Library of the American Philosophical Society*, Wilmington, Delaware. A most important source book of CD reference.

Carruthers, William 1830–1922. Botanist. FRS 1871. Keeper of Botany, British Museum (Natural History). Consulting botanist to Agricultural Society 1871–1910. 1878 CD to Torblitt in search of funds for potato blight work; C was against providing further money—MLi 373.

Cartmell, James 1810–1881. Master of Christ's College Cambridge 1849–1881. Chaplain to Queen Victoria 1855–1881. 1909 William Erasmus D's speech at Cambridge celebrations 'He [CD] spoke to me with pride and pleasure of walking, dressed in his scarlet gown, arm in arm with Dr. Cartmell'—EDii 171.

Carter, Alice 1885 A partially blind Downe cottager whom ED helped. She looked after old *Mrs* Osborn.

Carus, Julius Victor 1823–1903. German zoologist. 1860 Jun. was at British Association meeting at Oxford. 1866 C translated 3rd German *Origin*, which was published in 1867, from 4th English. 'The connection was cemented by warm feelings of regard on both sides'—LLiii 48. Later translated 12 other of CD's works. 1876 Mar.21 CD to C 'I can assure you that the idea of anyone translating my books better than you never even momentarily crossed my mind'—MLi 146.

Carver, Miss Alice Schoolmistress. Co-founder of Downe House School with *Miss* O. M. Willis.

Cary, William s of William C, 1759–1825, instrument maker of London. 1831 CD to Henslow about C making instruments for *Beagle*—Barlow, *Darwin and Henslow* 25, 41.

Case, Rev. G. Unitarian minister at Shrewsbury with a chapel in High St. 1817 CD went for a year, with sister Emily Catherine, to an infant school run by C.—Barlow, *Autobiography* 22.

Casks 1879 [letter] Rats and water casks, *Nature*, Lond.,19:481, supporting one from Arthur Nicols, *ibid.*, 433 (Bii 218, F1785).

Catasetum tridentatum 1861 *C.tridentatum, Monacanthus viridis* & *Myanthus barbatus* are male, female and hermaphrodite flowers of the same species of orchid MLii 280. 1862 On the three remarkable sexual forms of *Catasetum tridentatum*, an orchid in the possession of the Linnean Society, *J.Proc.Linn.Soc. Lond,(Bot.)*, 6:151–157 (Bii 63, F1718). 1863 French translation in *Ann.Sci.nat.Bot.*, 19:204–295, with CD's papers on *Primula* & *Linum*.

Caton, John Dean 1812–1895. Chief Justice of Illinois & naturalist. 1868 CD thanks C for a paper on American deer —LLiii 102. 1871 CD to C, George, Howard & Francis D are touring USA, please aid them and show 'famous Deer-Park'—Carroll 402. Author of 1877 *The antelope and deer of America*, New York.

Cattell, J. Nurseryman of Westerham, Kent. 1860 CD to Maxwell Masters, the nurseryman CD generally dealt with—MLii 257.

Cavendish, Sir William, Duke of Devonshire 1808–1891. 7th *Duke* 1858. 1882 Pall Bearer at CD's funeral, as Chancellor of Cambridge University. 1845 Sep. or Oct. CD visited Chatsworth, the ducal seat, then of William C, 6th *Duke*. DNB.

Cecil, Robert Arthur Talbot Gascoyne, Marquis of Salisbury 1830–1903. Statesman. 3rd *Marquis* 1868. m 1857 Georgiana Alderson [II]. EB DNB.

Cecil, Lord Sackville Arthur 1865–1898. 5s of 3rd Marquis of Salisbury. Cambridge friend of CD's sons and neighbour in Kent. 1882 C was on 'Family Friends invited' list for CD's funeral.

Cerro Perico Flaco Argentine. A hill near river Beguelo, a tributary of Rio Negro. 1833 Nov.22–26 CD visited from estancia of *Mr* Keen and found skull of 'Megatherium' [actually *Toxodon*]. The hill now bears an obelisk commemorating CD's visit and a nearby village is called Darwin—J. H. Winslow, *J.hist.Geogr.*, 1:347–360, 1975.

Chaffers Master of *Beagle* on 2nd voyage.

Chagas' Disease A trypanosomiasis of South America, spread to man by the house bugs *Triatoma infestans* & *Conorhinus magistus*. The infective agent, *Trypanosoma cruzi*, was first described by Carlos Chagas, Nova tripanozomiaze humana, Ueber eine neue Trypanosomiasis des Menschen, *Mem.Inst. Oswaldo Cruz*, Rio de Janeiro, 1:159–218, 1909. Often suggested that CD had the disease from being bitten by *T.infestans*, the benchuca bug, at Luxan, Mendoza Province, Argentine, 1835 Mar.26. Others say that his symptoms were not those typical of the disease. *see* CD Health.

Chambers, Robert 1802–1883. Edinburgh publisher. Anonymous author of *Vestiges of the natural history of creation*, 1844, and of *Explanations; a sequel*, 1845. Public acknowledgement was not made until 12th edition 1884, after C's death. 1844 CD to Hooker, 'have been somewhat less amused at it than you appear to have been'—LLi 333. 1845 CD to Hooker, on *Explanations* and Kerguelen cabbage—MLi 48. 1847 CD to C on Glen Roy—MLii 177. 1847 CD to Hooker, 'Somehow I feel perfectly convinced he is the author'—LLi 356. 1848 CD to Lyell, 'if he be, as I believe, the Author of Vestiges this book [*Ancient sea margins*] for poverty of intellect is a literary curiosity'—Carroll 73. c1850 CD to Hooker, CD calls him 'Mr. Vestiges'—LLii 29. 1860 C was at Oxford British Association meeting. 1861 CD called at 'his very nice house in St. John's Wood. He is really a capital fellow'—MLi 186.

Chapman Cambridge friend of CD—LLi 181. Not traced.

Chapman, Dr John 1822–1894. Physician & publisher. 1865 CD tried his ice-cure, in spring & summer.

Charlesworth, Edward 1813–1893. Geologist. 1838 CD to Lyell, 'Charlesworth is to be pitied for many reasons'—Carroll 11. 1842 CD to Lyell, discussing a controversy between C and Buckland, Lyell and Owen on the Crag, 'it is not the wise who rule the universe, but the active rule the inactive and verily Charlesworth is . . . active'—Carroll 28.

Chator, William 1802–1885. Nurseryman of Saffron Walden, Essex. 1855 CD to Henslow [as Mrss Chator], on breeding of hollyhocks in which C specialized—Darwin-Henslow 189.

Chatsworth Derbyshire. Seat of the Dukes of Devonshire. 1845 Sep. or Oct. CD visited.

Chêne nr Vevey, Lac Léman, Switzerland. Home of J. C. L. Simonde de Sismondi.

Cherry blossoms 1876 Cherry blossoms, *Nature*, Lond., 14:28 (Bii 189, F1772).

Chester, Mr A friend of Fitz-Roy who was invited to go on *Beagle* before CD, but could not.

Chester, Colonel Joseph Lemuel 1821–1882. American genealogist. Worked on early history of the Darwin family. 1858 C settled in London. 1879 Henrietta Emma D 'My brothers had been having the pedigree of the Darwins made out by a certain Colonel Chester'—EDii 237. George Howard D's mss notes for C are in the Galton papers at University College London. DNB.

Chester Place No. 4, Regent's Park, London. 1868 Sarah Elizabeth Wedgwood's [II] 'little house'.

Chester Terrace No. 42, Regent's Park, London. Home of Hensleigh Wedgwood.

Chevening Kent. Seat of 4th & 5th Earls Stanhope q.v. 1849 CD visited.

Chiloe Island Chile. 1834 Nov.10–1835 Feb.4 *Beagle* surveying around. CD much ashore, including visits to Chonos Archipelago to south of C. 'Everyone was glad to say farewell to Chiloe'—*J.Researches* 1845, 297.

Chinese First edition in: *Origin of species* 1903 (Chs 3 & 4 only) (F634); whole work 1918 (F637).

Chlorophyll 1882 The action of carbonate of ammonia on chlorophyll bodies, *J.Linn.Soc.Lond.Bot.*, 19:262–284 (Bii 256, F1801); abstract by Francis D. who helped in the work, *Nature*, Lond., 25:489–490.

Chobham Surrey. 1853 Aug. CD visited military camp for Crimean war.

Chonos, Archipiélago de los Chile. 1834 Dec.18–1835 Jan.15 *Beagle* surveying off; CD ashore.

Christ's College Cambridge 1827 Oct.15 CD admitted, 'Admissus est pensionarius minor sub Magistro Shaw', but did not go up until Lent term. Set in front court, G staircase, traditionally the same as those of William Paley. The set now has commemorative Wedgwood plaque.

Cirripedia, British Fossil 1850 On British fossil Lepadidae, *Quart J.Geol.Soc.(Proc.)*, 6:439–440, abstract only; CD withdrew the paper (F1679). 1851, 1854, 1858 *A monograph of the fossil Lepadidae, or pedunculated cirripedes of Great Britain . . . A monograph of the fossil Balanidae and Verrucidae of Great Britain . . .* [Index to Vol.II 1858], Palaeontographical Society Vols 5, 8 & 12 [index to Vol.II], London (F342), Facsimile 1966 (F343).

Cirripedia, British Living *see* Albany Hancock.

Cirripedia, Living 1851, 1854 *A monograph of the sub-class Cirripedia . . . The Lepadidae; or, pedunculated cirripedes . . . The Balanidae (or sessile cirripedes), the Verrucidae*, 2 vols, Ray Society's Publ. Nos 21 & 25, London (F339) . Facsimile 1964 (F340). Foreign edition: extracts only Russian 1936 (F341). 1854 CD asks Huxley's advice on complimentary copies; these were sent to Bosquet, Milne Edwards, Dana, L. Agassiz, Müller, Dunker; possibly also to Von Siebold, Lovén, d'Orbigny, Kölliker, Sars, Kröyer. 1863 On the so-called auditory-sac in cirripedes, *Nat.Hist.Rev.*, 3:115–116 (Bii 85, F1722). 1873 On the males and complemental males of certain cirripedes, and on rudimentary structures, *Nature*, Lond., 8:431–432 (Bii 177, F1762).

Claparède, Jean Louis René Antoine Édouard 1830–1871. Swiss invertebrate zoologist. Professor Comparative Anatomy Geneva 1862– . Early convert to evolution—MNi 259. Articles on evolution in *Revue Germanique*, 1861.

Clapham Grammar School All CD's sons went there except William Erasmus D. 1834 Headmaster & founder Charles Pritchard; George & Francis educated by him. 1862 Headmaster Alfred Wrigley; Leonard & Horace educated by him. Closed 1885.

Clapham, Marianne Aunt of Laura Forster, known as Mone; wrote autobiography, with darwinian reference.

Clark, Sir Andrew, Bart 1826–1893. Fashionable London physician. 1st *Bart* 1883 FRS 1885. 1873 C first attended CD. 1876 attended William Erasmus D at Down House for concussion in a riding accident. 1881 C saw CD in London, 'some derangement of the heart'. 1882 Mar.10 C saw CD at Down House. 1882 Apr. C on 'Personal Friends invited' list for CD's funeral. DNB.

Clark, John Willis 1833–1910. Zoologist, archaeologist & Cambridge historian. Superintendant Zoology Museum Cambridge 1866–1891. Registrar Cambridge University 1891–1910. 1877 Nov. C fed ED on galantine when CD got honorary LL.D. 1882 C was on 'Personal Friends invited' list for CD's funeral. 1909 C organised CD centenary celebrations at Cambridge. DNB.

Clark, Dr 1837 CD's physician in London, perhaps *Sir* James C 1788–1870.

Clark, William 1788–1869. Prof. Anatomy Cambridge

1817–1866. FRS 1836. Rector of Guisely, Yorkshire 1826–1859. 1860 May 18 CD to Lyell, says anti-*Origin*, but son J. W. Clark says not so—LLii 308. DNB.

Clarke, William Branwhite 1798–1878. Physician of Ipswich. 1850 C edited *Narrative of the wreck of the 'Favorite'*, by John Nunn, a sailor.

Cleavage 1846–1847 CD's views on geological cleavage, with illustrations by CD—MLii 199–210. These were never published as a paper.

Clemson Gunsmith of Shrewsbury. 1831 C made CD's gun and spare parts for *Beagle* voyage—LLi 210.

Clift, William 1775–1849. Conservator Royal College of Surgeons Museum 1793–1844. 1825 his daughter married Richard Owen. DNB.

Climbing plants 1865 On the movements and habits of climbing plants, *J.Proc.Linn.Soc.Lond.*, 9, Nos 33 & 34, 1–118 (F833–834): also available as a book in paper wrappers (F835); 1866 reprinted in *Flora*, 49:241–252, 273–282, 321–325, 337–345, 375–378, 385–398. 1875 2nd edition *The movements and habits of climbing plants*, London (F836). 1882 2nd edition with appendix to preface by Francis D, London (F839). First foreign editions: USA (F838), German (F860) 1876; French (F858) 1877; Russian (F865) 1900; Romanian (F864) 1970.

Clive, William 1795–1883. Archdeacon of Montgomery 1844–1861. m Marianne d of George Tollet. 1855 CD to Henslow, CD had seen C in London and he had enquired after H—Darwin-Henslow 174.

Clough, Miss Anne Jemima 1820–1892. Sister of Arthur Hugh Clough, poet. First Principal of Newnham College Cambridge. 1883 C stayed at Down House. DNB.

Coal Club CD was interested in the savings club for Downe villagers—Darwin-Innes 203.

Coal, Origin of 1846 CD to Hooker, 4 letters on the subject—Mlii 217–220.

Cobbe, Miss Frances Power 1822–1904. Antivivisectionist. Editor of *The Echo and Zoophilist*. Secretary National Anti-Vivisection Society 1875–1884. 1881 C issued antivivisection circular which she sent to CD; letters by C to *The Times* Apr.19 & 23, by CD Apr.22 & by Romanes Apr.25 relate. CD to Romanes 'with the sweet Miss Cobbe—Good Heavens what a liar she is: did you notice how in her second letter she altered what she quoted from her first letter, trusting to no one comparing the two'—LLii 203. Reviewed *Descent* in *Theologi-cal Rev*. 1868 ED to her sister Elizabeth Wedgwood 'I dined over the way [at Hensleigh Wedgwood's] (and Charles also) to meet Miss Cobbe and Miss Lloyd. Miss Cobbe was very agreeable'—EDii 189. 1894 C to ED for permission to publish correspondence from CD which she had altered and printed in *The Echo*, about what C considered a miscarriage of justice, but was not—EDii 302. 1872 *Darwinism in morals and other essays*, London. *Autobiography* 1894. DNB.

Cobbold, Thomas Spencer 1828–1886. Parasitologist. 1885 C described CD's *Beagle* parasites in *J.Linn.Soc.Lond.Zool.*, 19:174–178.

Cocos Keeling Islands Indian Ocean. 1836 Apr.1–12 *Beagle* at. Apr.2–3 CD ashore on Direction Island, met *Captain* John Clunies Ross, the owner and his assistant *Mr* Liesk. They are coral atolls with lagoons and had an important influence on CD's views on the origin of such islands.

Cohn, Ferdinand Julius 1828–1898. German botanist. Prof. Botany Breslau. 1876 Aug. C visited Down House. 1882 C wrote of visit in *Breslauer Zeitung* Apr.23.

Colaptes campestris 1870 Notes on the habits of the pampas woodpecker, (*Colaptes campestris*), *Proc.zool.Soc.Lond.*, No. 47:705–706 (Bii 161, F1750).

Colburn, Henry ?–1855. Publisher of Great Marlborough St, London. Published 1st edition of *Journal of researches* 1839.

Coldstream, John 1806–1863. Physician at Leith. Naturalist friend of CD at Edinburgh. DNB.

Collier, Elizabeth 1747–1832. Natural daughter of Charles Colyear; mother was ?Collier, governess to the legitimate Children. m1 Edward Chandos Pole. m2 1781, as second wife, Erasmus Darwin [I] CD's step-grandmother, Francis Galton's grandmother.

Collier, Hon. John 1850–1934. Painter & rationalist. RA. s of *Sir* Robert Porrett C, *Baron* Monkswell. m1 1879, Marian Huxley. m2 1889, Ethel Gladys Huxley, both daughters of Huxley. Known as Jack. 1881 C painted CD three quarter length in oils. CD sat for him in Aug.—LLiii 223. 1881 CD thanks for sending copy of 'your Art Primer'. 'Everybody whom I have seen, and who has seen your picture of me is delighted with it. I shall be proud some day to see myself suspended at the Linnean Society [who commissioned it]'—MLi 398. 1887 'Many of those who knew his face most intimately think that Mr. Collier's picture is the best of the portraits'—LLiii 223. Now at Linnean Society, Burlington House, London. Replica by the artist with the family. Engraved by Leopold Flameng, the prints bearing the signatures of artist and engraver. 1882 C on 'Personal Friends invited' list for CD's funeral. DNB.

Collingwood, Dr Cuthbert 1826–1908. Botanist. 1861 CD to Bates, CD had corresponded with C on mimicry—MLi 197. 1855 *On the scope and tendency of botanical study*, London. 1868 *Rambles of a naturalist on the shores and waters of the Chinese seas*, London. DNB.

Colonia del Sacramiento Uruguay. 1833 Nov.17 CD at.

Columbarian Society A society for breeders of domestic pigeons, in which CD was much interested for *Variation*. 1855 & 1856 CD attended meetings near London Bridge—LLii 51. 1859 CD to Huxley. 'I sat one evening in a gin palace in the Borough amongst a set of pigeon fanciers'—LLii 281. 1859 CD to Huxley, 'I have found it very important associating with fanciers and breeders'—LLii 281. ?1859 CD to Huxley sending him a card to admit him to a pigeon show—MLi 125. *see also* Philoperistera.

Colon, Archipiélago de Official Ecuadorian name for Galápagos Islands q.v.

Colyear, Charles, Earl of Portmore 1700–1785. 2nd *Earl* 1730. Natural father of Elizabeth Collier. m 1732 Juliana, Dowager *Duchess* of Leeds. Known as Beau Colyear. CD's Step-great-grandfather in bastardy. Francis Galton's great-grandfather in bastardy. DNB.

Comfort Gardener-coachman at Down House c1842–1854.

Compilers CD considered his evolution books to be compilations. 1859 CD to Huxley, 'The inaccuracy of the blessed band (of which I am one) of compilers passes all bounds, The difficulty is to know what to trust. No one or two statements are worth a farthing'—LLii 281.

Concepcion Chile. 1835 Mar.4–7 *Beagle* at. Earthquake of Feb.20 had caused almost total destruction of the town and of its port Talcahuano.

Condy's ozonised water 1862 CD took for dyspepsia. CD to Hooker 'with, I think, extraordinary advantage—to comfort, at least'—MLi 472.

Conington EDii 19, misprint for Covington q.v.

Coniston Lancashire. 1879 Aug.2–27 CD had family holiday there.

Conway Caernarvonshire. 1831 Aug. CD visited with Sedgwick for geology.

Conway, Moncure Daniel 1832–1907. American Unitarian clergyman. Ardent abolitionist. Minister South Place Chapel, Finsbury, London 1863–1884. 1873 Jan. visited Down House. Sent *Col.* Higginson's *Collected essays* to CD—LLiii 176.

Cookson, Montague Hughes 1832–? Barrister. QC 1875. Cambridge friend of CD's sons. 1882 C was on 'Personal Friends invited' list for CD's funeral.

Cooper, Mr of 188 Strand, London. C cut woodblocks for *Insectivorous plants*.

Cope, Edward Drinker 1840–1897. American palaeontologist. Prof. Geology & Palaeontology Pennsylvania 1889– . 1872 CD to Alpheus Hyatt about Hyatt's and C's theories on evolution—MLi 338. 1876 CD to ?William Erasmus D, 'He writes very obscurely, but is an excellent naturalist'—Carroll 502. *The origin of the fittest*, 1887, New York.

Copiapó Chile. 1835 Jun.22 CD reached C on expedition from Valparaiso, via Coquimbo. Jun.26–Jul.1 CD took a short expedition into cordilleras from C. Jul.5 *Beagle* left C for Iquique.

Coquimbo 1835 May 14–Jun.2 CD visited C on expedition from Valparaiso; met Fitz-Roy there and stayed with *Mr* Edwards, whose silver mine at Arqueros they visited May 21. Small earthquake whilst they were there.

Coral islands 1843 Remarks on the preceding paper in a letter from Charles Darwin, Esq. to Mr. Maclaren, *Edinb.new Phil.J.*, 34:47–50 (Bi 171, F1662); preceding paper by Charles Maclaren, On coral islands and reefs as described by Mr. Darwin. 1962 Coral Islands, *Atoll Research Bull.*, No.88, 20 pp, 1 map (F1576); a transcript of CD's mss notes, with introduction by D. R. Stoddart.

Coral reefs Part 1 of geology of the voyage of the *Beagle*. 1842 *The structure and distribution of coral reefs*, London (F271). 1851 same text in a combination volume with the other 2 parts (F274). 1969 Facsimile (F306). 1874 2nd edition (F275). 1889 3rd edition (F277). First foreign editions, whole or part: Russian 1846 (F320); German 1876 (F311); French 1878 (F309); Italian 1888 (F318); USA 1889 (F278); Japanese 1949 (F319).

Corbet, Mr A blind friend of *Mrs* Marsh Caldwell. 1866 CD to Mrs C enclosing note for C about diet—Carroll 323.

Corfield, Mr of Pitchford, Shropshire, father of Richard

C—Darwin-Henslow 97.

Corfield, Richard Schoolfriend of CD living in Valparaiso. 1834 and again 1835 CD stayed with.

Cornford, Frances *see* Darwin.

Cornford, Francis Macdonald 1874–1943. FBA 1937. m Frances Crofts Darwin. Laurence Professor of Ancient Philosophy Cambridge.

Cotton, Mr 1822 'An old Mr. Cotton in Shropshire' had pointed out to CD the bell stone, an erratic boulder in Shrewsbury—Barlow—*Autobiography* 52.

Couper, William 1853–1942. Sculptor of New York. 1909 Bust in bronze by C of CD presented to Christ's College Cambridge by USA delegates to celebrations.

Covington, Syms c1816–1861 Feb.17. 'Fiddler and boy to the poop cabin' on 2nd voyage of *Beagle*. 1833 May 22 became personal servant to CD at 'under £60 per annum'. Remained in CD's employ as secretary servant until 1839 Feb.25, when CD's accounts show 'Present to Covington on leaving me £2'. 1839 May 29 CD wrote testimonial for. 1842 C rearranged CD's notes on volcanic islands—Journal. ?1843 C went to New South Wales. CD continued to correspond with C until 1859. CD's letters to C published in *Sydney Mail*, 38:254–255, 1884 Aug.9; 1959 reprinted in *Notes & Records Roy.Soc.*, 14:14–27.

Craik, Georgiana Marion, Mrs May 1831–1895. Novelist. 1858 C was a visitor to Moor Park Hydro. CD to ED 'I like Miss Craik very much though we have some battles'—LLii 114.

Cranworth, Baron *see* Rolfe.

Crawfurd, John 1783–1868. Orientalist & Army surgeon. 1856 CD to Hooker mentions C as being on selection committee of Athenaeum when Huxley was up for membership—MLi 89. 1859 C reviewed *Origin* in *Examiner*, hostile but free from bigotry—LLii 237. DNB.

Crawley, Charles 1846–1899. Cambridge friend of Francis D. 1872 C visited Down House. 1882 C was on 'Personal Friends invited' list for CD's funeral. C & wife, Augusta Emily Butcher, drowned while boating on river Wye.

Crellin, J. K. 1968 C was editor of *Darwin and evolution*, London, a Jonathan Cape Jackdaw card wallet with facsimilies and other material, including t.p. of 1859 *Origin*.

Creskeld Poole, Yorkshire. Seat of Francis Rhodes, later Darwin.

Cresselly Pembrokeshire. Home of John Bartlett Allen, from 1803 of John Hensleigh Allen, from 1843 of Seymour Phillips Allen.

Cresy, Edward 1825–1870. Architect. Neighbour at Downe 'was we believe an architect'—MLi 58. 1860 C helped CD with measurements for *Insectivorous plants*—LLiii 318. DNB.

Crewe, Frances ?–1845. m 1834 Robert Wedgwood as 1st wife.

Crick, W. D. of Northampton. 1882 Feb. C to CD about dispersal of fresh-water bivalve molluscs by water beetles —LLiii 252. *see Nature*, Lond., 529–530, 1882 Apr.6.

Cripps Corner Ashdown Forest, Sussex. 1900 Country home of Leonard D when he married Mildred Massingberd.

Crocker, Charles William 1832–1868. 1862 C had lately retired from being foreman at Kew. He was going to work on varieties of hollyhock—MLi 218. 1862 of Chichester, 'he has the real spirit of an experimentalist, but has not done much this summer'—MLii 261.

Crofton, Amy 1867 C was a family friend who went to May eights at Cambridge with ED and family.

Croll, James 1821–1890. Geologist of Edinburgh. FRS 1876. 1869 CD to Lyell about C's estimates of geological time—Carroll 364. 1869 CD sent him 5th edition of *Origin*. 1875 *Climate and time*, London. DNB.

Cross, Mary Ann *see* Evans.

Cross and Self Fertilisation 1876 *The effects of cross and self fertilisation in the vegetable kingdom*, (F1249). 1878 2nd edition (F1251). 1891 3rd edition, but really as 2nd (F1256). First foreign editions: French (F1265), German (F1266), USA (F1250) 1877; Italian (F1269) 1878; Russian (F1272) 1938; Polish (F1270), Romanian (F1271) 1964.

Cross Breeding 1856 Cross breeding, *Gdnr's Chronicle*, No.49:806, 812 (Bi 264, F1691, 1692). 1860 Cross bred plants, *Gdnr's Chronicle*, No.3:49 (Bii 31, F1704). 1861 [letter to D. Beaton] Phenomena in the cross-breeding of plants, *J.Hort.*, 1:112–113 (Bii 39, F1713). 1861 Cross-breeding in plants, *J.Hort.*, 1:151 (Bii 42, F1714).

Crüger, Dr Hermann 1818–1864. Botanist. 1857– Director of Botanic Garden, Trinidad. 1862 Mar. C helped CD with Melostomaceae—MLii 299. ?1863 C observed fertilisation in *Catasetum & Coryanthes*—LLiii 284. 1866 CD to Fritz Müller, 'I am sorry to say Dr. Crüger is dead from a fever'—MLii 262.

Cumberland Place No.1, Regent's Park, London. 1868 Hensleigh Wedgwood's house.

Cumming, Hugh 1791–1865. Collector, especially of molluscan shells. 1819 Sail maker at Valparaiso. 1839 C returned to England. 1846 C visited Galápagos Islands—MLi 52. 1854 CD arranged and identified C's barnacles for him. DNB.

Cupples, George 1822–1865. Popular writer. 1873 CD to C, long letter of general nature about people. CD had recommended Mrs (Anne J) C's book *Tappy's chicks and other links between nature and human nature*, London 1872, to Josiah Wedgwood's [III] family, with whom CD was staying—Carroll 428.

Cypripedium 1867 Fertilisation of cypripediums, *Gdnr's Chronicle*, No.14: 350 (Bii 134, F1738).

Cytisus scoparius 1866 The common broom (*Cytisus scoparius*), *J.Linn.Soc.Lond.Bot.*, 9:358; a note added to George Henslow's paper, Note on the structure of Indigofera etc., *ibid.*, 9:355–358 (Bii 134, F1737).

Czech First editions in: *Journal of researches* 1956 (F171); *Origin of species* 1914 (F641); *Descent of man* 1906 (F1048); *Expression of the emotions* 1964 (F1181).

D

Dallas, William Sweetland 1824–1890. Zoologist. 1868 CD to
Fritz Müller, 'Prof. Huxley agrees with me that Mr. Dallas is
by far the best translator' of *Für Darwin*—MLii 353. 1868 D
compiled index to *Variation under domestication*, holding the
publication up. 1872 D compiled glossary to 6th edition of
Origin.

d'Alton, Johann Samuel Eduard 1803–1854. Vertebrate
zoologist. Son of J.W.E.d'A. q.v.

d'Alton, Josef Wilhelm Eduard 1772–1840. Vertebrate
zoologist. Father of J.S.E.d'A. d'A is referred to in historical
sketch to *Origin* as J.S.E.d'A, their names being persistently
misprinted Dalton. *see Book Collector*, 25:257–258, 1976.

Dana, James Dwight 1813–1895. American geologist &
zoologist. Foreign Member R.S. 1884, Copley Medal 1877.
Silliman Prof. Natural History & Geology Yale 1850–1892.
1849 D sent CD his work on geology of US Expedition—LLi
374. 1849 CD to Lyell, 'Dana is dreadfully hypothetical in
many parts, and often as "d—d cocked sure" as Macaulay'
—MLii 225. 1854 CD sent D copy of *Living Cirripedia*. 1859
CD sent D copy of 1st edition of *Origin*. 1859 Dec. CD to
Lyell, CD had had a letter from D saying that he is 'quite
disabled in his head' from overwork—Carroll 188. 1860 D to
CD, from Florence, saying that his health was poor. 1863 CD
to Lyell on D's classification of mammals in *Silliman's J.*,
25:65–71 & *Ann.Mag.nat.Hist.*, 12:207–213, 'The whole seems
to me to be utterly wild'—MLi 236. 1881 Aug. CD to Hooker,
says D was first to argue for permanence of continents—LLiii
247. Biography: Gilman 1899.

Dandy A carriage horse at Down House, bought 1867, sold
1868.

Dangerous Archipelago *see* Tuamotu.

Danish First editions in: *Journal of researches* 1876 (F174); *Origin of
species* 1872 (F643); *Descent of man* 1874–1875 (F1050); *Autobiography* 1909 (F1512).

Darby, Yvonne 1st wife of *Sir* Robert Vere Darwin.

Dareste de la Chavanne, Gabriel Madeleine Camille
1822–1899. French biologist. Held various biological chairs in
Paris. Specialist on monstrosities. 1863 CD to D, D was pro-
Origin—LLiii 7. 1869 CD to D about his application for a chair
of physiology in Paris.

Darwin, Family of Burke, 1888, gives by far the most detailed
pedigree; he traces the family in the male line back to William
D [I] of Marton, Lincolnshire, who died before 1542; the male
descendents continue largely in that county. In 1680 William
D [VI] married Ann Waring who inherited Elston Hall in the
same county. The estate was inherited by their son Robert D
and is still held by the senior branch of CD's line of the family.
But it passed to a distaff on the marriage of Charlotte Maria
Cooper D to Francis Rhodes in 1849. The latter, in 1850,
changed his name to Darwin on inheriting Elston under the
will of his brother-in-law Robert Alvey D, who had died in
1847. The headship of the family, in the male line, then passed
back to the descendents of Erasmus D [I] who was the younger
brother of Charlotte D's father William Alvey D. Erasmus's
only surviving son Robert Waring D, CD's father, held it
briefly in 1847–1848 and, on his death in the latter year, it went
to his elder son Erasmus Alvey D, CD's brother. The latter
died in August 1881, unmarried, and CD himself held it for a
little over 6 months. From him it went to his eldest son
William Erasmus D who had no children. CD's second son,
Sir George Howard D, had died in 1912 and his eldest son *Sir*
Charles Galton D became head on William Erasmus D's death
in 1914. On *Sir* Charles's death in 1962, it passed to his eldest
son George P.D. Less detailed pedigrees are printed in *Emma
Darwin*, i, 1915, and in *Life letters and labours of Francis Galton*, i,
1914. There is also a brief one in *Period piece*, 1952, which
carries the pedigree one generation further into this century. A
pedigree in manuscript, compiled in 1978 by *Sir* Iain Mon-
crieffe of that Ilk, *Bart*, shows the relationship of CD to the
present *Queen* Elizabeth II, through her mother. The common
ancestor was Thomas Foley (1617–1677), great-great-
grandfather of Erasmus D's [I] first wife, Mary Howard,
whose mother was Penelope Foley. Her Majesty is thus CD's
fifth cousin four times removed. *Sir* Iain also gives a pedigree
to *King* Edward III (1312–1377), in 18 generations, and he
suggests a relationship to William Shakespeare, with one
doubtful link: both of these are through the *Hon.* Penelope

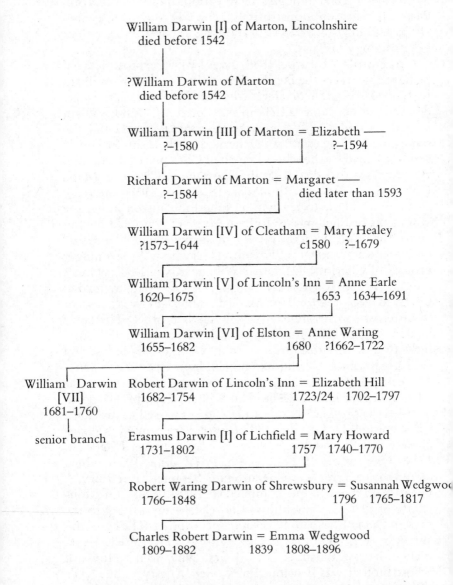

William Darwin [I] of Marton, Lincolnshire
   died before 1542

?William Darwin of Marton
   died before 1542

William Darwin [III] of Marton = Elizabeth ——
   ?–1580   ?–1594

Richard Darwin of Marton = Margaret ——
   ?–1584   died later than 1593

William Darwin [IV] of Cleatham = Mary Healey
   ?1573–1644   c1580   ?–1679

William Darwin [V] of Lincoln's Inn = Anne Earle
   1620–1675   1653   1634–1691

William Darwin [VI] of Elston = Anne Waring
   1655–1682   1680   ?1662–1722

William Darwin   Robert Darwin of Lincoln's Inn = Elizabeth Hill
   [VII]   1682–1754   1723/24   1702–1797
1681–1760

senior branch   Erasmus Darwin [I] of Lichfield = Mary Howard
                          1731–1802   1757   1740–1770

                      Robert Waring Darwin of Shrewsbury = Susannah Wedgwood
                          1766–1848   1796   1765–1817

                      Charles Robert Darwin = Emma Wedgwood
                          1809–1882   1839   1808–1896

Skeleton Pedigree of Charles Robert Darwin in the male line
(from H. Farnham Burke, 1888)

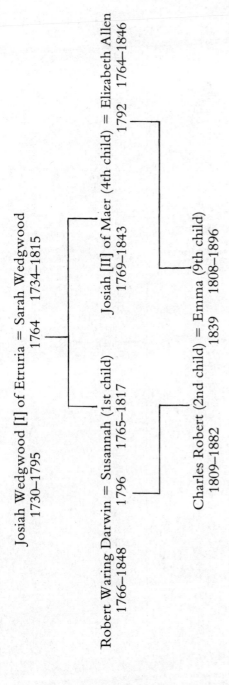

Josiah Wedgwood [I] of Etruria = Sarah Wedgwood
1730–1795   1764   1734–1815

Josiah [II] of Maer (4th child) = Elizabeth Allen
1769–1843   1792   1764–1846

Robert Waring Darwin = Susannah (1st child)
1766–1848   1796   1765–1817

Charles Robert (2nd child) = Emma (9th child)
1809–1882   1839   1808–1896

Pedigree to show Charles Robert Darwin's Relationship to his wife Emma Wedgwood
(From *Emma Darwin*, 1915)

67

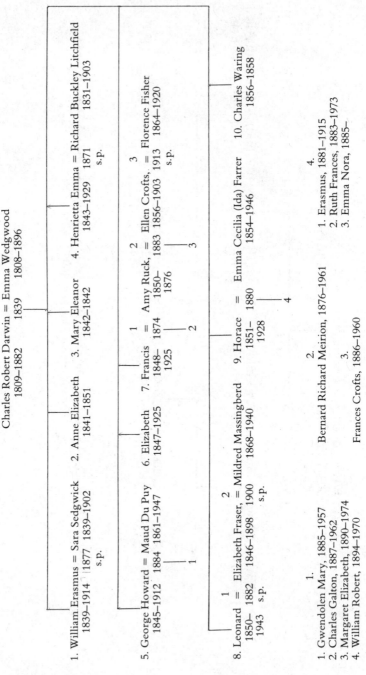

Charles Robert Darwin = Emma Wedgwood
1809–1882   1839   1808–1896

1. William Erasmus = Sara Sedgwick   2. Anne Elizabeth   3. Mary Eleanor   4. Henrietta Emma = Richard Buckley Litchfield
1839–1914 |1877| 1839–1902   1841–1851   1842–1842   1843–1929   1871   1831–1903
            s.p.   s.p.

5. George Howard = Maud Du Puy   6. Elizabeth   7. Francis   =   Amy Ruck,   =   Ellen Crofts,   =   Florence Fisher
1845–1912 1884 1861–1947   1847–1925   1848–   1   1850–   2   1883 1856–1903 1913 1864–1920
                                                          1925   1876   s.p.
                      1   1   2   3
                                                                        2   3

8. Leonard = Elizabeth Fraser, = Mildred Massingberd   9. Horace   =   Emma Cecilia (Ida) Farrer   10. Charles Waring
1850– 1882 1846–1898 1900 1868–1940   1851–   1880   1854–1946   1856–1858
1943 s.p.   1928
        1   2   4

1.   2.   3.   4.
1. Gwendolen Mary, 1885–1957   Bernard Richard Meirion, 1876–1961   Frances Crofts, 1886–1960   1. Erasmus, 1881–1915
2. Charles Galton, 1887–1962   2. Ruth Frances, 1883–1973
3. Margaret Elizabeth, 1890–1974   3. Emma Nora, 1885–
4. William Robert, 1894–1970

Pedigree of Charles Robert Darwin's Children and Grandchildren

68

Paget, mother of Paul Foley, grandson of Thomas Foley. Finally, there is an absurd single sheet, compiled by Francis Darwin Swift, about 1920, which gives a skeleton pedigree back to Isaac II, Angelus, Eastern *Emperor* 1185–1204. Three pedigrees are given here: one, abridged from Burke, shows the male Darwin line back to the 16c, as far as he was able to trace it: a second shows CD's children and grandchildren, although the latters' marriages and the CD great-grandchildren are intentionally omitted: and thirdly one to shew CD's relationship to ED. These pedigrees can be expanded, especially to the other 13 children of Erasmus Darwin [I], and to Wedgwoods and Allens, by reference to the text.

Arms and Crest of Robert Waring Darwin

Darwin, Family of, Arms Burke, 1888, records the arms of William D [IV], c1573–1644, as: Argent, on a bend gules between two cotises vert, three escallops vert. He illustrates the same coat for Robert D of Lincoln's Inn in 1717, with a cadency crescent for 2nd son. Erasmus D [I] used them without cadency, although he was also a second son. His son, Robert Waring D, shows a martlet for 4th son, although the pedigree gives him as 3rd son. There seems to be no record of

CD using arms, although he did use a signet with the crest. Crest in all these examples, a demi-griffin segreant vert, holding between the claws an escallop vert. Motto "E conchis omnia". Burke illustrates the arms of 2 of CD's sons, William Erasmus D & *Sir* George Howard D in both of which the coat is quartered 2 & 3, vert a chevron argent, between 3 herons heads erased (for Waring of Elston Hall, Lincolnshire); crest the same; motto 'Cave et aude'. Fairburn, for 4 of CD's sons, records the crests as having in front of the griffin three escallops fesseway argent. The senior branch of the family had slightly variant arms: ermine a leopard's face jessant-de-lys between 2 escallops, all within 2 bendlets gules. In 1849 Francis Rhodes married Charlotte Maria Cooper D, heiress of Elston Hall, the family seat. In 1850 he changed his surname to Darwin and was granted in the same year, by Queen Victoria, the Darwin arms quartering 2 & 3 those of Rhodes, per pale argent & azure, on a bend nebuly, a lion passant guardant, between 2 acorns slipped, all countercharged; twin crests, a demi-griffin segreant sable, semée of mascules or, resting the sinister claw upon an escutcheon argent, charged with a leopard's face jessant-de-lys gules (for Darwin), A cubit arm erect, vested of six argent & azure, cuffed gules, the hand holding in saltire an oak branch and a vine branch, both fructed proper (for Rhodes): Motto 'Cave et aude'.

Darwin, family, Charity *see* Brass Close.

Darwin, Amy Richenda *see* Ruck.

Darwin, Ann 1727–1813. 4c of Robert D. CD's great-aunt. unm.

Darwin, Anne [I] *see* Earle.

Darwin, Anne [II] *see* Waring.

Darwin, Anne [III] 1777–1859. c of William Alvey D [I]. m 1799 Samuel Fox. CD's 1st cousin once removed.

Darwin, Anne Elizabeth 1841 Mar.2–1851 Apr.23 midday. 2c of CD, born at 12 Upper Gower St. Known as Annie, Kitty Kumplings. CD's favourite child. Died at Malvern of a fever. Her character—LLi 132–134.

Darwin, Annie *see* Anne Elizabeth D.

Darwin, Babba *see* Charles Robert D.

Darwin, Babsey *see* Bernard Richard Meirion D.

Darwin, Backy *see* *Sir* Francis D.

Darwin, Bee *see* Fraser.

Darwin, Bernard Richard Meirion 1876 7 Sep.–1961 Oct.18.

Writer mostly on golf. Only c of *Sir* Francis D & Amy Richenda. CD's senior grandchild, the 1st of two born in CD's lifetime; his mother died in childbed and he was brought up at Down House until his father married again in 1882. Known as Babsey, Dubba, or Dubsy in infancy. m 1906 Elinor Mary Monsell 1s 2d. 1. *Sir* Robert Vere, 2. Ursula Francis Elinor, 3. Nicola Mary Elizabeth. Home Gorringes, Downe. Although best known as a writer on golf D also wrote the introduction to the excellent *Oxford dictionary of quotations*, 1941.

Darwin, Bessy *see* Elizabeth D [VI].

Darwin, Body *see* Henrietta Emma D.

Darwin, Boofy *see* Ruth Francis D.

Darwin, Budgy *see* Henrietta Emma D.

Darwin, Caroline Sarah 1800 Sep.14–1888 Jan.5. 2c of Robert Waring D. m 1837 Josiah Wedgwood [III]. CD's sister.

Darwin, Catherine *see* Emily Catherine D.

Darwin, Charles 1758 Sep.3–1778 May 15. 1c of Erasmus D & Mary. unm. CD's uncle and CD named after him. Medical student, died from a dissecting room wound at Edinburgh. Author of *Experiments establishing a criterion between mucaginous and purulent matter*, Lichfield 1780, edited by his father.

Darwin, Sir Charles Galton 1887 Dec.9–1962 Dec.31. Physicist. 2c of *Sir* George Howard D. m. 1925 Katherine Pember 4s 1d. CD's grandson. KBE 1942 FRS 1922. Prof. Natural Philosophy Edinburgh 1923–1936. Director National Physical Laboratory 1938–1949. D owned Down House when Buxton Browne bought it in 1927. DNB WWH.

Darwin, Charles John Wharton 1894 Dec.12–1941 Dec.26. *Squadron Leader* & Businessman. s of Charles Waring D. m 1917 Sibyl Rose. Head of senior branch of the family, of Elston Hall, Notts. CD's remote cousin.

Darwin, Charles Robert Dates of birth, death, marriage and names of children are given first, followed by a few quotations to give some indication of CD's character. Other information is then given under the following heads:

Anniversaries	Eponyms
Appearance	Finance
Books by	Funeral
Books, autobiographies	Ghost
Books, bibliographies	Grave
Books, biographies	Habits
Degrees	Handwriting

Health   Order
Homes   Prize
Iconography   Religion
Itinerary   Society Membership
Manuscripts   Stamps
Medals

1809 Feb.12 Sun.–1882 Apr.19 Wed.c4 pm. Naturalist. 4c of
Robert Waring D. Born The Mount, Shrewsbury; died Down
House, Downe, Kent. When CD was born he had only one
grandparent living, Sarah Wedgwood his maternal grand-
mother who was ED's paternal grandmother. She died when
CD was 5/6. His mother died when he was 7 and his father
when he was 39. He had 1 brother & 4 sisters one of whom,
Caroline Sarah D, outlived him. Of his 10 children, 3 died in
infancy or childhood, the rest outliving him. He had 4 grand-
sons & 5 grand-daughters; 2, Bernard Richard Meirion D and
Erasmus D [III] were born in his lifetime. m 1839 Jan.29
Emma Wedgwood, by *Rev.* John Allen Wedgwood at St
Peter's Church, Maer, Staffs. 6s 4d. 1. William Erasmus, 2.
Anne Elizabeth, 3. Mary Eleanor, 4. Henrietta Emma, 5.
George Howard, 6. Elizabeth, 7. Francis, 8. Leonard, 9.
Horace, 10. Charles Waring. FRS 1839 JP 1857. 1859 CD's
only recorded attendance on the Bench—LLii 225. 1881 CD to
Romanes, he was, as a magistrate, giving orders daily to allow
pigs to cross roads, at a time of swine fever. Nicknames: Babba
(by Bernard Richard Meirion D in infancy), Dear old
philosopher (by officers on *Beagle*), F (by ED in writing to the
children when they were grown up), Flycatcher (by all ranks
on *Beagle*), Gas (at Shrewsbury School). 1834 to Emily
Catherine D, from E. Falkland I., 'there is nothing like Geology; the pleasure of the first day's partridge shooting or first
day's hunting cannot be compared to finding a fine group of
fossil bones, which tell their story of former times with almost
a living tongue'—*Darwin & the Beagle* 96. 1844 Aug.29 CD to
Horner, 'I always feel as if my books came half out of Lyell's
brain'—MLii 117. 1856 CD to Thwaites, asking for information, 'When a beggar once begins to beg he never knows when
to stop'—Carroll 125. 1859 CD to Lyell, 'It is a pity he [Fitz-
Roy] did not add his theory of the extinction of *Mastodon* etc.,
from the door of the Ark being made too small', about 2 letters
to *The Times* signed 'Senex'—MLi 129. 1860 Mar. CD to

Leidy, 'I have never for a moment doubted, that though I cannot see my errors, that much in my book [*Origin*] will be proved erroneous'—Carroll 202. 1862 Dec. Hooker to B. H. Hodgson of Darjeeling, 'First naturalist in Europe. Indeed I question if he will not be regarded as great as any that ever lived; his powers of observation, memory and judgement seem prodigious, his industry indefatigable and his sagacity in planning experiments, fertility of resources and care in conducting them are unrivalled, and all this with health so detestable that his life is a curse to him'—Allan 209. 1863 CD to Hooker, 'We are degenerate descendants of old Josiah W., for we have not a bit of pretty ware in the house'—LLiii 5. 1863 CD to Gray, 'the *Times* is getting more detestable (but that is too weak a word) [about slavery] than ever. My good wife wishes me to give it up, but I tell her that is a pitch of heroism to which only a woman is equal. To give up the "Bloody Old *Times*" as Cobbett used to call it, would be to give up meat, drink and air.'—LLiii 11. 1863 CD to Hooker, 'It is mere rubbish thinking at present of the origin of life; one might as well think of the origin of matter'—LLiii 18. 1869 CD to Bentham, 'How detestable are Roman numerals! Why should not the Presidents' addresses . . . be paged with Christian figures'—MLi 381. 1863 CD to J. Scott, 'Be sparing in publishing theory. It makes people doubt your observation'—MLii 323. 1867 CD to *Cannon* Farrer, 'I . . . would leave classics to be learnt by those alone who have sufficient zeal and high taste requisite for their appreciation'—MLii 441. ?1869 CD to Wallace, 'It is an aweful stretcher to believe that a peacock's tail was thus formed; but, believing it, I believe in the same principle somewhat modified applied to man'—MLii 90. 1870 CD to Fritz Müller, 'I have not yet met a soul in England who does not rejoice in the splendid triumph of Germany over France: it is a most just retribution against that vainglorious war-liking nation'—MLii 92. 1878 CD to G. A. Gaskell, 'No words can exaggerate the importance, in my opinion, of our colonisation for the future history of the world'—MLii 50. 1881 Jun.15 CD to Hooker, 'So I must look forward to Down graveyard as the sweetest place on earth'—MLii 433.

ANNIVERSARIES The following list contains the main dates which may have been celebrated with pleasure, or remembered with pain, in CD's immediate family circle, from his

birth in 1809 up to ED's death in 1896. One does not get the
impression that CD's household was much given to celebrat-
ing anniversaries.

January	3	Horace D, CD's son, married 1880.
	5	Caroline Sarah W, CD's sister, died 1888.
	15	Susannah D, CD's mother, born 1765.
	29	CD & ED's wedding day 1839.
February	2	Emily Catherine Langton, CD's sister, died 1866.
	12	CD born, 1809. Charlotte Wedgwood, ED's sister, married in this month
March	2	Anne Elizabeth D, CD's daughter, born 1841.
	11	Josiah W, ED's brother, died 1880.
	30	Frances Crofts D, CD's grand-daughter, born 1886.
	31	Elizabeth W, ED's mother died 1846. Henrietta Emma D, CD's daughter, married 1871.
April	7	Marianne D, CD's sister, born 1798.
	19	CD died 1882.
	22	Anne Elizabeth D, CD's daughter, died 1851.
May	2	ED born 1808.
	6	Robert Waring D, CD's father, born 1766.
	10	Emily Catherine D, CD's sister, born 1810.
	13	Horace D, CD's son, born 1851.
June	1	Hensleigh W, ED's brother, died 1891.
	28	Charles Waring D, CD's son, died 1858.
July	3	Susannah D, CD's mother, died 1843.
	8	Elizabeth D, CD's daughter, born 1847.
	9	George Howard D, CD's son, born 1845.
	11	Leonard D, CD's son, married 1882.
	12	Josiah W, ED's father, died 1843.
	18	Marianne Parker, ED's sister, died 1858.
	22	George Howard D, CD's son, married 1884.

August	2	Ruth Frances D, CD's grand-daughter, born 1883.
	3	Susan Elizabeth D, CD's sister, born 1803.
	16	Francis D, CD's son, born 1848.
	20	Frances W, ED's sister, died 1832.
	26	Erasmus Alvey D, CD's brother, died 1881.
		Gwendolen Mary D, CD's grand-daughter, born 1885.
September	7	Bernard Richard Meirion D, CD's grandson, born 1876.
	14	Caroline Sarah D, CD's sister, born 1800.
		ED moved into Down House, without CD, 1842.
	17	CD moved into Down House 1842.
	23	Mary Eleanor D, CD's daughter, born 1842.
	25	Henrietta Emma D, CD's daughter, born 1843.
October	1	Francis W, ED's sister, died 1888.
	2	*Beagle* reached Falmouth and CD disembarked 1836.
	3	Susan Elizabeth D, CD's sister, died 1866.
	16	Mary Eleanor D, CD's daughter, died 1842.
November	2	ED died 1896.
	7	Sarah Elizabeth W, ED's sister, died 1880.
	11	CD proposed marriage to ED and was accepted 1838.
	13	Robert Waring D, CD's father, died 1848.
December	6	Charles Waring D, CD's son, born 1856.
	7	Erasmus D, CD's grandson, born 1881.
	19	Charles Galton D, CD's grandson, born 1887.
	22	Emma Nora D, CD's grand-daughter, born 1885.
	27	*Beagle* sailed from Devonport 1831.
	29	Erasmus Alvey D, CD's brother, born 1804.

APPEARANCE The only full description of CD's physical appearance and of his dress is in Ch.3 of LLi, in Francis D's reminiscences of his father, but he omits much and only treats of CD in his later years. The picture can be amplified from portraits. The only one in his childhood is the pastel by Rolinda Sharples, when he was about 7 years of age. In early manhood, before he grew his beard, there are: a water colour by George Richmond, when he was 31, the earliest photograph, with his son William Erasmus D, when he was 33, the Ipswich engraving by Maguire when he was 40, the chalk drawing by Samuel Laurence when he was 44, and the Maull & Fox photograph, probably taken when he was 45. After he grew his beard, there are one bust and three oils taken from life, as well as numerous photographs, but his beard was so copious that his features were much obscured.

He was about 6 feet tall, sparely built with medium shoulders. In Francis D's recollection he had a tendency to stoop which increased with age; high forehead, much wrinkled in age, but his face otherwise unlined; wide-set eyes, iris bluish-grey according to Francis D but pale brown in the Richmond portrait; eyebrows very bushy in age; nose straight; mouth small; chin neither prominent nor receding. All the portraits show a very youthful face for his age, until he grew his beard, from which time he looked unchangingly old. His hair and side whiskers were light brown and the hair line started to recede before he was 30; by 60 he had only a fringe of hair at the back. He first grew a beard, as did everyone else, when the *Beagle* left Montevideo for the cold south, 1832 Nov., but they shaved when they returned to temperate waters, 1834 Jul. CD to his sister Emily Catherine 'With my great beard'—LLi 254. 'Whilst we all wore our untrimmed beards'—*J.Researches*, 1845, 209. CD finally grew beard and moustache in 1864–1865; the beard was copious and the moustache cut square across. 1864 May 28 CD to Gray, on sending a bearded photograph 'Do I not look venerable'—Darwin-Gray letters 54. 1866 Apr. 28 ED to Henrietta Emma D 'He was obliged to name himself to almost all of them [people at a Royal Society soirée], as his beard alters him so'—EDii 185. His complexion was ruddy. 1849 CD to Hooker, 'Everyone tells me that I look quite blooming and beautiful; and most think that I am shamming, but you have never been one of those'—LLi 111. His gait was springing and he always walked with a stick which he banged on the ground. He used his hands a good deal in conversation, although the crossed arms and legs shown in the 'Ape' cartoon were characteristic. His laugh was a 'free and sounding peal'—LLi 111. The portraits show that CD's dress was usually conventional and that of a man of his position, but in later years it became less so. He gave up wearing a tall hat even in London, wearing a soft black one with a rounded crown in winter and a big straw in summer. His clothes were dark and of a loose and easy fit. Outdoors he wore a short cloak: the cloak and winter hat are well shown in the Elliott & Fry photograph of c1880. Indoors, he normally wore a shawl and 'great loose cloth boots' over his indoor shoes—LLi 112. 1880 Jan. his sons bought him a fur coat. ED to Leonard D 'He has begun wearing it so constantly, that he is afraid it will soon be worn out'—EDii 239. He seems never to have worn spectacles and his hearing was unimpaired.

BOOKS, BY CD. These and his publications in serials, are entered in the main sequence under brief titles. The following list gives full titles of his main books in strict alphabetical order, except for first articles, followed by the date of first appearance under that title and any needed cross reference. Several of his books appeared under more than one title. Works printed from CD's manuscripts since his death have not been included, but will be found under the separate heading 'Manuscripts' and they are also present under abbreviated titles in the main sequence. Works to which he contributed only an article, preface, or letter, have also not been included. CD wrote seventeen works in twenty one volumes, or fifteen if the three volumes of geology of the *Beagle* are treated as one. They consist of more than 9,000 pages of text with a further 170 pages of preliminary matter. If the papers in serials are added, the total comes to well over 10,000 pages. This rough total does not consider the increase, or rarely decrease, in the length of the text in later editions, and represents about 230 pages a year for forty three years.

1   *The descent of man, and selection in relation to sex,* 2 vols, 1871 (F937).

2   *The different forms of flowers on plants of the same species,* 1877 (F1277).

3   *The effects of cross and self fertilisation in the vegetable king-dom,* 1876 (F1249).

4   *Erasmus Darwin. Translated from the German . . . with a preliminary essay by Charles Darwin*, 1879 (F1319). Text by E. Krause, but CD's essay is longer.

5   *The expression of the emotions in man and animals*, 1872 (F1141).

6   *The formation of vegetable mould through the action of worms, with observations on their habits*, 1881 (F1357).

7   *Geological observations on coral reefs, volcanic islands, and on South America*, 1851 (F274). Combination volume of Nos 8, 9 & 27, from the same sheets.

8   *Geological observations on South America*, 1846 (F273).

9   *Geological observations on the volcanic islands visited during the voyage of H.M.S. Beagle, together with some brief notices of the geology of Australia and the Cape of Good Hope*, 1844 (F272).

10   *Insectivorous plants*, 1875 (F1217).

11   Journal and remarks 1832–1836, 1839 (F10 part). Volume 3 of No.18, first issue of No.12.

12   *Journal of researches into the geology and natural history of the various countries visited by H.M.S. Beagle*, 1839 (F11).

13   *Journal of researches into the natural history and geology of the countries visited during the voyage of H.M.S. Beagle round the world*, 1845 (F13). 2nd edition of No.12.

14   *The life of Erasmus Darwin . . . Being an introduction to an essay on his scientific work*, 1887 (F1321). 2nd edition of No.4, same text but new preliminaries.

15   *A monograph of the fossil Lepadidae, or pedunculated cirripedes, of Great Britain. A monograph of the fossil Balanidae and Verrucidae of Great Britain*, 2 vols, 1851, 1854[=1855] (F342).

16   *A monograph of the sub-class Cirripedia, with figures of all the species*, 2 vols 1851, 1854 (F339).

17   *The movements and habits of climbing plants*, 1876 (F836). 2nd edition of No.20.

18   *Narrative of the surveying voyages of his Majesty's ships Adventure, and Beagle*, 3 vols & appendix to Vol.2, 1839 (F10). Edited by Robert Fitz-Roy. Vol.3 is CD's volume, titled Journal and remarks, =No.11, 1st edition of No.12.

19   *A naturalist's voyage. Journal of researches etc.*, 1879 (F34). An unchanged reprint of No.13.

20   *On the movements and habits of climbing plants*, 1865 (F834).

21   *On the origin of species by means of natural selection, or the*

preservation of favoured races in the struggle for life, 1859 (F373).

22 *On the various contrivances by which British and foreign orchids are fertilised by insects, and on the good effects of intercrossing,* 1862 (F800).

23 *The origin of species by means of natural selection, or the preservation of favoured races in the struggle for life,* 1872 (F391). 6th edition of No.21.

24 *The power of movement in plants,* 1880 (F1325).

25 *Queries about expression,* [1867] (F871, 873).

26 *Questions about the breeding of animals,* [1839] (F262).

27 *The structure and distribution of coral reefs,* 1842 (F271).

28 *The variation of animals and plants under domestication,* 2 vols, 1868 (F877).

29 *The various contrivances by which orchids are fertilised by insects,* 1877 (F801). 2nd edition of No.22.

30 *The voyage of the Beagle,* 1905 (F106). Unchanged reprint of No.13.

31 *The zoology of the voyage of H.M.S. Beagle . . . during the years 1832 to 1836,* 5 parts, 1838–1842 (F8). Edited by CD

BOOKS, AUTOBIOGRAPHIES The original publication of CD's autobiography is in LLi 26–107, but CD's description of his father, which is in the mss, is printed in Ch.1, 11–20, instead of in its correct place. It was written in 1876, between May 28 and Aug.3, with some additions and alterations in 1878 & 1881. The mss is headed 'Recollections of the development of my mind and character'. This version was bowdlerised by Francis D after consultation with CD's other children—'passages should occur which must have to be omitted'. One omitted passage, about CD's mother, is printed in MLi 30. A further autobiographical fragment of his first ten years, written in 1838, was printed in MLi 1–5. The first full transcription of the original mss appeared in Russian translation by S. L. Sobol' in 1957. Nora Barlow's version of it, which was independently transcribed, appeared in 1958, with an important appendix. In 1974 de Beer edited an edition of the Barlow transcription, with slight modifications after the mss had been re-examined by James Kirsley, in *Charles Darwin, Thomas Henry Huxley, autobiographies.* This edition also contains the fragment of 1838.

BOOKS, BIBLIOGRAPHIES There is no full bibliographical work

even of the first editions of CD's books. *The origin of species* has been surveyed in great detail by Morse Peckham in his comparative edition of 1959. He covers all English editions and issues up to 1890, and his descriptions include paper, type and binding cases, as well as summaries of John Murray's accounts. H. D. Horblit, in the Grolier Club volume *One hundred books famous in science*, 1964, gives another description of the 1st edition. A full description of *Living Cirripedia* is given in R.Curle, *The Ray Society a bibliographical history*, 1954, 48–49. There are several handlists: 1883 F.W.True, A darwinian bibliography, *Smithson. misc.Coll.*, 25:92–101. 1887 J.P. Anderson, i–xxxi in G. T. Bettany, *Life of Charles Darwin*, a good list which also contains list of early darwiniana and of reviews. 1887 Frances D, LLiii, 362–372, not so useful as Anderson. 1977 R. B. Freeman, *The works of Charles Darwin*, 2nd edition. 1977 P. H. Barrett, *The collected papers of Charles Darwin*, 2 vols, contains an almost complete collection of CD's works in serials, with their references, and notes.

BOOKS, BIOGRAPHIES Biographies of CD are numerous and include DNB. Those listed here all contain general biographical matter as well as considerations of his work and theories. Many more, which are concerned with darwinism from the biological, ethical or sociological viewpoints, contain some facts about his life, but usually nothing new: these have been ignored. The basic biography, on which most of the others draw strongly for facts, is Francis D's *Life and letters*, 3 vols, 1887. This is supplemented by Francis D & A. C. Seward, *More letters*, 1903, and, largely for family matters, by H. E. Litchfield, *Emma Darwin*, 1904. Much information has come to light since these early books which was not available to their editors, but no full scale biography containing it has appeared. The most important will be found under the entries for Barlow, de Beer, Gruber & Stecher.

1882 *Charles Darwin, memorial notices*, Nature Series. 6 obituaries from *Nature*, Lond.
1883 L. C. Miall, *The life and work of Charles Darwin; a lecture.*
1883 J. M. Winn, *Darwin.*
1884 E. Woodall, *Charles Darwin.*
1886 J. T. Cunningham, *Charles Darwin; naturalist.*
1887 G. T. Bettany, *Life of Charles Darwin.*
1887 Francis D, *Life and letters of Charles Darwin*, 3 vols.

1891 C. F. Holder, *Charles Darwin. His life and work.*
1892 Francis D, *Charles Darwin. His life told in an autobiographical chapter, and in a selected series of his published letters.* An abridged version of 1887, with some alterations and additions.
1903 Francis D & A. C. Seward, *More letters of Charles Darwin,* 2 vols.
1904 H. E. Litchfield, *Emma Darwin, wife of Charles Darwin,* privately printed edition. 1915 *Emma Darwin,* published edition.
1909 E. B. Poulton, *Charles Darwin and the Origin of species.*
1921 Leonard Huxley, *Charles Darwin.*
1923 Karl Pearson, *Charles Darwin, 1809–1882.* Questions of the day and of the fray, No.12.
1927 Henshaw Ward, *Charles Darwin. The man and his warfare.*
1937 Geoffrey West [pseud. of G. H. Wells], *Charles Darwin, the fragmentary man.*
1950 P. B. Sears, *Charles Darwin, the naturalist as a cultural force.*
1955 William Irvine, *Apes, Angels and Victorians.*
1955 Dorothy Laird, *Charles Darwin. Naturalist.*
1959 Arthur Keith, *Darwin revalued.*
1963 G. de Beer, *Charles Darwin, evolution by natural selection.*
1966 Julian Huxley & H. B. D. Kettlewell, *Darwin and his world.*
1970 P. J. Vorzimmer, *Charles Darwin: the years of controversy.*
1977 Mea Allan, *Darwin and his flowers. The key to natural selection.*

DEGREES: Bonn   1868 Hon.D.Med.& Chirurg.
          Breslau   1862 Hon.D.Med.& Chirurg.
          Cambridge   1831 Apr.26 B.A., 10th in list of candidates who did not seek honours. 1837 MA. 1877 Nov.17, Hon. LL.D.
          Leyden   1875 Hon.MD.
          [Oxford   1870 Jun.17, CD declined Hon.DCL, on grounds of ill health.]

EPONYMS Gathered under this heading are all objects, names, places in which 'Darwin' referring to CD occurs. In most, the association is obvious and the great majority relate to the *Beagle* voyage. In a few, particularly amongst the place names, the connection is obscure and may not relate to CD. The only 'Darwin' eponym known to me which does not relate to CD is the plant genus *Darwinia*; this relates to Erasmus D [I] q.v. There are doubtless many street names, of which there are five in London alone; these have been ignored. Eponyms in the genitive, e.g. Darwin's bulldog, will be found at the end of the CD entry. Animals named after; the orthography of the specific names has been modernized:

Agonum darwini Van Dyke, a ground beetle.

Alleloplasis darwini Waterhouse, a bug of the family Derbidae.

Amphisbaena darwini Duméril & Bibron, a legless lizard.

Astarte darwini Forbes, a bivalve mollusc.

Attus darwini White, a jumping spider.

Bulimus darwini Pfeiffer, a land snail.

Calosoma darwinia van dyke, a ground beetle.

Carabus darwini Hope, a ground beetle.

Chthamalus darwini Bosquet, a fossil barnacle from the Chalk.

Colymbetes darwini Babington, a water beetle.

Cossyphus darwini Jenyns, a wrasse.

Crocodilus darwini Ludwig, a tertiary fossil crocodile.

Cubinia darwini Gray, a gekko.

Diplolaemus darwini Bell, an iguana.

Docema darwini Mutchler, a beetle of the family Hydrophilidae.

Dorcus darwini Hope, a stag beetle.

Felis darwini Martin=*F. yaguarundi* Desmarest.

Fissurella darwini Reeve, a keyhole limpet.

Foenus darwini Westwood, an ichneumonid wasp.

Galapagodacnum darwini Blair, a plant beetle of the family Chrysomelidae.

Gryphaea darwini Forbes, a fossil oyster.

Hesperomys darwini Wagner in Schreber, a cricetine rodent.

Hydroporus darwini Babington, a water beetle.

Idiocephalus darwini Saunders, a chrysomelid beetle.

Leiolaemus darwini (Bell) Gray, an iguana.

Mactra darwini Sowerby in CD, a bivalve mollusc.

Migadops darwini Waterhouse, a carabid beetle.

Monophora darwini Agassiz, a fossil sea urchin.

Mus (Phyllotis) darwini Waterhouse, a cricetine rodent.

Mylodon darwini Owen, a fossil giant sloth.

Nyctelia darwini Waterhouse, a heteromeran beetle.

Odontoscelis darwini Waterhouse, a pentatomid bug.

Ostraea darwini Forbes in d'Orbigny, as *Gryphaea,* a fossil oyster.

Pholas darwini Sowerby, a piddock bivalve mollusc.

Pleurodema darwini Bell, a tree-frog.

Polycaldus darwini Diesing, a flatworm.

Proctotretus darwini Bell, an iguanid lizard.

Rhea darwini Gould, the southern rhea.

Rhinoderma darwini Duméril & Bibron, a dwarf frog.

Sclerostomus darwini Burmeister

Spirifer darwini Morris in Strzelecki, a fossil brachiopod.

Tanagra darwini Gould, Darwin's tanager.

Taraguira darwini Gray, an iguana.

Mytilus darwinianus d'Orbigny, a fossil mussel.

Mastotermes darwinianus Froggatt, a primitive termite named after Port Darwin, Northern Territories, Australia.

Pecten darwinianus d'Orbigny, a scallop.

Testudo darwini Van Denburgh=*Geochelone darwini*, a giant tortoise, Galápagos Is, James I.

Turbonilla darwiniensis Laseron, small turk's head gastropod.

Darwin College, Cambridge: 1964 Jul.28 founded for postgraduate and postdoctorate students. First buildings were conversions of Newnham Grange and the Old Granary, home of *Sir* George Howard D.

Darwin Foundation: A USA organization, founded 1959, which runs the D Research Station.

Darwin medal: Royal Society; first struck 1890, effigy reduced from a medallion by Allen Wyon. Awarded to Wallace 1890, Hooker 1892, Huxley 1894.

Darwin Memorial Fund: Committee set up 1882 May 16, with W. Spottiswoode PRS in Chair. 1883 Huxley took over the Chair as PRS on S's death. 1888 Printed *Report*, 12 pp, Spottiswoode, London, lists about 700 subscribers; £5,128 raised; £2,100 paid to Boehm for a statue at British Museum (Natural History), and a further £150 for the relief in Westminster Abbey; £9.0.6 paid to Whymper for a woodcut of a bust which illustrates *Report*. £2,608.8.8 remained, after expenses, some of which, although the *Report* does not refer to it, went to funding the Darwin medal, which was first awarded in 1890.

Places:

Bay, coast of Chonos Archipelago, Aysen Province, Chile.

Bay, southwest side of Tower Is, Galápagos Is.

Channel, leading to Port Aysen, Chile.

Cordilleras *see* Mountains.

District, Rhodesia, named after the mountain.
Island, official Ecuadorian name of Culpepper Is., most northerly of Galápagos group.
Mountain, Antarctica, 84.55S,160.,58E, above Beardmore Glacier, Ross Dependency.
Mountain, Isla Grande, Tierra del Fuego, Chile, w of Ushuaia on Beagle Channel. 1834 CD to Emily Catherine D, 'Mount Sarmiento, the highest mountain in the south, excepting !! Darwin !!'—MLi 252. But, not so; Sarmiento is the higher.
Mountain, Peru.
Mountain, Rhodesia; the district is named after the mountain.
Mountains, Magallanes-Patagonia provinces, Chile/Argentina, contain Mounts Fitz-Roy & Stokes; also called D Cordilleras.
Port, Northern Territory, Australia, named on 3rd voyage of Beagle.
Sound, Tierra del Fuego, Chile, continuing nw arm of Beagle Channel.
Town, small town in Sierra Nevada, California, USA.
Township, on Choiseul Sound, E. Falkland Is.
Township, on Port Darwin, Northern Territory, Australia.
Village, Uraguay, on r. Beguelo, a tributary of r. Negro, near Cerro Perico Flaco where CD collected fossils 1833.
Volcano, Albemarle Is, Galápagos Is.

Plants:
The following list is based on B. D. Jackson, *Darwiniana*, 1910, with additions and altered orthography:
Abutilon darwini Tweedie, Malvaceae, Brazil. 'Named by John Tweedie to whom Darwin was a hero'—Allan 286.
Asterina darwini Berkeley, Fungi, Chiloe, Chile.
Asterolampa darwini Greville=*Asteromphalus darwini*.
Asteromphalus darwini Ehrenberg, Algae, Antarctica.
Aulacodiscus darwini Pantocsek, Algae (Diatom), fossil Russia.
Baccharis darwini Henslow, Compositae, Patagonia, Argentine.
Berberis darwini W. J. Hooker, Berberidaceae, Chiloe, Chile, now a garden plant.
Bonatia darwini Weale=*Habenaria cassidea* Reichenbach, Orchidaceae.
Calceolaria darwini Bentham, Scrophulariaceae, Patagonia, Argentine. Grown as an alpine.

Catasetum darwinianum Rolfe, Orchidaceae, Guiana.

Cheilosporum darwini De-Toni, Algae, Chile.

Chiliotrichum darwini J. D. Hooker,=*Nardophyllum darwini*.

Clinopodium darwini Kuntze=*Micromeria darwini*.

Coldenia darwini Gürke=*C.dichotoma* Lehmann, Boraginaceae, Charles Is., Galápagos.

Cortinarius darwini Spegazzini, Fungi, Patagonia, Argentine.

Cytarria darwini Berkeley, Fungi, Tierra del Fuego. Eaten by natives.

[*Darwinia* Rudge 1813, Rafinesque 1817, Dennstedt 1818 *see* Erasmus D [I].]Darwin auricula 1882 Apr.25 Charles Turner named an alpine auricula strain 'Charles Darwin' at Royal Agricultural Society's show—*The Times*, Apr.26.

Darwin clematis 1887 Apr.25 C.Noble named a clematis strain 'Darwin in memoriam' at Royal Agricultural Society Show—*The Times*, Apr.26.

Darwin potato 1834 Dec. CD saw and ate tubers of *Solanum maglia*, Solonaceae, in Chonos archipelago. Named D potato by George Nicholson, *Illustrated dictionary of gardening*, 1885–1889—Allan 224.

Darwin tulip 1889 J. C. Lenglart of Lille raised the first and named it 'Princesse Aldobrandini'. He sold it to E. H. Krelage of Krelage N.V. of Haarlem who asked Francis D if he might name the strain in honour of CD.

Darwinothamnus Gunnar Harling, for *Erigeron lancifolium* J. D. Hooker, Compositae, Albemarle Is, Galápagos.

Eugenia darwini J. D. Hooker, Myrtaceae, Chile.

Fagelia darwini Kuntze=*Calceolaria darwini*.

Galapagoa darwini J. D. Hooker=*Coldenia darwini*=*Coldenia dichotoma*.

Gossypium darwini Watt, Malvaceae, Galápagos.

Hebe darwiniana Colenso, Scrophulariaceae, New Zealand.

H glaucophylla Hort. Grown as an alpine.

Hymenophyllum darwini W. J. Hooker, Fern, Antarctica.

Hypocopra darwini Spegazzini, Fungi, Patagonia, Argentine.

Laboulbenia darwini Thaxter, Fungi, Brasil.

Laelio-Cattleya darwiniana × hort. Orchidaceae.

Lippia darwini Spegazzini=*Neosparton darwini*.

Lithophyllum darwini Foslie, Algae, S.Australia.

Micromeria darwini Bentham, Labiatae, Patagonia, Argentine.

Myrtus darwini Barnéoud, Myrtaceae, Chile.

Nardophyllum darwini A.Gray, Compositae, Patagonia.

Nassauvia darwini O.Hoffmann & Dusén, Compositae, Tierra del Fuego.
Neosparton darwini Bentham & J. D. Hooker, Verbenaceae, Brasil.
Opuntia darwini Henslow, Cactaceae, Patagonia, Argentine.
Panagyrus darwini W. J. Hooker & Arnott=*Nassauvia darwini*.
Pisonia darwini Hemsley, Nyctaginaceae, Fernando Noronha.
Pleuropetalum darwini J. D. Hooker, Amarantaceae, Galápagos.
Polygala darwini A. W. Benn, Polygalaceae, Patagonia, Argentine.
Satureia darwini Briquet=*Micromeria darwini*.
Scalesia darwini J. D. Hooker, Compositae, James Is, Galápagos.
Senecio darwini W. J. Hooker & Arnott, Compositae, Tierra del Fuego.
Torula darwini Spegazzini, Fungi, Tierra del Fuego.
Ulota darwini, Mitten, moss, Patagonia.
Urtica darwini J. D. Hooker, Urticaceae, Chonos Archipelago=*U. megallanica* Jussieu.
Veronica darwiniana Colenso=*Hebe darwiniana*.
Zinnia darwiniana Haage & Schmidt=*Glossogyne pinnatifida* De Candolle, Compositae, Malaya.
Darwin-Wallace Medal, Linnean Society of London, first struck 1908, designed by Frank Bowcher. Seven were awarded in that year, Wallace, Hooker, Haeckel, Weismann, Strasburger, F.Galton, Ray Lankester, in that order.

FINANCE CD kept detailed accounts from the time of his marriage, as did ED for household expenditure. These, although preserved at Down House, have not been published in full. Extracts are given in Keith, *Darwin revalued*, 221–223, 1955, and in Atkins, *Down the home of the Darwins*, 95–100, 1976. Until his father's death in 1848, CD was wholly dependent on him, except for ED's marriage settlement and £150 which he received for the sale of his copyright in *J.Researches* in 1845. In his early manhood years, he received £400 p.a. which was increased to £500 on marriage. ED's dowry brought £400 p.a. He had saved and invested a little, so that his total income in 1839 was £1,244. His father left him more than £40,000. From 1859 until 1881, his books brought in a total of £10,248, an average of about £465 p.a. His farm, at Beesby, Lincolnshire, was bought in 1845 for £13,592 borrowed from his father at interest of £461.16s.10d, about 3 per cent. At that time the rent was £377, but by 1877 it had increased to £555.16. In 1854 CD's total income was £4,603; by 1871 it had risen to around £8,000 and it continued at this level until his death. He was able to save a considerable sum each year, the highest being £4,819 in 1873. His investments, which were looked after by his banker son William Erasmus D, were largely in railways and government bonds. On the death of his brother Erasmus Alvey D in 1881, he inherited half of his fortune, perhaps the £9,354.19s.6d shown as extraordinary receipts in his summary of income for 1881. In that year, he had an income of £17,299.1s.4d., a bank balance of £2,968 and £165.19s.4d in hand. His expenses were £4,880.16s.6d; he invested £10,218.6s.6d. and gave £3,000 to his children. Rates and taxes were always small; in the sixties a little over £60 p.a., in the seventies over £70. His highest income tax was £52 in 1872. 1881 Sep.8 William Erasmus D wrote to his father that the total estate was about £282,000 and that, calculated at 7 to 12, his daughters would inherit about £34,000 and sons £53,000. *See also* Down House, household expenditure.

FUNERAL 1882 Apr.25 Mon., pm. CD's body was carried from Down House, in a hearse drawn by four black horses, accompanied by Francis, Leonard & Horace D. Vigil in St Faith's Chapel, where they were joined by William & George D. The undertakers were T. & W. Banting—*The Times*, Apr.26. CD was the first and only naturalist to be buried in Westminster Abbey. Apr.26 Wednesday at noon, the mourners invited for 11 am. Apr.21 Letter to the Dean, G. G. Bradley, on House of Commons paper—'Very Rev. Sir, We hope you will not think we are taking a liberty if we venture to suggest that it would be acceptable to a very large number of our countrymen of all classes and opinions that our illustrious countryman Mr. Darwin should be buried in Westminster Abbey, We remain your obedient servants', signed by Lubbock and nineteen other MPs. The Dean was abroad and replied by telegram 'Oui sans aucune hésitation regrette mon absence'. Service conducted by Canon George Prothero, Senior Canon. Pall bearers, to left of body, Lubbock, Huxley, J. R. Lowell (as American Ambassador), *Duke* of Devonshire (as Chancellor of Cambridge), Wallace, to right of body, Canon Farrar (Rector of St Margaret's Westminster), Hooker, W. Spottiswoode (as President of Royal Society), *Earl* of Derby, *Duke* of Argyll. Chief Mourner William Erasmus D, followed by thirtyone relatives, including all surviving children, servants Parslow & Jackson at rear followed by representatives of scientific bodies. ED not present. *Queen* Victoria in Council was represented by *Earl* Spencer, the President. Ambassadors of France, Germany, Italy, Russia & Spain were present. There is a printed list of mourners, one copy of which is marked by George Howard D 'very erroneous'. There are manuscript lists by George Howard D at Cambridge including one of 'Personal Friends invited' with 108 names 'and other old servants and inhabitants of Down'. Anthem specially composed by *Sir* Frederick Bridge 'Happy is the man that findeth wisdom, and the man that getteth understanding'—Proverbs iii 13-17. Memorial Service: May 1 Westminster Abbey, sermon by Harvey Goodwin, *Bishop* of Carlisle. The *Archbishop* of Canterbury, A. C. Tait, had withdrawn at short notice—H. D. Rawnsley, *Harvey Goodwin*, 223–225, 1896.

GHOST One of several said to haunt Downe Court, opposite Down House—A. D. H. Coxe, *Haunted Britain*, 79, 1973, with photograph.

GRAVE Westminster Abbey, 'north-east corner of the nave next to that of Sir John Herschel', 7ft deep in a coffin of white oak—*The Times* Apr.27 1882. 'A few feet from the grave of Sir Isaac Newton'—LLiii 361. Memorial plaque by *Sir* Joseph Boehm 1887.

HABITS The only detailed account of CD's day to day pattern of life is in Francis D's reminiscences of his father—LLi 108–160. This stems from his middle and later years when he had developed a rigid pattern, seldom changed even when there were visitors in the house. His own autobiography tells little about his habits, except something of his hobbies and enthusiasms. A typical day at Down House may be summarized as follows:

7 am	Rose and took a short walk.
7.45 am	Breakfast alone.
8–9.30 am	Worked in his study; he considered this his best working time.
9.30–10.30 am	Went to drawing-room and read his letters, followed by reading aloud of family letters.

10.30–12 or 12.15 am	Returned to study, which period he considered the end of his working day.
12 noon	Walk, starting with visit to greenhouse, then round the sandwalk, the number of times depending on his health, usually alone or with a dog.
12.45 pm	Lunch with whole family, which was his main meal of the day. After lunch read *The Times* and answered his letters.
3 pm	Rested in his bedroom on the sofa and smoked a cigarette, listened to a novel or other light literature read by ED.
4 pm	Walked, usually round sandwalk, sometimes farther afield and sometimes in company.
4.30–5.30 pm	Worked in study, clearing up matters of the day.
6 pm	Rested again in bedroom with ED reading aloud.
7.30 pm	Light high tea while the family dined. In late years never stayed in the dining room with the men, but retired to the drawing-room with the ladies. If no guests were present, he played two games of backgammon with ED, usually followed by reading to himself, then ED played the piano, followed by reading aloud.
10 pm	Left the drawing-room and usually in bed by 10.30, but slept badly.

Even when guests were present, half an hour of conversation at a time was all that he could stand, because it exhausted him.

Alcohol:
Francis D records that CD 'drank very little wine, but enjoyed and was revived by the little he did drink'—LLi 118. However he admitted to him that 'he had once drunk too much at Cambridge' as his enthusiastic membership of the Gourmet Club perhaps indicates. 'Darwin had once told him [Hooker] that he had got drunk three times in early life, and thought intoxication the greatest of all pleasures'—M. E. Grant Duff, *Victorian vintage*, 144, 1930. CD's accounts show a considerable consumption of brandy and of beer at Down House, but the former was probably for guests and the latter for growing sons and the staff.

Research Notes on Insectivorous Plants, 1860

Hobbies and pastimes:
CD's beetle collecting whilst at Cambridge seems to have
been little more than collecting, but the techniques learnt were
useful on the *Beagle* voyage. He was not good at ball games,
although he records that he enjoyed bat fives whilst at
Shrewsbury School. He enjoyed watching his family play
lawn tennis and billiards. In his youth, he was an enthusiastic
shot, especially when visiting Maer and the Owens at nearby
Woodhouse. He shot for the pot and for scientific need during
the *Beagle* voyage, but gave it up entirely on his return. He
rode for pleasure in his youth and as the only way of covering
ground on inland trips from the *Beagle*. He took up riding
again for health reasons on his quiet cob 'Tommy', on the
recommendation of Dr Bence Jones, but gave it up after he had
been rolled on in 1869. He played Van John (Vingt-et-un) at
Cambridge a lot, but does not seem to have played cards later.
His evening recreation, other than reading, being read to and
listening to ED play the piano, was backgammon. He and ED
played two games every evening when they were alone. He
won most games, she most gammons. 1876 Jan.28 CD to Gray
records 5285 games played—EDii 221.

Tobacco:
CD started taking snuff when he was a student at Edinburgh
and continued to do so, finding it a stimulant. He smoked a
few cigarettes when travelling with gauchos in South
America, and restarted late in life when he was relaxing.

Charles Darwin's Full Signature 1854

HANDWRITING CD's handwriting, even at its best, is notori-
ously difficult to read. The specimen given opposite, written
in 1860, is typical of his research notes, written for himself.
Francis D comments of rough notes such as this that they
'were almost illegible, sometimes even to himself'—LLi 119.

Final manuscript for the press was, for many years, transcribed by the Downe schoolmaster, Ebenezer Norman, and long letters were dictated, often to ED and later to Francis D. He was considerate to foreign correspondents, remarking to Francis D 'You'd better try to write well, as it's to a for-eigner'—LLi 119. His formal signature was 'Charles Darwin', as in the example given above, from the Maull and Fox photograph of 1854, but on letters he often signed 'Ch. Darwin'. He seems never to have used his second initial.

HEALTH A great deal has been written on CD's ill-health, but it is all guess-work based on what he himself wrote in his auto-biography and on a few remarks by Francis D in LLi ch.3. No case notes from any of the physicians he consulted have ever been published, nor, so far as is recorded, was an autopsy carried out at his death. Barlow, in her edition of the *Autobiography*, 240–243, 1958, gives an appendix on the subject with the main references. She concludes that the following causes have been suggested 'Appendicitis, a duodenal ulcer, pyorrhea, or the damaging effects of sea-sickness during the voyage; but recent emphasis has been in the direction of neurotic or psychotic causes'. Other suggestions have been Chagas' disease and a toxic state arising from bad medication. de Beer, *Charles Darwin*, 114–117, 1963, puts most weight on Chagas' disease, but Woodruff, *The Times*, Dec.17, 1963, refutes this suggestion on the grounds that the symptoms were not at all typical. *see* 1971 J. H. Winslow, *Darwin's Victorian malady*, Philadelphia, 1971. R. Colp, *To be an invalid: the illness of Charles Darwin*, Chicago, 1977.

CD does not refer to any illnesses in childhood or youth and he lived an active and outdoor life. His first entry of illness is for 1831 Oct.–Dec., just before the *Beagle* sailed 'I was also troubled with palpitation and pain about the heart, and like many a young ignorant man, especially one with a smattering of medical knowledge, was convinced that I had heart disease. I did not consult any doctor'.—LLi 64. During the voyage, apart from a few minor accidents, some mild fever and con-tinuing sea-sickness, he had only one serious illness. This was at Valparaiso, 1834 Sep.19 until the end of October. Sep.19 'During the day I felt very unwell'. He reached Valparaiso on 27th 'with great difficulty', 'and was there confined to my bed till the end of October'. *J.Researches*, 1845, 268–269. For most of the voyage he was fit and lived an extremely energetic life.

During his residence in London, 1839–1842, 'I did less scientific work', 'This was due to frequent recurring unwellness, and to one long serious illness'—LLi 69. Again he gives no symptoms. When he had moved to Down House, he explained that after entertaining company 'my health almost always suffered from the excitement, violent shivering attacks and vomiting being thus brought on'—LLi 79. This condition continued for the rest of his life, although the attacks seem to have been less frequent or less violent in his later years.

During Dec.1881 he began to suffer anginal pains which became more frequent in Feb.–Mar.1882. He had a severe attack with fainting on Apr.18. Francis D records his father's last words, on 18th, as 'I am not afraid to die'—LLiii 358.

HOMES CD's home was his father's house, The Mount, Shrewsbury, until after his return from the *Beagle* voyage in 1836. He was however away for much of the year whilst an undergraduate student at Edinburgh, and Cambridge, and for almost 5 years when on the *Beagle*. On his return, he stayed in Cambridge with Henslow or in lodgings in Fitzwilliam St, and in London with his brother Erasmus Alvey D at 43 Great Marlborough St. In 1837, Mar. 13, he took furnished rooms at 36 Great Marlborough St with his secretary servant Syms Covington: this house can perhaps be regarded as his first personal home. After his engagement to ED, he rented a furnished house, 12 Upper Gower St, into which he moved in 1838, Dec.31, and where he and his bride took up residence the day after their wedding, 1839, Jan.30. They lived there until 1842, Sep. On 14th ED moved to Down House and CD followed on 17th. There they lived for the rest of their lives, although after 1882 ED spent the winters in Cambridge. The following list summarizes CD's homes and dates:

1809 Feb.12–1837 Mar.13 The Mount, Shrewsbury.
1825 Oct.22–1827 Apr.23 11 Lothian St, Edinburgh, in term time.
1828 Jan.   –1831 Jun.   Christ's College, Cambridge, in term time.
1831 Dec.10–1836 Oct.2   HMS *Beagle*
1837 Mar.13–1838 Dec.30 36 Great Marlborough St, London.
1838 Dec.31–1842 Sep.16 12 Upper Gower St, London.
1842 Sep.17–1882 Apr.19 Down House, Downe, Kent.

ICONOGRAPHY Portraits taken from life include one bust, three
oils, one each water colour, pastel, chalk, inkwash, and pencil.
There is one print, a lithograph, a number of photographs and
many caricatures. There are at least fifteen further works in
three dimensions ranging from full-scale statues to heads for
medallions which were not taken from life, but made between
his death and the 1909 celebrations of his birth. These are listed
below, but the artists are also entered in the main sequence.
The most comprehensive exhibition of portraits and related
material was that at Christ's College Cambridge. This was
held in the summer of the centenary year, 1909. A similar
exhibition, with some of the same material, was held at the
British Museum (Natural History) in that autumn. There are
printed catalogues of both.

Three dimensions:
1 1869 Bust by Thomas Woolner, now in Botany School
Cambridge. 1868 Nov. CD sat for. Francis D comments 'It has
a certain air, almost of pomposity, which seems to me foreign
to my father's expression'—LLiii 106.
2 1883 Statue in stone by *Sir* Joseph Boehm, at British
Museum (Natural History). 1885 Jun.9 unveiled by Huxley in
presence of Prince of Wales. B was paid £2,100 for it.
3 1883 statuette by *Sir* Joseph Boehm. From No.2, about half
size.
4 1887 Bust in terracotta by *Sir* Joseph Boehm, 24″. Copy in
National Portrait gallery. *See also* No.34.
5 1887 Deep medallion by *Sir* Joseph Boehm, in Westminster
Abbey. B was paid £150 for it.
6 1905 Statue in stone, seated, by Horace Mountford, outside
Old School, Shrewsbury. There is a life size plaster cast of this.
7 ?1905 Statuette in bronze by Horace Mountford, based on
No.6. Copies were for sale in 1909.
8 1905 Bust by Horace Mountford, 27½″, based on No.7.
Copy in terracotta in National Portrait Gallery. 1909 a copy in
plaster was with the artist.
9 before 1887 but not from life. Bust by Christian Wilhelm
Jacob Lehr, at University Museum Oxford.
10 before 1887 but not from life. Plaque by Thomas Woolner,
in green Wedgwood ware. Copy in CD's set at Christ's College Cambridge; another at American Philosophical Society,
Philadelphia.

11 1882 Medallion in bronze by Allan Wyon. The Royal Society's Darwin Medal was reduced from this; the die made in 1890. There is an electrotype from the original wax at British Museum (Natural History).

12 1909 or before. Medallion in bronze by Horace Mountford.

13 1909 or before. Medallion in bronze by William Rothenstein.

14 1909 Bust in bronze by William Couper of New York, at Christ's College Cambridge. Presented by USA delegates to 1909 centenary celebrations.

15 n.d. Statue by H. R. Hope-Pinker, at University Museum, Oxford; model for at Down House.

16 n.d. Bust by Charles L. Hartwell, at Down House. Commissioned by Joseph Leidy. Inscription reads 'Presented by Dr. Joseph Leidy II of Philadelphia, to the British Nation in memory of those American naturalists who came to the support of Charles Darwin upon the publication of "The origin of species" in 1859'.

Oils:

17 1875 by Walter William Ouless. CD sat for in Feb.–Mar. In family; copy by the artist at Christ's College Cambridge. Engraved by Paul Rajon, No.29. Francis D's opinion 'Mr. Ouless's portrait is, in my opinion, the finest representation of my father that has been produced'—LLiii 195.

18 1879 by *Sir* William Blake Richmond. CD sat for in Jun. Copy by the artist in the family. Cambridge Philosophical Society. Subscribed for by members of the University, £400 being raised. CD is in his Hon.LL.D. robes. ED's opinion in 1881 Oct. 'The red picture, and I thought it quite horrid, so fierce and so dirty'. Francis D's opinion 'according to my own view, neither the attitude nor the expression are characteristic of my father'—LLiii 222.

19 1881 by *Hon.* John Collier. CD sat for in Aug. At Linnean Society and commissioned by them. 1883 copy by the artist, presented 1896 to National Portrait Gallery by William Erasmus D. Francis D's opinion 'many of those who knew his face most intimately think that Mr. Collier's picture is the best of the portraits'—LLiii 223.

Water colours and drawings:

20 1816 Pastel of CD with his sister Emily Catherine. Reproductions always describe it as by 'Sharples', perhaps Rolinda

Sharples (d.1838); not her father James S who died in 1811. In the family.

21 ?1840 Pencil sketch for No.22 by George Richmond. Found in cellars of Botany School Cambridge in 1929.

22 ?1840 Water colour by George Richmond. Unsigned but note on back of frame reads March 1840. In the family.

23 1853 Chalk drawing by Samuel Laurence, a sketch for No.24.

24 1853 Chalk drawing by Samuel Laurence. In the family.

25 Between 1873 and 1880 Washed India ink by Louisa Ann Nash. Owned by L.A.N's grand-daughter at Corvallis, Oregon. This is the only picture of CD done in his lifetime which is in USA.

26 1878 Pencil sketch, 7"×5", by Marian Huxley, in National Portrait Gallery. Signed with a monogram MH.

Prints:

27 ?1850 Lithograph by T. H. Maguire. Printed by M. & N. Hanhart. Ipswich Museum British Association Portraits. Lithograph signature of CD below and blind stamp of Ipswich Museum. CD is seated in a Down study chair. This is the only print in any form from life. *See also* George Ransome.

28 1874 Steel engraving by C. H. Jeens, from Rejlander photograph No.40. For Nature, Lond. Jun.4. Fpce, *Charles Darwin memorial notices*, 1882.

29 ?1875 Copper engraving by Paul Rajon, from Ouless oil No.17. There is a proof at American Philosophical Society, Philadelphia.

30 1884 Wood engraving by G. Kruell, from Maull & Fox photograph, the profile, No.43, for *Harper's Mag.,* Oct.

31 1882 Wood engraving from Leonard D photograph, No.41, for *Century Mag.,* Jan.

32 1883 Copper engraving by Leopold Flameng, from Collier portrait, No.19. Copies are dated March 10, Fine Art Society (Limited) London, and have engraved signatures of artist and engraver.

33 1887 Wood engraving by G. Kruell, from Elliott & Fry photograph, No.43, for Fpce LLiii.

34 1886 or 1887 Wood engraving by Edward Whymper, from Boehm bust, No.4.

Photographs:

35 1842 Aug.23. Photographer unknown. CD with first child

William Erasmus D. A studio portrait with drop background.
36 c1854 Maull & Fox. *a*. Profile to third waistcoat button or to knees, seated in bentwood chair, check waistcoat and trousers; long available as a commercial photogravure. *b*. Full face, dark embroidery waistcoat and dark trousers; also available as a commercial photogravure but less often seen. The two versions were probably taken at the same session because the table and drapes are the same.
37 c1864 London Stereoscopic Co. There are at least three versions of these pairs.
38 1868 Aug. Julia Margaret Cameron; taken at Freshwater, Isle of Wight. *a*. profile, *b*. almost full face. Authentic copies should be signed by *Mrs* Cameron and bear Colnaghi's blind authentication stamp. CD's opinion of 'I like this photograph very much better than any other which has been taken of me'—LLiii 92, but he does not say which one.
39 c1868 CD on his cob 'Tommy'.
40 c1870 O. G. Rejlander, a profile facing right. *see* No.28.
41 c1874 Leonard D, CD sitting in a basket chair on verandah at Down House. A version of this printed on china was shown at Christ's College exhibition of 1909.
42 ?1878 Lock & Whitfield, *Men of Mark*, 3rd ser., 1878. A half-face head and shoulders; reproduced on free end paper of Eiseley, *Darwin's century*, 1958. This photograph is not otherwise recorded.
43 c1880 Elliott & Fry. *a*. On verandah at Down House in cloak and hat with round crown; *b*. same place but without cloak or hat. British Museum (Natural History) exhibition of 1909 showed four versions of this photographic session. Version *a*, at least was long available as a commercial photogravure.

Caricatures:
There are many of these and no list has ever appeared. The best known, and that most often reproduced is 'Natural Selection' by Carlo Pellegrini, 1871, Men of the Day No. 33, *Vanity Fair*, Sep.30. Pellegrini signed his caricatures 'Ape' from 1869 onwards, but this is not signed. It occurred for sale in two sizes, 31 cm & 18 cm, the former much better coloured. Others which were shown at the Christ's College exhibition of 1909 were 1881 Punch's Fancy Portraits No. 64, after publication of *Vegetable mould*, *Hornet*, CD with Monkey body, *Simplissimus*,

Lalune, La petite Lune, Fun, Once a week, Figaro. There is at least one caricature in pottery, a monkey body with CD's head.

ITINERARY Where CD was at any one time in his life is well documented except for the earliest years. For these the auto-biographical fragment, printed in MLi 5, is the most helpful; this was probably written in 1838 when he started his personal journal. The journal contains only a little on the *Beagle* voyage, but *J. Researches* and Fitz-Roy's Vol. 2 of the *Narrative* gives the details; for much of the time CD was ashore whilst the ship was surveying so that his whereabouts are by no means the same as hers. After 1838, all important visits from home are noticed in detail in his journal, except that some brief trips to London for a night or so may be omitted, or else he does not say where he stayed. After his move to Down House in 1842, CD was away from home for a considerable part of each year; much of the time was spent at hydropathic establishments, but there were also holidays and journeys for scientific business. From 1842 to 1881 he was away for a total of about 2000 days, exceeding 50 days in 23 of these 40 years.

1809–1912 No information about his being away from The Mount, Shrewsbury.

1813 Family summer holiday at Gros, Abergele, N. Wales.

1814–1816 No information about his being away from The Mount.

1817 In the spring, CD went with his sister Emily Catherine D to *Mr* G. Case's day school in Shrewsbury.

1818 In the summer CD went to Shrewsbury School as a boarder, stayed 7 years, *Dr* Samuel Butler being head-master all the time. Jul. CD went to Liverpool with his brother Erasmus Alvey D.

1819 Jul. Summer holiday at Plas Edwards, Towyn, N. Wales.

1820 Jul. CD went on riding tour with his brother to Pistyll Rhayader, N. Wales.

1822 Jun. CD went to Downton, Wilts with sister Caroline Sarah D. Jul. CD went to Montgomery & Bishop's Castle, Shropshire with sister Susan Elizabeth D.

1825 Jun. 17 left Shrewsbury School. Oct. 22 signed matricula-tion book Edinburgh University as a medical student. First lecture on Oct. 26. Lodged at 11 Lothian St.

1826 At Edinburgh all this year in term time. Jun. 15 N. Wales, walking tour with N. Hubbersty, climbed Snowdon.

1827 Apr.c.24 finally left Edinburgh, toured Dundee, St Andrew's, Stirling, Glasgow, Belfast, Dublin (only visit to Ireland). May, end of, visited Paris with Josiah Wedgwood [III] & Caroline Sarah D (only visit to continental Europe). Autumn, paid many visits to Woodhouse, Shropshire, especially for the shooting. Sep. at Maer and visited *Sir* James Mackintosh. Oct.15 admitted to Christ's College Cambridge, but did not go up until Lent term.

1828 Jan. went to Christ's College for Lent term and rest of academic year, lodging above Bacon's, tobacconist, in Sidney St. Summer to Barmouth, N.Wales with J. M. Herbert & T. Butler for private coaching by G. A. Butterton. Sep. at Maer and then at Osmaston Hall, nr Derby, home of William Darwin Fox.

1829 At Cambridge in term time, living in College. Feb.19 2 days in London to talk about beetles with F. W. Hope. Feb.24 to Cambridge. Jun. to Barmouth with F. W. Hope. Jun.–Jul. Shrewsbury. Jul. Maer one week. Oct. Birmingham with Wedgwoods for music meeting. Oct.16 to Cambridge.

1830 At Cambridge in term time, living in College. Aug. to N.Wales collecting beetles and fishing. Nov. Cambridge, passed BA examinations.

1812 Jan.23 to Cambridge for 3 months to keep terms, stayed with J. S. Henslow. Jun. left Cambridge at end of May term. Aug. to Llangollen, Ruthin, Conway, Bangor, Capel Curig, with Adam Sedgwick for geology, then alone to Barmouth. Sep.1 Maer for shooting. Sep.2–4 Cambridge. Sep.5 London, 17 Spring Gardens. Sep.9 left by Packet with Fitz-Roy for Plymouth. Sep.11 arrived Plymouth to see *Beagle*. Sep.19 Cambridge. Sep.22 Shrewsbury. Oct.2 London, 17 Spring Gardens. Oct. 21 Shrewsbury. Oct.24 Plymouth. Dec.10 sailed but put back. Dec.21 sailed but put back. Dec.27 sailed.

1832 Jan.6–Feb.8 Cape Verde Is, Feb.16–17 St Paul's Rocks, Feb.20 Fernando de Noronha, Feb.28–Mar.18 Bahia Blanca, Mar.19 Abrolhos archipelago, Apr.5–Jul.5 Rio de Janeiro, Jul.26–Aug.19 Monte Video, Sep.6–Oct.17 Bahia Blanca, Nov.2–26 Monte Video, Dec.16 Tierra del Fuego.

1833 –Feb.26 Tierra del Fuego, Mar.1–Apr.6 Falkland Is,
Apr.28–Jul.23 Maldonado, Aug.3–Dec.6 Rio Negro &
Monte Video, Dec.23– Port Desire.

1834 –Jan.4 Port Desire, Jan.9–Jan.19 Port St Julian,
Jan.29–Mar.7 Straits of Magellan via Falkland Is.,
Mar.10–Apr.7 Falkland Is., Apr.13–May 12 Santa Cruz
River, Jun.28–Jul.13 Chiloe, Jul.31–Nov.10 Valparaiso,
Nov.21– Chiloe.

1835 –Feb.4 Chiloe, Feb.8–22 Valdivia, Mar.4–7 Concepcion,
Mar.11–Jul.6 Valparaiso–Copiapo, Jul.12–15 Iquique,
Jul.19–Sep.7 Callao for Lima, Sep.16–Oct.20 Galápagos
Is., Nov.15–26 Tahiti, Dec.21–30 Bay of Islands, New
Zealand.

1836 Jan.12–30 Sydney, Feb.2–17 Hobart, Mar.3–14 St
George's Sound, Apr.2–12 Cocos Keeling Is., Apr.
29–May 9 Mauritius, May 31–Jun.18 Cape of Good
Hope, Jul.7–14 St Helena, Jul.19–23 Ascension.
Jul.19–23, Aug.1–6 Bahia Blanca, Aug.12–17 Pernam-
buco, Sep.4–8 Porto Praya, Cape Verde Is, Sep.20 Ter-
ceira, Azores, Oct.2 Falmouth, Cornwall, Oct.4
Shrewsbury, Oct. end of, Greenwich unloading *Beagle*,
Nov.6 London, 43 Great Marlborough St, Nov.c.21
Maer, Dec.2–13 London, Dec.13– Cambridge, J. S.
Henslow & Fitzwilliam St.

1837 –Mar.6 Cambridge with 2 trips to London one on Jan.4,
Mar.6–12 London, 43 Great Marlborough St,
Mar.13–Jun.25 London, 36 Great Marlborough St,
Nov.21 Isle of Wight 2 day visit to W. D. Fox, Nov.23
London.

1838 May 10 Cambridge 3 days, Jun.23 London to Leith by
steamer, Edinburgh 1 day Salisbury Crags, Loch Leven,
Glen Roy 8 days, Glasgow, Liverpool. Jul.12 Overton-
on-Dee, Flintshire 1 night, Jul.13–31 Shrewsbury &
Maer, Aug.1 to London, Oct.25 Windsor for 2 days rest,
Nov.9 Maer, Nov.11 proposed to Emma Wedgwood
and was accepted, Nov.12 Shrewsbury, Nov.17 Maer,
Nov.20 to London, Dec.6 Emma W came to London,
Dec.21 to Maer, Dec.31 slept at 12 Upper Gower St.

1839 Jan.11 to Shrewsbury, Jan.15 to Maer, Jan.18 to London,
Jan.25 to Shrewsbury, Jan.28 to Maer, Jan.29 CD married, Jan.30 to London 12 Upper Gower St, Apr.26–May
12 Maer, May 13–19 Shrewsbury, May 20 to London,

Aug.23 to Maer, Aug.26 to Birmingham for British Aassociation, Sep.12 to Shrewsbury, Oct.2 to London.

1840 Apr.3 to Shrewsbury, Jun.10 to Maer, Nov.10 to London.

1841 May 28 to Maer & Shrewsbury, Jul.23 to London.

1842 May 7–17 Shrewsbury, May 18–Jun.14 Maer, Jun.15 to Shrewsbury, Jun.18 Capel Curig, Bangor, Caernarvon, Capel Curig, 10 days, Jul.18 to London, Jul.24 CD & ED first saw Down House slept at inn, Sep.14 ED slept at Down House, Sep.17 CD slept at Down House.

1843 Jul.8 Maer & Shrewsbury 1 week, Oct.12 Shrewsbury 10 days.

1844 Apr.23 to Maer & Shrewsbury, May 30 to Down House, Oct.18–29 Shrewsbury.

1845 Apr.29–May 10 Shrewsbury, May 11 Down House, Sept. 15 Shrewsbury, Beesby (CD's farm), Manchester to visit W. Herbert, Walton Hall to visit C. Waterton, Chatsworth, Camp Hill to visit Sarah Elizabeth W [I]. Oct.26 to Down House.

1846 Feb.21–Mar.2 Shrewsbury, Jul.21–Aug.8 Shrewsbury, Sep.9–16 Southampton for British Association, 12 visited Portsmouth and Isle of Wight, 13 Winchester & St Cross, 14 Netley Abbey & Southampton Common, Sep.22 day at Knole Park, Sevenoaks with ED & Susan D. Oct. London 10 days in two visits.

1847 Feb.19–Mar.4 Shrewsbury, Jun.22–Jun.30 Oxford for British Association, visited Newnham Courtney, Dropmore, Burnham Beeches, Jul.22– Swanage by Wareham & Corfe Castle, returned by Poole & New Forest, Oct.10–24 Shrewsbury, Nov.17–25 Shrewsbury after death of CD's father on 13.

1849 Mar.10–Jun.30 Malvern Wells with whole family & servants (CD's 1st hydropathic visit), Sep.11–21 Birmingham for British Association, day visit to Malvern.

1850 Jun.11–18 Malvern Wells, Aug.10–16 Leith Hill Place to visit Josiah W [III], Oct.14–21 Hartfield, Sussex, The Ridge to visit Sarah Elizabeth W [II], 18 Ramsgate for the day.

1851 Mar.24–31 Malvern with Anne Elizabeth D, Apr.16–24 Malvern with Anne Elizabeth D who died there on 23, Jul.30–Aug.9 London 7 Park St to see Great Exhibition.

1852 Mar.24–Apr.15 Rugby 1 day to see William Erasmus D

at school then to Barlaston, Batley & Shrewsbury to his sister Susan, Sep.11–16 Leith Hill Place, home by Godstone & Reigate.

1853 Jul.14–Aug.4 Eastbourne with family, to Brighton & Hastings on day visits, Aug.13–16 The Hermitage nr Woking to visit Henry Allen W with ED, George Howard D & Henrietta Emma D, visited military camp for Crimean war at Chobham.

1854 Jan. visited London, Mar.13–17 The Ridge, Hartfield, Sussex, Jul.13–15 The Ridge, Hartfield, Sussex, Oct.9–14 Leith Hill Place, Dec.1 in London for breakfast.

1855 Jan.18–Feb.15 London 27 York Place, Baker St, Sep.10–18 Glasgow for British Association with ED, Sep.19 slept Carlisle, Sep.20 to Shrewsbury by Rugby, Sep.22 to Down House.

1856 Sep.13–18 Leith Hill Place.

1857 Apr.22–May 5 Moor Park Hydro, Jun.16–29 Moor Park Hydro, 27 visited Selborne, Nov.5–12 Moor Park Hydro, Nov.16–20 London.

1858 Apr.20–May 3 Moor Park, Jul.9–13 The Ridge, Hartfield, Jul.17–26 via Portsmouth, Sandown, Isle of Wight, King's Head Hotel with family, Jul.26–Aug.12 Norfolk House, Shanklin, I.O.W., Oct.25–31 Moor Park.

1859 Feb.5–18 Moor Park, May 21–28 Moor Park, Jul.19–26 Moor Park, Aug.20–23 Leith Hill Place, Oct.2–Dec.7 Wells Terrace, Ilkley (CD there when *Origin* published), Dec.8–9 London.

1860 Feb.27–Mar.3 London, Apr.14 London, Jun.28–Jul.6 Sudbrook Park, Petersham, Surrey, Jul.10–Aug.1 The Ridge, Hartfield, Sep.22–Nov.10 15 Marine Parade, Eastbourne.

1861 Apr.1–4 London, Queen Anne St, Jul.1–Aug.26 2 Hesketh Terrace, Torquay, Nov.21 London.

1862 Apr.1–4, London, Queen Anne St, May 15–21 Leith Hill Place, Aug.12–31 1 Carlton Terrace, Southampton, Sep.1–27 Cliff Cottage, Bournemouth, Sep.29 London, Queen Anne St.

1863 Feb.4–14 London, Queen Anne St, Apr.27–May ?10 Hartfield, May ?11–14 Leith Hill Place, Sep.2–Oct.13 Malvern Wells.

1864 Aug.25–?31 London, 4 Chester Place.

1865 Nov.8–?17 London, Queen Anne St.

1866 Apr.21–May 4 London, Queen Anne St, May 29–Jun.2 Leith Hill Place, Nov.22–29 London, Queen Anne St.

1867 Feb.13–21 London, Queen Anne St, Jun.17–24 London, Queen Anne St, Sep.18–24 London, Queen Anne St, Nov.28–Dec.3 London, Queen Anne St.

1868 Mar.3–9 London, Queen Anne St., Mar.10–31 London, 4 Chester Place (Sarah Elizabeth W [II]), Jul.16 Bassett, Southampton on way to Isle of Wight, Jul.17–Aug.20 Dumbola Lodge, Freshwater, I.O.W.

1869 Feb.16–24 London, Queen Anne St, Jun.10 Shrewsbury on way to Barmouth, Jun.11–29 Caerdeon, Barmouth, N. Wales, to recuperate from fall from his pony 'Tommy', Jun.30 Stafford on way home, Nov. 1–9 London, Queen Anne St.

1870 Mar.5–10 London, Queen Anne St, May 20–24 Bull Hotel, Cambridge, Jun.24–Jul.1 London, Queen Anne St, Aug.13–26 Bassett, Southampton, Oct.13–20 Leith Hill Place, Dec.8–14 London, Queen Anne St.

1871 Feb.23–Mar.2 London, Queen Anne St, Apr.1–5 London, Queen Anne St, May 11–19 Bassett, Southampton, Jun.24–30 London, Queen Anne St, Jul.28–Aug.24 Haredene, Albury, Guildford, family holiday. Nov. 3–10 Leith Hill Place, Dec.12–22 London, Queen Anne St.

1872 Feb.13–Mar.21 London, 9 Devonshire St, a rented house. Jun.8–20 Bassett, Southampton, Aug.13–21 Leith Hill Place, Oct.5–26 Sevenoaks Common (Horace D had lodgings in Sevenoaks), Dec.17–23 London, Queen Anne St.

1873 Mar.15–Apr.10 London, 15 Montague St, a rented house, Jun.4–12 Leith Hill Place, Aug.5–9 Abinger Hall visiting *Sir* Thomas Farrer, Aug.10–21 Bassett, Southampton, Nov.8–18 London, 4 Bryanston St visiting R. B. Litchfield who had recently married Henrietta Emma D.

1874 Jan.10–17 London, Queen Anne St, Apr.21–29 London, 4 Bryanston St, Jul.25–30 Abinger Hall, Jul.31–Aug.24 Bassett, Southampton, Dec.3–12 London, 4 Bryanston St.

1875 Mar.31–Apr.12 London, Queen Anne St & Bryanston St. Jun.3–Jul.5 Abinger Hall, Aug.28–Sep.11 Bassett,

Southampton, Nov.4–5 London, Queen Anne St (for Vivisection Commission), Dec.10–20 London, Bryanston St.

1876 Feb.3–5 London, Queen Anne St, Apr.7–May 3 London, Queen Anne St, May 6–Jun.6 Hopedene, Dorking (home of Hensleigh W), Jun.7–9 Hollycombe, Midhurst (home of *Sir* John Hawkshaw), Oct.4–6 Leith Hill Place, Oct.7–19 Bassett, Southampton, Dec. ? London to Roy. Soc.

1877 Jan.6–15 London, Bryanston St, Apr.12–28 London, Bryanston St then Queen Anne St, Jun.8–12 Leith Hill Place, Jun.13–Jul.3 Bassett, Southampton, visited Stonehenge, Aug.20–25 Abinger Hall, Oct.26–29 London, Queen Anne St, Nov.16–18 Cambridge for award of Hon.LL.D.

1878 Jan.17–23 London, Queen Anne St, Feb.27–Mar.5 London, Bryanston St, Apr.27–May 3 Bassett, Southampton, Jun.7–?14 Leith Hill Place & Abinger Hall, Jun.?15 Barlaston to visit Francis W., Nov.21–26 London, Bryanston St.

1879 Feb.27–Mar.5 London, Queen Anne St, May 6–7 Worthing to see Anthony Rich, May 8–20 Bassett, Southampton, May 21–25 Leith Hill Place, Jun.26 London, Queen Anne St, Jun.28–30 West Hackhurst, Abinger Hammer, home of Miss L. M. Forster, Aug.1 London, Queen Anne St, Aug.2–27 Coniston, Lake District, family holiday, 1 day expedition to Grasmere, Dec.2–12 London, 5 days Bryanston St, 5 days Queen Anne St.

1880 Mar.4–8 London, Queen Anne St, Apr.8–13 Abinger Hall with Horace D and his wife Emma Cecilia (Ida) Farrer, May 25–Jun.8 Bassett, Southampton, Aug.14–18 Cambridge, Botolph Lane to visit his sons, Aug.19–20 London, Queen Anne St, Oct.20–Nov.2 London Bryanston St, Dec.7–10 London, Queen Anne St, Dec.11–14 Leith Hill Place.

1881 Feb.24–Mar.3 London, Bryanston St, Jun.2–Jul.4 Glenrhydding House, Patterdale, Ullswater, Aug.3–5 London, Queen Anne St, Sep.8–10 West Worthing Hotel, Worthing, Sussex, visiting Anthony Rich, Oct.20–27 Cambridge, stayed with Horace D., Dec.18–20 London, Bryanston St.

1882 CD did not leave Down House in this last year of his life.

MANUSCRIPTS Much material which was left in manuscript at CD's death has been published since. Most of it was never intended for publication and is in note or abbreviated form, although some is from early drafts of what he hoped eventually to prepare for the press. The autobiographical manuscripts have been considered above and published letters will be found in the main sequence. Other mss material which has been published will also be found in the main sequence under brief title, but is summarized here in date order of first publication:

1882 In George J. Romanes, *Animal intelligence*, contains extracts from CD's notes on behaviour, published with his permission and in press before his death.

1883 In George J. Romanes, *Mental evolution in animals*, contains an appendix which is from ch.10 of the 2nd part of CD's intended big book on evolution. *See also* Stauffer, 1975.

1885 Über die Wege der Hummel-Männchen, in *Gesammelte kleinere Schriften*, 2:84–88 (F1584, 1602). *See also* Freeman 1968 below.

1909 *The foundations of The origin of species, a sketch written in 1842*, transcribed & edited by Francis D. Printed for private distribution.

1909 *The foundations of The origin of species, Two essays written in 1843 and 1844*, transcribed & edited by Francis D. Published edition. The sketch of 1842 is from the same setting of type as previous entry.

1933 *Charles Darwin's diary of the voyage on H.M.S. Beagle*, transcribed and edited by Nora Barlow.

1959 Darwin's journal, *Bull.Brit.Mus.(nat.Hist.)*, hist.Ser., 2:1–21. Transcribed by G. R. de Beer. There is a Russian translation of an earlier and independent transcription by S. L. Sobol', 1957.

1960–1967 Darwin's notebooks on transmutation of species, *Bull.Brit.Mus.(nat.Hist.)*, hist.Ser., 2:23–73, 75–113, 119–150, 151–183, 185–200; 3:129–176. Transcribed and edited by G. R. de Beer, M. J. Rowlands & B. Skramovsky. Notebooks B–E.

1962 Coral islands, *Atoll.Res.Bull.*, No.88, transcribed by D. R. Stoddart.

1963 Darwin's ornithological notes, *Bull.Brit.Mus.(nat.Hist)*, hist.Ser., 2:201–278, transcribed by Nora Barlow.

1963 Darwin's manuscript of pangenesis, *Brit.J.Hist.Sci.*, 1:251–263, transcribed by R. C. Olby.
1968 Charles Darwin on the routes of male humble bees, *Bull.Brit.Mus.(nat.Hist.)*, hist.Ser., 3:177–189. Translation of 1885 German paper above, with transcription of field notes by R. B. Freeman.
1974 Howard E. Gruber, *Darwin on man*, contains transcription of M & N notebooks on behaviour, with other mss, by Paul H. Barrett.
1975 R. C. Stauffer, *Charles Darwin's Natural selection*, transcribed from what was intended by CD to be Part 2 of his big book on evolution, *Variation under domestication* being Part 1.
1979 Charles Darwin's red notebook, *Bull.Brit.Mus.(nat. Hist.)*, hist.Ser., 7: transcribed by S. Herbert. Contains CD's earliest notes on evolution, covering the period June 1836– June 1837.

MEDALS Copley (Royal Society) 1864, CD was proposed in 1862 but failed; Daly (Royal College of Physicians) 1879; Royal (Royal Society) 1853; Wollaston (Geological Society) 1859, which from 1846–1860 was made of palladium.

ORDER Pour la Mérite, Prussia 1867.

PRIZE Bressa, Reale Accademia della Scienze, Turin 1879; 12,000 francs. CD gave £100 from it to the Zoologische Station at Naples.

RELIGION CD's religious views are summarized in LLi – 304–317. Francis D states 'My father spoke little on these subjects, and I can contribute nothing from my own recollection'. CD considered religious views to be a deeply personal matter and took great pains not to offend ED. 'Whilst aboard the *Beagle* I was quite orthodox'. 'But I had gradually come by this time, *i.e.* 1836–1839, to see that the Old Testament was no more to be trusted than the sacred books of the Hindoos'. 1879 CD to Fordyce, 'In my most extreme fluctuations I have never been an Atheist in the sense of denying the existence of a God. I think that generally (and more and more as I grow older), but not always, that an Agnostic would be the more correct description of my state of mind'—*Aspects of scepticism*, 1883. 1881 CD discussed his views with Aveling who published what he thought CD meant in *The religious views of Charles*

Darwin, Freethought Publishing Company, 1883: Francis D
felt that Aveling had misunderstood. For CD's imaginary
deathbed conversion to a fundamentalist orthodoxy *see*
Atkins, 51–52, and for his fictitious book on the subject, *My
apology for my unformed ideas, see* Freeman, 18–19.

SOCIETY MEMBERSHIP As was customary, CD joined those
London societies whose meetings might be of interest to him,
although, after he left London in 1842, his attendance at their
meetings was infrequent. He was a founder member of the
Entomological Society in 1831, his beetle collecting days, and
joined the Zoological Society as a corresponding member in
the same year before the *Beagle* left England, becoming a
Fellow in 1839. As soon as he returned in 1836 he joined the
Geological Society and was its Honorary Secretary from 1838
Feb.16 to 1841 Feb.19. He added the Geographical Society in
1838. He was elected to the Royal Society in 1839 Jan.24, at the
age of 29, and he served on its Council in 1850–1851 and again
in 1855–1856. He *did not* join the Linnean *until* 1854, apparently largely so that he could get books by post from its
excellent library. Finally he joined the Ethnological Society in
1861. He used the periodical publications of all these societies,
except those of the Entomological and Ethnological Societies,
for his own papers. His Honorary memberships included the
Royal Society of Edinburgh, the Royal Medical Society of
Edinburgh of which he was particulary proud for he had been
an ordinary member when a medical student there, and the
Royal Irish Academy. He was an Honorary of 13 in the
Americas and of about 40 in Europe. Of local natural history
societies in England, he was elected to only 2, the Watford
Natural History Society, later the Hertfordshire, in 1877, and
the Epping Field Club, later the Essex, in 1880. Almost all
these are listed by countries in LLiii 373–376, but their titles
are sometimes translated into English. The following list
is in alphabetical order with names in the original lan-
guages:
Academia Nacional de Ciencias de las República Argentina,
Cordova. CD Honorary Member 1878.
Academia Caesarea Leopoldino-Carolina Germanica Naturae
Curiosorum. CD Honorary Member 1857, cognomen Forster.
Academia Scientiarum Imperialis Petropolitana (Imperators-

kaya Akademiya Nauk). CD Corresponding Member 1867.
Académie Royale des Sciences, des Lettres et des Beaux-Arts de Belgiques, CD Associate 1870.
Academy of Natural Sciences, Philadelphia, CD Correspondent 1868.
American Academy of Arts and Sciences, Boston, CD Foreign Honorary Member 1873.
American Philosophical Society, Philadelphia, CD Member 1869.
Anthropologische Gesellschaft, Vienna, CD Honorary Member 1872.
Asiatic Society of Bengal, Calcutta, CD Honorary Member 1871.
Berliner Gesellschaft für Anthropologie, CD Corresponding Member 1877.
Boston Society of Natural History, CD Honorary Member 1873.
California Academy of Sciences, CD Honorary Member 1872.
California State Geological Society, CD Corresponding Member 1877.
Canterbury [New Zealand] Philosophical Institute, CD Honorary Member, 1863.
Entomological Society of London, CD original Member 1831.
Epping Field Club, CD Honorary Member 1880.
Ethnological Society of London, CD Fellow 1861.
Franklin Literary Society, Indiana, CD Honorary Member 1878.
Gabinete Portuguiz de Leitura, Pernambuco, CD Corresponding Member 1879.
Geological Society of London, CD Fellow 1836.
Institucion Libre de Enseñanza, Madrid, CD Honorary Professor 1877.
Institut de France, CD Correspondent, Section of Botany 1878.
Kaiserliche-Koenigliche Zoologische-Botanische Gesellschaft, Vienna, CD Honorary Member 1867.
Kaiserliche Akademie der Wissenschaften, Vienna, CD Corresponding Member 1871, Honorary Foreign Member 1875.
Koeniglich-Bayerische Akademie der Wissenschaften, Munich, CD Foreign Member 1878.

Koeniglich-Preussiche Akademie der Wissenschaften, Berlin, CD Corresponding Member 1863, Fellow 1878.

Kongeligt Dansk Videnskabernes Selskab, Copenhagen, CD Fellow 1879.

Kongliga Svenska Vetenskaps-Akadamien, Stockholm, CD Foreign Member 1865.

Kongliga Vetenskaps-Societeten, Uppsala, CD Fellow 1860.

Koninklijke Akademie van Wetenschappen, Amsterdam, CD Honorary Fellow 1872.

Koninklinke Natuurkundige Vereeniging in Neder-landische-Indie, Batavia, CD Corresponding Member 1880.

Linnean Society of London, CD Fellow 1854.

Magyar Tudományos Akademia, Budapest, CD Member 1872.

Manchester Literary & Philosophical Society, CD Honorary Member 1868.

Medicinische-Naturwissenschaftliche Gesellschaft zu Jena, CD Honorary Member 1878.

Medico-Chirurgical Society of London, CD Honorary Member 1868.

Naturforschende Gesellschaft zu Halle, CD Honorary Member 1879.

New York Academy of Sciences, CD Honorary Member 1879.

New Zealand Institute, CD Honorary Member 1879.

Real Accademia dei Lincei, CD foreign Member 1875.

Reale Accademia della Scienze, Turin, CD Honorary Member 1873.

Royal Geographical Society, CD Fellow 1838.

Royal Irish Academy, Dublin, CD Honorary Member 1866.

Royal Medical Society, Edinburgh, CD Member 1826–1827, Honorary Member 1873.

Royal Society, London, CD Fellow 1839 Jan.24.

Royal Society of Edinburgh, CD Fellow 1865.

Royal Society of New South Wales, Sydney, CD Honorary Member 1879.

Schlesische Gesellschaft für Vaterlandische Cultur, Breslau, CD Honorary Member 1878.

Senkenbergische Naturforschende Gesellschaft, Frankfurt-am-Main, CD Corresponding Member 1873.

Siebenburgische Verein für Naturwissenschaften, Hermann-stadt, CD Honorary Member 1877.

Sociedad Cientifica Argentina, Buenos Aires, CD Honorary Member 1877.

Sociedad de Naturalistas Neo-Granadinos, CD Honorary Member 1860.

Sociedad Zoológica Argentina, Cordova, CD Honorary Member 1874.

Sociedade de Geographia de Lisboa, CD Corresponding Member 1877.

Società dei Naturalisti in Modena, CD Honorary Member 1875.

Società Geografica Italiana, Florence, CD Honorary Member 1870.

Società Italiana di Antropologia e di Etnologia, Florence, CD Honorary Member 1872.

Società La Scuola Italica Pitagorica, Rome, CD Presidente Onorario 1880.

Societas Caesarea Naturae Curiosorum (Société Imperiale des Naturalistes), Moscow, CD Honorary Member 1870.

Société d'Anthropologie, Paris, CD Foreign Member 1871.

Société des Sciences Naturelles, Neuchatel, CD Corresponding Member 1863.

Société Entomologiques, Paris, CD Honorary Member 1874.

Société Geologiques, Paris, CD Life Member 1837.

Société Hollandaise des Sciences à Haarlem (Hollandische Maatschappij der Wetenschappen), CD Foreign Member 1877.

Société Royale de Botanique de Belgique, Brussels, CD Associate Member 1881.

Société Royale des Sciences Médicales et Naturelles, Brussels, CD Honorary Member 1872.

Society of Naturalists of the Imperial Kazan University (Obschchestvo Estestvoispuitateleĭ pri Imperatorskon Kasanskom Universitetys), CD Honorary Member 1875.

Watford Natural History Society, CD Honorary Member 1877.

Zeeuwsch Genootschap der Wetenschappen te Middleburg, CD Foreign Member 1877.

Zoological Society of London, CD Corresponding Member 1831, Fellow 1839.

STAMPS Ecuador 1935, to commemorate CD's landing on Galápagos Is., 20 sucre, head of CD.

Darwin's bull-dog 'I am Darwin's bull-dog' he once said. 1871 Nov.2 Huxley to Haeckel, 'The dogs have been barking at his heels too much of late'—*Life of Huxley*, 2nd edition, ii 62.

Darwin's Farm At Beesby, Lincolnshire q.v.

Darwin's Finches The sub-family Geospizinae of the Galápagos Is. Coined by Robert T. Orr, *Bull.N.Y.zool.Soc.*, 45:42–45, 1942. Used by David Lack, *Proc.zool.Soc.Lond.*, pt.5, No.53, 49, 1944, and title of his book 1947.

Darwin's Hero CD's name for an exceptionally vigorous plant of morning glory (*Ipomoea purpurea*) in *Cross and self fertilisation*. Heading ch.15 in Allan.

Darwin's Peak Another name for Angulus woolneri q.v., *see also Nature*, Lond., Apr.6 1871.

Darwin's True Knight Hooker's description of Wallace.

Darwin's Window A window in Hooker's retirement house at Sunningdale, so-called because CD suggested its insertion on seeing the plans, to improve the view of the garden.

Darwin, Colonel Charles Waring [I] 1855 Aug.28–1928 Aug.1. m 1894 Mary Dorothea Wharton. CD's remote cousin. Head of the senior branch of the D family, of Elston Hall.

Darwin, Charles Waring [II] 1856 Dec.6–1858 summer. 10th & last c of CD. Died of scarlet fever, ?had Down's syndrome. 'He had never learnt to walk or talk'—EDii 162.

Darwin, Charlotte Maria Cooper 1827–1885. c of William Brown D. m Francis Rhodes, later Darwin. CD's remote cousin. Last of the senior branch of family. Elston Hall, the family seat, was left to her husband.

Darwin, Charlotte Mildred *see* Massingberd.

Darwin, Chucky *see* Susan D.

Darwin, Doddy *see* William Erasmus D.

Darwin, Dubsy *see* Bernard Richard Meirion D.

Darwin, Edward 1792–1829. 1c of Erasmus D [I] & Elizabeth. unm. CD's half uncle. Officer in 3rd Dragoon Guards.

Darwin, Edward Levett 1821–?. 2s of *Sir* Francis Sacheveral D. CD's half first cousin. Author on sporting matters under pseudonym 'High Elms'; *The game-preservers manual*, 1858.

Darwin, Elinor Mary *see* Monsell.

Darwin, Elizabeth [I] 1725–1800. 2c of Robert D. m 1751 *Rev*. Thomas Hall, Rector of Westborough, Lincolnshire. CD's great aunt.

Darwin, Elizabeth [II] *see* Collier.

Darwin, Elizabeth [III] 1763–1764. 3c of Erasmus D & Mary Howard. CD's aunt.

Darwin, Elizabeth [IV] *see* Hill.

Darwin, Elizabeth [V] *see* St Croix.

Darwin, Elizabeth [VI] 1847 Jul.8–1928. 6c of CD. unm. Known as Bessy. 'Very stout and nervous . . . not good at practical things . . . and she could not have managed her own life without a little help and direction . . . but she was shrewd enough . . . and a very good judge of character'—*Period Piece*, 146–147.

Darwin, Elizabeth *see* Susan Elizabeth D, CD's sister.

Darwin, Elizabeth Frances *see* Fraser.

Darwin, Ellen Wordsworth *see* Crofts.

Darwin, Emily Catherine 1810 May 10–1866 Feb.2. 6c of Robert Waring D. m Charles Langton as 2nd wife. dsp. CD's sister. Known as Catty. 'Had neither good health nor good spirits'—EDii 180. 'Failed to work out her capabilities either for her own happiness or that of others (perhaps)'—EDii 184.

Darwin, Emma *see* Wedgwood.

Emma Darwin 1904 [Mrs] H. E. Litchfield editor, *Emma Darwin, wife of Charles Darwin. A century of family letters*, 2 vols, Cambridge (F1552), 250 copies printed for family and friends. 1915 *Emma Darwin. A century of family letters, 1792–1896*, 2 vols, London (F1553), text as 1904 with some alterations. USA 1915 from stereos (F1554).

Darwin, Emma Cecilia *see* Farrer.

Darwin, Emma Georgiana Elizabeth 1784–1818. 3c of Erasmus D [I] & Elizabeth. unm. CD's half aunt.

Darwin, Emma Nora 1885 Dec.22– .3c of *Sir* Horace D. m *Sir* James Allen Noel Barlow *Bart.* CD's grand-daughter. Known as Nora. 1932 editor *Diary of the voyage of the Beagle* (F1566); 1945 *Charles Darwin and the voyage of the Beagle* (F1571); 1963 Darwin's ornithological notes, *Bull.Brit.Mus. (nat.Hist.)*, hist.Ser., 2:201–278 (F1577); 1967 *Darwin and Henslow* (F1598).

Darwin, Erasmus [I] 1731 Dec.12–1802 Apr.17. Physician & scientist. 4c of Robert D. m1 1757 Mary Howard 4s 1d. 1. Charles, 2. Erasmus, 3. Elizabeth, 4. Robert Waring, 5. William Alvey. m2, 1781, Elizabeth Chandos Pole née Collier 4s 3d. 1. Edward, 2. Frances Anne Violetta, 3. Emma Georgina Elizabeth, 4. Francis Sacheveral, 5. John, 6. Henry, 7. Harriet. He also had 2 illegitimate daughters, their names and mother

unrecorded, the *Misses* Parker. CD's grandfather. FRS 1761.
Born at Elston Hall, Lincolnshire; practised at Lichfield
1756–1781; Radburn Hall, Derby 1781–1783; Full St, Derby
1783–1802; Breadsall Priory, Derby 1802, where his relict
continued to live until her death 1832. Main works: *Botanic
garden*, 1791, 1790; *Zoonomia*, 1794, 1796; *Phytologia*, 1800;
Temple of nature, 1803. Biography: DNB; Seward, 1804; Dow-
son, 1861; Krause & CD, 1879; Pearson, 1930; King-Hele,
1963, 1977. Portraits: two in oils, one by Joseph Wright of
Derby in National Portrait Gallery, London, one by Rawlin-
son of Derby in Derby Museum. Medallion in Lichfield
Cathedral after Wright portrait. His commonplace book is
now at Down House. The genus *Darwinia* Rudge, 1813, was
named for D, (Myrtaceae) c. twenty-five species of Australian
heath-like shrubs. *Darwinia* Rafinesque 1817 & *Darwinia*
Dennstedt 1818 are junior homonyms.

Erasmus Darwin 1879 Ernst Krause, *Erasmus Darwin . . . with
a preliminary notice by Charles Darwin* (F1319), CD's notice,
1–127, is longer than Krause essay on D's scientific work;
facsimile 1971 (F1322). 1887 *The life of Erasmus Darwin*
(F1321), sheets of the first edition with new preface. Krause's
paper first appeared in German in *Kosmos*, 3, 1879 Feb., but his
text was revised for the translation. This book started the
one-sided row with Samuel Butler. B's copy with mss notes is
in the British Library. First foreign editions of CD's notice:
German 1880 (F1323); Russian 1959 (F1324).

Darwin, Erasmus [II] 1759–1799. 2c of Erasmus [I] & Mary.
unm. CD's uncle. Solicitor & genealogist. Committed suicide
by drowning.

Darwin, Erasmus [III] 1881 Dec.7–1915 Apr.24. 1c of *Sir*
Horace D. unm. CD's grandson, the second of the two born in
CD's lifetime. Director Cambridge Instrument Co. Killed at
Ypres. Obituary in *Emma Darwin* ii–vi, 1915.

Darwin, Erasmus Alvey 1804 Dec.29–1881 Aug.26. 2c of
Robert Waring D. unm. CD's only brother. Known as Ras.
Trained as a physician at Edinburgh but never practised.
Invalid. Trustee Bedford College, University of London from
its foundation, *see Bedford Coll.Mag.*, 1902 Jun. 1859 Nov. D to
CD 'In fact the *à priori* reasoning is so entirely satisfactory to
me that if the facts won't fit in, why so much worse for the
facts is my feeling'—LLii 234. 1881 CD to *Sir* Thomas Farrer,
'He was not I think a happy man'—MLi 395. 'He had some-

thing of original and sarcastically ingenious in him, one of the sincerest, naturally truest, and most modest of men'—Carlyle, *Reminiscences*, ii 208. 24 Regent St, 43 Great Marlborough St, 7 Park St, 6 Queen Anne St. His only recorded staff were Surman, his secretary and Pearce his manservant. Buried Sep.1 in Downe Churchyard.

Darwin, Etty *see* Henrietta Emma D.

Darwin, Florence Henrietta *see* Fisher.

Darwin, Frances *see* Fraser.

Darwin, Frances Anne Violetta 1783–1874. 2c of Erasmus D [I] & Elizabeth. m 1807 Samuel Tertius Galton. Mother of *Sir* Francis Galton. CD's half great aunt.

Darwin, Frances Crofts 1886 Mar.30–1960. Only c of *Sir* Francis D & Ellen. m Francis Macdonald Cornford. Mother of Francis Cornford, the poet. CD's grand-daughter.

Darwin, Francis [I] *see* Rhodes.

Darwin, Sir Francis [II] 1848 Aug.16–1925 Sep.19. Botanist. 7c of CD. m 1 1874 Amy Richenda Ruck 1s Bernard Richard Meirion. m 2 Ellen Crofts 1d Frances Crofts. m 3 Florence Henrietta Fisher sp. Kt. 1913 FRS 1882. Qualified as a physician but did not practice. Known as Baccy, Frank & Franky. Assisted CD with his botanical work, including drawing figures of *Aldrovanda* & *Utricularia* for *Insectivorous plants*. Reader in Botany Cambridge. On first marriage lived at vicarage Downe. After 1st wife's death, moved into Down House with infant son. Wintered until 2nd marriage with ED in Cambridge, then 80 Huntingdon Rd. 1887 editor *Life and letters* (F1452); 1903 editor, with A. C. Seward, *More letters* (F1548); editor 1909 *Sketches of 1842 and 1844* (F1555, 1556). Main work: *The elements of botany*, 1895. DNB WWH.

Darwin, Sir Francis Sacheveral 1786–1859, Physician & traveller. 4c of Erasmus D [I] & Elizabeth. m Jane Harriet Ryle and had offspring, eldest s Reginald D. CD's half uncle.

Darwin, Frank, Franky *see Sir* Frances D [II].

Darwin, Gas *see* Charles Robert D.

Darwin, Sir George Howard 1845 Jul.9–1912 Dec.7. Mathematician. 5c of CD. m 1884 at Erie, Pennsylvania, Maud du Puy 2s 2d 1. Gwendolen Mary, 2. Charles Galton, 3. Margaret Elizabeth, 4. William Robert. KCB 1905 FRS 1879. 2nd Wrangler Cambridge 1868, Smith Prize 1868. Trained as a barrister but never practised. Professor of Astronomy & Experimental Philosophy Cambridge. Interested in heraldry in youth 'the young herald'—MLi 287. Drew figures of *Dros-era* and *Dionaea* for *Insectivorous plants*. 1882 inherited Down House. The only remaining male line of CD's family comes through him. Newnham Grange, Cambridge. Biography: DNB WWH, Frances D in Vol.5 of *Scientific papers*, 5 vols 1916. Main work: *The tides*. 1898.

Darwin, Georgiana Elizabeth 1823–before 1888. c of *Sir* Francis Sacheveral D. m *Rev.* Benjamin Swift. Mother of Francis Darwin Swift. CD's half cousin.

Darwin, Granny *see* Susan Elizabeth D.

Darwin, Gwendolen Mary 1885 Aug.26–1957. 1st c of *Sir* George Howard D. m Jacques Raverat 2d. CD's grand-daughter. Artist, trained at Slade School, University College London. Main work: *Period piece*, 1952; illustrated published edition of *The bird talisman*, 1939.

Darwin, Harriet 1790–1825. 7c Erasmus D [I] & Elizabeth. m 1811 *Admiral* Thomas James Malin. dsp at Valparaiso.

Darwin, Harriot *see* Henrietta Emma D.

Darwin, Henrietta Emma 1843 Sep.25–1930. 4c of CD. m 1871 Aug.31 R. B. Litchfield dsp. CD's only married daugh-ter. Known as Body, Budgy, Harriot (she tried to use this name in 1865, ED objected 'the pertest of names'), Rhadaman-thus minor or just Rhadamanthus (by Huxley), Trotty Veck, Etty. Was sickly as a child. 1856 when ill had breakfast in bed, 'she never got up to breakfast again in all her life'—*Period piece*, in which ch.7 gives a description of her valetudinarian habits. 1861 CD to Hooker, 'Poor H . . . she has now come up to her old point, and can sometimes get up for an hour or two twice a day'—LLii 360. Helped CD with writing *Descent of man*—EDii 196. Did some editing of CD's part of *Erasmus Darwin* —King-Hele 1977. Editor *Emma Darwin*, 1904 (F1552) & 1915 (F1553). On death of husband 1903 moved to Burrow's Hill, Gomshall, Surrey.

Darwin, Henry 1789–1790. 6c of Erasmus D [I] & Elizabeth. CD's half uncle.

Darwin, Sir Horace 1851 May 13–1928 Sep.22. 9c of CD. m 1880 Emma (Ida) Cecilia Farrer 1s 2d 1. Erasmus [III], 2. Ruth Francis, 3. Emma Nora. Known as Jemmy or Skimp. KBE 1918 FRS 1903. Founder & Director of Cambridge Instrument Co., Botolph Lane, Cambridge. 66 Hills Rd, Cambridge. DNB WWH.

Darwin, Ida *see* Emma Cecilia Farrer.

Darwin, Jane *see* Brown.

Darwin, Jane Harriet *see* Ryle.

Darwin, Jemmy *see Sir* Horace D.

Darwin, John [I] ?–1542. brother of William D [II]. 9th generation uncle of CD.

Darwin, Rev. John [II] 1730–1805. 6c of Robert D. unm. CD's great uncle. Rector of Elston, Lincolnshire.

Darwin, Rev. John [III] 1787–1818. 5c of Erasmus D [I] & Elizabeth. unm. CD's half uncle. Rector of Elston, Lincolnshire.

Darwin, Katherine *see* Pember.

Darwin, Kitty Kumplings *see* Anne Elizabeth D.

Darwin, Major Leonard 1850 Jan.15–1943 Mar.26. 8c of CD. m1 1882 Elizabeth Frances Fraser sp. m2 1900 Charlotte Mildred Massingberd sp. Royal Engineers, commissioned 1870 Dec. 1892 Jul.–1895 Jul. MP Liberal-Unionist, for Lichfield. 1895 stood again but not re-elected. c1874 photographed CD in basket chair on verandah at Down House, engraved for *Century Mag.* 1883 Jan., also occurs printed on china. 12 Egerton Place, Brompton Rd, London. 1900 on 2nd marriage moved to Cripp's Corner, Forest Row, Sussex. Main works: 1897 *Bimetallism*; 1926 *The need for eugenic reform*; Memories of Down House, *Nineteenth Century*, 106; 108–123, 1929. Biography: M. Keynes (niece), Cambridge 1943.

Darwin, Margaret Elizabeth 1890–1974. 3c of *Sir* George Howard D. m 1917 *Sir* Geoffrey Keynes 4s. CD's granddaughter. D wrote biography of Leonard D, 1943.

Darwin, Marianne 1798 Apr.7–1858 Jul.18. 1c of Robert Waring D. m 1824 Henry Parker 4s 1d. CD's sister. On her death the grown up family was adopted by her sister Emily Catherine and lived at The Mount, Shrewsbury.

Darwin, Martha Haskins *see* Du Puy.

Darwin, Mary [I] *see* Healey.

Darwin, Mary [II] *see* Howard.

Darwin, Mary Dorothea *see* Wharton.

Darwin, Mary Eleanor 1842 Sep.23–1842 Oct.16. 3c of CD. Born at Down House and died there. ED had moved into Down House on Sep.14.

Darwin, Maud *see* Du Puy.

Darwin, Mildred *see* Massingberd.

Darwin, Monica *see* Slingsby.

Darwin, Nigger *see* Charles Robert D.

Darwin, Nora *see* Emma Nora D.

Darwin, Polly *see* Mary Darwin [II].

Darwin, Ras *see* Erasmus Alvey D.

Darwin, Reginald 1818–? eldest c of *Sir* Francis Sacheveral D. CD's half first cousin. 1879 lent CD documents, including a commonplace book, on Erasmus D [I], which CD used for his notice in E. Krause's *Erasmus Darwin*. The commonplace book now at Down House.

Darwin, Richard ?–1584. 3c of William D [III]. m before 1580 Margaret ? 3s 1d. Inherited Torksey from his uncle and held Marton. 8th generation in male line to CD.

Darwin, Robert 1682–1754 Nov.20. 2s of William D [VI]. m 1723–24 Jan. Elizabeth Hill of Sleaford, Lincolnshire, 4s 3d. 1. Robert Waring, 2. Elizabeth, 3. William Alvey, 4. Ann. 5. Susanna, 6. John [II], 7. Erasmus. CD's great grandfather. Barrister of Lincoln's Inn. Member of Spalding Club.

Darwin, Robert Alvey 1826 Apr.17–1847 Dec.7. 3c of William Brown D. Of Elston Hall & Exeter College Oxford. Last male in senior branch of family, he left Elston Hall to his sister Charlotte Maria Cooper D.

Darwin, Sir Robert Vere 1910–1973. Painter. 1st c of Bernard Richard Meirion D. m1 Yvonne Darby sp. m2. Ginette Hewitt sp. CD's great grandson. Kt 1964 RA 1972. Known as Robin. Principal Royal College of Art. Painted portrait of *Sir* George Buxton Browne for Down House. WWH.

Darwin, Robert Waring [I] 1724–1816. lc of Robert D. unm. CD's great uncle. Of Elston Hall. Author of *Principia botanica*, 1787.

Darwin, Robert Waring [II] 1766 May 30–1848 Nov.13. 4c of Erasmus D [I] & Mary. m 1796 Apr.18 Susannah Wedgwood 2s 4d. 1. Marianne, 2. Charlotte Sarah, 3. Susan Elizabeth, 4. Erasmus Alvey, 5. Charles Robert, 6. Emily Catherine. CD's father. FRS 1788. Physician, MD Leyden 1785 Feb.26. Had a large practice in Shrewsbury and around, where he built The Mount c.1800. 6'2", very corpulent, 'when he last weighed himself he was 24 stone, but afterwards increased much in weight'—LLi 11. Strictly teetotal. CD's description of his father, which belongs to his autobiography, is printed in LLi 11–20 instead of in ch.2. Buried in Montford churchyard, Shropshire.

Darwin, Sir Robin *see* Robert Vere D.

Darwin, Ruth Frances 1883 Aug.2–1973. 2c of *Sir* Horace D. m

W. Rees Thomas. CD's grand-daughter. Known as Boofy.

Darwin, Sarah *see* Sedgwick.

Darwin, Sarah Gay Forbes 1830–? 7c of William Brown D. m.1848 Edward Noel. CD's cousin.

Darwin, Sibyl *see* Rose.

Darwin, Skimp *see Sir* Horace D.

Darwin, Susan Elizabeth 1803 Oct.3–1866 Oct.3. 3c of Robert Waring D [II]. unm. CD's sister. 'My father [CD] told me that anything in coat and trousers from eight years to eighty was fair game to Susan'—EDi 141. Continued to live at The Mount, Shrewsbury until her death. After the death of her sister Marianne in 1858, she adopted the grown-up Parker children who lived with her. 1836 CD called her Granny.

Darwin, Susanna 1729–1789. 5c of Robert D. unm. CD's great aunt.

Darwin, Susannah *see* Wedgwood.

Darwin, Trotty Veck *see* Henrietta Emma D.

Darwin, Violetta *see* Frances Anne Violetta D.

Darwin, William [I] died before 1542. 2s, 1. ?William, 2. John Of Marton, Lincolnshire, Yeoman. The earliest ancestor given by Burke. 10th generation to CD in male line.

Darwin, ?William [II] died before 1542. Eldest s of William [I] 2s 4d. 9th generation to CD in male line. Of Marton, Lincolnshire, Yeoman. Burke is not certain of christian name.

Darwin, William [III]–1580. Eldest son of ?William [II]. m Elizabeth ?, 3s. 8th generation to CD in male line. Inherited Marton from his uncle John D.

Darwin, William [IV] c1573–1644. 3s of Richard D. m as 2nd husband Mary Healey of Cleatham, Lincolnshire. 6th generation to CD in male line. Yeoman of the Royal Armoury, Greenwich. Also held Marton.

Darwin, William [V] 1620–1675. Eldest s of William D [IV]. m 1653 Anne Earle, d of Erasmus Earle 5s 1d. 5th generation in male line to CD. Barrister. Recorder of Lincoln. Royalist. Erasmus became a family name through his wife.

Darwin, William [VI] 1655–1682. Eldest s of William [V]. m 1680 Anne Waring, heiress of Robert Waring of Elston Hall, Newark, Nottinghamshire, 2s. 4th generation in male line to CD. Portrait 'at Elston shows him as a good-looking young man in a full-bottomed wig'—LLi 3. Waring became a family forename through his wife, and Elston Hall the family seat.

Darwin, William [VII] 1681–1760. Eldest son of William D

[VI]. m1 1706 Elizabeth D (1st cousin) 2s 2d. m2 1715/16 Mary
Secker 1s 4d. m3 1749 Mary Hurst sp. Of Cleatham & Elston
Hall.

Darwin, William Alvey [I] 1726–1783. 2c of Robert D. m Jane
Brown 1s 1d. CD's great uncle. Inherited Elston Hall.

Darwin, William Alvey [II] 1767–1767. 5c of Erasmus D [I] &
Mary. CD's uncle.

Darwin, William Brown 1774–1841. s of William Alvey D [I].
m Elizabeth de St Croix 3s 4d. CD's first cousin once
removed.

Darwin, William Erasmus 1839 Dec.27–1914 Sep. 1c of CD.
m 1877 Sarah Sedgwick sp. Called Hoddy Doddy in infancy.
Educated at Mr Wharton's preparatory school and Rugby.
Partner in Grant & Maddison, Bankers of Southampton, also
called Southampton & Hampshire Bank, 1862–1902. He is the
child in CD's paper in *Mind*, 2, 1877. Looked after CD's
financial affairs with great success. Ridgemount, North
Stoneham, Bassett, Southampton. 1902, after death of wife, 12
Egerton St, London, next door to brother Leonard D. Gwendolen Mary D lived with him whilst at Slade School. Obituary: Francis D, *Christ's College Mag.*, 1914.

Darwin, William Robert 1894–1970. 4c of *Sir* George Howard
D. m Monica Slingsby. CD's grandson.

Darwin, Yvonne *see* Darby.

Darwinia Used three times for genera of plants. see Erasmus
Darwin [I].

Darwinian *adj.*1 relating to the verse or views of Erasmus D [I].
1794 OED suppl.
adj.2 relating to CD's theories. 1860 OED suppl. Huxley 'The
Darwinian hypothesis has the merit of being eminently simple
and comprehensible'—*Westminster Rev.*, Apr.566.
*sb.*1 one who holds the views of, or imitates the verse of
Erasmus D [I]. 1809 OED suppl.
*sb.*2 one who holds the views of CD. 1896 OED suppl. Wallace
'and it is very interesting to Darwinians'—*Malay Archipelago*,
1,iv,61.

Darwinian Tubercle = Angulus Woolneri, Darwin's peak qq. v.

Darwinianism *sb.*1 obs. or nonce-word, relating to Erasmus D
[I]. 1804 OED.
*sb.*2 rare, relating to CD's theories=Darwinism. OED 1893 J.
H. Stirling, *Darwinianism: workmen and work* [title].

Darwinism *sb.*1 obs. relating to Erasmus D [I]. 1856 OED.

sb. 2 relating to CD's theories. 1864 OED suppl. Huxley 'What we may term the philosophical position of Darwinism'—*Nat.Hist.Rev.*, Oct.567.

Darwinism, CD's papers on 1871 [letter] A new view of Darwinism, *Nature*, Lond., 4:180–181, refers to letter by Henry B. Howorth of same title, *ibid.*, 4:161–162 (Bii 167, F1754). 1872 Bree on Darwinism, *Nature*, Lond., 6:279 (Bii 168, F1756), relates to a review by Wallace of Bree's book, *An exposition of the fallacies in the hypothesis of Mr Darwin*, 1872.

Darwinism 1889 by Wallace q.v.

Darwinism and Modern science 1909 edited by A. C. Seward q.v.

Darwinism Stated by Darwin Himself 1884 edited by Nathan Shepperd q.v.

Darwinist *sb.* one agreeing with CD's theories. 1883 OED 'Interesting to every sincere Darwinist'—*Sci.& Lit.Gossip*, 1:79

adj. Darwinistic. 1875 OED 'Decisive in favour of Darwinistic views'—Schmidt, *Descent & Darwinism*, 292.

Darwinite *sb.* 1 one agreeing with CD's theories. 1862 OED 'Here are Darwinites . . . reviving the doctrine of Lord Monboddo that man and monkeys are of the same stock'—*Illustr.Lond.News*, 41:41.

adj. 1867 OED C. Kingsley (letter) 'Can you tell me where I can find any Darwinite lore about the development of birds?'—*Life*, 2:280, 1883.

sb. 2 a natural copper arsenite, reddish white, from N.America, synonym of Whitneyite. 1861 coined by D. Forbes.

Darwinize *vb.* 1 *intrans.* to write verse like that of Erasmus D [I]. OED 1880, but said to have been coined much earlier by S. T. Coleridge.

vb. 2 *intrans.* to follow CD's theories, to work on them. 1920 OED G.B.Shaw 'It has restored faith in Providence to a Darwinized world'—*Public Opinion*, Aug.13, 160.

Daubeny, Charles Giles Bridle 1795–1867. Botanist. FRS 1822. Prof. Chemistry Oxford 1882, Prof. Botany 1834, Prof. Rural Economy 1840. 1860 Jun.30 conversazione held in his rooms after British Association scene—LLii 323. 1860 D commented on *Origin* in *Rep.Brit.Assoc.* CD on 'very liberal and candid, but scientifically weak'—LLii 332. 1860 *Remarks on the final causes of the sexuality of plants*. 1867 *Miscellanies*, 2 vols. DNB.

Davidson, Thomas 1817–1885. Palaeontologist. FRS 1857. Specialist on brachiopods. 1861 CD corresponded with. Anti-*Origin*.

Davis, Richard Missionary at Waimate, N.Island, New Zealand, arrived 1819. Not in orders, but ran a farm to teach the natives agriculture. 1835 Dec. CD met. CD spells 'Davies'—*J.Researches* 1845, 425.

Davy, Dr John 1790–1868. Army surgeon. FRS 1834. Brother of *Sir* Humphry D. Inspector General of Army Hospitals. Friend of *Sir* James Mackintosh. 1855 CD to D on salmonid eggs; 2 long replies printed in *Phil.Trans.*, 1855 and *Proc.Roy.Soc.*, 1856, as well as in his *Physiological Researches*, 251–269, 1863. DNB.

Dawes, Richard 1793–1867. Educationalist. Tutor at Emmanuel College Cambridge. Dean of Hereford. Older friend of CD at Cambridge. 1831 spring, CD & D talked of a trip to Teneriffe with Ramsay & Kirby. 1867 CD subscribed £2.2s. through J. M. Herbert for some memorial to him. DNB.

Dawkins, Sir William Boyd 1837–1929. Geologist. Kt 1919 FRS 1867. CD was friendly with and 1873 wrote testimonial for an application for Chair of Geology at Cambridge, which D did not get. Prof. Geology Owen's College Manchester 1872–. WWH.

Dawkins Testimonials [1873] *Testimonials in favour of W. Boyd Dawkins . . . a candidate for the Woodwardian Professorship of Geology* [at Cambridge], Cambridge, University Press printed (F1216). CD's letter p.2.

Dawson, Sir John William 1820–1899. Canadian geologist. Kt 1884 FRS 1862. Prof. Geology and Principal McGill 1855–1893. 1855 D was describer of *Eozoon* q.v. Anti-*Origin*—MLi 210, 466, 468. 1862 CD to Hooker, 'Lyell had difficulty in preventing Dawson reviewing the *Origin* on hearsay, without having looked at it'—MLi 468. 1860 D reviewed *Origin* in *Canad.Nat*. DNB.

Dawson, Robert 1776–1860. Cartographer to Ordnance Survey. 1831 CD met at Llangollen when on geological tour with Sedgwick. DNB.

De Bary, Heinrich Anton 1831–1888. German fungologist. Prof. Botany Strasbourg. 1879 D sent CD *Utricularia*—FUL 87.

de Beer, Sir Gavin Rylands 1899–1972. Zoologist & general writer. Kt 1954 FRS 1940. Director British Museum (Natural

History) 1950–1960. Writer on CD and transcriber of mss. 1959 d prints 38 CD letters in *Notes & Records Roy. Soc.*, 14:12–66 (F1595). 1960–1967 transcribed, with collaborators, B–E notebooks on transmutation, *Bull. Brit.Mus.(nat.Hist.)*, hist.Ser. 2–3 (F1574). 1961 d prints 42 CD letters in *Ann.Sci.*, 17:81–115 (F1596). 1963 *CD biography*, London. 1974 *Charles Darwin, Thomas Henry Huxley, autobiographies,* London (F1580), based on the Barlow edition with a re-reading of the mss by James Kinsley. Obituary: *Mem.Fellows Roy.Soc.*, 19:65–93. WWH.

De la Beche, Sir Henry Thomas 1795–1855. Geologist. Kt 1842 FRS 1819. Director Geological Survey 1832– . 1848 CD listened to D's Presidential address to Geological Society, 'a very long and rather dull address'—MLi 65. DNB.

De la Rue, Warren 1815–1889. Astronomer & inventor. FRS 1850. 1851 Feb. CD met D at Royal Institution. DNB.

Decaisne, Joseph 1807–1882. French botanist. 1859 CD probably sent D copy of 1st edition of *Origin*—LLii 172.

Defence of Science 1881 Mr Darwin in defence of science, *Brit.med.J.*, 2:917 (Bii 235, F1799).

Delpino, Federico 1833–1905. Italian botanist. Prof. Botany Genoa & later at Naples. Frequent correspondent.

Denny, Henry 1803–1871. Entomologist, specialist on lice and minute beetles. Undated, CD to D about races of human lice and on a Mr Martial's observations on them—Carroll 35. 1871 *Descent* i, 219 mentions D's work on lice of pigeon, fowl & dogs.

Derbishire, Alexander Mate on 2nd voyage of *Beagle*. 1832 Apr. D returned to England.

Derby, Countess of *see Lady* West.

Derby, 13th Earl of *see* Edward Smith Stanley.

Derby, 15th Earl of *see* Edward Henry Stanley.

Descent of man 1870, 1871 *The descent of man, and selection in relation to sex,* 2 vols (F936). CD's copy of Vol.1 dated 1870 is the only one known. 1871 Feb. normal issue of both vols, 25 errata on verso of title leaf of Vol.2, 1st issue (F937); 1871 Mar. 2nd issue, text changes and no errata, works by the author on verso of title leaf of Vol.2 (F938); 1871 Apr. 7th thousand, with textual changes (F939), facsimile of this issue 1969 (F1042); 1871 Dec. 8th thousand, with textual changes (F940); 1874 2nd edition, 10th thousand (F944); 1875 2nd edition corrected, 11th thousand (F945); 1877 2nd edition revised and

augmented, 12th thousand (F948). First foreign editions:
Dutch (F1053), German (F1065), Italian (F1088), Russian
(F1107), USA (F941) 1871; French (F1058), Swedish (F1136)
1872; Danish (F1050), Polish (F1101) 1874; Hungarian (F1084)
1884; Spanish (F1123) ?1902; Czech (F1048) 1906; Portuguese
(F1104) 1910; Yiddish (F1138) 1921; Bulgarian (F1047) 1927;
Japanese (F1100) 1949; Slovene (F1122) 1950; Romanian
(F1106) 1967; Turkish (F1137) 1968. The last sentence of the
work reads '. . . we must acknowledge, as it seems to me, that
man with all his noble qualities, with sympathy for the most
debased, with benevolence which extends not only to other
men but to the humblest living creature, with his god-like
intellect which has penetrated into the movements and con-
stitution of the solar system—with all these exalted powers—Man still bears in his bodily frame the indelible stamp of
his lowly origin'.

Descent of man (paper) 1871 The descent of man, *Hardwicke's
Science Gossip*, 7:112 (Bii 168, F1693). This, the shortest of all
CD's writings in serials, contains the essence of the idea given
above, in blunter morphological terms, 'The early progenitors
of man were no doubt once covered with hair, both sexes
having beards; their ears were pointed and capable of movement; and their bodies were provided with a tail, having the
proper muscles' etc.

Deseado Patagonia, Argentine=Port Desire. 1833 Dec.23 *Beagle*
at, when it was a deserted Spanish settlement.

Devonport Town and naval dockyard w of and contiguous
with Plymouth, Devon. 1831 Sep.14 CD with Fitz-Roy and
Musters arrived after 3 days by packet from London; CD
returned to London Sep.17. Oct.30 CD back and stayed at 4
Clarence Baths until *Beagle* finally sailed Dec.27, after two
unsuccessful attempts to put to sea.

Devonshire, 7th Duke of *see* William Cavendish.

Dianthus hybrids 1857 Hybrid dianths, *Gdnr's Chronicle*,
No.10:155 (Bi 273, F1693).

Diary of the voyage of the Beagle *see Charles Darwin's diary*.
. . .?

Dicey, Albert Venn 1835–1922. Barrister. Vinerian Prof. Law
Cambridge 1882–1902. D was on 'Personal Friends invited'
list for CD's funeral.

Dicky A small male dog of ED's widowhood, given to her by
Mrs (Margaret) Vaughan Williams in 1885.

Ditchfield Field at Downe, just n of Little Pucklands.

Dobbin A pony in CD's childhood—MLi 5.

Dobell, Horace Benge 1828–1917. Physician and medical author, 1863 CD to, thanking for a copy of his *On the germs and vestiges of desease*, 1861, and on regeneration—MLi 234.

Dogs The following family dogs are entered by name: Bobby, Button, Dicky, Pepper, Polly, Quiz, Tony, Tyke.

Dogs (paper)1882 On the modification of a race of Syrian street dogs by means of sexual selection, by *Dr* [W.] Van Dyck, with a preliminary notice by CD, *Proc. zool. Soc. Lond.*, No.25:367–370 (Bii 278, F1803). Read Apr.18 by the Secretary: CD died on Apr.19.

Dohrn, Felix Anton 1840–1909. German zoologist. Founder of Zoologische Station at Naples 1873, later Stazione Zoologica. 1870 Sep.26 D visited CD at Down House, and perhaps again later—MLi 323. 1872 Apr.3 CD wrote to D about success of *Descent of man* in Germany—LLiii 133. 1875 CD wrote to D about Naples station and invited D & wife to visit Down House, 'I have often boasted that I have had a live Uhlan in my house!'—LLiii 198. 1879 CD gave D £100 for the station from his Bressa Prize money—LLiii 225.

Don, David 1800–1841. Botanist. Prof. Botany King's College London 1836–1841. 1836 CD approached about identifying *Beagle* plants.

Donders, Frans Cornelius 1818–1889. Physiologist. Prof. Physiology Utrecht. 1871 D gave CD information for *Expression of the emotions*—LLiii 134. 1872 Apr. D wrote to CD to tell him of his election to Koninklijke Akademie van Wetenschappen—LLiii 163. 1874 CD wrote to D, to thank him for entertaining his son George Howard D—LLiii 325.

Dorking Surrey. 1876 May 6–Jun.6 CD had family holiday there.

Double Flowers 1843 Double flowers—their origin, *Gdnr's Chronicle*, No.36:628 (Bi 175, F1663). CD's first botanical publication.

Doubleday, Henry 1808–1875. Entomologist & quaker. Correspondent with CD on insect matters. Sent CD plants of true oxslip *Primula elatior*.

Doveleys, The Frances b 1806 and Emma b 1808 Wedgwood in childhood.

Down The village was so spelt before 1842. *see* Downe.

Down House Luxted Road, Downe, Orpington, Kent. 1842

Jul.22 CD & ED first saw. Bought from *Rev*. J.Drummond, Vicar of Downe, for £2020 with 18 acres of which 12 were then the paddock. ED moved in Sep.14; CD moved in Sep.17. Ordnance datum 565 ft, the well is 325 ft deep, to the clay below the chalk of the North Downs.

ACCOUNTS OF: 1842 Jul. CD's own account of house, estate & district, written to his sister Catherine, is printed in MLi 31–36. 1929 Leonard D, Memories of Down House, *Nineteenth Century*, 106:118–123. 1952 Raverat, *Period Piece*, ch.8. from personal experience in childhood, but not in CD's lifetime. 1955 Keith, *Darwin revalued*, chs 4 & 24. 1974 Atkins, *Down House*.

ALTERATIONS TO HOUSE 1843 Bow front to all 3 Storeys of W front added; 1845–1846 Kitchen area rebuilt and butler's pantry added, with schoolroom and 2 small bedrooms above; 1846 Outhouses rebuilt; 1858 New drawingroom added at N end, with 2 bedrooms above it, cost £500; 1859 Billiard table set up; 1872 Verandah added to drawingroom; 1877 New billiard room added and new main entrance of E side. 1881 billiard room converted to new study.

ALTERATIONS TO LAND: 1844 New garden wall built; 1845 Mound under yews on W side removed, mound added at E side as wind protection; 1846 Sandwalk wood planted on land rented from *Sir* John William Lubbock; 1862 Feb. New greenhouse completed, superintended by Horwood, *Sir* John W. Lubbock's gardener; 1874 Sandwalk wood exchanged for a piece of pasture with *Sir* John Lubbock; 1881 Bought strip of field beyond orchard from Sydney Sales for hard tennis court, new wall built.

FURNISHINGS In the present shrine, the old study and the new drawingroom are furnished, as nearly as possible, as they were when CD was alive; this includes the original study chairs, the portrait of Lyell given to CD by *Lady* Lyell in 1847, the portrait of Hooker given to CD by Julia Cameron, the photographer of it, and the print of Josiah Wedgwood II given back by Francis D in 1927. The drawingroom piano, bought in 1839, was bought back from the Positivist Society for £20 in 1929.

HOUSEHOLD EXPENDITURE: CD & ED kept detailed accounts from the date of their marriage. These, although preserved at

Down House, have not been published in full. Keith, 221–232, and Atkins, 95–100, give extracts. The latter gives a detailed breakdown for 1867–1881. In 1867, when there were four dependent sons and two daughters, only the eldest son being away and employed, probably eight indoor servants and the garden staff, expenditure was as follows: meat £250, butter £5, cheese £18, candles £16, oil £7, bacon £10, soap £10, grocery £53, sugar £16, bread £63, fish & game £20, servants £71, poultry £38, tea £27, coffee £11, washing £6, dresses for ED & the girls £28, gifts £79, miscellaneous £75, dripping £3. These figures do not include those expenses which CD paid for himself, menservants wages, alcohol, snuff and later cigarettes and the clothing of the boys. *See also* entry under CD finance.

ICONOGRAPHY, House: 1 1880 painting by Albert Goodwin, back from sw in EDii 76. 2 1882 Aug. drawing by Alfred Parsons, back from sw, wood engraving from in *Century Mag.*, Jan.1883, also in LLi 320. 3 etching of whole sw front, not signed, not done in CD's lifetime—Moorehead 261. 4 photograph from sw by *Col*.James Creedy, modern—Atkins 24. 5 photograph from sw by J. Dixon Scott, modern—Keith 46. 6 plan of ground floor—Keith 46. 7 another plan of ground floor—Atkins 22. 8 1882 Apr. new study, copper engraving by Axel H.Haig—Moorehead 256.

ICONOGRAPHY, Grounds: 1 plan—Keith 47; 2 plan—Atkins 22. 3 Sandwalk and wood—Freeman, *Bibliographical handlist*, 1965, 70 (captions in German); 4 Sandwalk and wood—*Bull.Brit.Mus.(nat.Hist.)*, hist Ser., 3:180, 1968 (captions in English).

STAFF: The details are scanty, especially for those of junior staff and full names and dates are almost never available, however *see* the following: Butlers; Jackson, Parslow, Price. Coachmen; Comfort, John. Cooks; Brummidge, Evans. Custodians; Harold, Samuel & Sydney Robinson. Footmen; Jackson, Moffatt. Gardeners; Comfort, Hills, Horwood, Lettington. Governesses; Barellien, Beob, Grant, Latter, Ludwig, Pugh, Thorley. Maids; Anne, Betsy, Emily Jane, Jane, Matheson. Nursemaid; Harding. Nurses; Brodie, Evans, Mary, Maryann, Sara.

HISTORY: earlier given in Atkins, 12–17, with list of owners or tenants back to 1651; later 1900–1906 rented from George Howard D by a *Mr* Whitehead about whom nothing seems to be known except that he owned the first motor car in Downe; 1907–1922 rented by Downe House School q.v.; 1924–1927 run as an unsuccessful girl's school by a *Miss* Ram; 1927 bought from the Darwin heirs by *Sir* George Buckston Browne for £4,250; after spending c£10,000 on repairs and giving £20,000 as an endowment, he handed it over to the British Association in 1929; it was formally opened at a tea on Jun.7. 1953 given free to Royal College of Surgeons of England who have administered it since, although they attempted to transfer it to the National Trust in 1958. The Surgeons' research establishment marches with the grounds to the sw.

VISITORS: ED entertained considerably at Down House, although seldom large gatherings. Casual calling, which was customary in cities, was confined to near neighbours; John Lubbock, who was 8 years old when CD came to Downe, was the most frequent. Visitors from London and elsewhere came for weekends, or for Sunday lunch. The following list omits relatives and neighbours and it is probably far from complete. The numbers of visitors increase in later years when the children were grown up and brought their own friends and when CD's health had improved. The following were frequent visitors: F. M. Balfour (in 1870–1880), T. Bell (early), Hugh Falconer (after his return to England), E. Forbes (before 1854), J. D. Hooker, T. H. Huxley, C. Lyell, G. J. Romanes (after 1874), Margaret J. Shaen, S. W. Strickland (after c1860), A. R. Wallace & G. R. Waterhouse.
The following are recorded only once or twice: 1846 Leonard Horner; 1847 Leonora Horner; 1850 A. C. Ramsay, R. H. Schomburgk; 1854 J. S. Henslow; 1857 R. Fitz-Roy; 1861 W. B. Carpenter, G. B. Sowerby II; 1862? R. A. von Kolliker; 1866 E. H. Haeckel; 1867 V. O. Kovalevskiǐ, H. Parker, R. Trimen; 1868 H. W. Bates, E. Blyth, A. Gray, G. Smith, J. Tyndall, J. J. Weir; 1869 A. E. Agassiz, T. Woolner; 1870 V. O. Kovalevskiǐ, A. Newton; 1871 Arabella, B. Buckley, M. E. G. Duff, R. Lowe, J. Hague, V. Lushington, R. Swinhoe; 1872 C. L. Brace, C. Crawley, T. Woolner, C. Wright; 1873 M. D. Conway, F. A. Dohrn; 1875 W. W. Ouless, R. L. Tait, G. Young; 1876 F. J. Cohn, W. E. Gladstone, J. Morley, C. E. Norton, L. Playfair; 1877 Ann Pertz; 1878 L. A. Errera, Theodora Sedgwick; 1879 W. B. Richmond; 1880 E. Barbier, A. L. P. P. de Candolle, E. Sarcey; 1881 E. B. Aveling,

J. Collier, Laura M. Forster, Marianne North, H. Richter; 1882 A. H. Haig, *Countess* of Derby (both after CD's death). The following are recorded without date: J. W. Judd, K. Ludwig, W. Ogle. The following groups of people visited: 1873 onwards Working Men's College, groups of fifty or sixty for the day; 1881 onwards J. W. C. Feegan's street boys from his homes, for the day or camping; 1882 onwards 'Sunday tramps', led by L. Stephen, came for the day.

Downe Village, Orpington, Kent, BR6 Post Office spelling was Down before 1842. Census of 1841 total population 444; of 1881 555. Postal addresses, nr Bromley in 1845, nr Farnborough 1845–early 1855, nr Bromley late 1855–late 1869, nr Beckenham 1869 Sep. Present address is in the Bromley postal code. Church; St Mary the virgin, illustration 1786, before drastic restoration—Atkins 25. Inn; The George; 1842 Jul. CD to his sister Catherine, 'The little pot-house where we slept is a grocer's shop and the landlord there is the carpenter . . . there is one butcher and baker and the post-Office. A carrier goes weekly to London and calls anywhere for anything in London and takes anything anywhere'—MLi 31–36. Schoolmasters; Norman, Skinner. Physician: Engleheart. Vicars: Drummond, Innes, ffinden. Curates: Hoole, Horsman, Humphreys, Powell, Robinson, Salin, Stephens. Churchwarden: Lovegrove. 1933 Howarth & Howarth give a detailed description of the village and its history. Newman, in Pevsner's *Buildings of England, West Kent*, 251, 1969, describes the architecturally worthwhile buildings.

Downe Court Original manor house of Downe, opposite E side of Down House, dated 1690. 1842 Jul. CD to his sister Catherine, 'There is a most beautiful old farm-house with great thatched barns and old stumps of oak trees . . . one field off'—MLi 31–36. 1973 A. D. H. Coxe, *Haunted Britain*, 79; CD's ghost is one of the several said to haunt it.

Downe Friendly Club CD helped to found, probably in 1852, and acted as its Treasurer for 30 years—LLi 142. 1852 Mar. Rules for the Club printed at CD's expense—CD's mss accounts. 1877 *To members of the Down Friendly Club*, a single sheet printed for CD to dissuade members from disbanding (F1303). The annual general meeting was held at Down House every year, usually on Whit Monday.

Downe House School Always spelt with an 'e'. Occupied Down House 1907 Feb.–1922 Apr.1. Headmistress Olive

Margaret Willis was co-founder with her friend Alice Carver; started with one girl and 5 mistresses, but was at once successful. 1922 moved to larger premises Hermitage Rd, Cold Ash, Newbury, where it flourishes.

Downes, John 1810–1890. Cambridge friend of CD. Vicar of Horton & Piddington, Northants 1834–1863. 1831 Jul.11 CD to Henslow, 'Do you by any chance recollect the name of a fly that Mr. Bird sent through Downe—Darwin-Henslow 27.

Downton Wiltshire. 1822 Jun. CD had a holiday there with his sister Caroline Sarah D.

Drewe brother of Edward Drewe; squire of Grange, nr Honiton, Devon.

Drewe, Adèle see Prévost.

Drewe, Caroline see Allen.

Drewe, Charlotte ?–c1817. 5c of Edward D. unm.

Drewe, Edward 1756–1810. Vicar of Broadhembury, Devon. m 1793 Caroline Allen 2s 5d 1. Harriet Maria, 2. Marianne, 3. Georgiana, 4. Edward Simcoe, 5. Charlotte, 6. Francis, 7. Louisa.

Drewe, Edward Simcoe 1805–1877. 4c of Edward D. m. 1828 Adèle Prévost and had children. c1820 D inherited The Grange, nr Honiton, Devon.

Drewe, Gorgiana c1800–? 3c of Edward D. m 1823 *Sir* Edward Hall Alderson; mother of *Lady* Salisbury.

Drewe, Harriet Maria 179?1857. 1c of Edward D. m 1816 Robert, *Lord* Clifford and had offspring. 1837 was living at 1 Atholl Crescent, Edinburgh.

Drewe, Louisa ?–c1817. 7c of Edward D.

Drewe, Marianne 179?–1822. 2c of Edward D. m 1820 *Rev*.Algernon Langton. Died in childbed.

Dring Acting Purser on return of *Beagle* from 2nd voyage.

Dropmore Buckinghamshire, 1847 CD visited on day trip from British Association meeting at Oxford.

Drummond, Rev.J. Vicar of Downe before Innes. 1842 D sold Down House to CD for £2020.

Drummond, James 1763–1863. Botanist of Swan River, W Australia. D helped CD on fertilisation of *Leschenaultia*—MLii 259.

Drummond, Thomas 1797–1840. Army engineer & politician. Invented Drummond's light. DNB.

Drysdale, Lady ?–c1882 aged nearly 100. Friend of CD & ED through Moor Park Hydro. *Dr* Lane's mother-in-law.

Du Bois-Reymond, Emil 1818–1896. German electrophysiologist. Prof. Physiology Berlin 1858– . 1860 CD to Gray telling him that D agrees with CD's views—LLii 354. 1878 D writes to CD to tell him of his election to K.-P.Akademie der Wissenschaften, Berlin, as Corresponding Member. 1876 *Darwin versus Galiani*, Berlin. 1884 *Friedrich II in Englische Urtheilen, Darwin und Kopernicus*, Leipzig.

Dubarry, Amy 1866 Sunday school teacher at Downe —Darwin-Innes 231.

Dublin 1827 CD visited on spring tour.

Duck, Mr ?–1875. 1866 A trustee of Downe Friendly Club—Darwin-Innes 245.

Duff, Sir Mountstuart Elphinstone Grant 1829–1906. Politician. GCSI 1887 FRS 1901. Liberal MP for Elgin Burghs 1857–1881. Under Secretary for India 1868–1874. 1871 Jan. D visited Down House with Lubbock, Huxley & R. Lowe, from High Elms. DNB.

Dumbola Lodge Freshwater, Isle of Wight, a house owned by Julia Cameron. 1868 CD & Family stayed there in summer. CD was photographed by Mrs Cameron on this visit.

Duncan, Andrew 1773–1832. Prof. Materia Medica Edinburgh. FRS 1798. 1826 CD to his sister Catherine D, 'is so very learned that his wisdom has left no room for his senses. His lectures begin at eight in the morning'—MLi 7. 1847 CD to Hooker, 'a whole cold breakfastless hour on the properties of rhubarb'—LLi 355.

Duncan, Ethel d of Andrew Duncan of Liverpool. m G. J. Romanes. 1879 CD to Romanes, *Mrs* R is right to forbid the monkey from the nursery—Carroll 576.

Duncan, Peter Martin 1824–1891. Invertebrate palaeontologist & writer of popular natural history. c1869 CD to D, will send coral specimens from Keeling Islands—Carroll 272. 1876 CD to D, CD will return an overlooked coral and mss by William Lonsdale—Carroll 498.

Dundee Angus. 1827 CD visited on a spring tour.

Dunker, Wilhelm Bernhard Rudolph Hadrian 1809–1885. Palaeontologist especially of Mollusca. Lecturer Technical High School Cassel, later Prof. Geology Marburg. 1851 D sent fossil and recent cirripedes to CD. CD sent *Fossil cirripedes* to—*Lychnos*, 1948–1949:206–210. 1854 CD sent *Living cirripedes* to D.

Dunns, Rev. J. Free Church minister and dabbler in natural history. 1860 D reviewed *Origin* in *North British Rev.*, 'very severe'—LLii 311.

Du Puy, Martha Haskins 1861–1947. d of Charles Meredith Du Puy & Ellen Reynolds of Philadelphia. m 1884 *Sir* George Howard Darwin. Niece of *Lady* Jebb (Caroline Reynolds) who was her mother's sister. Known as Maud. Pedigree in *Period piece*.

Du Puy, Maud *see* Martha Haskins Du P.

Dutch First editions in: *Journal of researches* 1891 (F176); *Origin of species* 1864 (F594); *Variation under domestication* 1889–1890 (F910); *Descent of man* 1871–1872 (F1053); *Expression of the emotions* 1873 (F1182).

Dyck, Dr W. Van Lecturer in Zoology at Protestant College of Beirut. 1882 D to CD on sexual selection in Syrian street dogs. Apr.2 CD to P. L. Sclater submitting it, with covering note, for *Proc.zool.Soc.Lond.*, Apr.18 read, No.25: 367–370 (Bii 278, F1803); last publication in CD's lifetime; he died on Apr.19.

Dyer, Sir William Turner Thiselton 1843–1928. Botanist. KCMG 1899 FRS 1880. Director of Royal Botanical Garden, Kew 1885–1905 in succession to Hooker. m Harriet Anne Hooker. D helped CD with botanical material from Kew, e.g. 1879 CD to D, on a species of *Oxalis*—FUL 109. 1882 D was on 'Personal Friends invited' list for CD's funeral. DNB.

E

E *see* Katherine Euphemia Wedgwood.

Earle, Anne d of Erasmus Earle. m 1653 William Darwin II. CD's maternal 5th generation ancestor.

Earle, Augustus Draughtsman on 2nd voyage of *Beagle*. 1832 Aug. left owing to continuous ill-health. Replaced by C. Martens.

Earle, Erasmus 1590–1667. Serjeant-at-Law. CD's maternal 6th generation ancestor. Father of Anne Earle. Origin of name Erasmus in D family. MP for Norwich, Recorder of Lincoln. 1890 Oct. William Erasmus D & George Howard D went on a visit to 'General Bulwer, a beautiful place in Norfolk [Heydon Hall], to see the picture of Erasmus Earle, an ancestor'. Also a monument to E in Sts Peter & Paul Church. DNB.

Earth, Age of 1877 CD's views on in MLii 211–212.

Earthworms *see Vegetable mould and worms* and Wormstone.

Eastbourne Sussex. 1853 Jul.14–Aug.4 CD had family holiday there. 1860 Sep.22–Nov.11 family holiday there.

Eaton, Bertha m 1848 Edmund Edward Allen, sister of Dorothea Hannah E.

Eaton, Dorothea Hannah ?–1868. m 1846 George Baugh Allen, sister of Bertha E.

Eddowes' Newspaper Shrewsbury. 1880 *Mrs* Haliburton [Sarah Owen of Woodhouse] had reminded CD of his saying as a boy that if Eddowes' Newspaper ever alluded to him as 'our deserving fellow townsman' he would be amply gratified—LLiii 335. Opening sentence of a leading article of 1880 is given.

Edgeworth, Maria 1767–1849. Author. d of Richard Lovell Edgeworth. Friend of Erasmus D [I] & Josiah Wedgwood [I]. 1840 E described the character of ED—EDii 56. DNB.

Edgeworth, Michael Packenham 1812–1881. s of Richard Lovell E. Half brother of Maria E. Botanist & Indian Civil Servant. 1861 CD met at Linnean Society—MLi 184. DNB.

Edible fungus from Tierra del Fuego 1845 in Berkeley, M. J.,

On an edible fungus from Tierra del Fuego, *Trans. Linn.Soc.Lond.*, 19:37–43, summary in *Proc.*, 1:97–98 (F1671). Contains extracts from CD's notes.

Edinburgh Midlothian. Apart from his time at the University, CD visited 1838 Jun. on his way to Glen Roy.

Edinburgh University 1825 Oct.–1827 Apr. CD was at as a medical student, but did not qualify. 1825 Oct. stayed briefly at Star Hotel, Princes St, moving to 11 Lothian St, lodgings run by *Mrs* Mackay. *See* 1888 Feb.16 *St James's Gaz.*, 1888 May 22 *Edinburgh Weekly Dispatch*, 1935 Ashworth, *Proc.Roy.Soc.Edinb.*, 55:97–113.

Edmonston, John 'A negro lived in Edinburgh, who had travelled with Waterton, and gained his livelyhood by stuffing birds . . . he gave me lessons for payment'—LLi 40. Waterton, *Wanderings in South America*, 153, 1825 identifies him as John, a slave of Charles Edmonston of Demerara. On coming to Scotland and being freed, he took the surname of Edmonston or Edmonstone. E lived at 37 Lothian St; CD lived at No.11. *see* Freeman, *Notes & Records Roy.Soc.*, 33: 83–86, 1978.

Edmonston, Laurence 1795–1879. Physician & naturalist. Correspondent with CD from Unst, Shetland. Eldest son Thomas, 1825–1846, visited Galápagos Is in HMS *Herald*; accidentally shot in Peru.

The education of Darwin 1908 *The education of Darwin, the first section of Darwin's autobiography, written in 1876*, Boston, Directors of the Old South Works Leaflets, 8, No.194 (F1478). Extracts from earlier part of CD's autobiography.

Edward A manservant at 12 Upper Gower St. 1839 Feb.3 'Edward is such a perfect Adonis in his best livery, that he is quite a sight'—EDii 33. 1839 May, E occurs in CD's accounts. 1840 E had left and Parslow had arrived.

Edward VII 1841–1910. *King* of Great Britain *etc* 1901–1910. 1866 Apr.27 CD presented to when Albert Edward, *Prince* of Wales, at Royal Society Soirée. CD said nothing because he could not hear what the Prince said, 'A nice good-natured youth'.

Edwards, Mr A resident at Downe—Darwin-Innes 207.

Edwards, Henry 1830–1891. American entomologist and amateur actor. 1873 Correspondent with CD—FUL 87. c1876 CD to E, thanking for photograph and glad E approved of Wiesmann's essay—Carroll 486.

Edwards, Henry Milne 1800–1885. Zoologist. Belgian of British parents, he also used Henri as first name. FRS 1845. Prof. Zoology Paris 1841–. Frequent correspondent. 1854 CD sent *Living Cirripedia* to.

Egan, James Hungarian agriculturist of Budapest. 1858 CD corresponded with on colour of horses—Carroll 160, 161.

Egerton St Westminster, London. No.12 home of Leonard D 1882–1900. No.10 or No.14 home of William Erasmus D after death of wife in 1902, 1902–1914. Gwendolen Mary D lived with him there when she was a student at Slade School of fine Art.

Egerton, Sir Philip de Malpas Grey, Bart 1806–1881. Palaeontologist. 10th *Bart*. FRS 1831. 1885 Oct. CD met at Shrewsbury, 'He asked me why on earth I instigated you [C. Darwin Fox] to rob his poultry yard'. E was a neighbour of F at the time. DNB.

Eiseley, Loren C. 1906–1977. Prof. Anthropology Pennsylvania. 1958 author of *Darwin's century*, and several books on evolution.

Ehrenberg, Christian Gottfried 1795–1876. Protozoologist. Prof. Zoology Berlin. Examined fine dust from *Beagle* in Atlantic for Protozoa—*J.Researches* 1845, 5. 1838 *Die Infusionstierchen*, Leipzig.

Electric fish 1881 CD to Romanes, parable about evolution of electric organs to get rid of parasites—*Life of Romanes* 106.

Elephant 1836 May 5 CD rode one in Mauritius from *Capt.* Lloyd's country house half way to Port Louis, 'The circumstance which surprised me most was its quite noiseless step'—*J. Researches* 1845, 486. It was the only one in the island.

Elephant Tree Large beech on the sandwalk at Down House, also known as Bismarck and the rhinoceros. Cut down almost dead in 1969, but main trunk preserved.

Elephants 1869 [letter] Origin of species [on the reproductive potential of elephants], *Athenaeum*, No.2174:861 (Bii 136, F1746). 1896 [letter with same title], *ibid.*, No.2177:82 (Bii 137, F1747).

Elevation and Subsidence in the Pacific and Indian Oceans 1837 On certain areas of elevation and subsidence in the Pacific and Indian Oceans *Proc.geol.Soc.*, 2:552–554 (Bi 46, F1647).

Elevation on the Coast of Chile 1837 Observations of proofs of recent elevations on the coast of Chile, made during the survey of His Majesty's Ship *Beagle*, commanded by Capt. Fitzroy R.N., *Proc.geol.Soc.*, 2:446–449 (Bi 42, F1645).

Élie de Beaumont, Jean Baptiste Armand Louis Léonce 1798–1874. French geologist. Perpetual Secretary of the Académie des Sciences 1853→. Influentially anti-*Origin*. 'Damned himself to everlasting fame' by coining the term 'la science moussante' for evolutionism—LLii 185. 1870 CD to Quatrefages, É calls CD's science 'frothy', his own bubbles first of craters of elevation and second of direction of mountain chains according to age have 'burst and vanished into thin air' everywhere but France—Carroll 382.

Eliot, George *pseudonym see* Mary Ann Evans.

Elliot, Sir Walter 1803–1887. Indian Civil Servant & archaeologist. KCSI 1866 FRS 1877. 1855 CD met at British Association, Glasgow. 1856 CD writes to E in India asking for information on variation—Carroll 123, 162. 1857 E sent poultry skins from Madras to CD—MLi 99. 1873 Title of CD's 1827 contribution to Plinian Society first printed by E in *Trans.bot.Soc.Edinb.*, 11:1–42, 17 footnote; also in *Nature*, Lond., 9:38. DNB.

Elliott and Fry Commercial photographers of London, later incorporated in Bassano & Vandyck Studios, now Bassano's Ltd. c1880 photographed CD on verandah at Down House: *a*. standing by pillar in cloak and hat. *b*. head and shoulders without cloak or hat. *c*. seated on verandah in tightly wrapped cloak and with hat. *d*. head and shoulders from same negative as *a*. All, especially *a*., have been often reproduced and *a*. was long available as a commercial photograph. 1909 Brit. Mus.(Nat.Hist.) exhibition showed four different E & F photographs, dating them 1882.

Elliott, Mary 1887 ED to Henrietta Emma D, a villager at Downe.

Elston nr Newark, Notts. Elston Hall, seat of William Darwin VI whose wife, Anne Waring, had inherited from her mother, and present seat of senior branch of D family. Many early Ds are buried in All Saints' churchyard. Erasmus D [I] was born there.

Embury, George *see* Tollet.

Emily Jane Domestic servant at Down House ?1865–1879.

Englefield nr Theale, Berkshire. Seat of the Benyon family—Darwin-Innes 256.

Engleheart, Stephen Paul ?1830–1885. 1865 E was the village physician at Downe, known to D family as Spengle. Died by drowning in Old Calabar, Africa, trying to visit a patient.

Entomological Society of London (Royal 1933) CD Fellow (founder member) 1931. 1867 'No body of men were at first so much opposed to my views as the members of the London Entomological Society'—LLiii 69. 1856 CD to *Mrs* Lyell, 'You might trust Mr. Waterhouse implicitly, which I fear as [illegible] goes, is more than can be said for all entomologists'—MLi 85.

Eozoon A supposed fossil protozoan described by J. W. Dawson, *Quart.J.geol.Soc.*, 15:54. Later shown not to be of organic origin, but still described as a foraminiferan by A. Sedgwick, *Student's textbook of zoology*, 1:15, 1898. 1882 CD to D. Mackintosh, 'As far as external form is concerned, *Eozoon* shows how difficult it is to distinguish between organised and inorganised bodies'—MLii 171.

Epping Field Club 1880 Jan. CD to William Cole, declining joining at foundation, but sending a guinea 'in aid of your preliminary expenses'. Feb. CD to same, accepting Honorary Membership—*Essex Nat.*, 21:14, 1927. Later Essex Field Club.

Erichsen, Sir John Eric, Bart 1818–1896. Surgeon. *Bart* 1895 FRS 1876. Prof. Surgery University College London. 1885 E was member of Vivisection Commission. DNB.

Errera, Léo Abram 1858–1905. Belgian botanist. 1877 CD to and from on heterostyly especially in *Primula elatior*—Carroll 520–524. 1878 CD to and from, E had visited Down House, but CD was away—Carroll 544, 545. 1879 CD thanks for offprint on heterostyly—Carroll 563. 1879 E to CD sending photograph which CD had asked for; E asks for one in return—Carroll 563.

Erratic Boulders of South America 1841 On the distribution of erratic boulders and on the contemporaneous unstratified deposits of South America, *Proc.geol.Soc.*, 3:425–430 (Bi 145, F1657); *Trans.geol.Soc.*, 415–431 (F661).

Erratic Boulders, Transportal of 1848 On the transportal of erratic boulders from a lower to a higher level, *Quart. J.geol.Soc.(Proc.)*, 4:315–323 (Bi 218,F1677).

Erskine, Frances m *Sir* (later *Baron*) Thomas Henry Farrer as 1st wife.

Erskine, William m Maitland Mackintosh. Issue included Frances E.

Essay on Instinct 1883 in G. J. Romanes, *Mental evolution in animals*, posthumous essay on instinct by CD, 355–384, index 405–411 (F1434). Complete transcript of original mss in R. C.

Stauffer editor, *Charles Darwin's Natural selection*, 466–527, 1975 (F1440). First foreign editions: French (F1441), USA (F1435) 1884; German (F1443) 1885; Russian (F1449) 1894; Italian (F1447) 1907; Romanian (F1448) 1967.

Essays of 1842 & 1844 *see* Sketches of 1842 & 1844.

Estonian First edition in: *Journal of researches*, 1949 (F179).

Ethnological Society CD Fellow 1861.

Etruria Hall Staffordshire, home of Josiah Wedgwood I.

Evans CD's father's butler at The Mount, Shrewsbury.

Evans, Mrs Nurse to Leonard D then cook at Down House 1871–1882. The *Mrs* is honorary, but E married later. 1881 wages were £36 p.a. 1882 E attended CD's funeral; had a ticket for Jerusalem Chamber, but was asked to join family mourners in the Choir.

Evans, Mary Ann 1819–1880. Novelist under pseudonym George Eliot. m 1880 J. W. Cross, a New York Banker. 1854–1878 E was common law wife of G. H. Lewes. 1874 E attended seance with CD & ED at R. D. Litchfield's house. DNB EB.

Evolution First use of the word in CD's sense is in *Descent of man*, 1871. First use in *Origin* is in 6th edition, 1872, 201 twice & 424 three times. Evolved is the last word in all editions of *Origin*. Geological use 1832, Lyell, *Principles* 2:11.

Evolution by Natural Selection 1959 *see* Loewenberg, B. J.

Ewald, Julius Wilhelm 1801–1891. German geologist. 1878 E seconded CD's election to Berlin Academy as Corresponding Member.

Ewart, Rev. Henry C. Anglican priest. 1882 article by in *Sunday Mag.* on sermons preached about CD, after Westminster Abbey memorial service of 1 May—Atkins 50.

Ewart, James Cossor 1851–1933. Zoologist. FRS 1893. Prof. Zoology Edinburgh 1882–1927. 1881 CD to Romanes, unable to give E a testimonial [for Edinburgh chair] because he has already given one for E. R. Lankester; thinks that E is fit for the appointment; remembers interesting interview with E on bacteria at University College London laboratory—Carroll 604, 614. *Pennycuik experiments*, 1899, on telegony in horses, a theory in which CD once believed.

Expression of the Emotions 1872 *The expression of the emotions in man and animals*. First issue has last signature $2B^2 2C^3$ (F1141); second issue $2B^1 2C^4$ (F1142). First issue has plates numbered in Arabic; second issue, sometimes Arabic, some-

times Roman. Facsimile 1969 (F1175). 1890 2nd edition
(F1146), edited by Francis D. First foreign editions: German
(F1187), Russian (F1206) 1872; Dutch (F1182), Polish (F1203),
USA (F1143) 1873; French (F1184) 1874; Italian (F1200) 1878;
Spanish (F1214) ?1902; Hungarian (F1199) 1963; Czech
(F1181) 1964; Romanian (F1205) 1967). *See also Queries about
expression.*

Extinct Mammalia in the Neighbourhood of the Plata 1837
A sketch of the deposits containing extinct Mammalia in the
neighbourhood of the Plata, *Proc.geol.Soc.*, 2:542–544 (Bi44,
F1646).

Eyre, Edward John 1815–1901. Australian explorer. Governor
of Jamaica 1864. 1865 E put down a negro insurrection. 1866
CD supported J. S. Mill's attempt to prosecute E for murder.
CD subscribed to Jamaica Fund—LLiii 53. DNB.

Eyton, Thomas Campbell 1809–1880. Ornithologist &
specialist in skeletal variation. At Cambridge with CD and
shot with him in vacations. Donnerville House, Wellington,
Shropshire; 23rd heir of the Eytons of Eyton. Anti-*Origin*.
1839 E examined birds from *Beagle* voyage for *Zoology of
Beagle*, and wrote appendix to Pt III, 147–156. Much correspondence with CD on skeletal variation. 1868 E sent CD his
Osteologia avium, Wellington 1867. CD remembers hunting
and fishing with him in their youth—Carroll 353. DNB.

F

F = Father, used by ED in writing to her sons when they were grown up, after 1868. 'I would as soon be called Dod'—CD.

Fabre, Jean Henri 1823–1915. French entomologist. 1880 CD to F, praising *Souvenirs entomologiques,* 1879–1907. 1880–1881 CD letters to—MLi 385.

Falconer, Hugh 1808–1865. Physician & palaeontologist. FRS 1845. 1830 went to India as Assistant Surgeon, Bengal. 1832 Superintendant of Botanic Garden, Saharunpur; 1848 Superintendant of Botanic Garden, Calcutta. 1859 was living at Torquay for his health—MLi 455. 1861 F offered a live *Proteus anguinus* to CD. 1864 F proposed CD for Copley Medal of Royal Society. Often at Down House on his return from India. 1868 *Palaeontological memoirs,* 2 vols.

Falkland Islands British colony in S Atlantic. 1834 Mar.16 *Beagle* at Berkeley Sound in E Falkland, Port Louis at head of sound. CD explored and returned Mar.19. Port Darwin, at head of Choiseul Sound, named after CD; he crossed the isthmus near to it on Mar.17.

Falkland Islands geology 1846 On the geology of the Falkland Islands, *Quart.J.geol.Soc.(Proc.),* 2:267–279 (Bi 203,F1674).

Farrar, Frederic William 1831–1903. Anglican priest. FRS 1866. Rector of St Margaret's Westminster. 1883 Archdeacon & Rural Dean of Westminster. 1865 CD to F, congratulating him on *Origin of language.* 1882 Pall Bearer at CD's funeral. 1858 *Eric or little by little.* DNB EB.

Farrer, Cecilia Frances m *Sir* Stafford Henry Northcote, 8th *Bart,* 1st *Earl* of Iddesleigh 1885. 1882 F was on 'Family Friends invited' list for CD's funeral.

Farrer, Emma Cecilia 1854–1946. Only d of *Sir* Thomas Farrer. m 1880 *Sir* Horace Darwin. Known as Ida. CD's daughter-in-law. CD liked to hear her singing Sullivan's 'Will he come'—LLi 124.

Farrer, Ida *see* Emma Cecilia Farrer.

Farrer, Katherine Euphemia *see* Wedgwood.

Farrer, Mary ?–1905. Sister of *Sir* Thomas Henry F. m Arthur, *Baron* Hobhouse, 1819–1904. 1878 CD to Romanes, *Lady* Hobhouse is trustworthy—Carroll 547.

Farrer, Sir Thomas Henry, Bart 1833–1884. *Bart* 1883 *Baron* 1893. Barrister & Civil Servant. m1 Frances Erskine 3s 1d Emma Cecilia (Ida). m2 Katherine Euphemia Wedgwood s.p. Abinger Hall, Dorking, Surrey. 1873 Aug. CD visited there for first time and often later which he much enjoyed. DNB EB.

Farrington, Benjamin 1966 *What Darwin really said*, London. Selections by F.

Fawcett, Henry 1833–1884. Political economist & statesman. FRS 1882. Blind. Prof. Political Economy Cambridge 1863–1884. Postmaster General 1880–1884. 1860 F was present at Oxford British Association meeting. 1861 F was at Manchester British Association meeting and spoke in defence of *Origin*. 1861 F to CD, on J. S. Mill's opinion of the logic of *Origin*—MLi 189. 1862 On the method of Mr. Darwin in his treatise on the origin of species, *Rep.Brit.Assoc.Adv.Sci.*, for 1861, 141. Biography: Leslie Stephen, 1885. DNB.

Fayrer, Sir Joseph, Bart 1824–1907. Physician & toxicologist in India. 1st *Bart* 1896 FRS 1877. F provided cobra venom for *Insectivorous plants*.

Fegan, James William Condell 1852–1925. Evangelical worker amongst poor boys in South London, founder of Fegan's Homes, Deptford 1872. 1880 his parents moved to Downe on retirement; CD lent him the village Reading Room, which he called the Gospel Room. 1881 and later years F brought boys from his home to camp at Downe; they sang for CD who gave them 6d each. F also reclaimed drunks in the village and 'did much good there'—EDii 244, Atkins 52. Biography: W. Y. Fullerton [1930], contains letter from CD to F about the Reading Room.

Fellowes, Catherine ?1900. d of Isaac Fellowes, 5th *Earl* of Portsmouth & *Lady* Evelina Alicia Juliana Herbert. m 1843 Seymour Phillips Allen.

Fernando de Noronha Atlantic oceanic islands, belonging to Brazil. 1832 Feb.20 *Beagle* anchored off and CD ashore.

Ferrier, Sir David 1843–1928. Physician. Kt 1911 FRS 1877. Prof. Neuropathology King's College London. 1881 F was prosecuted under Vivisection Act. CD had met at C. L. Brunton's house and offered to subscribe towards the expenses of the case—MLii 437, *Brit.med.J.*, 2:917, 1881.

Fertilisation of Flowers 1883 Hermann Müller, *The fertilisation of flowers*, London; preface, vii–x, by CD (F1432). Translation, by D'Arcy W. Thompson, of *Befruchtung der Blumen durch Insekten*, Leipzig 1873. Foreign edition, CD's preface only: Russian (F1433) 1950.

Fertilisation of Orchids *see* Orchids.

Fertilisation of Plants 1877 *Gdnr's Chronicle*, 7:246 (Bii 191, F1780).

Fertilisation of winter-flowering plants 1869 *Nature*, Lond., 1:85 (Bii 160).

ffinden, George Skertchley Anglican priest. 1871–1911 ff was Vicar of Downe; he was generally disliked. 1896 *Mrs* ffinden is mentioned with nursemaid and baby in an elegant goat-carriage—ED. Olive Willis described him as 'that wicked man'—Atkins 48.

Fife, George 1807–1857. Physician of Newcastle-on-Tyne. Naturalist friend of CD at Edinburgh.

Findon, Mr Mr Findon's son, then a schoolboy at boarding school, of Downe—Atkins 104. ?= ffinden.

Fine Dust Which Falls on Vessels in the Atlantic 1846 An account of the fine dust which often falls on vessels in the Atlantic ocean, *Quart.J.geol.Soc.(Proc.)*, 2:26–30 (Bi 199, F1672). The dust was analysed for protozoan content by Ehrenberg q.v.

Finnish First edition in: *Origin of species* (F653) 1928.

Fish, David Taylor 1824–1901. Professional gardener & horticultural journalist. 1882 Apr.29 F wrote fine obituary tribute to CD, *Gdnr's Chronicle*—Allan, 295–296, Boulger & Britten.

Fisher, Mrs *see* A. B. Buckley.

Fisher, Florence Henrietta 1864–1920. m1 Frederic William Maitland. m2 *Sir* Francis Darwin as 3rd wife s.p. Author of *Six plays*, Cambridge 1921.

Fiske, John 1842–1901. American evolutionist & theoretical biologist. 1871 CD to F, with invitation to visit Down House when he came to England—LLiii 193. 1874 F sent CD *Outlines of cosmic philosophy*, 2 vols, 'I never in my life read so lucid an exposition'—MLi 333. 1879 *Darwinism and other essays*, London. 1884 *Excursions of an evolutionist*, London. 1884 *The destiny of man viewed in the light of his origin,* Boston. 1885 *The idea of God as affected by modern knowledge*, London.

Fitton, William Henry 1780–1861. Physician & geologist. FRS 1815. 1838 Aug. CD dined with at Athenaeum.

Fitz-Roy, Robert 1805–1865. R.N., hydrographer & meteorologist. s of *Lord* Charles Fitz-Roy, 2nd s of 3rd *Duke* of Grafton, bastard descendent of Charles II. FRS 1851. 1828 Nov.13–1830 Nov. F was in command of *Beagle* from death of *Commander* Stokes until end of 1st voyage. 1831 Sep.–1836 Nov. in command of *Beagle* for whole of 2nd voyage. *Commander* 1828, *Captain* 1835 Dec. *Rear Admiral* 1857, *Vice Admiral* 1863. 1843–1845 Governor-General New Zealand. 1854 Chief of Meteorological Department, Board of Trade. 1857 F visited Down House, the last time he and CD met. 1859 Dec. CD to Lyell, enclosing a letter printed in *The Times* signed Senex, 'It is I am sure by Fitz-Roy . . . It is a pity he did not add his theory of the extinction of *Mastodon*, etc., from the door of the Ark being made too small'—MLi 129. 'What a mixture of conceit and folly, and the greatest newspaper in the world inserts it'—Carroll 182. 1860 F was at Oxford meeting of British Association; strongly anti-*Origin*, he is said to have walked out of the lecture room holding a bible over his head and exclaiming 'The Book! the Book!'; the story comes from George Griffith and A. G Vernon Harcourt, who were both present—Poulton, *Darwin and the Origin*, 66. 1865 Apr.30 F committed suicide at his home at Norwood, Surrey. CD's opinion of his character 'Fitz-Roy's character was a very singular one, with many noble features: he was devoted to his duty, generous to a fault, bold, determined, indomitably energetic, and an ardent friend to all under his sway': 'Fitz-Roy's temper was a most unfortunate one'—Barlow, *Autobiography* 72–73. DNB EB. F's name is variously spelt; I have used that given in DNB. F's opinions of CD's character are given in his letters to Beaufort, 1832 Apr.28 'Darwin is a regular trump'. Aug.15 'He has a mixture of necessary qualities which make him feel at home, and happy, and makes everyone his friend'—Francis D, *Nature*, Lond., 88:547–548, 1912; Barlow, *Cornhill*, 72: 493–510, 1932, which also contains the best account of CD's relationship with F. F edited *Narrative of the surveying voyages of . . . Adventure and Beagle*, 1839, and also wrote an earlier brief account of the 2nd voyage, with a little on the 1st, *J.R.geogr.Soc.*, 6:311–343, 1836.

Flameng, Leopold 1831–1911. French engraver. 1881 F engraved the John Collier oil portrait of CD; copies are signed by artist and engraver.

Fletcher, Mr 1844 F was schoolmaster at Downe. CD sent F his mss of species theory for fair copy, now at Cambridge.

Flourens, Marie Jean Pierre 1794–1867. French physiologist. 1883→ F was Perpetual Secretary Academy of Sciences. Influential anti-*Origin*. 1864 *Examen du livre de M.Darwin sur l'origene des espèces*, Paris.

Flower, Sir William Henry 1831–1899. Mammalogist. KCB 1892 FRS 1864. Director British Museum (Natural History) 1884–1898. 1864 CD to F, about supposed 6th toe in frogs—MLi 251. 1877 F to CD, he had examined a pig's foot with an extra digit sent to CD by O. Zacharias—Carroll 510–512. 1873 On palaeontological evidence of gradual modification of animal forms, *J.Roy.Instn*, pp. 94–104. 1882 F was on 'Personal Friends invited' list for CD's funeral.

Flowers and Insects 1877 Fritz Müller on flowers and insects, *Nature*, Lond., 17:78, introducing a letter from Müller, *ibid.*, 17:78–79 (Bii 211, F1781).

Flowers and Their Unbidden Guests 1878 Kerner [Von Marilaun, *Freiherr*], Anton, *Flowers and their unbidden guests*, London, prefatory letter by CD v–vi (F1318); translation by W. Ogle of *Die Schützmittel der Blüthen gegen unberufene Gaste*, Innsbruck 1876.

Flowers 1861 Cause of variation of flowers, *J.Hort.*, 1:211 (Bii 43, F1715). 1866 Partial change in sex in unisexual flowers, *Gdnr's Chronicle*, No.6:127 (Bii 130, F1735).

Flycatcher CD's nickname used by all ranks on *Beagle*.

Flyer A cob used for pulling the coach at Down House.

Foliation 1846–1856 CD's views on geological foliation—MLii 199–210.

Forbes, David 1828–1876. Geologist. FRS 1856. 1860 CD to Hooker, CD praises F's work on geology of Chile. Geological correspondent of CD in general. Brother of Edward F. DNB.

Forbes, Edward 1815–1854. Naturalist. FRS 1845. m 1848 Emily Ashworth 2s 1d 1. Edward b 1849 died at birth, 2. Edward b 1850, 3. Jane Teare b 1852. Prof. Botany King's College London 1843–1854. Prof. Natural History Edinburgh 1854. A brilliant natural historian, but less sound on theoretical matters. Founder and moving spirit of the Red Lion Club, a convivial group of the British Association. Died prematurely of kidney failure. b of David F. Often at Down House. 1849 Nov.20 CD to Lyell, 'after more doubt and misgiving than I almost ever felt, I voted to recommend Forbes for Royal Medal, and that was carried, Sedgwick taking the lead—MLii

131. 1854 CD praised his introductory lecture at Edinburgh—MLi 78. 1855 CD to Hooker, 'poor Forbes', 'of course I shall wish to subscribe as soon as possible to any memorial'—MLi 95. 1856 CD to Hooker, 'but I must confess (I hardly know why) I have got to mistrust poor dear Forbes'—MLi 95. 1868 CD to Hooker, 'false theories . . . that of polarity, by poor Forbes'—MLi 305. Biography: Wilson & Giekie 1861. DNB.

Forbes, Emily *see* Ashworth.

Forbes, James David 1809–1868. Physicist & glaciologist. FRS 1832. Prof. Natural Philosophy Edinburgh 1833–1868. CD sent specimens of rocks to F—FUL 105.

Ford 1817 CD remembers that, when he was at *Mr* Case's school, aged 8½, he went for a walk with F on the Church Stretton road.—MLi 4.

Ford Cut most of the blocks for *Descent of man*. 1870 CD to A. Günther, praising their quality—LLiii 121.

Fordyce, John 1879 CD to F on theism—LLi 304, FUL 88. Author of *Aspects of scepticism*, London 1883, which prints the letter.

Forel, Auguste Henri 1848–1931. Swiss entomologist, especially of ants. 1874 CD to F, having read *Les fourmis de la Suisse*, Zurich—LLiii 191.

Forms of Flowers 1877 *The different forms of flowers on plants of the same species*, London (F1277), facsimile (F1294) 1969. 1878 2nd edition (F1279). 1884 2nd edition, 3rd thousand (F1281), with new preface by Francis Darwin. First foreign editions: German (F1297), USA (F1275) 1877; French (F1296) 1878; Italian (F1299) 1884; Russian (F1302) 1948; Japanese (F1297) 1949; Romanian (F1301) 1965.

Forster, Johann Reinhold 1729–1798. FRS 1772, and his son Johann George Adam F 1754–1797. Both were naturalists on *Commander* James Cook's 2nd voyage, 1772–1775. 1857 CD's cognomen as Member of Academia Caesarea Leopoldino-Carolina Germanica Naturae Curiosorum was Forster.

Forster, Miss Laura May 1839–1924. A lifelong friend of Henrietta Emma D. 1879 Jun. F lent her house, West Hackhurst, Abinger Hanger, nr Dorking, Surrey to CD for a holiday. 1881 Mar. F stayed at Down House to recuperate from an illness. 1892 Jul. F stayed at Down House—E. M. Forster (nephew) *Marianne Thornton*, 1956.

Forster, William Edward 1818–1886. FRS 1875. Liberal MP

1861–1886. 1875 member of Vivisection Commission—LLiii 201. DNB.

Forsyth, Charles 1836 Oct. Midshipman on *Beagle* on return from 2nd voyage.

Foster, Sir Michael 1836–1907. Physician. KCB 1899 FRS 1872. Prof. Practical Physiology University College London 1869–1883. Prof. Physiology Cambridge 1883–1903. F edited *Scientific memoirs* of Huxley. 1871 CD asks F for curare for experiments for *Insectivorous plants*, and inviting to Down House: F sent it—Carroll 400, 401. 1872 CD again invites to Down House—Carroll 419. 1875 F saw and agreed to R. B. Litchfield's draft sketch for a vivisection bill—LLiii 204. 1882 F was on 'Personal Friends invited' list for CD's funeral. DNB.

Foundations of The Origin of species *see* Sketches of 1842 & 1844.

Fox, Anne *see* Darwin [III].

Fox, Frances d of William Darwin Fox. m 1852 *Rev*. J. Hughes.

Fox, Samuel m Ann Darwin [III]. f of William Darwin F.

Fox, William Darwin 1805–1880. s of Samuel F. m 1834 & had 11 children by 1853. CD's second cousin. Vicar of Delamere, Cheshire 1838–1873. At Christ's College, Cambridge, with CD and kept up correspondence. 1827 'became acquainted with Fox & Way and so commenced Entomology'—Journal. 1828 CD stayed at family home, Osmaston nr Derby. 1859 CD sent 1st edition of *Origin*. 1868 CD thanks F for a return on sheep and cattle—Carroll 357. 1870 Nov. CD to F, will send copy of *Descent* when published. 'It is very delightful to me to hear that you, my very old friend, like my other books'—Carroll 385.

Franke, Constance Rose *see* Wedgwood.

Franke, Hermann 1847–? German geologist. m 1880 Constance Rose Wedgwood.

Frankland, Sir Edward 1825–1899. Organic chemist. KCB 1897 FRS 1853. Prof. Chemistry College of Chemistry London 1865– . F did experiments for *Insectivorous plants*. DNB.

Franklin Literary Society, Indiana CD Honorary Member 1878.

Fraser, Elizabeth Frances 1846–1898. m 1882 Leonard D, s.p. Sister of *General Sir* Thomas Fraser, a brother officer. Known as Bee. CD's daughter-in-law.

Freeman, Richard Broke 1915–   *see* CD bibliography, 1965,

1977; Humble bees; *Queries about expression; Questions about the breeding of animals*.

Freke, Henry ?–1888 Irish eccentric theoretical evolutionist. 1860 CD to Henslow, 'Dr Freke has sent me his paper, which is far beyond my scope'—MLi 175. 1861 CD to Hooker, his results have been arrived at by 'induction', whereas all my results are arrived at only by 'analogy'—LLii 359. 1860 *Origin of species by means of natural affinity*.

French First editions in: *Journal of researches* (extracts only) 1860 (F180), complete 1875 (F181); *Coral reefs* 1878 (F309); *Volcanic islands* 1902 (F310); *Origin of species* 1862 (F655); *Fertilisation of orchids* 1870 (F818); *Climbing plants* 1877 (F858); *Variation under domestication* 1868 (F912); *Descent of man* 1872 (F1058); *Expression of the emotions* 1874 (F1184); *Insectivorous plants* 1877 (F1237); *Cross and self fertilisation* 1877 (F1265); *Different forms of flowers* 1878 (F1296); *Biographical sketch of an infant* 1877 (F1311); *Movement in plants* 1882 (F1342); *Vegetable mould and worms* 1882 (F1403); *Life and letters* 1888 (F1514).

Freshwater Isle of Wight. 1868 Jul.17–Aug.20 CD had family holiday at. Photographed by Julia Margaret Cameron there.

Friendly Club, Downe *see* Downe Friendly Club.

Frog 1879 Fritz Müller on a frog having eggs on its back—on the abortion of hairs on the legs of certain caddis-flies, etc., *Nature*, Lond., 19:462–463; introducing a letter from Müller, *ibid.*, 19:463–464 (Bii 216, F1784).

Fuegians The Indian tribes of Tierra del Fuego. The best account of those encountered by the crew of the *Beagle* as well as the history of Fuegia Basket, Jemmy Button, Boat Memory and York Minster, the Fuegians brought to England on the first voyage, 3 returned on the second, is in Fitz-Roy's *Narrative*, 2, esp. 1–16, 119–227. Their later history and that of Fuegians in general is in E. L. Bridges, *Uttermost part of the earth*, 1947.

Fumariaceae 1874 Fertilisation of the Fumariaceae, *Nature*, Lond., 9:460 (Bii 182, F1769).

G

Gabinete Portuguiz de Leitura, Pernambuco CD Corresponding Member 1879.

Galápagos Islands Ecuadorean Pacific islands, 90'–91' W, 0'–1' S. The whole archipelago was renamed by Ecuador in 1892 Archipélago de Colón, but the old names are still used in English writings on the group. The equivalent names are; Abingdon = Pinta, Albemarle = Isabela, Barrington = Santa Fé, Bindloe = Marchena, Charles = Santa Maria, Chatham = San Cristóbal, Culpepper = Darwin, Duncan = Pinzón, Hood = Española, Indefatigable = Santa Cruz, James = San Salvador, Jervis = Rabida, Narborough = Fernandina, South Seymour = Baltra, Tower = Genovesa, Wenman = Wolf. 1835 Sep.16 *Beagle* arrived, CD landed St Stephen's Bay, Chatham; Sep.23 Charles for 4 days; Sep.30 Albemarle; Oct.4 Abingdon; Oct.7 Bindloe; Oct.8 James; Oct.14 Hood for a week; Oct.20 *Beagle* sailed for Tahiti. 1835 there was a penal settlement on Charles. The importance of the fauna of these islands, especially of the ground finches now called Darwin's finches q.v., to the development of CD's early thoughts on evolution has often been stressed. There is a large biological literature on them, e.g. 1959 J. R. Slevin, *Occ.Pap.Calif.Acad.Sci.*, No.25, 1–150; 1963 *Occ.Pap. Calif.Acad.Sci.*, No.44:1–154; 1967 *Nat.geogr.Mag.*, 131:540–585.

Galápagos Islands Finches John Gould, *Proc.zool.Soc.Lond.*, pt.5, No.53, 1837. Members of the sub-family Geospizinae of the buntings, Emberizidae, with special evolution on the islands. 1837 CD, Remarks on the habits of the genera *Geospiza,Camarhynchus, Cactornis* and *Certhidea, Proc.zool.Soc.Lond.*, Pt 5:49 (Bi 40, F1644). 1839 *J.researches*, 378–380. 1946 D. Lack, *Occ.Pap.Calif.Acad.Sci.*, No.21. 1947 D. Lack, *Darwin's finches*, London.

Galápagos Islands Monument Wreck Bay, Chatham. Erected in 1935 with inscription by Leonard D; illustrated in Slevin,

136, 138. 'Charles Darwin landed on the Galapagos Islands in 1835 and his studies of the distribution of animals and plants thereon led him for the first time to consider the problem of organic evolution. Thus was started the revolution in thought on this subject which has since taken place'.

Galápagos Islands Research Station Built by Charles Darwin Foundation at Academy Bay, Indefatigable I.; dedicated 1964.

Galápagos Islands Stamps 1935 commemorative issue by Ecuador, centenary of CD's visit; 2, 5, 10 & 20 centavos, with map, marine iguana, giant tortoise & head of CD respectively.

Galileo Galilei 1564–1642. The comparison of CD with Galileo, so often made, stems from Asa Gray's obituary notice, 1882 Apr., *Amer.J.Sci* & May, *Proc.Amer.Acad.*, 'What Galileo was to physical science in his time, Darwin is to biological science in ours'.

Galton, Frances Anne Violetta *see* Darwin.

Galton, Sir Francis 1822–1911. Eugenicist & statistician. Kt 1909 FRS 1860. 9c of Samuel Tertius G. m 1853 Louisa Jane Butler s.p. CD's half first cousin. 1873 G sent CD a questionnaire on education & background—LLiii 177. 1879 CD answered F's questions on the faculty of visualising for *Inquiries into human faculty*, 1883, 'I am inclined to agree with Francis Galton in believing that education and environment produce only a small effect on the mind of anyone, and that most of our qualities are innate'—Barlow, *Autobiography* 43. G was a voluminous writer on many topics. 1869 *Hereditary genius*, London. 1874 *English men of science*, London. Autobiography: 1908. Biography: K. Pearson, 1914–1930; D. W. Forest, 1974. Archive calendar: M. Merrington & J. Golden, 1976. DNB EB.

Galton, Lucy *see* Barclay.

Galton, Mary Anne 1778–1856. 1c Samuel G. m 1806 Lambert Schimmelpennick. s.p. Known as *Mrs* Skim. Strict Moravian, a most tedious woman. Biography: C. C. Hankin, 2 vols, London 1858.

Galton, Samuel John 1753–1832. Armament manufacturer & Quaker. FRS 1785. m Lucy Barclay. f of Samuel Tertius G. Great Barr House, Stafford. Member of Lunar Society of Birmingham. Anonymous author of *Natural history of birds*, 4 vols, London 1786–1791, a children's book.

Galton, Samuel Tertius 1783–1833. c of Samuel John G. m 1807 Frances Anne Violetta Darwin. f of Francis G. c1824 G taught CD how to use a vernier on a barometer at Shrewsbury.

Galton, Violetta *see* Darwin.

Gardening 1864 Ancient gardening, *Gdnr's Chronicle*, No.41: 965 (Bii 93, F1732).

Gaudry, Jean Albert 1827–1908. French palaeontologist. 1868 CD to G, on reception of *Origin* in France and on paper in *Geol.Mag.*, 372, 1868—LLiii 87. 1868 G was pro-*Origin*—LLiii 103.

Garth 1851 Jan. G went to British Museum with CD to look at W. P. Cocks' Irish cirripedes—FUL 93. ?misreading of mss.

Gautrey, Peter Jack Cambridge University Library, responsible for CD archive. *see Queries about expression.*

Geach, Frederick F. Mining engineer in Malacca, introduced to CD by Wallace: answered queries about expression for Malays & Chinese, *see Emotions*, 21.

Gegenbaur, Karl 1826–1903. Prof. Anatomy Heidelberg. An early convert to CD's views, 1864—MLi 257.

Geikie, Sir Archibald 1835–1924. Geologist. Kt 1891 KCB 1907 FRS 1865 PRS 1908–1913 OM 1914. Director General Geological Survey 1881–1901. b of James G. Autobiography: *A long life's work*, London 1924. DNB EB.

Geikie, James 1839–1915. Geologist. FRS 1875. b of *Sir* Archibald G. Prof. Geology & Mineralogy Edinburgh 1882– . 1881 *Prehistoric Europe*, London, contains extracts from 2 letters from CD, 141–142 (F1351). DNB EB.

Geographical Society, Royal CD Fellow 1838– .

Geological Notes on Coasts of South America 1836 Geological notes made during a survey of the east and west coasts of South America, in the years 1832, 1833, 1834 and 1835, with an account of a transverse section of the cordilleras of the Andes between Valparaiso and Mendoza, *Proc.geol.Soc.,* 2:210–212 (Bi 16, F1642); CD's first paper under his own name alone.

Geological Observations on Volcanic Islands and Coral Formations 1838 advertised as a book, but title abandoned and work issued as two books, *Coral reefs & Volcanic islands* qqv.

Geological Society of London 1836 Sep.8 CD proposed by Sedgwick & Henslow; Nov.2 elected; Nov.4 admitted. 1838 Feb.16–1841 Feb.19 CD was Secretary; *Sir* Henry T. De la Beche was Foreign Secretary at the time. 1859 CD awarded Wollaston Medal, which from 1846 to 1860 was made of palladium.

Geology of the Voyage of H.M.S. Beagle Intended as one volume in 3 parts, but issued as 3 books, *Coral reefs*, 1842, *Volcanic islands*, 1844 & *South America*, 1846 qqv. 1851 First appearance of the three bound in one volume, a remainder from unsold sheets (F274). 1890 Ward Lock edition of the three parts printed together (F279).

Georgian First edition in: *Journal of researches* 1951 (F187).

Geospiza, Camarhynchus, Cactornis and Certhidea of Gould 1837 *Proc.zool.Soc.Lond.*, pt 5:46 (Bi 40, F1644). CD's notes on habits of Darwin's finches, following John Gould's descriptions of CD's specimens from Galápagos Islands. There are four other papers by Gould in part 5 on CD's South American birds, but without notes by CD.

German CD had great difficulty in understanding the German language. 1880 CD to R. L. Tait, 'German, which to almost all Englishmen is a great trouble and sorrow'—N&R 81. Also CD to Hooker 'I have begun German'; Hooker to CD 'I have begun it many times'. *see also* Wien. First editions in: *Letters on geology* 1891 (F6); *Journal of researches* 1844 (F188); *Coral reefs* 1876 (F311); *Volcanic islands* 1877 (F312); *South America* 1878 (F313); *On the tendency of species to form varieties* 1870 (F365); *Origin of species* 1860 (F672); *Fertilisation of orchids* 1862 (F820): *Climbing plants* 1876 (F860); *Variation under domestication* 1868 (F914); *Descent of man* 1871–1872 (F1065); *Expression of the emotions* 1872 (F1187); *Insectivorous plants* 1876 (F1238); *Cross and self fertilisation* 1877 (F1266); *Different forms of flowers* 1877 (F1297); *Biographical sketch of an infant* 1877 (F1343); *Erasmus Darwin* 1880 (F1323); *Movement in plants* 1881 (F1343); *Vegetable mould and worms* 1882 (F1404); *Essay on instinct* 1885 (F1443); *Life and letters* 1887–1888 (F1515).

Gibbs, George 1815–1873. Ethnologist of Smithsonian Institution. 1867 Mar. G wrote to CD about *Queries about expression*, which S. F. Baird had shown him.

Gifford, Lady Harriet *see* Drewe.

Gifford, Robert, Baron Judge & M.P. 1st *Baron* 1824. m Harriet Drewe 7c. Woodchester, Stroud, Glos.

Gilbert, Sir Joseph Henry 1817–1901. Agricultural chemist. Kt 1893 FRS 1860. At Rothamsted Experimental Station 1843–1901. 1876 CD to G on soil without organic matter; CD had met at Linnean Society—LLiii 342. DNB EB.

Glaciers of Caernarvonshire 1842 Notes on the effects produced by the ancient glaciers of Caernarvonshire, and on the boulders transported by floating ice, *Phil.Mag.*, 21:180–186 (Bi 163, F1660). CD visited Caernarvonshire in May & June 1842.

Gladstone, Helen 1849–1925. Youngest c of William Ewart G. Vice-Principal Newnham College Cambridge 1882-1896. 1882 G was on 'Personal Friends invited' list for CD's funeral.

Gladstone, William Ewart 1809–1898. Statesman. FRS 1881. 1876 G visited Down House in company with Huxley, *Lord* Morley, & Playfair, whilst staying at High Elms. How honoured CD was 'that such a great man should come and visit me'—Atkins 85. 1877–1879 CD corresponded with, mostly on behaviour—FUL 88–90. 1880 G arranged a Civil List pension for Wallace. 1881 Jan. G wrote personally to CD about Wallace pension. DNB EB.

Glasgow 1827 May CD visited on a spring tour—Journal. 1838 Jun. CD visited at end of geological trip to Glen Roy. 1855 CD & ED went to British Association meeting.

Glass, Dr Director of Botanic Garden, Rio de Janeiro, Brazil. 1881 G wrote to CD about graft hybrids of sugar cane. 1882 CD to Romanes, about preparing a paper by Villa Franca & G, *Proc.Linn.Soc.Lond.*, 1880–1882: 30–31.

Glen Roy Lochaber, Inverness-shire. 1838 end of Jun. CD spent '8 good days there'—LLi 290. 1839 Observations on the parallel roads of Glenroy, and of other parts of Lochaber, with an attempt to prove that they are of marine origin, *Phil. Trans.*, 129:39–81 (Bi 89, F1653). 1841–1880 Full discussion and letters about—MLii 171–193. 1861 'my paper was one long gigantic blunder from beginning to end. Eheu! Eheu!'—MLi 188. 1861 'I do believe every word in my Glen Roy paper is false'—MLii 192. 1876 'A good lesson never to trust in science to the principle of exclusion. A great failure'—LLi 69. 1880 CD to Prestwich 'I gave up the ghost with more sighs and groans than on almost any other occasion in my life'—*Life of Prestwich* 300.

Glenie, Rev. Samuel Owen 1810–?. Anglican clergyman. Chaplain at Trincomalee, Ceylon, retired 1871. 1868 G to CD, answering Queries about expression, and on weeping in elephants—*Emotions* 167. 1868 CD to Thwaites asking him to thank G for 'excellent letter'—Carroll 354, 358.

Glutton Club *see* Gourmet Club, of which it was a nickname.

Goddard 1873 Priest at Chislehurst who annoyed ED by preaching about Louis Napoleon as if he were a saint.

Goodacre 1880 G sent CD hybrids between common goose and Chinese goose which were apparently fertile—LLiii 240, *Nature*, Lond., 21:207. The offspring of this cross are fertile.

Goodwin, Rev. Harvey 1818–1891 Anglican priest & mathematician. *Bishop* of Carlisle 1869–1891. 1882 May 1 G preached sermon at CD's memorial service, Westminster Abbey, in place of *Archbishop* of Canterbury, Archibald Campbell Tait, who withdrew at short notice—Atkins 49. DNB.

Goose 1880 Fertility of hybrids from the common and Chinese goose, *Nature*, Lond., 21:207 (Bii 219, F1786). *see also* Goodacre.

Goree Roads At eastern end of Beagle Channel, Tierra del Fuego. 1833 *Beagle* at Jan.15–Feb.9.

Gorringes A house near Downe. A *Sir* Hugh Lubbock and a *Mrs* Forrest are recorded as living there—Atkins 104. Later home of Bernard Richard Meirion Darwin.

Gosse, Philip Henry 1810–1888. Naturalist & Plymouth brother. FRS 1856. 1861 CD read some book of his; Francis D suggests *Naturalist's sojourn in Jamaica*, 1851, but more likely *Letters from Alabama*, 1859. 1863 CD to G, on fertilisation of orchids, which G cultivated. Biography: Edmund Gosse (son), 1890 *Life*; 1907 *Father and son*. DNB.

Gould, John 1804–1881. Ornithologist. FRS 1843. Taxidermist to Zoological Society of London. Producer of sumptuous bird books. 1837 G described CD *Beagle* birds in *Proc.zool. Soc.Lond.* (F1643, 1644) with notes on habits by CD and others without. 1838–1841 *Zoology of Beagle,* Pt III, *Birds* q.v. (F8). DNB.

Gourmet Club Formed by CD and friends at Cambridge, nicknamed Glutton Club. CD was at one time President. Members included Blane, Lovett Cameron, Heaviside, Herbert, Lowe, Watkins & Whitley qq.v.—N&R 65.

Gower Street No.110 *see* Upper Gower St No.12.

Graham, John 1794–1865. 1829 G was an examiner for Little-go at Cambridge. Master of Christ's College 1830–1848.

Graham, William 1839–1911. Prof. Jurisprudence Queen's College Belfast. 1881 CD to G, on reading his *Creed of science*, London—LLi 315. DNB.

Grange estate c1830 inherited by Edward Simcoe Drewe, nr Honiton, Devon.

Grange, The *see* Newnham Grange.

Grant & Maddison Bankers, Southampton. William Erasmus D a partner 1862–1902. Looked after CD's investments. Taken over by Lloyd's in 1902.

Grant, Miss 1857 Governess at Down House for 6 months.

Grant, Robert Edmond 1793–1874. Zoologist & physician. FRS 1836. Prof. Zoology & Comparative Anatomy University College London 1827–1874. G was with CD at Edinburgh and they collected on the sea-shore together. 1836 G was willing to examine *Beagle* corallines. 1861 G dedicated his *Tabular view of the primary divisions of the animal kingdom* to CD, with a long letter about G's early views on evolution. G is mentioned in the historical sketch of 1861, but not in the USA & German versions of 1860. 1876 'He did nothing more in science, a fact which has always been inexplicable to me'—Autobiography. Huxley of G 'I met nobody, except Dr.Grant, of University College, who had a word to say for Evolution—and his advocacy was not calculated to advance the cause—LLii 188. Biography: Freeman 1964. DNB.

Grasmere Westmorland. 1879 Aug. CD visited on day trip from Coniston.

Gray, Asa 1810–1888. American botanist. For.Mem.RS 1873. Fisher Prof. Natural History Harvard 1842– . Intimate friend and correspondent of CD. 1855 or before CD met at Kew. 1859 CD sent 1st edition *Origin*. 1861 Natural selection not inconsistent with natural theology, *Atlantic Monthly*, Jul., Aug., Oct. Later in same year produced in London as a pamphlet at CD's expense. Letters on its distribution; CD presented thirtytwo copies—Darwin-Gray 92–93. 1868 Oct.24 dined at Down House and stayed. 1877 *Forms of flowers is dedicated* to G. 1876 *Darwiniana*, New York. Biography: Jane Loring Gray (wife), 2 vols, 1894. Correspondence with CD calendared by Historical Records Survey with introduction by Bert Loewenberg 1939, reprint 1973. Letters are at Gray Herbarium, Harvard. EB.

Gray, George Robert 1808–1872. Zoologist. FRS 1866. Assistant Natural History Department, Bristish Museum. 1839–1841 G wrote much of the text for J. Gould's *Birds*, pt III of *Zoology of Beagle*, when Gould was in Australia. 1869 CD refused to write testimonial for G on grounds that he did not know enough of G's work—Ful 90–93. DNB.

Gray, John Edward 1800–1875. Zoologist. FRS 1832. Keeper of Zoology, British Museum 1840–1874. 1854 CD to G—FUL

93. 1856 to *Mrs* Lyell, suggesting that she offer a collection of beetles to G for the Museum—MLi 84. Biography: *Ann.Mag.nat.Hist.*, 15:218, 1875. DNB.

Great Cumberland Street London, No.14 home of *Sir* James Mackintosh and his daughter, *Mrs* Rich, in 1830.

Great Marlborough Street London, No.36 CD's lodgings 1837 Mar.13–1838 Dec.30 No.43 home of Erasmus Alvey D from before 1837.

Great Pucklands *see* Pucklands.

Greek First editions in: *Journal of researches* 1900 (F206); *Origin of species* 1915 (F698).

Green, Rev. John Richard 1837–1883. Historian. Librarian at Lambeth Palace 1869–. 1860 G was present, as an undergraduate student, at British Association Oxford meeting; he described the scene to Boyd Dawkins, then a fellow student—LLii. 322. DNB.

Greg, William Rathbone 1809–1881. Social essayist. 1878 CD to G, on G's son's views on and objections to CD's views on evolution—Carroll 557.

Gresson, Rev. G. T. Of Worthing. 1863 Innes suggested G as a possible tutor to CD's sons—Darwin-Innes 216. Earlier 2nd master at Bradfield College, 'a great dandy who wore white flannel trousers, a delicately tinted shirt, a purple velvet cap with tassel and primrose gloves for football'—Blackie, *Bradfield 1850–1975*, 37, 1976.

Greville House Paddington Green, London. 1822 Jan. ED and sister Frances at school there for one year. Headmistress *Mrs* Mayer—EDi 142.

Grieve, Symington 1848–1932. Ornithologist, expert on great auk. 1882 Mar.22 CD to G, on floating stones supporting fuci.

Griffin, R. & Co. Publishers, London. 1860 CD corrected his own entry in their *Comprehensive dictionary of biography*—FUL 94.

Grisebach, A. W. 1864 B. D. Walsh to CD, G introduced W to CD at Christ's College, Cambridge 'more than thirty years ago'—MLi 249. Not in Venn.

Gros nr Abergele, Denbighshire. 1813 CD went with family for sea bathing—Journal.

Grote, George 1794–1871. Historian & educationalist. FRS 1857. Vice-Chancellor University of London 1862–. In the 40s CD met at *Lord* Stanhope's—LLi 76. DNB.

Grove, The Hartfield, Sussex. Home of Charles Langton until 1862.

Grove, The Huntingdon Rd, Cambridge. 1882–1896 ED moved there for the winters and died there.

Grove, Sir William Robert 1811–1896. Physicist & barrister. Kt 1871 FRS 1840 Judge 1880. 1866 CD to Hooker, G as President of British Association, Nottingham, 'disappointed in the part about Species; it dealt in such generalities that it would apply to any view or no view in particular'—LLiii 48.

Growth 1877 Growth under difficulties, *Gdnr's Chronicle*, 8:805 (Bii 213, F1782).

Gruber, Howard E. 1974 *Darwin on man. A psychological study of scientific creativity; together with Darwin's early and unpublished notebooks*, London. Transcriptions by Paul E. Barrett of M & N notebooks with extracts from B–E, Essay on theology and natural selection, Questions for Mr. Wynne (F1582).

Günther, Albert Karl Ludwig Gotthilf 1830–1914. Zoologist. FRS 1867. On staff of British Museum (Natural History). 1869 G gave CD information on sexual differences in fish. 1870 G arranged for cutting of blocks for *Descent* by Ford. 1871 Feb. G at Down House—FUL 95. 1882 G was on 'Personal Friends invited' list for CD's funeral.

Gullick, John Thomas 1832–1923. USA missionary & naturalist. 1872 CD to G, G to CD, about extremely limited distribution of species, especially land molluscs in the Sandwich Islands (Hawaii)—Carroll 421–423.

Gully, James Manby 1808–1883. Physician. In charge of cold water cure at The Lodge, Malvern. 1849, when CD first went to Malvern, G made him give up snuff. DNB.

Gunville Tarrant Dorset. Home of Josiah Wedgwood III 1800–1805.

Gurney, Edmund 1847–1888. Writer on music & psychic research. 1876 CD to G on music—LLiii 186. 1881 G wrote on vivisection in *Fortnightly Rev.*, 30:778. 1882 on same subject, *Cornhill*, 45:191, referred to—LLiii 210. 1882 G was on 'Personal Friends invited' list for CD's funeral. DNB.

H

Haast, Sir John Francis Julius von 1824–1887. New Zealand geologist. Kt 1885 FRS 1867. Prof. Geology New Zealand University, Canterbury 1866. 1863 CD to H on New Zealand geology and natural history—LLiii 6. DNB.

Hacon, William Mackmurdo Solicitor. Practised 1843–1885; his partners varied, but Hacon & Turner 1870–84, 101 Leadenhall St, London. H acted for CD, although they never met. 'Everything I did was right, and everything was profusely thanked for'—H's feeling for CD in Francis D's reminiscences—LLi 120.

Haeckel, Ernst Heinrich 1834–1919. German biologist & physician. 2s of Karl H & – Sethe. m1 1862 Anna Sethe dsp. m2 1867 Agnes Huschke 1s 2d. Prof. Zoology Jena 1865– . The apostle of darwinism in Germany. 1863 Mar. CD to Lyell, 'A first rate German naturalist (I now forget the name)'—LLiii 16. 1867 CD complains to Huxley of excess of neonyms in H's *Generelle Morphologie*, 1866—MLi 277. 1868 CD to H 'your boldness sometimes makes me tremble'—LLiii 105. 1866 Oct. H stayed at Down House. 1869 Huxley 'The Coryphaeus of the Darwinian movement in Germany'—LLiii 67. H's wild, and mostly unsupported, phylogenetic speculation, combined with his popular reputation, held back experimental scientific work on evolution. Main works: *Generelle Morphologie*, 2 vols,1866; *Natürliche Schöpfungeschichte*, 1868. *Die systematische Phylogenie,* 1894; *Anthropogenie,* 1874; *Die heutige Entwickelungslehre in Verhältnisse zur Gesammtwissenschaft,* 1877; *Gesammelte populäre Vorträge aus dem Gebiete der Entwickelungslehre,* 1878–1879; *Die Naturanschauung von Darwin, Goethe, und Lamarck,* 1882. Biography: Bölsche 1900.

Hägg, Axel Hermann *see* Haig.

Hague, Duncan James 1836–1908. USA geologist. 1871 Feb. visited Down House. 1884 H wrote reminiscences of visit in *Harper's Mag.;* concerning *Descent*, 'everybody is writing about it without being shocked'—LLiii 133.

Haig, Axel Hermann 1835–1921. Swedish artist & architect. 1882H engraved new study at Down House a week after CD's death, when it had not been disturbed. His name is also spelt Hägg.

Haile, Peter A bricklayer at Parkfield, the home of CD's aunts Sarah Elizabeth Wedgwood [I] and Catherine W. A recollection of him was one of CD's earliest memories in his childhood—MLi 2.

Haliburton, Sarah *see* Owen

Haliburton, Thomas Chandler 1796–1865. Nova Scotian judge. m Sarah Owen. Author of *Sam Slick*, 1837–1840. DNB.

Hall, 1829 Cambridge friend of CD. ?Jeffrey Bock H, 1807–1886.

Hall, Basil 1788–1844. Captain R.N. & anthropologist. FRS 1816. 1838 Athenaeum acquaintance of CD. DNB.

Hamond 1882 one of CD's surviving shipmates from *Beagle*—LLi 221.

Hancock, Albany 1806–1873. Invertebrate zoologist, of Newcastle-on-Tyne. 1849 On the occurrence on the British coast of a burrowing barnacle, being a type of a new order of the class Cirripedia, *Athenaeum*, No.1143: 966 (Bi 250, F1678), with notes by CD, read to British Association meeting 1849. 1855 CD thought him a 'higher class of labourer than J. O. Westwood' and suggested him for a Royal Medal of Royal Society, which he received in 1858—MLi 80. 1886 CD's letters to H published in *Trans.nat.Hist.Soc.Northumberland, Durham & Newcastle*, 8:263–265. DNB.

Hanley, Dr 1825 CD & Erasmus Alvey D called on him on their arrival in Edinburgh, Oct.26.

Harbour, Mr A man employed by CD to collect beetles for him around Cambridge. 1829 CD to Fox, 'I have caught Mr. Harbour letting——have the first pick of the beetles; accordingly we have made our final adieus'—LLi 177.

Hardie Physician, Friend of CD at Edinburgh when a student, went on natural history trips together. Ashworth, *Proc.Roy. Soc. Edinb.*, 55:112, 1934, identifies him as Willoughby Arding q.v., but CD says that he died young in India.

Harding, Elizabeth 1846 nursery maid at Down House, aged 13, from Staffordshire. Got lost with William D, aged 3, and Frances Julia Wedgwood, aged 9, in Cudham Wood—Atkins 40.

Haredene Albury, nr Guildford, Surrey. 1871 Jul.–Aug. CD &

family spent a holiday there. The house belonged to Henry Drummond an Irvingite.

Harley, Agnes m 1907 Rowland Wedgwood as 2nd wife.

Harris A gentleman farmer of Orange Court, Downe.

Harris, Sir William Snow 1791–1867. Electrical engineer. Kt 1848 FRS 1831. 1831 H's type of lightning conductor was fitted to all masts of *Beagle*, long before they were adopted by the navy for all ships. CD met at Plymouth. Known as 'Thunder and lightning Harris'. DNB.

Harrison, Frederic 1831–1923. Popular writer. 1871 CD to H on beauty—Carroll 392.

Harrison, Lucy Caroline *see* Wedgwood.

Harrison, Matthew James m 1874 Lucy Caroline Wedgwood and had offspring.

Hartfield Village in E. Sussex. In biography usually means The Ridge, Hartfield, home of Sarah Elizabeth Wedgwood [II], built for her 1847, left 1868. 1855 George Howard D, aged 10, was allowed to ride the 20 miles from Downe alone—Atkins 41. Also means Hartfield Grove, a quarter of a mile from The Ridge, home of Charles Langton & family ?1840–1863. The houses are on the edge of Ashdown Forest.

Hartfield Grove House at Hartfield, Sussex, q.v.

Hartung, Georg ?1822–1891. German geologist, specialist on geology of Atlantic islands. 1858 CD corresponded with, through Lyell, on Azores—LLii 112.

Harvey, William Henry 1811–1866. Algologist. FRS 1858. Prof. Botany Trinity College Dublin 1856– . CD was a friendly correspondent with from at least 1858. 1860 Feb.17 H read a 'serio-comic squib' to Dublin University Zoological & Botanical Association—LLii 314. This was published as a pamphlet *An inquiry into the probable origin of the human animal* etc., Dublin; CD's copy, at Cambridge, is marked 'With the author's repentance, Oct.1860'. 1860 H wrote courteous but anti-*Origin* review in *Edinb.Rev.* 1860 Aug. CD to H about Whale-bear story, 'I struck it out in the second edition'—MLi 162. 1860 CD to Gray, 'Even [H] . . . is not nearly so savage against me as . . . when he published his foolish pamphlet'—Darwin-Gray 90. 1861 H wrote another review in *Dublin Hosp.Gaz.*, May 15. DNB.

Hastings Sussex. 1853 Jul. CD visited for day from Eastbourne.

Hatherly, Baron *see* W. P. Wood.

Haughton, Rev. Samuel 1821–1897. Man of science. FRS

1858. Prof. Geology Trinity College Dublin 1851–1881. 1858 Feb.9 H's address to Geological Society of Dublin is the first comment on the CD & Wallace statement to Linnean Society 'If it means what it says it is a truism; if it means anything more, it is contrary to fact'—LLii 157. 1860 CD to Gray, with footnote CD to Hooker, 'A review in the last Dublin *Nat.Hist.Review* is the most unfair thing which has appeared—one mass of misrepresentations', 'Do you know whether there are two Rev. Prof. Haughtons at Dublin', 'Can it be my dear friend?'—MLi 153. DNB.

Hawkins, Benjamin Waterhouse 1807–1889. Artist. H drew and put on stone the plates for *Fish & Reptiles* in *Zoology of H.M.S. Beagle*. H. made the Crystal Palace giant reptile replicas.

Hawkshaw, Sir John 1811–1891. Civil engineer. Kt 1873 FRS 1855. His s John Clarke H m 1865 Cecily Mary Wedgwood. 1876 Jun. CD visited his home, Hollycombe, nr Midhurst, Surrey.

Hawkshaw, John Clarke 1841–1921. s of *Sir* John H. brother of Mary H. m 1865 Cicely Mary Wedgwood, 3c. Known as Clarke.

Hawkshaw, Mary d of *Sir* John H. brother of John Clarke H. m Godfrey Wedgwood as 1st wife.

Healey, Mary ?–1679. m c1600 William Darwin [I] as 2nd husband. 6th generation ancestor of CD in male line.

Heathcote, Miss 1874 CD to Lyell, 'I was glad to hear at Southampton from Miss Heathcote a good account of your health'—MLii 237.

Heathorn, Henrietta Anne 1825–1915. Of Sydney. m 1855 Jul.25 Thomas Henry Huxley. Known as Nettie. 1882 H was on 'Personal Friends invited' list for CD's funeral.

Heaviside, Rev. James William Lucas 1808–1897. Fellow of Sidney Sussex College Cambridge 1833–1838. Prof. Mathematics H.E.I.C. Haileybury 1838–1857. Canon of Norwich. Cambridge friend of CD, member of Gourmet Club. 1836 CD met in Cambridge.

Hebrew First editions in: *Journal of researches* 1930 (F207); *Origin of species* 1960 (F700); *Autobiography* 1948–1949(F1520).

Hedgehogs 1867 Hedgehogs, *Hardwicke's Science Gossip*, 3:280 (Bii 137, F1740).

Heer, Oswald 1809–1883. Swiss palaeobotanist & entomologist. Prof. Botany Zurich. 1850 H went to Madeira for his health. 1878 Royal Medal of Royal Society. 1878 H seconded CD's election to Fellowship Koenliglich-Preussiche Akademie der Wissenschaften, Berlin.

Hellyer, Edward H. Clerk on 2nd voyage of *Beagle*. 1833 May, drowned at Falkland Is.

Helmholtz, Hermann Ludwig Ferdinand von 1821–1894. Prof. Physiology Heidelberg 1858– . 1878 H seconded CD's election to Fellowship Koenlich-Preussiche Akademie der Wissenschaften, Berlin.

Hemmings, Henry Manservant to Sarah Elizabeth Wedgwood [I] at Petleys, Downe, until her death 1856; when he returned to Maer. 1872 H was alive but with a bad heart.

Henry, Isaac Anderson- 1800–1884. Lawyer & plant hybridiser, of Edinburgh. 1849 CD to H, on *Phlox* & *Mimulus*—Carroll 86. 1863 CD to H, on cross & self fertilisation and on the uselessness of the compound microscope—MLii 297. 1867 H offered to lend CD De Maillet's *Telliamid*, 1748—MLi 280.

Hensleigh, Elizabeth 1738–1790. m 1763 John Bartlett Allen as 1st wife. CD's maternal great-grandmother. Of Panteague; origin of name H in Wedgwood family.

Henslow, Anne d of J. S. Henslow. m – Barnard. 1871 H to CD, telling him of a visit to Colchester mental asylum, seeing a girl with pointed ears—Carroll 389. 1871 CD to H, thanking her for information and praising John Stevens H—Carroll 390.

Henslow, Frances ?–1874. d of John Stevens H. m 1851 as his 1st wife Hooker. 1856 CD to Hooker, on her 'pedestrian feats'—MLii 209. 1874 Dec.25 CD to Gray, 'The death of Mrs Hooker has indeed been a terrible blow. Poor Hooker came here [Down House] directly after the funeral and bore up manfully'—Darwin-Gray 62.

Henslow, Rev. George 1835–1925, Botanist. Only s of John Stevens H. Hon. Prof. to Royal Horticultural Society. 1882 H was on 'Personal Friends invited' list for CD's funeral. 1873 *The theory of evolution of living things*, London.

Henslow, Rev. John Stevens 1796–1861. m 1s 3d. Father-in-law of *Sir* Joseph Dalton Hooker. FRS 1818. Prof. Mineralogy Cambridge 1822–1827, Botany 1827–1861. Vicar of Hitcham, Suffolk 1837–1861. CD, when at Cambridge, was known as 'the man who walked with Henslow'. CD regularly attended his Friday evening gatherings, which continued every week in term until 1836 and were the forerunners of the Cambridge Ray Club 1837– . H became a strong personal friend of CD and

looked after specimens sent back from *Beagle* voyage. 1835 H
edited CD's letters to him as *Letters on geology*, privately
printed for members of the Cambridge Philosophical Society
(Bi 3, F1). 1830 CD to Fox, of *Mrs* H, 'she is a devilish odd
woman, I am always frightened whenever I speak to her, yet I
cannot help liking her'. 1836 CD at Sydney to H, 'my master
in natural history'—LLi 264. 1854 H visited Down House
when Hooker was staying for a fortnight. 1855 CD paid little
girls in H's parish to collect seeds of *Lychnis* etc.—MLi 419.
1859 CD sent 1st edition of *Origin* to. 1860 Jun. 30 Sat. H was in
the chair of Section D at British Association Oxford scene.
1861 CD to Hooker, on H's death and the question of a
biography, 'The equability and perfection of Henslow's whole
character'—MLi 188. 'His judgement was excellent and his
whole mind well-balanced; but I do not suppose that anyone
would say that he possessed much original genius'—Barlow,
Autobiography 64. 1871 CD to Anne Barnard (H's daughter),
'To the last day of my life I shall think of your father with the
deepest respect and affection, and gratitude for his invariable
kindness towards me'—Carroll 390. Biography: 1862 Leonard
Jenyns, with recollections by CD, 51–55 (F130); 1967 Barlow,
Darwin and Henslow (F1598). DNB.

Herbert, John Maurice 1808–1882. County Court judge on
Monmouth & Cardiff circuit. Cousin of C. T. Whitley. Close
friend of CD at Cambridge and member of Gourmet Club.
Nicknamed Cherbury, from *Lord* Herbert of Cherbury. 1828
CD collected beetles with H at Barmouth, N. Wales. 1839 H
sent CD a silver forficula, i.e. asparagus tongs, as a wedding
present—EDii 24. 1856 CD to H, thanking him for a book of
poetry, 'I shall keep to my dying day an unfading remem-
brance of the many pleasant hours, (especially at Barmouth)
which we have spent together'—Carroll 121. 1867 May, CD
invites H to Down House—Carroll 327. 1868 H had given CD
his old microscope—Carroll 344. 1872 CD sent H 1st edition
of *Emotions*—Carroll 425.

Herbert, S. *see* CD's manuscripts, 1978.

Herbert, Hon. & Rev. William 1778–1847. Poet & plant
breeder. Dean of Manchester. 1845 CD visited. 1844 CD to
Hooker mentions him in relation to heaths from Cape of Good
Hope. DNB.

Hermitage House nr Woking, Surrey. Home of Henry Allen
Wedgwood c1847.

Hero CD's name for a plant of morning glory, *Ipomoea purpurea*, of exceptional vigour—*Cross and self*, Allan 252.

Herschel, Sir John Frederick William, Bart 1792–1871. Astronomer & chemist. 1st *Bart* 1838 FRS 1813. Master of the Mint 1850–1855. 1836 Jun. CD dined with at Cape of Good Hope, at *Lady* Caroline Bell's house. Her comment on him 'he always came into a room as if he knew that his hands were dirty, and that his wife knew that they were dirty'—Barlow, *Autobiography* 107. CD also dined with him in London. 1849 H edited *Manual of scientific enquiry*, to which CD contributed the geology (F325). 1859 CD sent H copy of 1st edition of *Origin*. 1861 CD to Gray, on evolution as stated in H's *Physical geography of the globe*, 1861—LLii 373. DNB.

Heterogamy 1863 [letter] The doctrine of heterogamy and the modification of species, *Athenæum*, No.1852:554–555 (Bii 78, F1729).

Hewitt, Mr A pheasant and poultry breeder of Birmingham. 1868 Mar. CD to J. J. Weir on sexual preferences of pheasant cocks when crossed with poultry hens—MLii 69. 1868 Apr. CD to the same, H says 'the common hen prefers a salacious cock, but is quite indifferent to colour'. H is much quoted in *Descent*.

Hewitt, Ginette m *Sir* Robert Vere Darwin as 2nd wife.

Heywood Lodge Heywood Lane, Tenby, S. Wales. 1843–1864 Emma Allen and her sister Frances lived here after the death of their brother John Hensleigh A.

Higginson, Colonel Thomas Wentworth 1823–1911. 1873 CD to H, he had enjoyed his *Life with a black regiment*, 1870, and also had his *Atlantic essays*, 1871. Of Newport, Rhode Island, USA.

High Elms Home of, and rebuilt by, c1842 *Sir* John William Lubbock, and then of his son *Sir* John L, *Baron* Avebury. Estate of c3000 acres marched with Down House grounds.

'High Elms' Pseudonym of Edward Darwin [II] as an author.

Hildebrand, Friedrich Hermann Gustav 1835–1915. Prof. Botany Frieburg. CD often praised H for writing German which was as clear as French. 1866 CD to H, on his papers on fertilisation of Fumariaceae and *Salvia*—LLiii 280. 1868 CD to H, on graft hybrids—MLi 285.

Hill, The nr Abergavenny, Wales. Home of John Wedgwood in 1830.

Hill, Elizabeth 1702–1797. d of John H. m 1723/24 Robert

Darwin. CD's great-grandmother.

Hill, John Of Sleaford, Lincolnshire. m Elizabeth Alvey. f of Elizabeth H. 4th generation ancestor of CD in male line.

Hill, Major Richard Noel 1800–1861. 5th *Baron* Berwick 1848. A cousin of *Capt.* Owen of Woodhouse. A shooting companion of CD in the 1820s; took part in a shooting joke at CD's expense—Barlow, *Autobiography* 54.

Hills, Mrs 1887 ED to Henrietta Emma Litchfield, 'Old Mrs' H, a villager at Downe; ?wife of the next.

Hills Gardener at Down House after CD's death. 1899 Apr. H gave notice.

Hindi First edition in: *Origin of species*, 1964 (F702).

Hindmarsh, L. 1861 CD to, about *Earl* of Tankerville's wild white cattle at Chillingham, Northumberland—MLi 187. *See Ann.Mag.nat.Hist.*, 2:274, 1839.

Historical sketch Of previous studies and ideas on evolution. First added to 3rd English edition of *Origin*, 1861, in answer to criticisms by reviewers. It had previously appeared in a shorter version, written before Feb.20, in 1st German edition and 4th USA printing, both 1860.

Hitote Tahitian Chief. 1835 Nov.26 CD discussed lightning conductors with H and several other Chiefs.

Hobart Tasmania. 1836 Feb.5–17 *Beagle* anchored in Storm Bay; CD landed.

Hobhouse, Mary *see* Farrer.

Hochstetter, Ferdinand Christian, *Baron* von 1829–1892. Austrian geologist. Prof. Mineralogy & Geology, Imperial Polytechnic Institute Vienna. 1861 H wrote to Hooker that evolution was making 'very considerable progress' in Germany—LLii 327.

Hodgson, Bryan Houghton 1800–1894. Vertebrate naturalist of Darjeeling, India. 1862 Hooker wrote to H, who was a personal friend, in succinct praise of CD.

Höchberg, Karl Of Lugano, Switzerland. 1879 CD to H, answering his queries on diet in relation to activity—Carroll 491.

Hofmann, Augustus Wilhelm von 1818–1892. Chemist. FRS 1851. Director College of Chemistry London. Prof.Chemistry Berlin 1864. H helped CD with experiments for *Insectivorous plants*.

Holden, Rev. James Richard 1807–1876. Cambridge friend of CD. Rector of Lackford, Suffolk.

Holland 1877 [letter of thanks by CD] in P. Harting, Testimonial to Mr Darwin—Evolution in the Netherlands, *Nature*, Lond., 15:410–412 (F1776). CD had received an album of portrait photographs for his 68th birthday.

Holland, Mr 1857 CD to James Buckman, CD had asked 'my cousin Mr. Holland of Dumpleton to make the enquiries, but as he is not on the spot, I have ventured to ask you'. The enquiry was about a rare breed of pigeon—Letter from CD, unpublished.

Holland, Sir Henry, Bart. 1788–1873. 1st *Bart* 1853 FRS 1815. Physician to *Queen* Victoria. Constantly kind to the D family in their illnesses. 1859 CD to W. B. Carpenter, 'I do not think (privately I say it) that the great man has knowledge enough to enter on the subject [evolution]'—LLii 223. 1859 Oct. CD to Lyell, CD hopes that H will not review *Origin* in *Quart.Rev.* because he 'is so presumptuous & knows so little'. 1859 Dec. CD to Lyell, CD had 'found him going an immense way with us (i.e. all Birds from one)—good'—Carroll 184. DNB.

Holly berries 1877 Holly berries, *Gdnr's Chronicle*, 7:19 (Bii 189, F1774). 1877 [The scarcity of holly berries and bees], *ibid.*, 7:83 (Bii 190, F1775).

Hollycome nr Midhurst, Surrey. Home of *Sir* John Hawkshaw. 1876 Jun. CD stayed there—Journal.

Holmgren, Frithiof 1831–1897. Prof. Physiology Uppsala. 1881 CD letter to H on vivisection, *The Times*, Apr.18; *Nature*, Lond., Apr.21; *Brit.med.J.*, 1:660; also in a pamphlet by George Jesse and several times in Sweden. Also in LLiii 208 and Bettany 160–162, both 1887. (F1352–1356).

Holmwood House $1\frac{1}{2}$ miles from Downe. 1865 home of Robert Rolfe, *Baron* Cranworth. George Bentham visited Down House from—LLiii 39. Atkins 103 says that the estate belonged to *Earl* of Derby.

Home, David Milne *see* Milne.

Homefield A small house 400 yards NW of Down House. On 2 acres originally part of little Pucklands field. Bought by the Ds and in the Downe House School period a convalescent dormitory. Leased and added to by *Sir* Arthur Keith, 1930 until his death.

Hooker, Harriet Anne 5c of *Sir* Joseph Dalton H & Frances Henslow. m *Sir* William Thiselton Dyer, H's successor as Director at Kew.

Hooker, Sir Joseph Dalton 1817 Jun.30–1911 Dec.10. Botan-

ist. KCSI 1878 GCSI 1897 FRS 1847 PRS 1873–1878 OM
1907. Royal Medal of Royal Society 1854. Copley Medal 1887,
Darwin Medal 1892. Darwin-Wallace Medal of Linnean Society 1908. VMH of Royal Horticultural Society 1897. 2nd s of
Sir William Jackson H. m1 1851 Frances Henslow e.d. of J. S.
Henslow 4s 2d. m2 Hyacinth Symonds, widow of *Sir* William
Jardine *Bart*, 2s. Harriet Anne H, 5th c of first marriage, m *Sir*
William Thiselton Dyer. Director of Royal Botanic Garden,
Kew, Surrey 1865–1885, in succession to his father. H was
CD's greatest personal friend and confidant, much more so
than either Lyell or Huxley, and provided much plant material
for CD from Kew. H preserved all CD's letters, *see* Janet
Browne, *J.Soc.Biblphy nat.Hist.*, 8:351–366, 1978. Often at
Down House. CD and H first met 1839 in London, either in
Park St or in Trafalgar Square. 1844 Sep. CD to Lyell, 'Young
Hooker talks of coming here [to Down House]; I wish he
might meet you,—he appears to me a most engaging young
man'—MLii 120. 1859 CD sent 1st edition of *Origin*. 1859
Nov. H accepted CD's theory in print in introductory essay to
Flora Tasmaniae, I, pt 3, ic–xxviii; this is Vol.3 of *Botany of
H.M.Discovery Ships Erebus and Terror, 1839–1843*, 3 vols
1849–1860. The introductory essay was also available separately. 1866 Aug.27 H satirized Oxford meeting of British
Association with allegory of new moon and savages' medicine
men at Nottingham meeting—LLiii 48. 1882 H was Pall
Bearer at CD's funeral. 1885 H retired to The Camp,
Sunninghill, Berkshire. Biography: L. Huxley 1918; Turrill
1963; Allan, *The Hookers of Kew*, 1967. DNB.

Hooker, Sir William Jackson 1785–1865. Kt of Hanover 1836
FRS 1812. Prof. Botany Glasgow 1820–1841. Director Royal
Botanic Gardens, Kew, Surrey 1841–1865. m 1815 Maria Sara
Turner eldest d of Dawson Turner, banker & naturalist, 2s 3d.
f of *Sir* Joseph Dalton H. CD knew and met often but was not
familiar with. Biography: J. D. H., *Ann.Bot.*, 16:ix-ccxxi,
1902; Allan, *The Hookers of Kew*, 1967. DNB.

Hoole, Rev. 1877 curate at Downe church, presumably as a
locum for ffinden, then the vicar. H's wife Alice 'poor Mrs
Hoole' was an invalid—Darwin-Innes 243.

Hope, Lady 'of Northfield' H was involved in CD's so-called
death-bed conversion, *see* Atkins 51–52. Alive in 1992 when a
Mr Tucker, of the Salvation Army asked her for details.
Perhaps is *Lady* [Elizabeth Reid] Hope, widow of *Admiral of*

the Fleet Sir James Hope, writer of evangelical tracts and on temperance.

Hope, Rev. Frederick William 1797–1862. Entomologist & print collector. FRS 1834. Founder of Hope Chair of Zoology (Entomology) Oxford. 1829 Feb. H gave CD specimens of c160 species of beetles in London—LLi 174. 1829 Jun. CD visited Barmouth with H to collect beetles, but CD was ill and had to return to Shrewsbury after 2 days. 1837 CD to H, about Australian insects. CD gave him many which are now in Hope collection, Oxford—Poulton, *Darwin and the Origin*, 202. 1838 CD to Lyell, 'How much I disliked the manner [Hope] referred to his other works, as much as to say 'you must . . . buy everything I have written'—LLi 292, Carroll 10. DNB.

Hope, Thomas Charles 1766–1844. FRS 1804. Prof. Chemistry Edinburgh 1799–1843. The only teacher at Edinburgh of whose lectures CD approved. DNB.

Hopedene A house nr Dorking, Surrey, which was lent to Hensleigh Wedgwood. 1876 Jun.5 CD stayed there—MLii 12.

Hopkins, William 1793–1866. Mathematician & geologist. FRS 1837. Mathematical coach at Cambridge. 1860 H reviewed *Origin* in *Fraser's Mag.*, Jun., Jul., against but friendly. DNB.

Hordern, Ellen Frances ?–1879. d of *Rev.*Peter H. m 1856 *Sir* John Lubbock as 1st wife.

Horner, Anne Susan *see* Lloyd.

Horner, Frances 1814–? 2c of Leonard H. m 1844 *Sir* Charles James Fox Bunbury. Author of biography of her husband, London [1894], privately printed.

Horner, Francis [I] 1778–1817. Barrister & statesman. Elder b of Leonard H. Statue by Chantry in Westminster Abbey. DNB.

Horner, Francis [II] 1820–1824. 6c & only son of Leonard H.

Horner, Joanna ?1822–? 7c of Leonard H. unm. 1856 H wrote to CD about some beetles which she had—MLi 84.

Horner, Katherine Murray 1817–1915. 4c of Leonard H. m 1848 *Lt-Col.* Henry Lyell, *Sir* Charles Lyell's younger b. 1875 H asked CD to be a Pall Bearer at Lyell's funeral; CD declined on grounds of ill-health—LLiii 197. 1882 H was on 'Personal Friends invited' list for CD's funeral. Author of: *Life, letters and journals of Sir Charles Lyell*, 2 vols,1881; *Memoir of Leonard Horner*, 2 vols, privately printed, 1890.

Horner, Leonard 1785–1864. Linen draper & geologist. FRS

1813. s of John Horner, linen draper of Edinburgh. m Anne
Susan Lloyd 1s 6d. 1. Mary Elizabeth, 2. Frances, 3. Susan, 4.
Katherine Murray, 5. Leonora, 6. Francis, 7. Joanna. First
Warden of University of London 1827–1831. Factory Com-
missioner 1833–1860. Fairly frequent correspondent of CD
and met when CD was in London. Member of whig circle and
friend of Erasmus Alvey D. 1826 H took CD to meeting of
Royal Society of Edinburgh—LLi 40. 1846 H visited Down
House with wife. 1860 CD sent 1st edition of *Origin* to.
Biography: K. M. Lyell (daughter), 2 vols, privately printed
1890. DNB.

Horner, Leonora 1818–? 5c of Leonard H. m 1854 *Chevalier*
Georg H. Pertz. 1839 H dined with CD & ED at Upper Gower
St. 1847 Sep. H visited Down House with the Lyells.

Horner, Mary Elizabeth 1808–1873. 1c of Leonard H. m 1832
Sir Charles Lyell.

Horner, Susan 1816–? 3c of Leonard H. unm.

Horses The following family horses are entered by name:
Dandy, Dobbin, Flyer, Tara, Tommy.

Horsman Curate at Downe c1868. H got, after a prison sentence, another curacy in Kent.

Horwood *Sir* John Lubbock's head gardener. 1862–1863 H
superintended building of CD's hothouse.

Hoskins Botanist. 1845 CD to Henslow, CD was disappointed
that H had not got some post at Edinburgh.

Hotham, Harriet 1810–1873. m 1833 *Sir* John William Lubbock.

Houghton, Baron *see* Richard Monckton Milnes.

Houseman, Emma m 1871 Lawrence Wedgwood.

Howard, Mary 1740 Feb.12–1770 Jun.30. d of Charles H &
Penelope Foley. m 1757 Erasmus Darwin [I] as 1st wife.
Known as Polly. CD's grandmother. Drank gin and died of
doing so.

Howarth, Osbert John Radcliffe 1878–1954. Secretary British
Association for the Advancement of Science 1909–1946.
Curator Down House 1929–1954. H & Eleanor K. H. (wife), *A
history of Darwin's parish*, Southampton 1933.

Hubbersty, Nathan 1803–1881. Assistant master Shrewsbury
School 1826–1828. Headmaster Wirksworth Grammar School
1832–1851. 1826 CD went on walking tour in N.Wales with
H. 1839 CD suggested to H that he should do some plant
breeding experiments—4th notebook on transmutation.

Hudson, William Henry 1841–1922. Ornithologist & popular writer. *see* Pampas woodpecker.

Hughes, Frances *see* Fox.

Hughes, Thomas McKenny 1832–1917. Geologist. FRS 1889. Woodwardian Prof. Geology Cambridge 1873–1917. 1880 CD to H, about award to CD of a medal by Chester Natural History Society. 1880 Oct. took tea with CD & ED in Cambridge. WWH.

Humble Bees 1841 Humble bees, *Gdnr's Chronicle*, No.34:550 (Bi 142, F1658). 1885 Ueber die Wege der Hummeln-Männchen, 84–88 in *Gesammelte kleinere Schriften*, Leipzig (F1584). 1965 1885 paper translated as On the flight paths of male humble bees, 70–73 in R. B. Freeman, *The works of Charles Darwin*, London (F1580). 1968 Charles Darwin on the routes of male humble bees, *Bull.Brit.Mus.(nat.Hist.)*, hist.Ser., 3:177–189; as 1965 translation but with transcript of CD's field notes added (F1568).

Humboldt, Friedrich Heinrich Alexander, Baron von 1769–1859. German naturalist & traveller. Corr.Mem.RS 1815. CD once met, when CD was resident in London, at Murchison's house. 1881 CD to Hooker, 'the parent of a grand progeny of scientific travellers'.

Humphrey, Philip E. *see* Marston Bates.

Humphreys Of 32 Sackville St, London. c1868 supplied curates for Downe Parish.

Hungarian First editions in: *Journal of researches* (F208) 1913; *Origin of species* (F703) 1873–1874; *Variation under domestication* (F919) 1959; *Descent of man* (F1084) 1882; *Expression of the emotions* (F1199) 1963; *Autobiography* (F1521) 1955.

Hunt, Robert 1807–1887. Scientific writer. FRS 1854. 1868 CD sent a third person summary of his life for inclusion in *Biographical memoirs of men of science,* [1868]. DNB.

Hutton, Frederick Wollaston 1836–1905. Army Officer & geologist. FRS 1892. Curator of Canterbury Museum, Christchurch, New Zealand. 1861 H reviewed Origin in *The Geologist*, 132—LLii 362. 1861 CD to H, on his review, praising it—MLi 183. 1867 CD to Kingsley, 'a very acute observer'—Carroll 330. *Author of Darwinism and Lamarckism, old and new*, London 1899.

Hutton, John Balfour 1808–1884. Botanist. Regius Keeper of Royal Botanic Garden Edinburgh. 1861 CD sent H Gray's *Natural selection not inconsistent with natural theology,*

1861—Darwin-Gray 76.

Hutton, Richard Holt 1826–1897. Unitarian clergyman, which he later abandoned. Man of letters. 1875 H was a member of Vivisection Commission.

Huxley, Henrietta Anne *see* Heathorn.

Huxley, Sir Julian Sorrell 1887–1975. Zoologist. Kt 1958 FRS 1938. Eldest s of Leonard H & Julia Frances Arnold. m 1919 Marie Juliette Baillot. 1909 Feb.12 H was present at CD celebrations at Oxford. Author of works on evolution and biological popularizer. 1939 *The living thoughts of Darwin*, selected by H, translated into many languages. WWH.

Huxley, Leonard 1860–1933. 3c Thomas Henry H. m1 1885 Julia Frances Arnold (1862–1908) 2s 1d, 1. Julian Sorrell, 2. Aldous. m2 1912 Rosalind Bruce 2s, 1. Andrew. Biographer of his father and of Hooker.

Huxley, Marian 1859–1887. m 1879 John Collier. 1878 H made pencil sketch of CD, now at National Portrait Gallery.

Huxley, Thomas Henry 1825 May 4–1895 Jun.29. Man of science & educationalist. FRS 1850 PRS 1883–1885 PC 1892. 7c of George H & Rachel Withers. m 1855 Jul.25 Henrietta Anne Heathorn 3s 5d, 1. Noel 1856–1860; 2. Jessie Oriana 1858–1927; 3. Marian q.v.; 4. Leonard q.v.; 5. Rachel 1862–1934 m 1884 Alfred Eckersley; 6. Henrietta 1863–1940 m 1889 Harold Roller, known as Nettie; 7. Henry 1865–1965 m 1890 Sophia Stobart; 8. Ethel Gladys 1866–1941 m 1889 John Collier (as deceased wife's sister), known as Babs & Pabelunza. 1845 MB London. 1846–1850 Surgeon on HMS *Rattlesnake*, mostly in Australian waters. 1854 Prof. Natural History School of Mines London. Frequent correspondent and often at Down House, but was never on such close personal terms with CD as was Hooker *see* Bartholemew, M., *Ann.Sci.*, 32:525, 1975. H was known as Darwin's bull-dog. 'I am Darwin's bull-dog' he once said. 1871 Nov.2 H to Haeckel 'The dogs have been barking at his heels too much of late'—*Life of Huxley*, 2nd edition ii 62. 1854 Apr. CD to H on archetypes. 1854 CD to Hooker, about H's Royal Institution lectures 'I think his tone is much too vehement'—MLi 89. 1859 CD sent 1st edition of *Origin* to. 1860 Apr. H reviewed *Origin* in *The Times* and *Westminster Rev*. 1860 Jun.30 Sat. H defended *Origin* against *Bishop* Samuel Wilberforce's attack at Oxford meeting of British Association—LLii 32–323. 1873 £2100 subscribed by CD and other friends to let H have a long rest after nervous breakdown. All H's children were looked after by ED at Down House whilst he was away—MLi 72.

1875 H was member of Vivisection Commission; he saw and agreed to Litchfield's draft for bill—LLiii 204. 1880 H lectured to Royal Institution on The coming of age of the *Origin*, published in *Nature*, Lond. & in *Science & Culture*. CD sorry that he could not attend—LLiii 240. 1882 CD left him £1000 in his will—MLi 72. 1882 H was Pall Bearer at CD's funeral. 1887 H on the reception of *Origin* in 1859–1860, 'How extremely stupid of me not to have thought of that'—LLii 179–204. 1890 H retired to Hodslea (a name which he invented and believed related to the origin of his surname), Stavely Rd, Eastbourne, Sussex, which he designed and had built. 1891 Anthony Rich left H his house, Chapel Croft, Heene, Worthing, Sussex, and contents. H sold house for £2800. 1908 E. R. Lankester of H 'the great and beloved teacher, the unequalled orator, the brilliant essayist, the unconquerable champion and literary swordsman'—Darwin-Wallace celebrations at Linnean Society 29. 1909 E. B. Poulton of H 'the illustrious comparative anatomist, Huxley, Darwin's great general in the battles that had to be fought, but not a naturalist, far less a student of living nature'—*Darwin and the Origin* 58. Main works: 1863 *Evidence as to man's place in nature*; 1863 *On our knowledge of the causes of the phenomena of organic nature*; 1873 *Lay sermons, addresses and reviews*; 1873 *Critiques and addresses*; 1881 *Science and culture and other essays*; 1893–1894 *Collected essays*, 9 vols. Biography: L. Huxley (son) 1900; F. Chalmers Mitchell 1900. DNB. EB.

Huxley Testimonials [1851] *Testimonials for Thomas H. Huxley, F.R.S., candidate for the Chair of Natural History at the University of Toronto*. London, Richard Taylor printed. CD's letter at p.4 (F344). The Chair went to William Hincks, brother of *Sir* Francis Hincks, then Prime Minister of Upper Canada.

Hyatt, Alpheus 1838–1902. Palaeontologist. 1881 Curator of Museum of Boston Natural History Society. H worked especially on fossil cephalopods. Pupil of L. Agassiz and friend of Cope. 1872 CD to H about H's and Cope's ideas on acceleration and retardation in evolution. CD wrote on the back of one of H's papers 'I cannot avoid thinking this paper fanciful'—LLiii 154, MLi 338. 1877 CD to H on inheritance of acquired characters—LLiii 232.

Hybrids 1868 On the character and hybrid-like nature of the offspring from the illegitimate unions of dimorphic and trimorphic plants, *J.Linn.Soc.Lond.(Bot.)*, 10:393–437 (F1742).

Hyman, Stanley Edgar 1919–. 1963 *Darwin for today the essence of his work*, New York. Selections by H (F1618).

I

Icebergs Making Grooves 1855 On the power of icebergs to make rectilinear uniformly-directed grooves across a submarine undulatory surface, *Phil.Mag.*, 10:96–98 (Bi 252, F1681).

Ilkley nr Otley, Yorkshire. 1859 Autumn CD to water cure there, stayed at Wells Terrace. CD was there when *Origin* was published.

Imperatorskaya Akademiya Nauk (Academia Scientarum Imperialis Petropolitana), St Petersburg. CD Corresponding Member 1867.

Impey CD's gyp (servant) at Christ's College, Cambridge. 1858 I was still there when William Erasmus D went up to Christ's.

Index Kewensis 1892–1895, 4 vols, with 12 subsequent supplements to 1959, and a supplement since quinquennially. List of plant genera and their contained species, with relevant literature. Wording of announcement in Vol.4 'The expense of preparing the work has been entirely defrayed by the members of the family of the late Charles Darwin'. 1882 Jan. CD sent a first £250 and left a letter desiring that his children should send a similar sum for 4 or 5 years. Originally supervised by Hooker and carried out by B. Daydon Jackson—LLiii 352, *Kew Bull.*, 29, 1896.

Ingall, Margaret Rosina m 1873 Alfred Allen Wedgwood.

Inglis, Sir Robert Harry, Bart 1786–1855. Politician. 2nd *Bart* 1820 FRS 1813. MP for Oxford University. 1854 CD took breakfast with him in company—MLi 79. I was legal guardian of Laura Forster's mother, Laura Thornton. DNB.

Inheritance 1881 Inheritance, *Nature*, Lond., 24:257 (Bii 230, F1795).

Innes, Rev. John Brodie Curate of Farnborough, Kent, 1842. Vicar of Downe 1846–1869. 1862 I retired to his ancestral home Milton Brodie, Forres; Downe was served by curates until G. S. ffinden became Vicar in 1871. ?1860 CD to I, 'I do not attack Moses, and I think Moses can take care of himself'.

'Brodie Innes and I have been fast friends for thirty years, and we have never thoroughly agreed on any subject but once, and then we stared hard at each other, and thought one of us must be very ill'—LLii 288. 1859 CD sent 1st edition *Origin* to. Letters to and from CD edited by R. M. Stecher, *Ann.Sci.*,17:201–258 (F1597); they contain a lot of information about people at Downe not contained in other sources. 1882 I was on 'Personal Friends invited' list for CD's funeral.

Innes, John William Brodie 1848–1923. s of J. B. Innes. Barrister & novelist. I occurs in letters between CD and his father, as a child and young man.

Insectivorous Plants 1875 *Insectivorous plants* (F1217); facsimile 1969 (F1235); 1875, 2nd thousand, with 6 line errata slip (F1218); 1875 3rd thousand, 6 errata corrected, but with a further 6 on slip (F1219); 1888, 2nd edition, revised by Francis Darwin (F1225). First foreign editions: USA 1875 (F1220), German (F1738), Russian (F1244) 1876; French (F1237) 1877; Italian (F1242) 1878; Romanian (F1243) 1965.

Instinct 1873 [letter] Inherited instinct, *Nature*, Lond., 7:281, introducing a letter without title from William Huggins, *ibid.*, 7:281–282 (Bii 170, F1757). 1873 Origin of certain instincts, *Nature*, Lond., 7:417–418 (Bii 172, F1760). 1883 The late Mr. Darwin on instinct, *Nature*, Lond., 29:128–129 (F1804), summary, with last 3 paragraphs in full, of a communication by Romanes to Linnean Society of London, published in full in *Mental evolution in animals*, 1883 q.v.

Institucion Libre de Ensenanza, Madrid CD Honorary Professor 1877.

Institut *see* Académie des Sciences.

Ipswich Museum portraits Set of 60 lithographs of distinguished scientists prepared 1850, for British Association meeting at Ipswich 1851. Paid for by G. Ransome, agricultural instrument maker. Portrait of CD is by T. H. Maguire, dated 1849, printed by M. & N. Hanhart. CD is seated in a Down House study chair. This is the only engraving of CD from life. Copies should carry a facsimile signature 'Charles Darwin' centre and a raised blind Ipswich Museum stamp with arms bottom right.

Iquique Peru. 1835 Jul.13–14 *Beagle* at; Jul.13 CD landed and made short journey to saltpetre mines.

Ireland 1827 May CD visited Belfast & Dublin at end of a tour in Scotland; his only visit to Ireland.

Isaac, Charlotte *see* Holland.

Irwin ? a local clergyman near Downe—CD–Innes 219.

Isle of Wight Hampshire. 1837 Nov. CD visited C. D. Fox there. 1846 Sep.12 CD & ED visited on day trip from British Association meeting at Southampton. 1858 Jul.17–Aug.12 Family holiday at Sandown & Shanklin. 1868 Jul.17–Aug.20 Family holiday at Freshwater.

Italian First editions in: *Journal of researches* (F211) 1872; *Coral reefs* (F818) 1888; *On the tendency of species to form varieties* (F368) 1960; *Origin of species* (F706) 1864; *Fertilisation of orchids* (F823) 1883; *Climbing plants* (F863) 1878; *Variation under domestication* (F920) 1876; *Descent of man* (F1088) 1871; *Expression of the emotions* (F1200) 1878; *Insectivorous plants* (F1242) 1878; *Cross and self fertilisation* (F1269) 1878; *Different forms of flowers* (F1299) 1884; *Movement in plants* (F1347) 1884; *Vegetable mould and worms* (F1407) 1882; *Autobiography* (F1522) 1919.

J

Jackson, Benjamin Daydon 1846–1927. Botanist on staff at Kew, in charge of *Index Kewensis*. Secretary to Linnean Society. *Darwiniana*, 1910, contains three essays published elsewhere, 1909, republished as a pamphlet with alterations; one gives a list of plants named after CD.

Jackson, William 1875 J was a manservant at Down House, succeeded Parslow as butler in that year. Retired c1882. 1882 J attended CD's funeral, walking in procession with Parslow behind the family mourners, but ahead of the official representatives. J made model of Down House in cork, once in Galton Collection at University College London, now at Down House.

Jäger, Gustav 1832–1917. Zoologist of Stuttgart. 1875 CD to J, thanking him for copy of his book *In Sachen Darwins insbesondere contra Wigand*, 1874. Author of *Die Darwin'sche Theorie und ihre Stellung zu Moral und Religion*, [1869].

Jameson, Robert 1774–1854. Mineralogist & natural historian. Prof. Natural History Edinburgh 1804–1854. CD found his lectures 'incredibly dull'—Autobiography. 1808 J founded Wernerian Society, Edinburgh. 1823 J founded Plinian Society, Edinburgh. 1854 CD to Hooker, about Forbes 'I wish, however, he would not praise that old dry stick Jameson'—MLi 79. DNB.

Jamieson, Thomas Francis 1829–1913. Geologist of Ellon, Aberdeen. Correspondent of CD. 1862 J was the first person to give correct solution to parallel roads of Glenroy, *Quart.J.geol.Soc.*, 19:235–259, 1863.

Jane Housemaid at Down House ?1865–1879. Not the same person as Emily Jane.

Janet, Paul 1823–1899. French philosophical writer & entomologist. Prof. Logic Lycée Louis le grand Paris 1857–1864. Prof. Philosophy Sorbonne Paris 1864– . 1866 CD to Wallace, 'As for M. Janet, he is a metaphysician, and such gentlemen are so acute that I think they often misunderstand common folk'—LLiii 46.

Japanese First editions in: *Journal of researches* (F216) 1954; *Coral reefs* (F319) 1949; *Origin of species* (F718) 1896; *Descent of man* (F1100) 1949; *Different forms of flowers* (F1300) 1949; *Autobiography* (F1524a) 1972.

Jardine, Sir William, Bart 1800–1874. Scottish cabinet naturalist, especially of birds. 7th *Bart*. 1860 CD to Lyell, CD had had a letter from J who opposed CD on evolution, but his attack on CD's ornithological accuracy is worthless—Carroll 201. J's relict Hyacinth Symonds m Hooker. DNB.

Jebb, Sir Richard Claverhouse 1841–1905. Greek scholar. Kt 1900 FBA 1902. Prof. Greek Glasgow 1875–1889, Cambridge 1887–1905. J's wife, Caroline Reynolds, was aunt of Maud du Puy, wife of *Sir* George Howard D. J was much in Cambridge Darwin circle after CD's death.—*Period piece*; DNB.

Jeens, Charles Henry 1827–1879. 1874 J made steel engraving from Rejlander photograph of CD for *Nature*, Lond. Jun.4.

Jeffreys, John Gwyn 1809–1885. Malacologist. FRS 1840. 1860 J was anti-*Origin*, letter referred to in LLii 260. DNB.

Jenkin, Henry Charles Fleeming 1833–1885. Electrician & engineer. FRS 1865. Prof. Engineering University College London 1865, Edinburgh 1868. 1867 CD to Kingsley, the review is telling and hostile, but lacking in knowledge. 1869 Francis D, 'my father, as I believe, felt the review to be the most valuable ever made on his views'—LLiii 107. 1869 CD to Hooker, 'Fleeming Jenkins [sic] has given me much trouble, but has been of more real use to me than any other essay or review'—MLii 379. DNB.

Jenner, Sir William, Bart 1815–1898. Physician. KCB 1877 1st *Bart* 1868 FRS 1864. Physician at University College London 1854–1879. 1863 CD consulted—Journal.

Jenyns, Leonard, *later* **Blomefield** 1800–1893. Anglican priest & naturalist. Vicar of Swaffham Bulbeck, Cambridgeshire. J changed his surname on inheritance, when he moved to Bath c1845. Henslow's brother-in-law. 1845 CD about J 'At first I disliked him, from his somewhat grim and sarcastic expression . . . but I was completely mistaken, and found him very kind-hearted and with a good stock of humour'. Also a biographical note—MLi 49. 1859 CD sent J 1st edition of *Origin*. 1862 J wrote *Memoir of John Stevens Henslow*, with recollections by CD 51–55 (F830). 1887 *Chapters in my life*, for private circulation, Bath; reprint with additions 1889, Bath.

Jesperson, P. Helveg 1949 Charles Darwin and Dr Grant,

Lychnos, 159–167. A useful source of information on CD's time at Edinburgh University.

Jesse, George Anti-vivisectionist. 1881 J had written, very politely, to CD on the subject. 1881 J's pamphlet (F1356) reprints CD's letter to Frithiof Holmgren, which had appeared in *The Times*, Apr.18 (Bii 226, F1352).

John Coachman at Down house in late 1880s.

John *see* Edmonston.

John *see* Jordan.

Johnson, Charles Richardson ?–c1882. Acting mate on return of *Beagle* from 2nd voyage. *Vice-Admiral* 1879—LLi 221.

Johnson, Henry Physician. 1826 J was at Edinburgh with CD. CD to his sister Caroline, saying that J had changed his lodgings for the 3rd time. 1880 CD to J about excavations at Wroxeter and about worms—N&R 74. J was still on Medical Register in 1883.

Jones 1838 CD to Lyell, 'old Jones' was going to quarrel at the Newcastle meeting of British Association, and an anecdote about J's liking for a lot of wine. CD dined with.—LLi 295, Carroll 10.

Jones, Henry Bence 1814–1873. Physician. FRS 1846. CD's physician for many years. Of St Georges Hospital. 1866 Apr.27 CD met at Royal Society soirée. DNB.

Jones, R. 1854 CD to Lyell, about a meeting of the Geological Society, J had told CD about Prestwich's views on red clay with flints. J may be the same as '– Jones' above. Perhaps Thomas Rymer J, 1810–1880, Physician & naturalist. FRS 1834. Prof. Comparative Anatomy King's College London 1836–1874; but why 'old Jones' when T. R. J. was younger than CD.

Jordan, John 1839 end of, Manservant at CD's house, 12 Upper Gower St, London.

Journal *see* Darwin's Journal.

Journal and Remarks *see Journal of researches* 1839.

Journal of Researches CD's first published book and probably his most read. He sold the copyright of the 2nd edition to John Murray in 1845 for £150 and so made no profit from it or from its many subsequent printings or translations. GB editions: 1839 as Vol.3 of R. Fitz-Roy, editor, *Narrative of . . . H.M.S. Adventure and Beagle*, sub-title Journal and Remarks (F10), CD's text was completed and printed in 1838; 1839 Independent issue of same text, *Journal of researches into the geology and* *natural history* etc. (F11); 1840 reissue (F12); 1845 2nd edition, *Journal of researches into the natural history and geology* etc. (F13); 1860 edition from stereos with postscript added (F20); 1890 edition with postscript incorporated in text, final definitive edition (F58); 1890 first Murray illustrated edition (F59); English braille edition, based on 1890, 1916 (F168). *See also Voyage of a naturalist, Voyage of the Beagle.* First foreign editions, in whole or in part; the 1st German is the only translation based on the 1st English: German (F188) 1844; USA (F16) 1846; French (F180) 1860; Russian (F226) 1870; Swedish (F259) 1872; German of 2nd edition (F189) 1875; Danish (F174) 1876; Italian (F211) 1877; Polish (F223) 1887; Dutch (F176) 1891; Greek (F206) 1900; Spanish (F249) 1902; Hungarian (F208) 1913; Hebrew (F207) 1930; Armenian (F169), Estonian (F179), Serbo-Croat (F244) 1949; Slovene (F248) 1950; Georgian (F187) 1951; Japanese (F216) 1954; Czech (F171) 1956; Romanian (F225) 1958; Lithuanian (F222) 1963; Bulgarian (F170) 1967.

Judd, John Wesley 1840–1916. Geologist. FRS 1877. Prof. Geology Royal College of Science London. Correspondent and visitor to Down House—LLiii 352, MLi 375. DNB.

Jukes, Joseph Beete 1811–1869. Geologist. FRS 1853. Director of the Geological Survey of Ireland 1850–1869. 1860 J was pro-*Origin*—LLii 293. 1848 CD to Hooker, 'The man, not content with moustaches, now sports an entire beard, and I am sure thinks himself like Jupiter tonans'—MLi 65. DNB.

Justice of the Peace 1857 CD appointed; his only recorded attendance on bench 1859—LLii 225. 1881 CD to Romanes, he was, as a magistrate giving orders daily to allow pigs to cross roads, at a time of swine fever

K

Kaiserlich-Koenigliche Zoologisch-Botanische Gesellschaft, Vienna CD Honorary Member 1867.

Kaiserliche Akademie der Wissenschaften Vienna. CD Foreign Corresponding Member 1871; Honorary Foreign Member 1875.

Karslake, Sir John Burgess 1821–1881. Barrister. Kt 1866. Attorney-General 1867–1868, 1874–1875. Member of Vivisection Commission 1875—LLiii 201. DNB.

Kay, James Phillips *see* Shuttleworth.

Kay, William 1807–1861. Physician of Clifton, Gloucestershire. Naturalist friend of CD at Edinburgh.

Kay-Shuttleworth, Sir James Phillips, Bart *see* Shuttleworth.

Keeling Islands *see* Cocos Keeling Islands.

Keen, Mr & Mrs British residents in Argentine. 1833 Nov.22–26 CD visited their estancia on r.Beguelo (CD spells Berguelo) and collected a skull of 'Megatherium', actually *Toxodon*, from a nearby hill, Cerro Perico flaco (CD calls it Cerro del Pedro Flaco)—Winslow, *J.hist.Geogr.*, 1:347–360, 1975.

Keith, Sir Arthur 1866–1955. Surgeon, anthropologist & darwinian. Kt 1921 FRS 1913. K was much involved in the purchase of Down House for the British Association and its later acquisition by the Royal College of Surgeons. K retired to Homefield, a small house on the w side of the Down House estate. 1942 A postscript to Darwin's Vegetable mould through the action of worms, *Nature*, Lond., 149:716. 1955 *Darwin revalued*, which contains a last chapter on the later history of Down House, as well as much other information which is not available elsewhere.

Kelvin, Baron *see Sir* William Thomson.

Kemp, William Scottish amateur geologist of Galashiels, Selkirk. 'Almost a working man', 'partially educated', 'a most careful and ingenious observer'. 1843 K sent CD seeds from a sandpit near Melrose, found under 25′ of white sand, which germinated into a common *Rumex*, an unrecognized species of *Atriplex* and two species of *Polygonum*. The case in the end not proven—MLii 243–244, Darwin-Henslow 151.

Kempson, Louisa Frances *see* Wedgwood.

Kempson, William John m 1864 Louisa Frances Wedgwood and had offspring.

Kendall, Thomas Early missionary for Church Missionary Society in New Zealand, arriving 1814. Not in holy orders but a schoolmaster. 1823 K was dismissed for living with a Maori girl and then went native. Author of the first book published in New Zealand, *The New Zealander's first book*, 1815, Sydney printed. 1835 CD mentions K (spelling Kendal) in Moral state of Tahiti, New Zealand etc., 1836, q.v. in company with John King, but CD did not meet.

Kennedy, Dr Benjamin Hall 1804–1889. Classical scholar. Headmaster of Shrewsbury School 1836–1866. Regius Prof. Greek Cambridge 1867–1889. 1881 Oct. CD saw 'old Dr. Kennedy of Shrewsbury' at Cambridge. DNB.

Kensington Square London, No.21, home of R. B. Lichfield 1883–1903.

Kent, William ?–1802 Assistant Surgeon on return of *Beagle* from 2nd voyage, 1836 Oct. Surgeon 1838.

Kerner von Marilaun, Anton, Freiherr 1831–1898. German botanist. 1878 CD wrote prefatory letter to translation by W. Ogle of K's book *Die Schützmittel der Blüthen gegen unberufene Gaste*, Innsbruck 1876, *Flowers and their unbidden guests*, London (F1318).

Kew Gardens *see* Royal Botanic Gardens, Kew.

Kew Index *see* *Index Kewensis*.

Keynes, Sir Geoffrey 1887– . Physician & bibliographer. Kt 1955. m 1917 Margaret Elizabeth Darwin 4s. WH.

Keynes, Richard Darwin 1919– s of *Sir* Geoffrey K. FRS 1959. Prof. Physiology Cambridge 1972– . The only member of the present generation of Ds to carry the continuous D Fellowship of Royal Society into 6th generation from Erasmus D [I]. WH.

Keyserling, Alexander Friederich Michael Leberecht Arthur von, Count 1815–1891. Russian palaeontologist. K is referred to in Historical sketch in *Origin*. *see* J. A. Roger, *Isis*, 64:487–488. 1860 K wrote to CD about *Origin LLii 261*.

King, Colonel of Hythe, Kent. CD corresponded with K about pigeons—*Variation* i 184.

King, Sir George 1840–1909. Physician & botanist. KCIE 1898 FRS 1887. Superintendent of Botanical Garden Calcutta 1871–1898. 1873 K sent CD *Aldrovanda* for *Insectivorous plants*, and also helped with *Worms*—LLiii 216. DNB.

King, John First missionary for Church Missionary Society in New Zealand, arrived 1810. Not in holy orders, a shoemaker by trade. 1835 Dec. CD met *Mrs* K and their son, but K was away—Moral state of Tahiti, New Zealand etc., 231.

King, Philip Gidley 1817–1904. Naval officer. Midshipman on 1st & 2nd voyages of *Beagle*. s of Philip Parker K. CD very friendly with. 1836 Feb. K left *Beagle* to remain with his father at Sydney. 1880– K was a member of Legislative Council of Sydney—LLi 221. K drew the diagrammatic layout of *Beagle* which first appeared in *Journal of researches* 1890; a photograph of the original with mss caption is at Down House.

King, Philip Parker 1793–1856. Naval Officer. FRS 1824. K's father was 1st Governor of New South Wales, 1758–1808. Father of Philip Gidley K q.v. K commanded, as *Captain*, *Adventure* on 1st voyage of *Adventure & Beagle*. Collected plants which Robert Brown was dilatory in identifying. Settled in Australia with rank of Rear Admiral. 1836 Jan.23 CD spent evening with K at Dunheved outside Sydney. DNB.

King, Richard ?1811–1876. Surgeon & naturalist. K was on *Sir George Back's* arctic expedition 1833–1835. c1850 CD listened to him and other arctic men discussing expeditions at Athenaeum—MLi 58. DNB.

King George's Sound Western Australia. 1836 Mar.6–14 *Beagle* anchored there, CD landed.

Kingsley, Charles 1819–1875. Anglican clergyman, author & naturalist. Curate and later Rector of Eversleigh, Hants; Canon of Westminster 1873. 1859 CD sent 1st edition *Origin* to, 'That the Naturalist . . . should have sent a scientist like me his book . . .'—LLii 287. 1860 CD to Henslow telling him that the 'celebrated author and divine' who is quoted in 2nd edition *Origin* was K—MLi 174. 1867 CD to K about *Duke* of Argyll's *Reign of law* and Fleeming Jenkin's review of *Origin*. Sent K 4th edition *Origin*—Carroll 330. EB DNB.

Kinnordy nr Kirriemuir, Forfarshire. Home of *Sir* Charles Lyell's father and later his.

Kippist, Richard 1812–1882. Botanist. Librarian of Linnean Society 1842–1881. CD often wrote to K to borrow books. DNB.

Kirby Cambridge friend of CD. 1831 K was interested in going with CD to Canary Islands. Not traced.

Klein, Rudolf Emmanuel Botanist. K helped CD with *Insectivorous plants*.

Knight, Thomas Andrew 1759–1838. Botanist. FRS 1805. A distinguished plant hybridizer. CD drew extensively on his work in *Variation*. Knight's Law, sometimes called Knight-Darwin Law, 'nature abhors perpetual self fertilisation' —MLii 250. *see* Francis D, *Ann.Bot.*, 13:13, 1899. *A selection from the physiological horticultural papers . . . a sketch of his life,* London 1841.

Knole Park Sevenoaks, Kent. Seat of *Baron* Sackville. 1846 Sep.22 CD, ED & Susan D made day trip to.

Koch, Fr. C. L. 1799–1852. German mineralogist. 1851 K sent CD fossil cirripedes. CD sent him copy of *Fossil Cirripedia—Lychnos*, 1948–1949: 206–210.

Kölliker, Rudolph Albert von 1817–1905. Swiss biologist. Prof. Physiology & Comparative Anatomy Zurich 1844. Prof. Physiology, Microscopy & Comparative Anatomy Würzburg 1847. At some time between 1860 & 1864 K visited Down House—LLiii 29. 1860 CD to Huxley who had suggested K as possible translator of *Origin* into German—MLi 139. 1861 *Entwicklungsgeschichte des Menschen und der höheren Thiere,* Leipzig.

Koeniglich-Bayarische Akademie der Wissenschaften Munich. CD Foreign Member 1878.

Koeniglich-Preussische Akademie der Wissenschaften Berlin. CD Corresponding Member 1863, Fellow 178.

Kollmann, Julius Constantin Ernst 1834–1918. 1876 K to CD on atavism and extra digits—MLi 393, *Variation* I 459.

Kongeligt Dansk Videnskabernes Selskab Copenhagen. CD Fellow 1879.

Kongliga Svenska Vetenskaps–Akademien Stockholm. CD Foreign Member 1865.

Kongliga Vetenskaps-Societeten Uppsala. CD Fellow 1860.

Koninklijke Natuurkundige Vereeniging in Nederlandsche-Indie Batavia. CD Corresponding Member 1880.

Korean First editions in: *Origin of species* (F732) 1957; *Autobiography* (F1525) 1965.

Kovalevskïi, Aleksandr Onofrievich 1840–1901. Embryologist. K was the first to point out the chordate affinities shown by ascidian tadpoles. Brother of V.O.K.

Kovalevskïi, Vladimir Onufrievich 1842–1883. Brother of A.O.K. Committed suicide. 1867 visited Down House and again in 1870. 1867–1868 K translated *Variation* into Russian.

Krause, Ernst 1839–1903. German botanist. 1879 Feb. K's biography of Erasmus Darwin [I] appeared in *Kosmos*, the number being a Gratulationsheft for CD's 70th birthday. 1879 An English translation, with introductory matter by CD had K's own alterations to his part (F1319). It was this edition which so offended Samuel Butler. Butler's copy with his mss notes is in the British Library. 1880 German translation of the 1879 English edition (F1323). 1885 *Charles Darwin und sein Verhältniss zu Deutschland*, Leipzig. 1885 *Gesammelte kleinere Schriften*, Bd I contains Humble bees, translated from CD's unpublished mss (F1584).

Krohn, August David 1804–1891. Invertebrate anatomist of Bonn. 1860 CD to Lyell, K had pointed out errors in interpretation of CD's anatomy of cirripedes 'with the utmost gentleness and pleasantness' in *Wiegmann's Archiv*, 25 & 26—LLii 345. CD's recanting of his views is in *Nat.Hist.Rev.*, 3:115 (F1722)—LLiii 2.

Kruell, Gustav Artist. 1843–1907. 1887 Wood engraving from Elliot & Fry photograph for LLiii fpce. 1884 Wood engraving from Maull & Fox photograph, the profile, for *Harper's Mag.*, Oct.—LLi fpce.

Kynaston, Sir Edward, Bart 1775–1839. 2nd *Bart* 1822. Vicar of Kinnerley, Shropshire. 1831 Sep.6 CD to his sister Susan, describes Fitz-Roy as a 'dark but handsome edition of Mr Kynaston'—LLi 206.

L

Lacaze-Duthiers, Felix Joseph Henri de 1821–1901. French invertebrate zoologist. 1872 CD to Quatrefages, 'I am gratified to hear that M. Lacaze-Duthiers will vote for me [for Académie des Sciences] for I have long honoured his name'—LLiii 155. The election was for the zoology section. CD did not get in, but was elected for the botany section in 1878.

Lack, David Lambert 1910–1974. Ornithologist. FRS 1951. Director Edward Grey Institute Oxford 1945–1974. 1946 The Galapagos finches, *Occ.Pap.Calif.Acad.Sci.*, No.21. 1947 *Darwin's finches*, London. WH.

Lacy, Dyson Australian, of Aramao, Bacao nr Rockhampton, Queensland. 1868 L answered CD's *Queries about expression*.

Lake District *see* Coniston, Patterdale.

Lamarck, Jean Baptiste Pierre Antoine de Monet, Chevalier de 1744–1829. French naturalist & evolutionist. 1861 CD discusses L's views in para.2 and footnote of Historical sketch, 'This justly celebrated naturalist'. 'He first did the eminent service of arousing the attention to the probability of all change . . . being the result of law, and not of miraculous interposition'. 1844 CD to Hooker, 'Heaven forfend me from Lamarck's nonsense of a "tendency to progression", "adaptations for the slow willing of animals", &c.!'—LLii 23. 1844 CD to Hooker, 'Lamarck's [book] which is veritable rubbish'—LLii 29. c1850 L 'In his absurd though clever work has done the subject much harm, as has Mr Vestiges'—LLii 29. L's main work, *Philosophie zoologique,* Paris 1809.

Lamont, Sir James, Bart 1828–1913. Sportsman, traveller & geologist. 1st *Bart* 1910. MP. Of Knockdow, Argyllshire. ?1860 Mar.5 CD to L about evolution—MLi 143. 1861 *Seasons with the sea-horses*, London; L sent CD a copy; CD replied about whales and bears. The book, p.17, contains an important statement about the relationship between British red grouse and Scandinavian willow grouse, and, p.277, quotes whale-bear story, from 1st edition of Origin p.184, in full, the only reproduction of it in CD's lifetime except in 1860 USA editions of *Origin*—MLi 179.

Lane, Edward Wickstead ?–1889. Proprietor of Moor Park hydropathic establishment, nr Farnham, Surrey; later at Sudbrooke Park. Petersham, Surrey. Son-in-law of *Lady* Drysdale. 1882 L was on 'Personal Friends invited' list for CD's funeral. L gives his recollections of CD in W. B. Richardson, *Lecture on Charles Darwin*—LLi 131 with quotation.

Lane, H. B. Australian of Belfast, Victoria, police magistrate and warden. 1867 L answered CD's *Queries about expression*.

Lane, Richard James 1800–1872. Physician. 1860 L was at Sudbrooke Park hydropathic establishment, Petersham, Surrey, which CD visited in that year. ? Brother of E.W.L.

Langdon, Miss Governess to the Wedgwoods at Maer. 1854 L was taken in by Sarah Elizabeth Wedgwood [II] at The Ridge, Hartfield. 'The most unattractive old lady I ever saw, nearly stone deaf, with a harsh countenance, and a voice like a parrot's'—EDii 155.

Langton, Algernon 1781–? Soldier, later Anglican clergyman. m 1820 Marianne Drewe 1s Bennet L. Uncle of Charles L.

Langton, Bennet 1822–? Only c of Algernon L.

Langton, Charles 1801–1886. Anglican clergyman. Nephew of Algernon L. m1 Charlotte Wedgwood 1s. m2 1863 Emily Catherine Darwin. s.p. L had before 1831 been tutor to *Lord* Craven's children. 1832–1841 Vicar of Onibury nr Ludlow. 1841 L lost his faith and resigned living. L lived at Maer 1841–1847. 1847–1863 L lived at Hartfield Grove, Hartfield, Sussex, which he left after death of 1st wife. 1863 CD & ED stayed there—MLi 240. L moved to Shrewsbury and, after death of 2nd wife, moved into lodgings 'at Mrs Tasker's'.

Langton, Charlotte *see* Wedgwood.

Langton, Edmund 1841–1875. Only c of Charles L & Charlotte Wedgwood. m 1867 Emily Caroline Langton Massingberd 1s 2d. 1. Mildred; 2. Steven Massingberd who m 1895 Margaret Lushington; 3. Diana who m 1896 *Capt.* A. A. Montgomery. CD's 2nd cousin.

Langton, Emily Caroline *see* Massingberd.   ·

Langton, Emily Catherine *see* Darwin.

Lankester, Sir Edwin Ray 1847–1929. Zoologist. KCB 1907 FRS 1875. Prof. Zoology & Comparative Anatomy University College London 1874–1890, Oxford 1891–1898. Director

British Museum (Natural History) 1898–1907. 1872 CD to L, about reproduction of elephants 'I can clearly see that you will some day become our first star in Natural History'—MLi 336. 1875 CD to ?, about L being blackballed for election to Linnean Society, 'he is not a personal friend only an acquaintance'—FUL 114. 1879 CD to L, CD is glad that L is to spend more time on original research, does 'splendid work'—Carroll 565. 1880 *Degeneration: a chapter on Darwinism*. 1881 CD wrote a testimonial for L's application for Edinburgh Chair, ?printed. L held it briefly in plurality—Carroll 604. DNB.

Larson, Dr Assistant to W. H. Flower at Royal College of Surgeons, although never on the official staff. 1878 Flower to CD, on deformity in goose wings, gives L's report—Carroll 551 & p.209. *See* R. A. Blair.

Latter, Mrs 1858 Governess at Down House for about a year.

Latvian First editions in: *Origin of species* (F736) 1914–1915; *Autobiography* (F1526) 1953.

Laugel, Antoine August 1830–1914. French geologist. 1860 L gave a favourable review of *Origin* in *Rev.deux Mondes*, Apr.—LLii 305.

Laurence, Samuel 1812–1884. Artist. 1853 Chalk drawing of CD is at Down House; there is a study for it at Botany School Cambridge.

Lawless, Hon. Mrs 1876 CD to Romanes, CD had corresponded with L about fertilisation of plants; she sent CD 'a very good manuscript'—*Life of Romanes* 56.

Layard, Edgar Leopold 1824–1900. Naturalist & traveller. L provided CD with information for *Variation*—Carroll 143.

Leaves 1881 [Letter] The movement of leaves, *Nature*, Lond., 23:603–604 (Bii 728, F1794). 1881 Leaves injured at night by free radiation, *Nature*, Lond., 24:459 (Bii 231, F1796).

Lecoq, Henri 1802–1871. French botanist. 1862 CD to Hooker, 'Here is a good joke: I saw an extract from Lecoq "Géograph.Bot." and ordered it and hoped it was a good sized pamphlet, and nine thick volumes have arrived'. The work is *Études sur la géographie botanique de l'Europe*, 9 vols, Paris 1854–1858—LLiii 301. 1863 CD to Hooker, L is a believer in change of species—LLiii 26.

Lee, Rev. Samuel 1783–1852. Historian & orientalist. Prof. Arabic Cambridge 1819–1831, Regius Prof. History Cambridge 1831–1848. 1838 CD dined with L at Trinity College.

Leggett, William Henry 1816–1882. Botanist of New York. L helped CD with information on forms of flowers.

Lehr, Christian Wilhelm Jacob 1856–?1898. Sculptor. Bust, not from life but before 1887, listed in LLiii without whereabouts. At Oxford University Museum.

Leidy, Joseph 1823–1891. American zoologist. Prof. Anatomy Pennsylvania 1853– . 1860 Feb. CD to L, welcoming L's partial acceptance of CD's views on evolution, 'I have never for a moment doubted, that though I cannot see my errors, that much in my book will be proved erroneous'—Carroll 202.

Leighton, William Allport 1805–1899. Anglican clergyman & lichenologist. Schoolfellow of CD at *Mr* Case's school, Shrewsbury—LLi 28.

Leith Midlothian, the port of Edinburgh, 1838 Jun. CD went to L by boat from London on his way to Glen Roy.

Leith Hill Place nr Dorking, Surrey. Home of Josiah Wedgwood [III] c1847–1880. Also of Margaret Susan W, *Mrs* Vaughan Williams.

Lepadidae, fossil of Great Britain *see* Cirripedia, British fossil.

Lesquereux, Leo 1806–1889. Swiss palaeobotanist, settled in USA. 1865 CD to Hooker, 'he says that he is converted [to evolution] because my books make the Birth of Christ, Redemption by Grace, etc., plain to him'—Mli 260.

Lessona, Michele 1823–1894. Prof. Zoology Turin. L translated four of CD's works into Italian. 1882 Commemorazione di Carlo Darwin, *Atti Accad.Sci.Torino*, 18:709–718. 1883 *Carlo Darwin*, Rome.

Lester, James Petty Officer Cooper on 2nd voyage of *Beagle*.

Letters Letters to and from CD, in whole or in part, are contained in the following main collections:

1887 *Life and letters*, 3 vols.

1903 *More letters*, 2 vols.

1904, 1915 *Emma Darwin*, 2 vols.

1909 Letters to Trimen in E. B. Poulton, *Darwin and the Origin*.

1915 Letters to Wallace in J. Marchant, *Alfred Russel Wallace*.

1939 Letters to Asa Gray, *Historical Records Survey*, Boston.

1959 de Beer, *Notes & Records Roy.Soc.*, 14:12–66, which also lists about thirty other sources of one or a few letters.

1961 de Beer, *Ann.Sci.*, 17:81–115, a continuation of de B's 1959 paper.

1961 Letters to Innes in R. M. Stecher, *Ann.Sci.*, 17:201–258.
1967 Letters to Henslow in Nora Barlow, *Darwin and Henslow*.
1969 Letters to Bates in R. M. Stecher, *Ann.Sci.*, 25:1–47, 95–125.
1976 Letters at American Philosophical Society, calendared by P. T. Carroll.

Letters on Geology Extracts from letters sent to Henslow by CD when on the *Beagle* voyage were read to the Cambridge Philosophical Society. 1835 these extracts were printed, without CD's knowledge, for private circulation amongst members of the Society, by Cambridge University Press. The pamphlet is not dated, although the preface is dated Nov.16, 1835 (F1). A type facsimile, also for private distribution, was issued in 1960 (F4). The letters are printed in full in *Darwin & Henslow* (F5, F1598), 1967. Foreign editions: German (F6) 1891; Russian (F7) 1959.

Lettington Gardener at Down House 1854–1872. Alive 1895 Jul. L of CD 'He moons about in the garden, and I have seen him standing doing nothing before a flower for ten minutes at a time. If only he had something to do I believe he would be better'—Lubbock, *Darwin-Wallace celebrations of the Linnean Society of London*, 57–58, 1908. 1882 L was on 'Personal Friends invited' list for CD's funeral.

Leuckart, Carl Georg Friedrich Rudolf 1822–1898. Prof. Zoology Leipzig. 1864 CD to Falconer, L was an early convert to evolution.

Lewes, George Henry 1817–1878. Man of letters. Common law husband of Mary Ann Cross [George Eliot] 1854–1878. 1868 Feb. L reviewed *Variation* favourably and 'gratifyingly'—LLiii 76. 1874 CD & ED attended a seance at Litchfield's house in London with L and George Eliot. DNB.

Lewy, Naphtali (Naphtali Hallevi). 1840–1894. Rabbi & humanistic writer of Radom, Russian Poland. 1876 L wrote to CD about his pamphlet *Toledoth Adam* [The descent of man], 60 pp, Vienna 1874, which is the first to introduce CD's views into rabbinical literature—MLi 365. 1891 L's book *Nachlat Naphtali*, Pressburg, prints extracts from his correspondence with CD. L died at Southport, Lancashire.

Leyden, University of 1875 CD Honorary MD.

Liebre, La 1832 Sep.11 Schooner hired by Fitz-Roy from James Harris, resident at Rio Negro, Argentine, for 8 lunar months, with Schooner *La Paz*. Commanded by *Lieut*. J. C. Wickham who had *Lieut*. B. J. Sulivan in *La Paz* under his command. Surveyed SE coast of Argentine.

Liesk, Mr Resident in Cocos Keeling Islands. 1836 Apr.3 CD met with J. C. Ross.

Life and letters 1887 Francis D, editor, *The life and letters of Charles Darwin, including an autobiographical chapter*, 3 vols, London; three other printings in 1887 and one in 1888 have small corrections (F1452–1457). Contains CD's autobiography in Vol.1, 26–160. Facsimile (F1507) 1969. Foreign editions of whole work: USA (F1456) 1887: German (F1515) 1887–1888; French (F1514) 1888; Norwegian (F1528) 1889. *See also Charles Darwin: his life*, 1892, which is largely, but not entirely an abridged version.

Lindley, John 1799–1865. Botanist FRS 1828. Prof. Botany University College London 1829–1860. 1843 CD sent L some seeds which had been found by W. Kemp under 25' of white sand—MLii 243. 1853 L was in competition with CD for award of Royal Medal of Royal Society. 1856 CD to Hooker, suggesting that L was worth a Copley Medal. L got a Royal in 1857, never a Copley—MLi 88. DNB.

Linnean Club Dining club of Linnean Society, 1861 CD dined at with Thomas Bell.

Linnean Society of London CD Fellow 1854– . He used the Library a great deal. 1856 CD sent £20 for some special purpose 'with heavy groans'—MLi 94. 1881 The Society commissioned John Collier's oil portrait of CD. It hangs in their rooms at Burlington House.

Linum 1863 On the existence of two forms, and on their reciprocal sexual relation in several species of the genus *Linum*, *J.Proc.Linn.Soc.(Bot.)*, 7:69–83 (Bii 93, F1723). French translation 1863 *Ann.Sci.nat.Bot.*, 19:204–295, with CD's 1862 papers on *Primula* & *Catasetum*.

Lion, The Inn, Wyle Cop, Shrewsbury. 1835 CD to his sister Susan, CD considered staying there when he got back from *Beagle* voyage, travelling by coach from Falmouth, to avoid waking family in middle of the night; in the event he reached Shrewsbury in the early morning. It is still there as an hotel.

Litchfield, Henrietta *see* Darwin.

Litchfield, Richard Buckley 1831–1903. Scholar & philanthropist. m 1871 Aug.31, at Downe Church, Henrietta Emma D. d.s.p. L worked on the legal side of the Ecclesiastical

Commission. A founder of the Working Men's College (later Birkbeck College) London. L lived at 4 Bryanston Square; 1883 moved to 21 Kensington Square. *See Period piece* ch.7.

Lithuanian First editions in: *Journal of researches* (F222) 1963; *Origin of species* (F738) 1959; *Autobiography* (F1527) 1959.

Little Etruria House nr Etruria Hall, 1st home of Josiah Wedgwood [II].

Liverpool Lancashire. 1818 Jul. CD visited with Erasmus Alvey D. 1838 CD passed through on return from Glen Roy.

Llangollen Denbighshire. 1831 Aug. CD visited with Sedgwick for geology.

Lloyd, Miss 1869 CD to L, sending letter from Boyd Dawkins about CD's visit to Caerdeon, Barmouth, ?owner of house where they stayed—Carroll 373.

Lloyd, Ann Susan 1789–1862. d of Gamaliel Lloyd of Yorkshire. m 1806 Leonard Horner.

Lloyd, Capt. John Augustus 1800–1884. FRS 1830. Surveyor General Mauritius 1831–1849. 1836 May 3 L entertained CD 'So well known from his examination of the Isthmus of Panama'—*J.Researches*, 1845, 485. *See also* Elephant. DNB.

Loch Leven Argyllshire. 1838 Jun. CD visited on way to Glen Roy.

Lock & Whitfield Commercial photographers of London. 1958 L. Eiseley, *Darwin's century*, has on front free end paper an oval photograph, from *Men of mark*, 3rd ser., 1878, attributed to this firm. It looks like a Julia Cameron rephotographed. No other evidence that they photographed CD.

Loddiges, Conrad Nurseryman. 1838 Sep. CD visited his garden in Hackney, saw 1279 varieties of roses—Allan 123.

Lowenberg, Bert James 1905–   . American historian of evolution. 1939 L wrote introduction to calendar of CD to Asa Gray letters. 1959 *Charles Darwin: evolution by natural selection*, Boston, selections by L from CD's works.

London Stereoscopic Company Three photographs of CD were shown at British Museum (Natural History) memorial exhibition, 1909; said to have been taken c1864. *See also* Stereoscopic Company.

Long, Professor Character in E. G. E. Bulwer Lytton's novel *What will he do with it*, 4 vols, 1858, Vol.1, 284–296. CD says, in Autobiography 81, that the character was modelled on him. 'Lecture on conchology to the Gatesboro' Athenæum and Literary Institute' for which the fee was £5.5.0. He had written

Researches into the natural history of limpets, 2 vols, Post Octavo.

Longfellow, Henry Wadsworth 1807–1882. Poet. 1868 L called on CD at Freshwater, I.O.W., with brother-in-law T. C. Appleton. L m 1843 Frances Elizabeth A.

Longley, Dr ?–1868. Resident at Downe. 1868 CD to Innes, 'I was sorry to lose'—Darwin-Innes 227. L is not on physicians register.

Longueville, Cecile m 1860 Henry Parker.

Lonsdale, William 1794–1871. Soldier & geologist. L served at Waterloo. 1829–1842 Curator & Librarian Geological Society of London. 1842 CD to Lyell, CD 'had a long talk with Lonsdale, who was cheerful for the first time in his life because of a gift, which he will use on coral work'. The gift was a moiety from the Wollaston Fund—Carroll 28.

Lothian St Edinburgh. No.11 CD lodged there when a medical student 1825 Oct.–1827 Apr. In the first year his brother Erasmus Alvey D was also there. *Mrs* Mackay charged £1.16.0 per week for two bedrooms and a sitting room. She regularly let to medical students, including earlier Edward Forbes. 1888 A tablet was put up on the house commemorating CD's stay, at suggestion of Francis D. Ashworth, 1935, wrongly, numbers the house 21. John Edmonston q.v. lived at No.37 during CD's time.

Lovegrove, Mr Churchwarden at Downe Church; he and *Mrs* L are mentioned in Darwin-Innes 220,231.

Low Archipelago *see* Tuamotu.

Lowe, Henry Porter 1810–1887. Cambridge friend of CD, later Sherbrooke. b of *Viscount* S. Member of Gourmet Club.

Lowe, Rev. Richard Thomas 1802–1874. Anglican clergyman & botanist. Chaplain at Madeira. 1866 Hooker to CD, H had a letter from L on distribution of plants in Atlantic islands which was of interest to CD. DNB.

Lowe, Robert 1811–1892. Statesman. *Viscount* Sherbrooke 1880. Liberal MP for Kidderminster, later for University of London. Chancellor of the Exchequer 1868–1873. Said by Allan to have been on Barmouth reading party with CD 1828, perhaps in confusion with his b Henry; R. L. was at Oxford. L visited Down House from High Elms with Lubbock, Huxley & M. E. G. Duff 1871. DNB.

Lowell, J. A. 1860 May L reviewed *Origin* in *Christian Examiner*, Boston, 449–464.

Lowell, James Russell 1819–1891. American author & diplomat. American Minister in London 1880–1885. Pall Bearer at CD's funeral. EB.

Lubbock, Lady [Alice] *see* Fox Pitt.

Lubbock, Lady [Ellen Frances] *see* Hordern.

Lubbock, Lady [Harriet] *see* Hotham.

Lubbock, Henry James 1838–? c of *Sir* John William L. b of *Sir* John L. m Frances Mary Turton. L visited Down House with his elder brother.

Lubbock, Sir John, Bart 1834–1913. Statesman, banker & man of science. 4th *Bart* 1865 1st *Baron* Avebury 1900 FRS 1858. lc of *Sir* John William L. m1 Ellen Frances Hordern 3s 3d 1. Amy Harriet; 2. John Birkbeck; 3. Constance Mary; 4. Norma; 5. Gertrude; 6. Rolfe Arthur. m2 Alice A. L. L. Fox Pitt 3s 2d. 1. Ursula; 2. Irene; 3. Harold Fox Pitt; 4. Eric Fox Pitt; 5.Maurice Fox Pitt. Home High Elms nr Downe. L was the closest of CD's younger friends and frequent visitor to Down House from childhood. 1859 CD sent 1st edition of *Origin* to. 1865 CD to Hooker, 'Many men can make fair M.P.'s; and how few can work in science like him'—MLii 157. 1882 L suggested Westminster Abbey funeral for CD and organized letter to the Dean; served as a Pall Bearer. Biography: Hutchinson 1914. DNB EB.

Lubbock, Sir John's Hundred Books Published by George Routledge. The set includes, 1891 *Journal of researches*, (F69) as No.2; and 1894(=1895) *Origin of species*, (F445) as No.88.

Lubbock, Sir John Birkbeck, Bart 1858–1929. 5th *Bart* 1913 2nd *Baron* Avebury 1913. Eldest s of *Sir* John L. & Ellen Frances Hordern.

Lubbock, Sir John William, Bart 1803–1865. Banker, barrister & astronomer. 3rd *Bart* FRS 1829. m 1833 Harriet Hotham. Home High Elms nr Downe, which he largely rebuilt. CD's neighbour, their land marching together; on friendly terms, but not close. f of Sir John L. DNB.

Lubbock, Ursula 1885–? 2c of *Sir* John L. & Alice Fox Pitt. m 1906 *Major* Adrian Grant Duff.

Ludwig, Miss Camilla Governess at Down House 1859–1865 or later; later *Mrs* Patrick. Sister of Karl L. 1868 L translated for CD C. L. Rütimeyer, *Die Grenzen der Thierwelt; eine Betrachtung zu Darwin's Lehre*, Basel.

Ludwig, Karl b of Camilla L; an officer of the Hamburg liner S.S. *Teutonia*. L visited Down House.

Ludwig, Rudolf August Birminghold Sebastian 1812–1880.

German palaeontologist of Darmstadt. 1877 CD to L, thanking for essay dedicated to CD and referring to *Crocodilus darwini*, Fossile Crocodiliden aus der Tertiär Formation des Mainzer Beckens, *Palaeontographica,* suppl.3, Lief. 4 & 5.

Luftschifferei der Spinnen 1839 Uber der Luftschifferei der Spinnen, *Froriep's Neue Notizen aus dem Gebiete der Natur-und Heilkunde*, 11:505–509 (F1654); a translation from *J. Researches*, 1845, 187–189.

Lumb, Edward English merchant at Buenos Aires. 1833 CD stayed with. 1834 L arranged for shipment to England of a 'Megatherium' skull, actually *Toxodon*, which CD had found near the estancia of *Mr* Keen q.v., on r. Beguelo—J. H. Winslow, *J.hist.Geogr.*, 1:347–360.

Lushington, Beatrice Ann Shore *see* Smith.

Lushington, Sir Godfrey 1832–1907. Barrister & Civil Servant. KCB 1892 GCMG 1899. 5s of Stephen L. m 1865 Beatrice Ann Shore Smith. 1868 CD & ED gave luncheon to him and his wife in London—EDii 189. 1882 L and *Mrs* L on 'Family Friends invited' list for CD's funeral.

Lushington, Jane *see* Mowatt.

Lushington, Vernon 1832–1912. County Court Judge for Surrey & Berkshire 1877–1900. 4th s of Stephen Lushington 1782–1873. MP 1806–1840. m 1865 Jane Mowatt 2d. Judge of High Court of Admiralty 1838–1867. 36 Kensington Square, London, & Borden, Hampshire. 1871 Spring & 1881 Jul. L visited Down House with wife. c1869 Henrietta Emma D first met R. D. Litchfield, her future husband, at the L's London house. The L's and their 2 daughters remained family friends. Katherine (Kitty) m Leopold James Maxse; Margaret m Stephen Massingberd s of Edmund Langton. 1882 L & *Mrs* L on 'Family Friends invited' list for CD's funeral. DNB.

Lyell, Charles [I] 1767–1849. Amateur botanist & country gentleman. m 1796 – Smith, 3s 7d. Of Kinnordy, Kirriemuir, Forfarshire. 1s Charles, 2s Thomas, 3s Henry.

Lyell, Sir Charles [II], Bart 1797 Nov.14–1875 Feb.22. Geologist. Kt 1848 1st *Bart* 1864 FRS 1826 Copley Medal 1858. 1st s of Charles Lyell [I]. m 1832 Mary Elizabeth Horner d.s.p. Family home Kinnordy , Kirriemuir, Forfarshire; in London 16 Hart St, Bloomsbury Square, later 53 Harley St. Called to the Bar and practised until 1827. Prof. Geology King's College London 1831–1833. L was of independent means and worked as a geologist, the most distinguished of his age. L was a close friend and correspondent of CD, but never on the same comfortable terms as Hooker, and never stated unequivocally in print his views on CD's position in regard to evolution. Blind in old age. 1836 Oct.29 CD first met at L's house in London. 1839 ED to her sister Sarah Elizabeth Wedgwood [II], 'Mr Lyell is enough to flatten a party, as he never speaks above his breath, so that everybody keeps lowering their tone to his'—EDii 40. 1845 CD dedicated 2nd edition of *Journal of researches* to L. 1844 CD to Hooker, 'I always feel as if my books [the geologies] came half out of Lyell's brain'—MLii 117. 1858 CD to Hooker, sending H notes on L's excellence to help him award Copley Medal—MLi 445. 1859 CD sent L 1st edition of *Origin*, copy now at Down House, presented by *Sir* George Buxton Browne. 1863 CD to Hooker, 'The Lyells are coming here . . . I dread it, but I must say how much disappointed I am that he has not spoken out on species, still less on man'—LLiii 9. 1865 Feb. CD broke 6th edition of *Elements of geology* into two halves in his dislike of fat books—LLiii 35. 1874 Sep.23 CD's last letter to Lyell about Judd's views on volcanoes—LLiii 190. 1875 CD was asked by *Mrs* Henry Lyell to be a Pall Bearer at L's funeral; CD declined on grounds of ill health. L's secretary for many years was Arabella Burton Buckley q.v. Most of CD's correspondence with L is at American Philosophical Society, Philadelphia, with Calendar 1976 by P. T. Carroll. L's seven notebooks on the species problem, at Kinnordy, edited by L. G. Wilson, Yale University Press 1970. Main works: *Principles of geology*, three vols, London 1830–1833; CD's copy of Vol.1 was presented to him by Fitz-Roy; Vol.2 reached him in S. America. *Elements of geology*, London 1838, *The geological evidence of the antiquity of man*, London 1863. Biography: *Mrs* K. M. Lyell (sister-in-law), 2 vols 1881; F. D. Adams 1933; E. Bailey 1962; L. G. Wilson 1972. EB DNB.

Lyell, Lady (Charles) *see* Mary Horner.

Lyell, Lt-Col. Henry ?–1875. Indian Army Officer. 3s of Charles Lyell [I]. m 1848 Katherine Murray Horner 3s 1d. 1. Leonard b 1850; 2. Francis b 1852; 3. Arthur b 1854; 4. Rosamund b 1856.

Lyell, Katherine Murray *see* Horner.

Lyell, Miss One of Charles [I] L's daughters, probably the eldest. 1875 CD to *Miss* Buckley mentions her—LLiii 196.

Lyell, Thomas Naval Officer. 2s of Charles L [I].

Lynch, Richard Irwin 1850–1924. Botanist. On staff at Kew 1867–1879. Curator Botanic Garden Cambridge 1879–1919. 1878 L supplied CD with plants—LLiii 331. *See* Francis D, *J.Linn.Soc.Lond.(Bot.)*, 22:102.

Lyne, Mrs ?–1881. A villager at Downe who died suddenly Feb.16. 'They wanted Francis D to see her corpse; he declined 'dirty old woman'.

Lythrum salicaria 1864 On the sexual relations of the three forms of *Lythrum salicaria, J.Linn.Soc.Lond.(Bot.)*, 8:169–196 (Bii 106, F1731).

Lytton, Edward George Earle Bulwer *Baron* Lytton *see* Bulwer.

M

M 'Old M', the village blacksmith in Downe, a notable drunkard. He was converted by J. W. C. Fegan—EDii 244.

MacArthur, Sir William 1800–1882. Australian amateur botanist. Kt 1885. Member of New South Wales Legislative Council. 1857 CD dined with M in London. CD to Gray, 'a clever Australian gardener'—MLii 253. DNB.

Macaulay, Thomas Babington 1800–1859. Historian & politician. 1st *Baron* 1857. c1842 CD met at *Lord* Stanhope's house in London. EB DNB.

Macaw Cottage 12 Upper Gower St, London q.v. So-called by CD from the gaudy curtains.

McCormick, Robert 1800–1890. Surgeon on 2nd voyage of *Beagle*. 1832 Apr. M returned to England, ostensibly sick, but had quarreled with Fitz-Roy and with Wickham—J. J. Keevil, *J.R.Naval Med.Serv.*, 29:36–62, 1943; J. W. Gruber, *Brit.J. Hist.Sci.*, 4:266–282, 1969.

M'Donnell, Robert 1828–1889. Comparative anatomist of Dublin. FRS 1865. 1860, CD to Lyell, 'a first rate man', M had written to CD about the difficulties of electric organs in evolutionary theory—LLii 352. M's observations on homologous structures in skate and torpedo published in *Nat.Hist.Rev.*, 57, 1861.

Macgillivray, William 1796–1852. Ornithologist & fine field naturalist. Conservator of Museum of Royal College of Surgeons of Edinburgh 1831–1841. 1841–1852 Prof. Natural History Aberdeen. CD knew him in Edinburgh and later met in London. DNB.

Mackay, Mrs Landlady of 11 Lothian St, Edinburgh, who specialized in medical students, Lothian St being near the University. 1825 Oct.–1827 Apr. CD lodged there. Erasmus Alvey D lodged there until he qualified in Summer 1826.

Mackintosh, Catherine [I] *see* Stuart.

Mackintosh, Lady [Catherine II] *see* Allen.

Mackintosh, Catherine [III] 3c of *Sir* James M. & Catherine

Stuart. m1 *Sir* William Wiseman. m2 G. H. Turnbull.

Mackintosh, Daniel 1815–1891. Geologist. M earned his living by tuition and lecturing. 1879 CD praises his work under difficulties and writes to on erratics—LLiii 235, MLii 166, 170. Author of *The scenery of England and Wales*, London 1869. Biography: *Geol.Mag.*, 432, 1891.

Mackintosh, Elizabeth 1799–1823. 1c of *Sir* James M. & Catherine Allen. unm.

Mackintosh, Frances 1800–1889. 2c *Sir* James & Catherine Allen. m 1832 Hensleigh Wedgwood. Known as Fan and Fanny Hensleigh by the CSs. 1851 M was a partisan of Mazzini—EDii 143. 1878 M stayed at Down House, 'quite an invalid'.

Mackintosh, Sir James 1765–1832. Philosopher & statesman. Kt 1803. m1 1789 Catherine Stuart 3d. 1. Maitland, 2. Mary, 3. Catherine. m2 1798 Catherine Allen 1s 2d. 1. Elizabeth, 2. Frances, 3. Robert. M was related to the D's through 2nd marriage and some of the children were family friends. 14 Great Cumberland St and Ampthill Park. 1827 Sep. CD visited—*Journal*. CD, 'The best converser I ever listened to'—Barlow, *Autobiography* 55. M died from a chicken bone in his throat. Biography: Robert M. (son) 1836. DNB EB.

Mackintosh, Maitland 1c of *Sir* James M & Catherine Stuart. m William Erskine.

Mackintosh, Mary [I] 3c of *Sir* James M & Catherine Stuart. m Claudius Rich. On being widowed in 1831, M lived with her twice widowed father. 1849 CD lent her Lyell's *Principles of geology*—MLii 125.

Mackintosh, Mary [II] *see* Appleton.

Mackintosh, Molly *see* Mary Appleton.

Mackintosh, Robert 1806–1864. 3c of *Sir* James & Catherine Allen. m Mary Appleton 2s 1d. 1846 ED called on M at a cottage near The Grange, *Lord* Ashburton's house, when CD went to British Association meeting at Southampton. 1836 M wrote biography of his father.

Mackintosh (M'Intosh), William Carmichael 1838–1931. Invertebrate zoologist. FRS 1877. Director of Gatty Marine Laboratory, St Andrew's University. 1881 CD to M 'of whose work I have a very high opinion'. CD refused to give a testimonial to M for the Edinburgh Chair of Natural History, on the grounds that he had already given one for E. R. Lankester—Carroll 604.

Maclaren, Charles 1782–1866. Editor of *The Scotsman* & geologist. 1847 CD corresponded with M. DNB.

Maclean, Sir Donald 1820–1877. New Zealand statesman & Maori scholar. KCMG 1874. 1850 Nov.23 CD mentions M in latter to Covington; M then living in Sydney—N&R 19.

Maclear, Sir Donald 1794–1879. Kt 1860 FRS 1831. Astronomer Royal at Cape of Good Hope 1834–1870. DNB.

Macleay, William Sharp 1792–1865. Cabinet naturalist. M invented the quinary system of classification. 1839 M emigrated to New South Wales. 1859 CD to Owen, 'I have thought that perhaps my book [sc. *Origin*] might be a case like Macleay's Quinarian system [i.e. laughed at]—FUL 104. DNB.

McNab, William Ramsay 1844–1889. Botanist. Scientific Superintendent Royal Botanic Gardens, Glasnevin, Dublin. Prof. Botany Dublin 1872–1889. 1862 CD to J. Scott, 'present my thanks to Mr. McNab'—MLii 308. 1863 CD to Hooker, Scott was not happy under McNab—MLii 319.

Madagascar Squib A description of a carnivorous plant supposed to subsist on human beings. 1874 CD to Gray, 'did not perceive it was a hoax till I came to the woman'—LLiii 325.

Madonna, The 1868 Julia Margaret Cameron's pretty maid, Mary Ryan, who often sat for her. CD & family met her at Freshwater, I.O.W.—EDii 191.

Maer Hall Maer, Staffordshire, 7 miles from Stoke-on-Trent. Home of Josiah Wedgwood [II], bought 1802, moved in 1807, left 1846, on death of his wife Bessy Allen. ED born there and married at St Peter's church from there. CD was a frequent visitor there in his youth especially for the shooting, and after his return from *Beagle* voyage, for his courting.

Magendie, François 1783–1855. Physiologist. Prof. Medicine Collège de France 1831–1855. 1881 Apr.22 CD in letter to *The Times* refers to the cruelty of his experiments 'some half a century ago'.

Maguire, Thomas Herbert 1821–1895. Irish lithographer. 1849 Portrait of CD drawn and put on stone by M, printed by M. & N. Hanhart. The only engraving in CD's lifetime. One of the Ipswich British Association portraits q.v.

Magyar Tudományos Akadémia CD Member 1872.

Mahon, Viscount *see* Stanhope, Philip Henry, 5th *Earl* of.

Maitland, Florence Henrietta *see* Fisher.

Maitland, Frederic William 1850–1906. FBA 1902. m 1886

Florence Henrietta Fisher. Downing Prof. Laws of England Cambridge 1888–1906. DNB.

Malden, Bingham Sibthorpe 1830–1906. Anglican clergyman & botanist. 1861 CD to M on orchids and insects—Carroll 254. 1862 M is acknowledged in *Orchids*.

Maldonado Uraguay. 1832 Jul.–Oct. CD stayed at; he used the mouth of La Plata River as base for inland expeditions.

Malin, Harriet *see* Darwin.

Malin, Thomas James Naval Officer. m 1881 Harriet Darwin d.s.p.

Malthus, Rev. Thomas Robert 1766–1834. Prof. Modern History & Political Economy, East India Company College Haileybury 1805–1834. 1838 Sep.13 CD started to read *An essay on the principle of population*, 1798, in the enlarged edition of 1803. M's statements on the geometrical increase in population and its relation to the availability of resources were extremely important in CD's formulation of the idea of natural selection. EB DNB.

Malvern Wells Herefordshire & Worcestershire. A spa town where *Dr* J. M. Gully had his water cure establishment at The Lodge. 1848 summer CD stayed for 'some months'—LLi 81. 1849 Mar.10–Jun.30 CD again had water cure there. 1849 Sep. CD visited for day from British Association meeting at Birmingham. 1851 Anne Elizabeth D, suffering from a fever, with Henrietta Emma D arrived there; *Miss* Thorley governess arrived a few days later; CD arrived on Apr.17; Anne died on Apr.23—EDii 132. 1863 CD took a house for whole family Sep.–Oct.—EDii 180.

Manchester Lancashire. 1845 Sep. CD visited W. Herbert, then Dean of the Cathedral.

Manchester Literary and Philosophical Society CD Honorary Member 1868.

Mansell, Henry Longueville 1820–1871. Anglican clergyman & metaphysician. Fellow of Magdalen College Oxford 1855–. Dean of St Paul's Cathedral, London 1868–1871. 1861 CD sent him Gray's *Natural selection not inconsistent with natural theology*—Darwin-Gray 76.

Manual of Scientific Enquiry 1849 CD's article on geology is Section VI in *A manual of scientific enquiry; prepared for the use of Her Majesty's Navy: and adapted for travellers in general*, edited by *Sir* John F. W. Herschel *Bart*, CD's article 156–195; early copies have a serious transposition of text 178–190 (F325); later copies are corrected (F326); CD's own copy, at Cambridge, has the correct section inserted in a pocket in back cover; 2nd edition 1861 (F328); 3rd edition 1859, superintended by R. Main (F329); 4th edition 1871, revised by J. Phillips (F331); 5th edition 1886 edited by *Sir* Robert S. Ball (F333). CD's article alone occurs as a pamphlet, 1st edition 1849 (F327); 3rd edition 1859 (F330); 4th edition 1871 (F332). First foreign editions: CD's article only, Russian 1860 (F336); whole book, Russian 1860 (F337).

Manures and Steeping Seed 1844 Manures and steeping seed, *Gdnr's Chronicle*, No.37:621 (Bi 196,F1666).

Marchant, Rev. Sir James 1867–1956. Religious writer. KBE 1921. 1915 editor, *Alfred Russel Wallace*, London, which prints the whole of the Darwin-Wallace correspondence.

Marindin, Samuel 1807–1852. *Captain*, Life Guards. 1835 Rector of Penselwood, Somerset. M was at Shrewsbury School and Cambridge with CD. 1834 M is mentioned in letter to Whitley—LLi 256.

Mark Coachman to Robert Waring Darwin [II] and later to Susan Elizabeth D until her death 1866. Alive 1875.

Marsh A carrier, London-Cambridge—Darwin-Henslow 123.

Marsh, Othniel Charles 1831–1899. American palaeontologist. Prof. Vertebrate Palaeontology Yale 1866–, where his uncle George Peabody endowed the Peabody Museum. 1880 CD thanks M for sending a copy of *Odontornithes*, 1880—LLiii 241.

Marshall, William 1815–1890. Solicitor & botanist of Ely. 1860 CD to Henslow, about spread of *Elodea canadensis*. 1852 M wrote a pamphlet on spread of *Anacharis alsinastrum*, London, reprinted from *Cambridge Independant Press*. CD had corresponded with—MLi 149, Darwin-Henslow 203. 1875 M provided information on *Pinguicula* in Cumberland for *Insectivorous Plants*. c1875 CD to M on oak trees—Carroll 459.

Marshall, William Cecil 1849–? Architect. Cambridge friend of CD's sons. 1876 CD to M, on adding billiard room at Down House—Carroll 499–501, Atkins 28.

Martens, Conrad ?–1878. Draughtsman of 2nd voyage of *Beagle*; M replaced Augustus Earle at Montevideo. Later a distinguished landscape painter in Australia. 'A pupil of C. Fielding and excellent landscape drawer', 'Our little painter'—Barlow, *Charles Darwin and the voyage of the Beagle*, 95,108. Self portrait in Moorhead, *Darwin and the Beagle*, 134.

Martial, Mr Surgeon on a whaling ship. M gave CD information of races of human lice—Descent i 219, where he is not named. 'Worthless and slightly educated'—Carroll 45.

Martha Sister of *Mrs* Morrey. Servant to Sarah Elizabeth Wedgwood at Petleys, Downe, until the latter's death 1856.

Martin, John Royle 1871 CD to R, asking for ten shares in Artisan's Dwelling Company for £100—Carroll 403.

Martin, Septimus Son of the Rector of an adjoining parish to Downe. 1853 M dined at Down House. M had emigrated to Melbourne before this and was visiting—N&R 22.

Martineau, Harriet 1802–1876. Feminist & author. 1833 CD met M at Hensleigh Wedgwood's in London, 'She is so happy, good-humoured and conceited that she will not much mind what people say of her'—EDi 257. 1841 Erasmus Alvey D tried to help her when she was ill and poor—EDii 58. CD's father Robert did not like her—EDi 776. EB DNB.

Martineau, James 1820–1871. Nonconformist minister. Prof. Philosophy New College London 1857–1869. Principal 1869–1871. 1861 CD sent M Gray's *Natural selection not inconsistent with natural theology*,—Darwin-Gray 76.

Marx, Heinrich Karl 1818–1883. German communist, living in London from 1848. CD never met, and some doubt has been thrown on the authenticity of M's letters to CD, *see* L. S. Feuer, *Ann.Sci.*, 32:1–12. Copy of 2nd edition of *Das Kapital*, Vol.1, 1873, inscribed to CD 'On the part of his sincere admirer' is at Down House. 1880 Oct.13 M wanted to dedicate the English translation of *Das Kapital* to CD; CD declined. See also E. B. Aveling.

Mary CD's children's nurse 1841.

Maryanne 1877 nurse to Bernard Richard Meirion D at Down House.

Mason, P. B. of Burton-on-Trent. 1871 CD to M, thanking for information about growth of hair on human back.

Massingberd, Charlotte Mildred 1868–1940. Grand-daughter of Charles Langton. m as 2nd wife Leonard D. CD's daughter-in-law. Known as Mildred. 1890 Nov. M was ED's companion 'or lady-in-waiting as we sometimes called it'—*Period Piece*.

Massingberd, Emily Caroline m Edmund Langton. Known as Lena.

Massingberd, Lena *see* Emily Caroline M.

Massingberd, Mildred *see* Charlotte Mildred M.

Masters, Maxwell Tylden 1833–1907. Plant teratologist. FRS

1870. s of William M. Editor *Gdnr's Chronicle* 1865–. 1860 CD to about evolution, mentioning that he had written to his father who was ill—MLi 147. 1860 CD to M, on papilionaceous flowers—MLii 256. ?1860 CD to M, about peloric flowers and referring to M's father's plant breeding—N&R 76. 1862 CD to M, about M's approval of *Origin*. 1869 *Plant Teratology*, Ray Society, London.

Masters, William 1796–1874. Nurseryman. f of Maxwell Tylden M. Friendly correspondent of CD.

Matheson ED's personal maid, when ED was a widow.

Matthew ?Frederick Hoskyns Matthews, so identified by de Beer in FUL, but seems much too old, b 1778. 1834 CD to Whitley, M is mentioned amongst other Cambridge friends. 1836 CD saw a Cambridge friend of this name—LLi 256.

Matthew, Patrick 1790–1874. Author on political & agricultural subjects. Of Gourdiehill, Errol, Scotland. His surname is sometimes misspelt Mathew or Matthews. One of CD's predecessors in the idea of natural selection. The main statement is in an appendix to his *Naval timber and arboriculture*, London 1831, and there are further remarks in *Emigration fields*, London 1839. 1860 M drew attention to his priority in *Gdnr's Chronicle*, Apr.7, with an extract from *Naval timber*, and reinforced it in *Saturday Analyst & Leader*, Nov.24. CD's reply to 1st paper is in *Gdnr's Chronicle*, Apr.21:362–363. 1865 CD to Hooker, about W. C. Wells' work, 'So poor old Patrick Matthew is not the first, and he cannot, or ought not to put on his title pages 'Discoverer of the principle of Natural Selection'—LLiii 41. ?No copies of M's books known with this on title pages. 1912 *Miss* Euphemia M, daughter, visited W. T. Calman at British Museum (Natural History) with copies of CD-M correspondence; copies are in the Museum. *see* Calman, *J.Bot.Brit.foreign*, 192–194, with portrait of M. de Beer prints the letters—N&R 39–43.

Matthews, Frederick Hoskyns 1778–? de Beer FUL 111, identifies a Cambridge friend of CD named Matthew as M. This man was of Shrewsbury School & Trinity, but seems too old—LLi 256.

Matthews, Richard Missionary from Church Missionary Society to Fuegians. Carried there on 2nd voyage of *Beagle*. 1834 Jan.23 M landed at Woollya. Feb.6 M was taken off again because his life was in danger; finally landed at New Zealand where his brother was a missionary—*J.Researches*, 1845, 207.

Maull & Fox Commercial photographers of London. c1854 photographed CD at Down House. Usual versions are *a.* check waistcoat and trousers, profile; *b.* dark embroidery waistcoat, dark trousers, full face. Both are seated.

Maurice, John Frederick Denison 1805–1877. Anglican clergyman & educationalist. Prof. English History & Literature King's College London 1840– , Divinity added 1846, later dismissed for heterodoxy. Prof. Moral Philosophy Cambridge 1866–1872. M was a friend of Litchfield. 1863 Kingsley to M, on success of *Origin*—LLiii 2. EB DNB.

Mauritius Indian Ocean. 1836 Apr.29–May 9 *Beagle* at Port Louis; CD made several inland trips including one to *Captain* J. A. Lloyd's house May 4; CD returned part of the way on an elephant, the only one in the island.

Maw, George 1832–1912. Geologist & botanist. Of Benthall Hall. 1861 Jul. M reviewed *Origin* in *Zoologist*. CD to Lyell, 'evidently a thoughtful man'—LLii 376. M provided *Drosophyllum* for *Insectivorous plants*.

May, Jonathan Carpenter on 2nd voyage of *Beagle*.

Mayor, Mrs 1882 Jan. Headmistress of Greville House School, Paddington, London, where ED was for a year.

Mays, J. Aldous 1862 M took shorthand notes of Huxley's six lectures to working men, delivered at the Museum of Practical Geology, Jermyn St, London. These were used for the six blue pamphlets, issued at 4d each. 1863 they were published as a book, *On our knowledge of the causes of organic nature*, London; the spine title was *On the origin of species*.

Medicinisch-Naturwissenschaftliche Gesellschaft zu Jena CD Honorary Member 1878.

Medico-Chirurgical Society London. CD Honorary Member 1868.

Meehan, Thomas 1826–1901. American botanist. 1874 CD to M, about colours of diœcious flowers—MLi 354.

Meldola, Raphael 1849–1915. Entomologist. FRS 1886. Prof. Chemistry Finsbury Technical College, London. 1873 CD to M, about saltations—MLi 350. 1882 M translated F. L. A. Weismann, *Studien zur Descendenz-Theorie*, Leipzig 1875–1876, as *Studies in the theory of descent*, London, with prefatory note by CD, v–vi (F1414). 1896 CD's letters with M in E. B. Poulton, *Charles Darwin and the theory of natural selection*, London, 199f. WWH.

Mellersh, Arthur Midshipman on 1st & 2nd voyages of *Beagle*.

1832 Apr. M was given mate's warrant. *Vice-Admiral* 1878.

Melostomaceae This group of flowering plants has, in some species, two forms of stigmata. CD worked on them 1862–1881, but never published his results. MLii 292–302 summarizes his work.

Memorial to the Chancellor of the Exchequer 1866 *Memorial to the Chancellor of the Exchequer* [on transfer of natural history section of British Museum to South Kensington], May 14, signed by CD & twentyfour others (F869). The Chancellor was Benjamin Disraeli. 1873 [Letter from P. L. Sclater containing the text], *Nature*, Lond., 9:41 (F370).

Mendel, Johann Gregor 1822–1884. Johann was his baptismal name; Gregor was taken with his monk's vows. Augustinian monk at Brno, Moravia, *Abbot* 1868– . CD had never heard of M and, although his famous paper on inheritance in peas, 1865, Versuche über Pflanzenhybriden, *Verh.naturforsch.Verein Brünn*, 4, was available at the Royal Society and at the Entomological Society, it was ignored until 1900.

Mendoza Argentine. 1835 Mar.27 CD visited from Valparaiso, crossing the Andes by the southern, Portillo, pass; Mar.29 returned by northern, Uspallata or Aconcagua, pass, crossing the Incas' bridge on Apr.4.

Mental Evolution in Animals 1883 G. J. Romanes, *Mental evolution in animals*, London, contains posthumous Essay on instinct by CD, q.v.

Meteyard, Miss Elizabeth 1816–1879. Biographer of the Wedgwoods. 1871 *A group of Englishmen (1795–1815) being records of the younger Wedgwoods and their friends*, London, is an important sourcebook, including information about CD's mother and of Darwins and Allens.

Miall, Louis Compton 1842–1921. Zoologist. FRS 1892. Prof. Zoology Leeds 1876–1907. 1883 *The life and works of Charles Darwin; a lecture delivered to the Leeds Philosophical and Literary Society on February 6th, 1883*, Leeds; the first biography after the obituaries. WWH.

Microscopes 1863 CD to I. A. Henry, 'I have, as yet, found no exception to the rule, that when a man has told me he works with the compound alone his work is valueless'. 'Experience, however, has fully convinced me that the use of the compound without the simple microscope is absolutely injurious to progress of N[atural] History (excepting, of course, with

Infusoria)'—MLii 299. For CD's own instruments *see* under his entry.

Midhurst Sussex. 1876 Jun.7–9 CD visited *Sir* John Hawkshaw there.

Mill, John Stuart 1806–1873. Philosopher. In service of East India Company 1823–1858, until dissolution. 1865–1868 whig MP for Westminster. 1861 H. Fawcett to CD, 'He considers that your reasoning throughout is in the most exact accordance with the strict principles of logic. He also says that the method of investigation which you have followed is the only one proper to such a subject'—MLi 189. EB DNB.

Miller, Hugh 1802–1859. Geologist, stonemason & author. CD never knew this remarkable man, but he borrowed *Lady* Lyell's copy of *Footsteps of the Creator*, 1849, and then bought one himself—MLii 125.

Miller, William Hallowes 1801–1880. Mineralogist. FRS 1838. Prof. Mineralogy Cambridge 1832–1870. 1836 M helped CD with examination of rocks from *Beagle* voyage. 1859 M & CD corresponded on structure of cells of honeybee comb—MLi 121, Carroll 189. DNB.

Milmann, Henry Hart 1791–1868. Anglican clergyman & author. Dean of St Paul's Cathedral, London. c1842 CD met Sydney Smith at M's house in London—LLi 75. DNB.

Milne Edwards, Henri *see* Henry Milne Edwards.

Milne, David, afterwards Milne-Home 1805–1890. Geologist & mineralogist. 1847 M was against CD's interpretation of Glen Roy, and a frequent correspondent—MLii 177. *Trans.Roy.Soc.Edinb.*, 16:395, 1849. DNB.

Milner, Sir William, Bart Of Nunappleton, Tadcaster, Yorkshire. 1859 M to CD, on nuts which he had found in young petrels' crops at St Kilda—LLii 147.

Milnes, Richard Monckton 1809–1885. 1st *Baron* Houghton 1863. Politician. In youth M was a member of Cambridge Apostles Debating Society. Late 1830s CD met at *Lord* Stanhope's house. Known by Sydney Smith as 'the cool of the evening'—EDii 114, 121. DNB.

Mim With Abbety & Boo were Bernard Richard Meirion D's nicknames in infancy for members of family. None is ED.

Minerva Nickname for Athenæum Club, London, from bust on top of facade. 1838 CD 'I did not even taste Minerva's small beer today'—LLi 295.

Missionaries 1836 CD & Fitz-Roy, 'On the whole . . . we are

very much satisfied that they thoroughly deserve the warmest
support, not only of individuals, but of the British Government'—*S.Afr.Christian Recorder*, 2:238. *See also* Moral state of
Tahiti.

Mivart, St George Jackson 1827–1900. Barrister & biologist.
FRS 1869. Lecturer in Biology, St Mary's Roman Catholic
College, Kensington. Roman Catholic anti-Darwinian;
excommunicated 1900. 1871 *The genesis of species*, London.
1871 CD to Wallace, 'but he was stimulated by theological
fervour'—LLiii 135. 1871 CD to Chauncey Wright, 'I con-
clude with sorrow that though he means to be honourable, he
is so bigoted that he cannot act fairly'—LLiii 135. M's other
evolutionary works: 1873 *Apes and men, an exposition of struc-
tural resemblances bearing upon questions of affinity and origin*,
London; 1876 *Contemporary evolution; an essay on some recent
social changes*, London; 1882 *Nature and thought*, London. Biography: J. Gruber 1960. DNB.

Moffatt, or Moffat Liveried footman at Down House,
1858–1878.

Moggridge, John Traherne 1842–1874. Naturalist. M was
tubercular and lived in S France. 1865 CD to M, about fertilisation of bee orchis—LLiii 276. M sent orchis *Neotina intacta* to
CD—Allan. 1871 CD to M, about habits of ants and about
orchids—Carroll 399. 1872 CD to M, about trap-door spiders—MLi 337. 1874 CD describes M as 'One of our most
promising young naturalists'—*Nature*, Lond.,11:114. Author
of *Harvesting ants and trap-door spiders*, London 1873[–1874],
which rediscovered the habits of *Atta*, described in *Proverbs*
vi.6.

Mojsisovics von Mojsvár, Johann August Georg Edmund
1839–1907. Hungarian geologist. Vice-Director Imperial
Geological Institute, Vienna. 1878 M sent CD his *Die
Dolomit-Riffe von Südtirol und Venetien*, [1878–]1879, Vienna.
CD replied praising it.

Molly Nurse to ED and her brothers and sisters at Maer Hall.

Mone *see* Marianne Clapham.

Monk 1874 CD to Newton, about crossing in wagtails mentions
M—FUL 99. Not traced.

Monkeys 1876 Sexual selection in relation to monkeys, *Nature*,
Lond., 15:18–19 (Bii 207, F1773), reprinted in *Descent of man*,
12th thousand 1877 onwards.

Monro, Alexander 3rd of the name. 1773–1859. Anatomist.

Prof Anatomy Edinburgh, in succession to his father & grand-father. M is said to have lectured from his grandfather's notes. 1826 CD to sister Caroline Sarah, 'I dislike him and his lectures so much, that I cannot speak with decency about them'—MLi 7. 'Made his lectures on human anatomy as dull as he was himself, and the subject disgusted me'—Barlow, *Autobiography* 47. DNB.

Monsell, Elinor Mary m 1906 Bernard Richard Meirion D. CD's grand-daughter-in-law.

Montague 1862 CD to Innes, 'They [the John Lubbocks] gave us a good account of poor Montague'—Darwin-Innes 212. Not traced.

Monteagle, Baron *see* Thomas Spring Rice.

Monte Video Uraguay. 1832 Jul.26 CD took several inland trips from here and from Buenos Aires when *Beagle* was based on La Plata river, until 1833 Dec.6 when *Beagle* left for Patagonia.

Montgomery Wales. 1822 Jul. CD visited for holiday with sister Susan Elizabeth.

Moor Park nr Farnham, Surrey. A water cure establishment, run by E. W. Lane, which CD visited often. 1859 'Dr. Lane's delightful hydropathic establishment'—LLi 85. In 17c M was home of *Sir* William Temple and Esther Johnson, Swift's Stella.

Moore, Aubrey Lackington 1848–1890. Anglican clergyman. Rector of Frenchay, Bristol 1876–1881. Fellow of Keble College Oxford 1881– . 'The clergyman who more than any other man was responsible for breaking down the antagonism towards evolution then widely felt in the English Church'—Poulton, *Darwin and the Origin*, 11. DNB.

Moore, David, né Muir 1807–1879. Botanist. Director of Glasnevin Botanical Gardens Dublin 1838–1879. M provided *Drosophyllum* for *Insectivorous plants*, and gave information on *Pinguicula*.

Moore, Sir Norman, Bart 1847–1922. Physician & antiquary. 1st *Bart* 1919. Of St Bartholomew's Hospital; M attended CD in his last illness. Atkins says that CD had no confidence in him—Atkins 38. 'He [CD] once remarked to Dr. Norman Moore that one of the things that made him wish to live a few thousand years, was his desire to see the extinction of the Bee-orchis'—LLiii 276. 1882 M was on 'Personal Friends invited' list for CD's funeral. DNB.

Moral state of Tahiti New Zealand &c. 1836 A letter, containing remarks on the moral state of Tahiti, New Zealand &c., *S.Afr. Christian Recorder*, 2:221–238, by Robert Fitz-Roy & CD (Bi 19, F1640); CD's contributions are suffixed 'D'. CD's first publication except for beetle records in Stephens.

More, Alexander Goodman 1830–1895. Botanist. Assistant British Museum 1867–1880; Curator of Botany 1881. M lived in Isle of Wight. 1860 M helped CD with orchid work—MLii 263.

More letters 1903 Francis Darwin & A. C. Seward editors, *More letters of Charles Darwin. A record of his work in a series of hitherto unpublished letters*, 2 vols, London (F1548); facsimile 1972 (F1550). Foreign editions: USA (F1549) 1903; Russian, auto-biographical fragment and account of Down House only (F1551) 1959.

Moresby, Sir Fairfax 1786–1877. Naval Officer. GCB 1865. *Admiral of the Fleet* 1870. 1845 'Captain Moresby informs me about turtles, also about Chagos, Maldives & Seychel-les'—*J.Researches*, 459. DNB.

Morley, John, Viscount 1838–1923. Statesman & man of let-ters. *Viscount* Morley of Blackburn 1908 OM 1902. 1871 M reviewed *Descent* in *Pall Mall Gazette* Mar.20 CD wrote to anonymous reviewer. 1876 M visited Down House with Gladstone, Huxley & Playfair, whilst staying at High Elms. EB DNB.

Morrey, Mrs Cook to Sarah Elizabeth Wedgwood [I] at Petleys, Downe, until *Miss* W's death 1856. Sister of Martha, the housemaid.

Morris, Francis Orpen 1810–1893. Anglican clergyman & naturalist. This good field naturalist was stridently anti-evolution, in a series of pamphlets; 1869 *The difficulties of darwinism*, London; [1870] *A double dilemma in darwinism*, Lon-don; 1875 *All the articles of the Darwin faith*, London; 1880 *The Darwin craze*, London; [1890] *The cui bono of hereditism*, Lon-don; [1890] *The demands of darwinism on credulity*, London. M seems never to have been mentioned by CD.

Morse, Edward Sylvester 1838–1925. American zoologist & Japanophile. Director Peabody Museum Yale 1880– . 1873? CD to M on supposed relation of brachiopods to annelids—*Proc.Boston.nat.Hist.Soc.*, 15; *Proc.Amer.Soc. Adv.Sci.*, 19:272, 1870; *Ann.Mag.nat.Hist.*, 6:267, 1870—MLi 350. 1877 CD to M, on his Presidential Address to American Association for the Advancement of Science, on the advance of evolutionary work in USA, published in *Proc. Amer.Assoc.Adv.Sci.*, 25, 1876—LLiii 233.

Moseley, Henry Nottidge 1844–1891. Zoologist. FRS 1877. Prof. Zoology & Comparative Anatomy Oxford 1881– . Naturalist on Challenger 1872–1876. 1879 CD to M, about M's book *Notes of a naturalist on the 'Challenger'*, London 1879, which is dedicated to CD.

Mosley, Frances ?–1874 d of Rector of Rolleston, Staffordshire. m 1832 Francis Wedgwood.

Motley, John Lathrop 1814–1877. American historian. 1840's CD met M at *Lord* Stanhope's house. Author of *History of the Dutch Republic*, 1856. EB.

Mould 1838 On the formation of mould, *Proc.geol. Soc.*, 2:574–576 (Bi 49, F1648); 1840 On the formation of mould, *Trans.geol.Soc.*, 5:505–509 (F1655); 1844 On the origin of mould, *Gdnr's Chronicle*, No.23:380 (Bi 195, F1665); 1869 The formation of mould by worms, *Gdnr's Chronicle*, No.20:500 (Bi 195, F1745). 1881 *The formation of vegetable mould through the action of worms see Vegetable mould and worms*.

Mount, The Parish of St Chad, Shrewsbury, Shropshire. Home of *Dr* Robert Waring D [II]; built by him c1800; late Georgian, red brick, 5 bays and 2½ storeys, quite plain, deep Tuscan porch; lower wings of different length and height, that on the left of four bays, one-storeyed with windows in blank arches—Pevsner, *Buildings of England, Shropshire*, 289, 1958. S face looks down Frankwell which comes up from Welch bridge ; N face looks down steeply over the river Severn. Photographs of S face and view from terrace of N face in Keith, *Darwin revalued*, 46, 1955. CD was born there. After CD's father's death, Susan Elizabeth D lived there until her death 1866. 1869 CD visited, then owned by Spencer Phillips—LLi 11.

Mountford, Horace Sculptor. ?1909 M carved statue of CD in stone, seated, outside old school Shrewsbury, now public library, also a plaster cast for it. There is also a bust, 1905, and a statuette copy in bronze of which copies were available for sale in 1909. M also made a medallion in bronze. The usual photograph of the school statue is by W. W. Naunton.

Movements of Plants 1881 Movements of plants, *Nature*, Lond., 23:406, observations on a ms letter from Fritz Müller (Bii 224, F1791). 1881 The movements of leaves, *Nature*, Lond., 23:603–604, observations on a ms letter from Fritz

Müller (Bii 228, F1794). *see also Power of movement in plants.*

Mowatt, Jane d of Francis Mowatt. m 1865 Vernon Lushington.

Moxon, Walter 1836–1886. Physician of Guy's Hospital. 1882 Apr.19 M was sent for to Down House, but CD was dying when he arrived. M was on 'Personal Friends invited' list for CD's funeral.

Müller, Sir Ferdinand Jacob Heinrich von 1825–1896. Botanist of German origin. *Baron* of Würtenberg 1871, KCMG 1879 FRS 1861. Government Botanist of Victoria, Australia 1852–1896. 1861 M answered CD's *Queries about expression*.

Müller, Friedrich Max 1823–1900. German philologist living in England. Privy Councillor. Curator of Bodley's Library. Corpus Prof. Comparative Philology Oxford 1868–. Friendly correspondent with CD—LLii 390, MLii 45. DNB.

Müller, Fritz *see* Johann Friederich Theodor M.

Müller, Hermann 1829–1883. Botanist. Younger b of Fritz M. Science teacher at Lippstadt 1855–. 1872 CD sent M ms of On the flight paths of male humble bees, which was translated by E. Krause as Über die Wege der Hummel-Männchen, *Gesammelte kleinere Schriften von Charles Darwin*, 1885–1886. Author of *Die Befruchtung der Blumen,* Leipzig 1873; translated, by D' A. W. Thompson, *The fertilisation of flowers*, 1883, with prefatory note by CD (F1432). Foreign edition: Russian, CD's preface only, 1950 (F1434). 1873 CD to M, saying that he is reading the German edition slowly—LLiii 281. 1872 *Anwendung der Darwinischen Lehre auf Bienen*, Berlin.

Müller, Johann Friederich Theodor known as and writing as Fritz. 1822–1897. German schoolmaster in Brazil & naturalist. Elder b of Hermann M. m with at least one d, Rosa who observed circumnutation in *Linum usitatissimum*—MLii 345. Teacher of mathematics at Gymnasium, Blumenae, S. Catherina 1852–. CD and M never met, but 'of all his unseen friends Fritz Müller was the one for whom he had the strongest regard'—LLiii 37. 'Uninterrupted friendship and scientific comradeship'—MLii 344. 'He had for Müller a stronger personal regard than that which bound him to his other unseen friends'—Francis D, *Ann.Bot.*, 13:xiii, 1899. CD to Hermann M, 'One of the most able naturalists living'.
1864 M was author of *Für Darwin*, Leipzig, translated by W. S. Dallas, at CD's expense on commission, 1869, *Facts and argu-*

ments for Darwin, London; it contains one of the earliest statements of the recapitulation theory and Haeckel took the
theory from here without acknowledgement; it also contains a
joke classification of the Crustacea. CD thought so highly of it
that he got Murray to have the copies cased in the same
binding style as *Origin* eds. 1–3, and later casings as edition
5—LLiii 86, MLii 92. Many letters, to and from M, first 1865
Aug.10, last 1881 Dec.19—MLii 370. 1880 M was nearly
drowned in a flood of the Hajahy river; CD to Hermann M,
offering financial help to replace books etc. (£100), but not
needed—LLiii 242, MLii 363, 369. CD wrote introductory
notes to six short papers by M in *Nature* Lond., 1874–1881.
Photograph MLii 344. Biography MLi 382.

Muñiz, Francisco Javier of Luxan, Argentina. 1845 M had
discussed Niata cattle, the pug-faced breed, with CD
—*J.Researches*, 145. 1845 CD to Owen on bones of *Machairodus*
sp. which M offered for sale and which British Museum
bought—FUL 101. 1845 M described it as *Muñi-Felis bonaren-
sis* in *Le Gaceta Mercantil*, Oct.9.

Murchison, Sir Roderick Impey, Bart 1792–1871. Geologist
& geographer. Kt 1846 KCB 1863 1st *Bart* 1866 FRS 1826.
Director General Royal School of Mines London 1855. CD
knew M fairly well during London period, calling him Don
Roderick. 1858 CD to M, about British Museum
enquiry—MLi 109. 'He was very far from possessing a
philosophical mind', 'The degree to which he valued rank was
ludicrous'—Barlow, *Autobiography* 102. *The Silurian system*,
London 1839. Biography: A. Giekie 1875. EB DNB.

Murray, Andrew 1812–1878. Advocate & naturalist. 1860 M
was anti-*Origin*, paper in *Proc.Roy.Soc.Edinb.*, 4:274–291. 1860
CD to Lyell, 'the entomologist and dabbler in Botany'—Carroll 191. 1867 CD to Hooker, CD had bought a second-hand
copy of M's *The geographical distribution of mammals*, 1866, 'It is
clear to me that the man cannot reason', 'He seems to me
conceited'—MLii 3. 1876 CD to Wallace, 'utter want of all
scientific judgement'—MLii 12. 1877 CD to Dyer, 'What
astonishing nonsense Mr. Andrew Murray has been writing
about leaves and carbonic acid'—MLii 412. DNB.

Murray, Charles Fairfax 1849–1919. Artist. 1887 ED sat for
him for portrait, pastel in wicker-work chair at Down House.

Murray, John [I] second of the name. 1808–1892. Publisher of
50 Albemarle St, London. CD's main publisher; they were on

personal terms from the first publication of *Origin*, 1859. 1845 M bought copyright of the 2nd edition of *J.Researches*, for inclusion in his Home and Colonial Library, for £150. M published 1st and subsequent editions of ten of CD's books, as well as 2nd edition of *Climbing plants*, 1875; E. Krause, *Erasmus Darwin*, 1879, with introductory essay by CD; 1869 F. Müller, *Facts and arguments for Darwin*; 1887 F. Darwin, editor, *Life and letters*, 3 vols; 1903 F. Darwin & A. C. Seward, editors, *More letters*, 2 vols; 1915 H. E. Litchfield, editor, *Emma Darwin*, 2 vols, 1st published edition. 1882 M was on 'Personal Friends invited' list for CD's funeral.

Murray, Sir John [II] 1841–1914. Marine biologist. KCB 1898 FRS 1896. Chief Naturalist on Challenger expedition 1872–1876, and editor of *Reports* 1882–1896. 1881 CD to A. Agassiz, on M's views on origin of coral reefs, in which CD was right and M wrong—LLiii 183, MLii 197. EB DNB.

Musters, Charles ?–1832. Volunteer 1st Class Royal Navy, on 2nd voyage of *Beagle*. 1831 Sep.11–14 M sailed with CD & Fitz-Roy from London to Plymouth. 1832 May M died of fever at Rio de Janeiro.

N

Nägeli, Carl Wilhelm von 1817–1891. Prof. Botany Munich 1857–. 1866 CD to N, praising *Entstehung und Begriff der Naturhistorischen Art*, 1865, which was given as a lecture, Mar.28, to Königlich-Bayerische Akademie der Wissenschaften, Munich—LLiii 49. CD to N, 'many of your criticisms are the best which I have met with'—LLiii 50.

Nancy CD's nurse at Shrewsbury. CD sent greetings to her in *Beagle* letters to his sisters—LLi 254.

Narrative of the surveying voyages of His Majesty's Ships Adventure and Beagle 3 vols & appendix to Vol.2, edited by Robert Fitz-Roy, 1839. Vol.1 is narrative of 1st voyage, 1826–1830, under *Captain* P. P. King; Vol.2 is narrative of 2nd voyage, 1831–1835, under Fitz-Roy, with tables of data in the appendix; Vol.3, entitled Journal & remarks, is by CD and is 1st issue of *Journal of researches*, which was issued separately at the same time; (F10) facsimile 1972 (F166). The whole work has never been translated. An earlier and brief narrative by Fitz-Roy is in *J.R.Geogr.Soc.*, 6:311–343, 1836.

Nash, Louisa Ann Wife of Wallis N q.v. c1875 N drew fine head and shoulders of CD in brushed india ink; it has never been reproduced and is still in the N family. 1910 N gave reminiscences of CD in *Overland monthly*, San Francisco, 404–408.

Nash, Wallis 1873–1926. Lawyer, later one of the founding fathers of the State of Oregon. 1873–?1880 N took George Wood's house, The Rookery, at Downe and became friendly with the D's. One of his four sons named L. Darwin Nash. Wife Louisa Ann N q.v. 1919 *A lawyers life on two continents*, Boston, has reminiscences of CD, 130–138. *see* K. G. V. Smith & R. E. Dimick, *J.Soc.Biblphy nat.Hist.*, 78–82, 1976.

Natural History Collections 1858 *Public natural history collections. Copy of a memorial addressed to the Right Honourable the Chancellor of the Exchequer,* [?London], signed by CD & eight others (F371); reprinted in *Gdnr's Chronicle*, No.48:861 (F372).

Natural History Review Founded 1860 largely by Huxley. 1860 CD to Huxley, warning him not waste his energies editing a review, but to get on with original work; a warning which Huxley did not heed—MLi 157.

Natural Selection 1859 phrase first used in title of *Origin*; ch.3 'I have called this principle, by which each slight variation, if useful, is preserved, by the term Natural Selection'. 1860 Natural selection, *Gdnr's Chronicle*, No.16:362–363 (Bii 32, F1705); in this paper CD recognizes Patrick Matthew's claim to priority in the idea, but not the expression. 1873 Natural selection, *Spectator*, 46:76 (Bii 169, F1758). 1880 Sir Wyville Thomson and natural selection, *Nature*, Lond., 23:32 (Bii 223, F1789). 1860 CD to Lyell, 'I doubt whether I use the term Natural Selection more as a Person, than writers use Attraction of Gravity as governing the movements of Planets &c but I suppose I could have avoided the ambiguity'—Carroll 198.

Naturalist on the River Amazons 1863, by H. W. Bates, review of in *Nat.Hist.Rev.*, 3:385–389, is attributed to CD in Dent's Everyman edition 1910 and later printings, also in British Museum, *Catalogue of printed books*; it is almost certainly not by CD. *see* Amazon valley fauna.

Naturforschende Gesellschaft zu Halle CD Member 1879.

Naudin, Charles Victor 1815–1899. French botanist. 1861 CD to Gray, N writes to say that he is going to publish on peloric flowers in *Pelargonium*—Darwin-Gray 84. 1864 CD to N, about N's work on Cucurbitaceae. 1868 *Variation* refers to N's work. 1880 CD to Romanes, 'Naudin, who is often quoted, I have much less confidence in', about plant hybrids—*Life of Romanes* 102. 1861 N is referred to in Historical sketch in *Origin*. CD says that he is unable to follow his arguments in *Rév.Horticole*, 1852—LLii 246, MLi 187.

Neale, Edward Vansittart 1810–1892. Co-operative reformer. 1861 CD to Hooker, 'a Mr. Neale has read a paper before the Zoological Society on "Typical Selection"; what it means I know not'—LLii 359. Paper in *Proc.zool.Soc.Lond.*, for 1861:1–11.

Nectar-secreting organs of plants 1855 Nectar-secreting organs of plants, *Gdnr's Chronicle*, No.29:487 (Bi 258,F1684).

Negro living in Edinburgh *see* John Edmonston.

Nelson, Richard John 1803–1877. Soldier & geologist. *Major-General* Royal Engineers. 1854 CD to Owen, CD had corresponded with on coral formations in Bermuda—N&R 50. DNB.

Netley Abbey Hampshire. 1846 Sep.14 CD visited on day trip from British Association meeting at Southampton.

Neumayr, Melchior 1845–1890. Palaeontologist. Prof. Palaeontology Vienna. N was an enthusiastic darwinian. 1877 CD to N, on inheritance of acquired characters and on his work with Carl Maria Paul, Die Congierenund Paludinens-chichten Slavoniens und deren Faunen, *Abhandl.K.-K.Geol.Reichs-Anstalt*, 7, Heft, 3, 1875—LLiii 232. 1878 CD to Judd, praising N's work and with brief biography—MLi 375.

Neville, Lady Dorothy Frances *see* Walpole.

Nevill, Reginald Henry ?–1878. m 1848 *Lady* Dorothy Frances Walpole. Of Dangstein, Rogate, Hampshire.

New Forest Hampshire. 1847 Jul. CD & family visited on return from holiday at Swanage.

New York Academy of Sciences 1879 CD Honorary Member.

New Zealand 1835 Dec.21–30 *Beagle* at Bay of Islands, North Island. CD landed and was entertained especially by missionaries. Dec.30 *Beagle* left for Sydney, 'I believe we were all glad to leave New Zealand. It is not a pleasant place' —*J.Researches* 1845, 430. 1836 Fitz-Roy, 'An Englishman may now walk alone . . . where, ten years ago, such an attempt would have been a rash braving of the club and the oven'—*J.R.geogr.Soc.*, 6:334. 1836 A letter, containing remarks on the moral state of Tahiti, New Zealand &c, *S.Afr.Christian Recorder*, 2:231–238 (Bi 19, F1640), by CD & Fitz-Roy, CD's contribution bear the suffix 'D'. This was CD's first publication except for beetle records in Stephens. 1843–1845 Fitz-Roy was Governor-General.

New Zealand Institute 1872 CD Honorary Member.

Newnham Courtney Oxfordshire. 1847 Jun. CD visited on day trip from British Association meeting at Oxford.

Newnham Grange House in Silver St, Cambridge, named by *Sir* George Howard D when he bought it in 1885. Now part of Darwin College q.v.

Newington, Samuel 1815–1883. Physician & botanist, of Hawkhurst, Sussex. N was joint proprietor of Ticehurst Private Asylum for Insane and Nervous Patients.

Newport, George 1803–1854. Surgeon & insect anatomist. FRS 1846. CD writes of watching this brilliant anatomist dissect a humble bee 'getting out the nervous system with a few cuts of a fine pair of scissors'; CD does not state where or when—LLi 110. DNB.

Newton, Alfred 1829–1907. Ornithologist. FRS 1870. 1st Prof. Zoology Cambridge. 1858 N was pro-evolution after reading Darwin-Wallace paper. 1860 Tristram to N, 'The infallibility of the God Darwin and his prophet Huxley'. 1865 CD refused to write a testimonial for N for the Cambridge Chair on the grounds that N knew only about birds—N&R 45. 1870 Feb.9 N spent Sunday at Down House—LLiii 79. 1870 May 23 CD visited N at Cambridge Museum. 1881 CD & ED took tea with N at Cambridge. 1882 N was on 'Personal Friends invited' list for CD's funeral. Biography: Wollaston 1921. DNB.

Nichols Retired postman at Downe, aged 87 in 1851—Atkins 103.

Nigger ED's nickname for CD—Keith, *Darwin revalued* 275.

Nilsson, Sven 1787–1883. Swedish naturalist & anthropologist of Lund. 1868 N provided CD with information about growth of reindeer antlers—*Descent* i 288, S. Lindroth, *Lychnos*, 1948:144–158.

Noel, Edward 1825–1899. Magistrate & Deputy Lieutenant of Derbyshire. m 1849 Sarah Gay Forbes D, of Elston Hall.

Noel, Sarah Gay Forbes *see* Darwin.

Norgate, F. Of Sparham, Norfolk. 1881 Mar. N to CD, about dispersal of fresh-water bivalve molluscs by water beetles, *Nature*, Lond., 25:529–530, 1882.

Norman, Ebenezer Village schoolmaster at Downe from 1854; for many years copyist for the press of CD's mss. 1857 CD to Hooker, 'I am employing a laboriously careful schoolmaster'—MLi 99. 1858 CD to Hooker, 'I can get the Down schoolmaster to do it [i.e. transcribe] on my return'—LLii 128.

Norman, George Warde 1793–1882. Writer on finance. Resident at Bromley Common nr Downe. 1860 CD to Hooker, 'My clever neighbour, Mr. Norman, says the article [*Edinb.Rev.*, on *Origin*] is so badly written, with no definite object, that no one will read it'—LLii 304. 1874 CD on increase of numbers of starlings 'Mr.Norman a well-known man in Kent'. 1876 CD to N, thanking for condolences on death of Amy Richenda D—Carroll 497. 1881 Romanes to his sister, recounts an episode about CD and N's liking for snuff—*Life of Romanes* 129. 1882 N was on 'Personal Friends invited' list for

CD's funeral.

North, Marianne 1830–1890. Author of *Recollections of a happy life*, 1892. N visited Down House 1881 Jul.16. 1882 N was on 'Personal Friends invited' list for CD's funeral.

Northcote, Lady (Cecilia Frances) *see* Farrer.

Norton, Charles Elliot 1827–1908. Prof. Italian Harvard. s of Andrews N, Prof. Theology Harvard. m Theodora Sedgwick, sister of Sara Sedgwick who married William Alvey D. 1868 N spent 4 months staying at Keston Rectory nr Downe, in summer. 1876 CD to Gray, two detachments of Nortons had visited Down House, 'I then verified a grand generalisation, which I once propounded to you, that all persons from the U States are perfectly charming'—Darwin-Gray 94.

Norton, Sara d of Charles Elliot N, niece of Sara Sedgwick. 1884 N visited ED at The Grove, Cambridge.

Norton, Theodora *see* Sedgwick.

Norwegian First edition in: *Life and letters*, 1889 (F1528).

Notebooks on transmutation of species *see* Darwin's notebooks etc.

O

Oakley, Mr 'A joiner with red hair'. 1833 CD met at Monte Video. O provided at least one fossil bone. Probably the same man who had collected for *Sir* Woodbine Parish—*Buenos Aires*, London 175–177, 1839.

Ogle, William 1827–1912. Physician & naturalist. Superintendant of Statistics to the Registrar General. 1865 CD advised O on experiments on fertilisation of flowers—LLiii 277. 1868 O to CD on Hippocrates' views on pangenesis—LLiii 82. 1878 O translated A. Kerner *Flowers and their unbidden guests*, London. 1882 O sent CD his translation of Aristotle on the parts of animals. n.d. CD to O, CD had called on him in London, invites him to lunch—Carroll 460. 1882 O was on 'Personal Friends invited' list for CD's funeral. n.d. O visited Down House—*Nineteenth Century*, 106:118–123, 1929.

Ogleby 1849 W. Thompson, author of *Natural history of Ireland*, 1849–1856, had written to CD stating that O had views on the use of authors' names in nomenclature similar to those of CD, i.e. that they should not be used—MLi 68.

Oldfield, Henry Ambrose 1856 CD to O on breeds of dogs —Carroll 128. Author of *Sketches of Nepal*, London 1880.

Olinda *see* Pernambuco.

Oliver, Daniel 1830–1916. Botanist. FRS 1863. On staff at Kew. Prof. Botany University College London 1861–1888. ?1860 CD to Hooker, 'Remember me kindly to Oliver. He must be astonished at not getting a string of questions'—LLiii 299. 1861 CD to Hooker, 'How capitally Oliver has done the résumé of botanical books. Good heavens how he must have read'—LLii 358. 1862 CD to Hooker, 'the all-knowing Oliver'—MLii 290. 1862 CD to Hooker, 'Oliver the omniscient'—LLiii 307. O provided material for CD's botanical work and was a long-standing and important correspondent.

Omori shell mounds 1880 [Letter] The Omori shell mounds, *Nature*, Lond., 21:561, introducing one from E. S. Morse, *ibid.*, 561–562 (Bii 222,F1788) Omori is in Japan.

Onibury nr Ludlow, Shropshire. Family home of the Langtons. 1837 ED stayed there.

Orange Court A house in Downe. *Mr* Harris owned it, a gentleman farmer.

Orchard, The A house in Cambridge, built in 1884 by Horace D on part of the Grove field.

Orchids 1860 CD to Lyell, 'I showed the case [of Orchids] to Elizabeth Wedgwood, and her remark was "Now you have upset your own book, for you won't persuade me that this could be effected by Natural Selection"'—MLi 156. 1869 CD to Gray, 'It really seems to me incredibly monstrous to look at an orchid as created as we now see it. Every part reveals modification on modification'—Darwin-Gray 94.

Orchids, Fertilisation of [book] 1862 *On the various contrivances by which British and foreign orchids are fertilised by insects, and on the good effects of intercrossing*, London (F800); 2nd edition 1877 *The various contrivances by which orchids are fertilised by insects* (F801). First foreign editions: German (F820) 1862; French (F818) 1870 (see papers below 1869); USA (F802) 1877; Italian (F823) 1883; Russian (F825) 1900; Romanian (F824) 1964. 1861 Sep.24 CD to John Murray, 'I think this little volume will do good to the "Origin" as it will show that I have worked hard at details'—LLiii 254. 1862 Discussion in reviews of the book included the idea that, if it had appeared before *Origin*, the author would have been canonized rather than anathematized by the natural theologians. A reviewer in *Literary Churchman*, Oct. found only one fault, that Mr Darwin's expression of admiration at the contrivances of orchids is too indirect a way of saying 'O! Lord, how manifold are thy works'. Review by *Duke* of Argyll, *Edinb.Rev.*, Oct., is in much the same vein.

Orchids, Fertilisation of (papers) 1860 Fertilisation of British orchids by insect agency, *Gdnr's Chronicle*, No.23:528 (Bii 32, F1706); 1860. Fertilisation of British orchids by insect agency, *Ent.Wkly Intelligencer*, 8:93–94,107–103 (F1707); 1861 Fertilisation of British orchids by insect agency, *Gdnr's Chronicle*, No.6:127 (Bii 38, F1710); 1861 Fertilisation of orchids, *Gdnr's Chronicle*, No. 37:831 (Bii 41, F1712); 1869 Notes on the fertilisation of orchids, *Ann.Mag.nat.Hist.*, 4:141–159 (Bii 138, F1748). The last 2 were inserted in the French translation of the book, 1870 and occur in the 2nd English edition, 1877. *see also Catasetum* & *Cypripedium*.

Origin of species (book) The text of each of the 1st six editions
is much altered; the changes are given in detail in the variorum
edition, 1959, listed below. 1859 Nov.24 *On the origin of species
by means of natural selection, or the preservation of favoured races in
the struggle for life*, London, John Murray, 1250 copies (F373);
facsimile 1964 (F602); facsimile 1969 (F614). This is the only
one of CD's books for which details of author's presentation
copies are available. At least twenty-four, perhaps more than
thirtyfive, were sent out inscribed by one of Murray's clerks;
no copy inscribed by CD himself is known. The whereabouts
of the following copies is known: Agassiz (Harvard); Butler
(St John's College, Cambridge); Dana (Yale); Horner (British
Museum (Natural History)); Herschel (Texas); Innes (University of London); Jenyns (in the family); Lyell (Down
House); Owen (Shrewsbury School); Prestwich (University
Library, Cambridge); Sedgwick (Trinity College, Cambridge); Wallace (*Sir* Geoffrey Keynes), Linnean Society of
London, Royal Society. Copies were sent to the following, but
their present whereabouts are unknown: Bunbury, de Candolle, Milne Edwards, Falconer, Fox, Gray, Henslow,
Hooker, Huxley, Kingsley, Lubbock, Ramsay. Galton's copy,
at University College London, is said to be author's presentation, but is not inscribed. CD's own copy is in University
Library, Cambridge. The print run was 1250 without overs;
CD had twelve free copies, five were for copyright and forty-
one were sent out for review. If CD bought another twenty-
four for presentation, then the number available for purchase.
was 1167. The story that the book sold out on publication
day stems from a letter from CD to Huxley on Nov.24, 'I
have heard from Murray today that he sold whole edition of
my book the first day & he wants another instantly'—*Science*,
64:476, 1926. CD's diary entry for Oct.1 reads 'all copies sold
first day'. It is clear that CD made this entry on or after
Nov.24. These statements have often been construed as mean-
ing that all copies were bought by the public on the first day.
What they do mean is that the booksellers took up the whole
printing available to them as soon as it was offered by John
Murray.
1860 Jan.5 (a very few copies 1859) 5th thousand [2nd edition]
(F375, 376), 3000 copies; 1861 Apr. 3rd edition, 7th thousand,
with historical sketch added (F381), 2000 copies; 1866 4th
edition, 8th thousand (F385), 1500 copies; 1869 5th edition,

10th thousand (F387), 2000 copies; 1872 6th edition, 11th thousand (F391), title changes to *Origin of species* etc., 3000 copies; 1876 6th edition (with additions and corrections), 18th thousand (F401); the final definitive text as CD left it. 1934 English Braille edition (F629); 1959 Variorum edition, Philadelphia, edited by Morse Peckham (F588);. First foreign editions: German (F672), USA (F377) 1860; French (F655) 1862; Dutch (F594[=648]), Italian (F706), Russian (F748) 1864; Swedish (F793) 1869; Danish (F643) 1872; Hungarian (F703), Polish (F739) 1873; Spanish (F770) 1877; Serbian (F766) 1878; Japanese (F718) 1896; Chinese (part)(F634) 1903, (whole)(F638) ?1918; Czech (F641), Latvian (F736) 1914; Greek (F698) 1915; Portuguese (F743) ?1920; Finnish (F653) 1928; Armenian (F630), Ukrainian (F797) 1936; Bulgarian (F632) 1946; Romanian (F746) 1950; Slovene (F768) 1951; Korean (F732) 1957; Flemish (F654) 1958; Lithuanian (F738) 1959; Hebrew (F700) 1960; Hindi (F702) 1964; Turkish (F796) 1970.

The whole of LLii is devoted to the preparation, publishing and reception of *Origin*. The best source of reference to reviews is J. P. Anderson in Bettany, *Life of Darwin*, 1887, xxvi–xxvii. A. Ellegård, *Gothenburg Studies in English*, 8:1–394, 1958, covers reviews in popular journals in detail. 1880 Apr.9 Huxley address to Royal Institution 'On the coming of age of The origin of species', printed in *Nature*, Lond., 22:1–4; *Pop.Sci.Monthly*, 17:337–344. 1862 CD to John Scott, 'The majority of the criticisms on the *Origin* are, in my opinion, not worth the paper they are printed on'—MLii 311. 1868 CD to W. D. Fox, 'I must prepare a new edition of that everlasting Origin. I am sick and tired of correcting'—Carroll 357.

Origin of Species (papers) 1863 [Letter] Origin of species, *Athenæum*, No.1854:617 (Bii 81, F1730). 1869 [Letter] Origin of species [on the reproductive potential of elephants], *Athenæum*, No.2174:861 (Bii 136, F1746). 1869 same title, *ibid.*, No.2177:82 (Bii 137, F1747).

Ornithological Notes *see* Darwin's ornithological notes.

Osborn, Christopher ?–1860. A resident at Downe. 1885 ED helped Mrs O when she was stone deaf and being looked after by another cottager, Alice Carter, who was partially blind—Darwin-Innes 207.

Osmaston Hall nr Derby. Home of Samuel Fox. 1828 Sep. CD visited.

Ouless, Walter William 1848–1933. Painter. RA 1875. 1875 Feb.–Mar. O painted CD in oils, the earliest portrait in oils. Original in family, copy at Christ's College, Cambridge. O also painted ED. FD 'Mr. Ouless's portrait is, in my opinion, the finest representation of my father that has been produced'—LLiii 95. CD 'I look a very venerable, acute, melancholy old dog; whether I really look so I do not know'. Engraved by Paul Adolphe Rajon. DNB.

Overton-on-Dee Flintshire. 1838 Jul. CD visited for a night on return from Glen Roy.

Owen, Major of Woodhouse, Shropshire. eldest s of William Mostyn Owen. 1820s, then *Captain*, shooting companion of CD who records in *Autobiography* how O helped to play a trick on him, preventing CD from knowing how many birds he had shot—LLi 43. 1865 and again in 1881 CD's accounts show interest on a mortgage to *Major* O (?the same man)—Atkins 96. 1882 O was on 'Personal Friends invited' list for CD's funeral.

Owen, Edward Mostyn s of William Mostyn O. m 1866 Susan Parker. 5c.

Owen, Frances d of William Mostyn O, sister of Sarah O. 1830 belle of the ball at Woodhouse—Keith, *Darwin revalued,* 6. O married a *Mr* Biddulph. Barlow calls her 'poor dear Fanny'—*Darwin and the voyage of the Beagle*, 63.

Owen, Sir Richard 1804–1892. Zoologist. KCB 1884 FRS 1834. m 1835 d of William Clift. Conservator & Hunterian Prof. Royal College of Surgeons of England 1836–1856. First Director of British Museum (Natural History) 1881. The most distinguished vertebrate zoologist and palaeontologist of Victorian England, but a most deceitful and odious man. CD was on friendly terms with O until the publication of the *Origin*; after that, O was probably the only man that CD hated, if he could hate. When *Life and letters* was published in 1887 O was alive and very little was printed on the matter; More letters, 1903, contains a lot, and more recent publications have added to it. 1836 Oct.29 CD and O first met at Lyell's house in London. 1859 Nov.11 CD to O and O's reply on sending a presentation copy of *Origin*, both in friendly manner—N&R 76. 1859 Dec.10 CD to Lyell' 'REPEAT NOTHING. Under garb of great civility, he was inclined to be most bitter and sneering against me'. 'He was quite savage and crimson at me'. 'A degree of arrogance I never saw approached'. 'He is the most

astounding creature I ever encountered'—Carroll 184. 1859
Dec.13 CD to O, before O had shown his hand in public, 'I
should be a dolt not to value your scientific opinion very
highly'—FUL 104.

1860 Apr. O reviewed *Origin*, anonymously, in *Edinb. Rev.*,
487–532. 1860 Apr. CD to Lyell, 'It is painful to be hated in the
intense degree with which ———— hates me'—LLii 300. 1860
May, CD to Hooker, 'Owen is indeed very spiteful'. 'The
Londoners say that he is mad with envy because my book has
been talked about; what a strange man to be envious of a
naturalist like myself, immeasurably his inferior'—MLi 149.
1860 Jun. CD to Gray, 'No one fact tells so strongly against
Owen . . . that he has never reared one pupil or fol-
lower'—MLi 153. 1863 The editors discuss CD's relationship
with O and instance his conduct in relation of Falconer's fossil
elephants—MLi 226.

1863 CD to Hooker, 'There is an Italian edition of the *Origin*
preparing. . . Owen will not be right in telling Longmans that
the book would be utterly forgotten in ten years. Hurrah!'—MLii 338. 1863 CD to Lyell, 'He ought to be ostracised
by every naturalist in England'—Carroll 287. 1867 CD to
Trimen, about O's review in *Edinb.Rev.* 'The internal evidence made me almost sure that only Owen could have written it: *but when I taxed him with the authorship and he absolutely
denied it—then I was quite certain*'. Trimen told the story to
Poulton—*Quart.Rev*, 1909:4–6. 1868 CD to Hooker, 'Owen
pitches into me and Lyell in grand style in the last chapter of
Vol.3 of *Anat.of Vertebrates*. He is a cool hand. He puts words
from me in inverted commas and alters them'—MLii 377.
1887 'Mrs Carlyle said that Owen's sweetness reminded her of
sugar of lead'—Huxley to Tyndall, Huxley's *Life* ii:167, MLi
309. 1897 Huxley to Flower, 'Gladstone, Samuel [Wilber-
force] of Oxford, and Owen belong to a very curious type of
humanity, with many excellent and even great qualities and
one fatal defect—utter untrustworthiness'—*Life of Huxley*
iii:274. Biography: *Rev*. R. Owen (grandson) 1894. DNB.

Owen, Sarah d of William Mostyn O, sister of Frances O. m T.
C. Haliburton. O was a strong personal friend of CD's before
Beagle voyage. 1872 CD to O, 'for old times sake', sending
photograph and copy of *Expression*—LLiii 173. 1880 CD to O,
'My dear Sarah, see how audaciously I begin'. 'I have always
loved and shall ever love this name'. O had reminded him of

his old ambition about Eddowe's Newspaper q.v. They had met at Erasmus Alvey D's house in London—LLiii 334.

Owen, William Mostyn Squire of Woodhouse, Shropshire. f of *Major* O, Frances O & Sarah O. CD used to shoot on his estate in the 1820s.

Oxalis bowei 1866 *Oxalis bowei,Gdnr's Chronicle*, No.32:756 (Bii 132, F1736).

Oxford Oxfordshire. 1847 Jun.22–30 CD visited for British Association meeting. 1860 British Association meeting q.v. CD was not present.

Oxford University 1870 CD declined Hon.D.C.L. on grounds of ill-health—*Oxford Univ.Gaz.*, Jun.17—LLiii 126. It was offered at the instigation of the Marquis of Salisbury on his installation as Chancellor; his list was opposed by Hebdomadal Council. 1909 Feb.12 The University celebrated the centenary of CD's birth; William, Erasmus [III], George, Francis & Leonard D were present. Main speeches were by George & Francis D and by Poulton—Poulton, *Darwin and the Origin*, 78–83, 1909.

P

P, The Venerable *see* Parslow.

Packard, Alpheus Spring 1839–1905. American entomologist. 1872 CD to Gray, saying that he had invited P to Down House, but he may not have got letter—Darwin-Gray 84.

Paget, Sir James, Bart 1814–1889. Surgeon. 1st *Bart* 1872 FRS 1871. St Bartholomew's Hospital. 1871 CD to W. Turner, 'he is so charming a man', and notes that he had been seriously ill of a post-mortem infection—MLii 106. 1872 P gave CD information for *Expression*. 1875 P probably agreed to Litchfield's draft sketch for a vivisection bill—LLiii 204. 1875 CD thanked P for sending his *Clinical lectures and essays*, London—Carroll 467. 1880 CD to Hooker, on P's work on growth in plants and on galls—MLii 425. 1881 CD met P at breakfast party for International Medical Congress in London. 1882 P was on 'Personal Friends invited' list for CD's funeral. EB DNB.

Paget, Stephen 1855–1926. Surgeon & author. 4s of *Sir* James P. Surgeon Middlesex Hospital. 1882 P was on 'Personal Friends invited' list for CD's funeral. WWH.

Paine, or Payne *Sir* Thomas Farrer's gardener, trained at Kew. P helped CD on *Mimosa*. ?1873 CD to Farrer, 'As he is so acute a man, I should very much like to hear his opinion' on water damage to leaves—LLiii 340.

Paley, William 1743–1805. Theologian. DD. 1763 Senior Wrangler, Cambridge. Traditionally CD & P had the same set at Christ's College. Archdeacon of Carlisle 1782. Author of *Natural theology*, London 1802, which is largely a crib from John Ray's *Wisdom of God*, London 1691. 'The logic of this book [*Evidences of christianity*] and as I may add of his *Natural Theology* gave me as much delight as did Euclid'. 'I did not at this time trouble myself about Paley's premises'—Barlow, *Autobiography* 59. DNB.

Pampas woodpecker 1870 Notes on the habits of the pampas woodpecker (*Colaptes campestris*), *Proc.zool. Soc. Lond.*,

No.47:705–706 (Bii 161, F1750). The last sentence in this paper reads 'I should be loath to think that there are many naturalists who, without any evidence, would accuse a fellow-worker of telling a deliberate falsehood to prove his theory'. This refers to remarks by W. H. Hudson in the previous number of *Proc.zool.Soc.Lond.* 1872 in 6th edition of *Origin*, CD writes 'in certain large districts it does not climb trees'—LLiii 153.

Pampean formation 1863 On the thickness of the Pampean formation near Buenos Aires, *Quart.J. geol. Soc.(Proc.)*, 19:68–71 (Bii 74, F1724).

Pander, Christian Heinrich 1794–1865. Russian embryologist & palaeontologist. 1861 CD attributed P's ideas to d'Alton in a footnote to the historical sketch in 3rd edition of *Origin*.

Pangenesis 1867 CD to Gray, sending clean sheets of *Variation*, 'What I call Pangenesis will be called a mad dream . . . I think it contains a great truth'—Darwin-Gray 58. 1868 The term was coined by CD and first appears in print in *Variation*. He thought that the idea was new although it was not. 1868 CD to Hooker, 'You will think me very self-sufficient, when I declare that I feel *sure* if Pangenesis is now stillborn it will, thank God, at some future time reappear, begotten by some other father, and christened by some other name'—LLiii 78. 1868 CD to Wallace, 'It is a relief to have some feasible explanation of the various facts, which can be given up as soon as any better hypothesis is found'. 'I had given up the great god Pan as a stillborn deity'—LLiii 80. 1869 CD to Hooker, 'You will be surely haunted on your deathbed for not honouring the great god Pan'—MLi 303. 1868 CD to Lyell, 'An untried hypothesis is always dangerous ground'—Carroll 349. 1880 CD to Paget, 'To anyone believing in my pangenesis (if such a man exists)'—MLii 427. 1860 Jul. Elizabeth Barrett Browning's poem first published, 'What was he doing the great god Pan, Down in the reeds by the river'. 1871 Pangenesis, *Nature*, Lond., 3:502–503, a letter criticising a paper by Francis Galton, *Proc.Roy.Soc.*, 19:393–410 (Bii 165, F1751). *See also* Charles Darwin's manuscript of pangenesis.

Panteague Home of Elizabeth Hensleigh in second half of 18c.

Papilionaceous Flowers 1858 On the agency of bees in the fertilisation of papilionaceous flowers, and on the crossing of kidney beans, *Ann.Mag.nat.Hist.*, 2:459–465, *Gdnr's Chronicle*, No.46:828–829 (Bii 19, F1701).

Parallel Roads of Glen Roy 1839 Observations on the parallel roads of Glen Roy, and of other parts of Lochaber in Scotland, with an attempt to prove that they are of marine origin, *Phil. Trans.*, 129:39–81, two plates, (Bi 89, F1653). CD's only contribution to *Phil. Trans.* For CD's later opinions of this paper *see* Glen Roy.

Parfitt, Edward 1820–1893. Botanist. 1860 CD to Stainton, mentions P as a correspondent about orchids—FUL 107. DNB.

Paris 1827 spring, CD visited with his uncle Josiah Wedgwood [II], his only visit to continental Europe.

Park Street London, No.7 home of Erasmus Alvey D, 1845–1852.

Parker 1837 P forwarded to CD a chart of Diego Garcia, Indian Ocean, which related to *Coral reefs*, *see* 3rd edition, 1889, 90–95—Darwin-Henslow 130.

Parker, The Misses 7 illegitimate daughters of Erasmus Darwin [I], ?by a *Miss* Parker, CD's great aunts. Erasmus D set up a school for them at Ashbourne, Derbyshire, in the 1790s. His *A plan for the conduct of female education in boarding schools*, London 1797, Dublin 1798, Cincinnati 1798, relates.

Parker, Cecile *see* Longueville.

Parker, Charles 1831–? 4c of Henry Parker [I]. unm. CD's nephew.

Parker, Francis 1829–1871. 3c of Henry Parker [I]. m 1860 Cecile Longueville 3s. CD's nephew.

Parker, Henry [I] 1788–1856. Physician & surgeon. m 1824 Marianne Darwin 4s 1d. 1. Robert, 2. Henry [II], 3. Francis, 4. Charles, 5. Mary Susan. CD's brother-in-law. After P's death, the grown-up family was adopted by Catherine D and lived at The Mount until her death in 1866.

Parker, Henry [II] 1827–1892. 7c of Henry Parker [I]. unm. CD's nephew. Classical Fellow of Oriel College, Oxford. 1862 P reviewed *Orchids* in *Sat. Rev.* 1862 Dec.29 P visited Down House—LLiii 274.

Parker, Mary Susan 1836–1893. 5c of Henry Parker [I]. m 1866 Edward Mostyn Owen of Woodhouse. CD's niece.

Parker, Marianne *see* Darwin.

Parker, Robert 1825–? 1c of Henry Parker [I]. CD's nephew. Story about his idleness—Barlow, *Autobiography* 33.

Parkfield Cardiganshire. Home of *Mrs* Josiah Wedgwood [I] until her death in 1815. Home of Sarah Elizabeth W [I] and her sister Catherine. When the latter died in 1823, Sarah Elizabeth W went to Camp Hill.

Parle N. Wales. 1826 Oct. 30 CD visited on a riding tour with his sister Caroline Sarah D.

Parr An old miserly squire of Lyth nr Shrewsbury.

Parslow, Joseph 1809/1810–1898. Manservant at 12 Upper Gower St c1840 and Butler at Down House until 1875. Hooker described him as 'an integral part of the family, and felt to be such by all visitors to the house'—LLi 318. Known by the family as 'the venerable P' after 'the aged Parslow' in Dickens' *Great expectations*. P was living out by 1871, at Home Cottage, Back Lane, Downe. Wages 1841–1842 £25 p.a. all found; 1881 £60; after CD's death P had a pension of £50 p.a. and the rent of his house. *Mrs* P was ED's personal maid before marriage; later she ran a dress making school; she died 1881. They had one son who 'married comfortably'—Darwin-Innes 251. 1882 P was at CD's funeral, walking in procession with Jackson, behind the family mourners, then seated in Jerusalem Chamber. 1885 P went to unveiling of CD statue at British Museum (Natural History). 1893 'The little Parslows came to tea', presumably grandchildren. Interview in D. S. Jordan, *The days of a man*, i:273–274, New York 1922.

Parson, Arthur m 1880 Mabel Frances Wedgwood.

Parsons, Theophilus 1797–1882. Barrister. Prof. Law Harvard & Swedenborgian. 1860 P wrote on *Origin* in *Silliman's J.*,—LLii 331. EB.

Pasteur, Louis 1822–1882. French chemist & bacteriologist. 1863 CD to Bentham, 'I was struck with infinite admiration at his work'—LLiii 25. EB.

Patrick, Mrs Camilla *see* Ludwig.

Patten, John Wilson, Baron Winmarleigh 1802–1892. 1st *Baron* 1874. Politician. Conservative MP 1832–1874. 1875 P was member of Vivisection Commission to which CD gave evidence—LLiii 201. DNB.

Pattrick, Francis 1837–1896. Classical scholar. Magdalene College Cambridge, President 1876–1896. 1882 P was on 'Personal Friends invited' list for CD's funeral. Identification uncertain.

Payne, Mr *see* Paine.

Paz, La 1832 Sep. 11 Schooner hired for 8 lunar months by Fitz-Roy from James Harris, resident at Rio Negro, Argentine, with schooner *La Liebre*. Commanded by *Lieut.* B. J.

Sullivan under *Lieut.* J. C. Wickham. Surveyed SE coast of Argentine.

Peacock, George 1791–1858. Anglican clergyman & astronomer. FRS 1818. Lowndean Prof. Astronomy Cambridge 1836–1858. Dean of Ely 1839–1858. P wrote to Henslow about post of naturalist on *Beagle*, suggesting Jenyns and then suggesting CD. DNB.

Peacocke, Mr 1837 P was present at interview of CD by Rice about £1000 grant for publishing *Zoology of Beagle* —Darwin-Henslow 134.

Pearce, Mr Manservant to Erasmus Alvey D. 1882 P was on 'Personal Friends invited' list for CD's funeral.

Pearson, Mr Resident at Downe. 1875 P was elected a trustee of Downe Friendly Club—Darwin-Innes 242.

Pearson, Hesketh 1887–1964. Actor & biographer. 1930 *Doctor Darwin*, a biography of Erasmus D [I]. Erasmus D, S. Galton & James Keir were his great great grandfathers.

Peas 1862, *Gdnr's Chronicle*, No.45:1052 (Bii 70, F1719).

Pellegrini, Carlo 1839–1889. Caricaturist. P signed most of his work 'Ape' from 1869. 1871 Caricature of CD called 'Natural selection', Men of the Day, No.33, *Vanity Fair*, Sep.10, not signed 'Ape'. It occurred for commercial sale in two sizes 31 cm & 18 cm, the former better coloured. DNB.

Pember, Katherine m 1925 *Sir* Charles Galton Darwin. CD's grand-daughter-in-law.

Penally nr Tenby, S.Wales. 1846 Home of CD's aunts Frances Allen and her sister *Mdme* [Jessie] Simonde de Sismondi.

Pengelly, William 1812–1894. Geologist. FRS 1863. Explorer of Devon caves. 1861 Jul. CD met at Torquay—LLii 376. DNB.

Pennethorne, Dean Parker 1835–1894. Barrister of Lincoln's Inn & School Inspector. 1860 CD to P, acknowledging letter on descent of man—Carroll 350. WWH.

Pepper A dog belonging to George Howard D which bit gardeners. P was taken over by William Erasmus D but bit gardener again; then to *Sir* Leslie Stephen in London, where it bit children; finally to *Archbishop* A. C. Tait at Addington Palace, Surrey—Atkins 80.

Perception 1873 [Letter] Perception in the lower animals, *Nature*, Lond., 7:360 (Bii 171, F1759), supporting a letter from Wallace, *ibid.*, 7:303, *Zoologist*, 8:3488–3489.

Period Piece 1952 *Period piece: a Cambridge childhood*, London,

by Gwendolen Mary Raverat (née Darwin). The most important source of information on CD's children in their adult day
to day lives, and on ED in old age, written as through the eyes
of G.M.R. as a child; a most interesting and amusing book.

Pernambuco Brazil. 1836 Aug.6–19 *Beagle* at. CD visited old
city of Olinda and studied the sandstone bar off the harbour;
now called Recife. see 1841 Bar of sandstone off Pernambuco,
Phil.Mag., 19:257–260 (Bi 139, F1659).

Perristone, or Perrystone Nr Ross, Herefordshire. Home of
William Clifford, family friend of Wedgwood. Several family
letters 1824–1848 are addressed from there.

Pertz, Miss Ann 1856–? d of George P. 1877 Aug. when visiting
Down House, P drew a leaf of *Trifolium resupinatum* for CD to
send to Dyer—MLii 412 (with drawing).

Pertz, Chevalier Georg H. m 1854 Leonora Horner. 1d Ann.
Royal Librarian Berlin.

Peters, Wilhelm Carl Hartwig 1815–1883. German palaeontologist. 1878 P seconded CD's election as Corresponding
Member of Koenlich-Preussische Akademie Berlin.

Petleys House at Downe, N of Down House. 1847–1856 Home
of Sarah Elizabeth Wedgwood [I] until her death. The Petley
family came to Downe in c13.

Philippi, Rudolph Amandus 1808–1904. Prof. Natural History Technical High School Cassel. 1851 P sent fossil cirripedes to CD; CD sent P *Fossil cirripedes—Lychnos*,
1948–1949: 206–210.

Phillips 1860 *Mrs* P a resident at Downe. 1868 'Old Phillips'
would not sell land to Innes to build a vicarage on, ? a farmer.
Phillips of Orange Court, perhaps the son, would not either.
Orange Court seems to have been owned by a *Mr*
Harris—Darwin-Innes 205, 227.

Phillips, George Lort ?–1866. of Laurenny Park. m 1840
Isabella Georgina Allen.

Phillips, Isabella Georgina *see* Allen.

Phillips, John 1800–1874. Geologist. FRS 1834. Keeper of
Ashmolean Museum Oxford 1854–1870. ?1856 CD to P on
foliation and offers copies of three vols of geology of
Beagle—Carroll 122. 1858 P to CD, to tell him of award of
Wollaston Medal of Geological Society. 1859 CD sent 1st
edition of *Origin* to—Sollas, *The age of the earth*, 251–253, 1905,
J. M. Edmonds, *Proc.Ashmol.nat.Hist.Soc.*, for 1948–1950,
25–29, 1951. 1859 P to CD, 'the only true definition of a

species, any form which has ever had a specific name'—MLi 127. 1860 P gave Rede lectures at Cambridge, anti-*Origin*, but very fair. *Life on earth*, Cambridge 1860, contains substance of Rede lectures, CD wrote that they were 'unreadably dull'—LLii 385. 1869 P sent CD his *Vesuvius*, Oxford 1869—Carroll 360. 1870 CD to Herschel, recommending that P be asked to revise 4th edition of *Manual of scientific enquiry*, 1871, which he did—Carroll 384.

Philoperistera Club 1855 A pigeon fancy club of which CD was a member—LLi 51. *see also* Columbarian.

Philos CD's nickname for his brother Erasmus Alvey D.

Philosophical Club of Royal Society Founded 1847. 1854 CD elected. A dining club of fortyseven members. It met on Thursdays at 6pm and chair quitted at 8.15pm for members to attend meetings of the Society. 1855 Dec.20 CD attended. 1864 CD resigned.

Phisty see Mephistopheles.

Physiological Society Founded 1876, partly as a result of the anti-vivisection movement. 1876 Jun.1 CD elected the first, and at that time the only, Honorary Member—MLii 436.

Pictet de la Rive, François Jules 1809–1872. Swiss zoologist. Prof. Zoology Geneva 1835–1859. 1860 P was courteously anti-*Origin*, review in *Arch.Sci.Bibliothèque Universelle*, Mar.—LLii 184.

Piano 1839 ED was given a piano from Broadwoods by her father, shortly after her marriage. It had belonged to *Rev.* Thomas Stevens, who had married Caroline Tollett. 1929 It was bought for Down House, for £20, from the Positivist Society—Atkins 116.

Pigeons The races of domestic pigeon, *Columba livia*, are extensively drawn on in *Variation* and CD kept stocks himself as well as getting material from other breeders. 1855 CD to Hooker, 'I love them to that extent that I cannot bear to kill and skeletonize them'—MLi 87. 1859 CD to Huxley, offering drawings of pigeons from his portfolio—MLi 130. CD was a member of the Columbarian & Philoperistera Societies qq.v.

Pinguicula 1874 [Irritability of *Pinguicula*], *Gdnr's Chronicle*, 2:15 (Bii 187, F1767).

Pinker, H. R. Hope- 1850–1927. Sculptor. Statue in University Museum Oxford is by P; model for it at Down House.

Pistyll Rhayadar [Rhiadr] Denbigh, Wales. 1820 Jul. CD & Erasmus Alvey D went on a riding tour from P.

Plas Edwards nr Towyn, Merioneth. 1819 Jul. CD went on family holiday there for 3 weeks.

Playfair, Sir Lyon, Baron 1818–1898. Chemist & administrator. 1st *Baron* 1892 KCB 1883 FRS 1848 MP 1868–1892. Chemist to Geological Survey & Prof. School of Mines London 1845. 1876 P visited Down House whilst staying at High Elms in company of Huxley, Morley & Gladstone. DNB.

Plinian Society of Edinburgh 1823 A student society founded by R. Jameson, ended c1848. 1826 R. E. Grant Secretary. 1826 Nov.28 CD elected; he attended eighteen out of a possible nineteen meetings up until 1827 Apr.3. 1827 Mar. 27 CD made a communication to it, not 'at beginning of the year 1826' as stated in Autobiography 39. Title was 1 That the ova of *Flustra* possess organs of locomotion. 2 That the small black globular body hitherto mistaken for the young of *Fucus loreus* is in reality the ovum of *Pontobdella muricata*. CD was wrong in both these assertions; the 'ova of *Flustra*' were pilidium larvae, and the 'ovum of *Pontobdella*' was an egg case full of eggs. Barrett 1977 ii:285 gives a full transcript of CD's original notes, now at Cambridge. 1873 Title of communication first printed in W. Elliot, *Trans.bot.Soc.Edinb.*, 11:1–42, p.17 footnote (F1764); also in *Nature*, Lond., 9:38. *see also* 1888 *Edinburgh weekly Dispatch*, May 22; J. H. Ashworth, *Proc.Roy.Soc.Edinb.*, 55:97–113; 1949, P. H. Jesperson, *Lychnos*, 159–167.

Plymouth *see* Devonport.

Pole, Elizabeth Chandos *see* Colyear.

Polish First editions in: *Origin of species* 1873 (F739); *Variation under domestication* 1888–1889 (F922); *Descent of man* 1874 (F1101); *Expression of the emotions* 1873 (F1203); *Cross and self fertilisation* 1964 (F1270); *Autobiography* 1891 (F1529).

Pollock, Sir Frederick, Bart 1845–1937. Jurist. 3rd *Bart* FBA 1902. 1882 Jan. 8 P came to Down House on a 'Sunday tramp'. DNB.

Polly A white rough-haired female fox terrier, which belonged to Henrietta Emma D and attached herself to CD when H.E.D. married in 1871. 1870 ED to H.E.D. description of behaviour after her litter of puppies had been removed and illustration of Haeckelian joke phylogeny—EDii 198. 1882 P was put down shortly after CD's death and buried under the Kentish beauty apple tree in the orchard. 1927 A stuffed replica was placed in the reconstructed old study by Buckston

Browne, curled up in her basket. It soon got moth and was thrown out—Atkins 115.

Pomare IV Queen of Tahiti; 1827–1877; Pomare was a lineal name, real name Aimata. 1835 Nov.25 P was entertained on board *Beagle*; 'a large awkward woman without any beauty, grace or dignity'—*J.Researches*, 1845, 416.

Poole Dorset. 1847 Jul. CD visited on way home from family holiday at Swanage.

Port, Marianne ?–1849. *Mrs* Waddington, mother of Frances, *Baroness* de Bunsen. Grand-niece of *Mrs* Delany. *Mme* D'Arbley described her as 'the beautiful Miss Port'. P was a friend of the Allens, especially of Lancelot Baugh A—EDi 48. 1817 *Mrs* Josiah Wedgwood to her sister Emma Allen 'the inconceivable Mrs Waddington'—EDi 110.

Port Darwin E Falkland Island, named after CD. 1834 Mar 17 CD crossed the isthmus near it.

Port Desire *see* Deseado.

Port Famine Patagonia, on Magellan Straits, S of Punta Arenas. 1834 Feb.2–11, Jun.1–8 *Beagle* there.

Port Jackson New South Wales, Australia. 1836 Jan.12 *Beagle* arrived and anchored in Sydney Cove.

Port Louis Berkeley Sound, E Falkland Island. 1833 Mar.1–Apr.6; 1834 Mar.10–Apr.7 *Beagle* at or near. CD at only in 1834.

Port Louis Mauritius. 1836 Apr.29–May 9 *Beagle* at. CD made several short excursions.

Porter, George Richardson 1792–1852. Statistician. Secretary to the Board of Trade 1834– . 1849 CD went to British Association meeting at Birmingham with P—LLi 378. DNB.

Portmore, Earl of *see* Colyear.

Porto Praya Santo Jago, Cape Verde Islands. 1832 Jan.17–Feb.8 *Beagle* at and CD landed. 1836 Aug.31–Sep.5 *Beagle* visited again.

Portsmouth Hampshire. 1846 Sep.12 CD visited on way to Isle of Wight on day trip from British Association meeting at Southampton. 1858 CD stopped at on way to family holiday in Isle of Wight.

Portsmouth, Earl of *see* Newton Fellowes.

Portuguese First editions in: *Bar of sandstone off Pernambuco* (F268) 1904; *Origin of species* (F743) ?192–; *Descent of man* (F1104) 1910–1912.

Pouchet, Felix Archimede 1800–1872. French biologist. 1868

CD quotes in translation 'variation under domestication throws no light on the natural modification of species'; a review of *Variation* in *Athenæum*, Feb.15 refers.

Poulton, Sir Edward Bagnall 1856–1943. Entomologist. Kt 1935 FRS 1889. Hope Prof. Zoology (Entomology) Oxford 1893–1933. Specialist on mimicry in butterflies and author of many papers on evolution. 1908 *Essays on evolution*, Oxford. 1909 *Charles Darwin and the Origin of species*, London. DNB. *see also* G. W. Sleeper.

Pour la Mérite 1867 CD awarded this Prussian Order.

Powell, Rev. Henry 1869–1871 P was Curate at Downe, known as *Mr* Punch—Darwin-Innes 230.

Powell, Rev. Baden 1796–1860. Mathematician. FRS 1824. Father of *Lord* Baden Powell, Chief Scout. Savilian Prof. Geometry Oxford 1827–1860. Correspondent of CD and important critic of evolution. 1855 *Essays on the spirit of inductive philosophy*, London, is referred to in Historical sketch in 3rd edition of *Origin*, 1861. 1861 Article by P pro-natural selection in *Essays and reviews*, 7th edition, London; quotation from, 138–139—MLi 174. DNB.

Power of Movement in Plants (book) 1880 *The power of movement in plants*, London, two line errata slip p.x, assisted by Francis D (F1325); facsimile 1966 (F1339); 1880 2nd thousand, errata corrected (F1326); facsimile 1969 (F1340); 1882 3rd thousand, preface slightly altered (F1328). First foreign editions: German (F1343), USA (F1327) 1881; Russian (F1349) 1882; Italian (F1347) 1884; Romanian (F1348) 1970.

Power of Movement of plants (paper) 1881 Movement of plants, *Nature*, London., 23:409 (Bii 224, F1791).

Prehistoric Europe 1881 James Geikie, *Prehistoric Europe, a geological sketch*, London (F1351), extracts from two letters from CD 141–142. Published late in 1880, although dated 1881.

Prestwich, Sir Joseph 1812–1896. Geologist & wine merchant. Kt 1896 FRS 1853. Prof. Geology Oxford 1874–1888. 1859 CD sent 1st edition *Origin* to. 1859 CD to Lyell, 'I wish there was any chance of Prestwich being shaken; but I fear he is too much of a catastrophist'—Carroll 181. DNB.

Prévost, Adèle 1803–1881. m 1828 Edward Simcoe Drewe.

Preyer, Wilhelm Thierry 1841–1897. Physiologist & child psychologist. Prof. Physiology Jena 1869–1893. 1862 P wrote dissertation on great auk, *Alca impennis*, along darwinian lines, almost the earliest piece of special work based on *Origin*—LLiii 16. 1868 Mar.31 CD to P, that he is glad to hear that P is pro-*Origin*—LLiii 88. 1879 Feb. P compiled a list of darwinian papers in Gratulationsheft number of *Kosmos* for CD's 70th birthday.

Price, James Butler at Down House c1882– . 1891 ED 'Parslow wants me to raise Price's wages again'—Atkins 74.

Price, John 1803–1887 Botanist. P sent CD *Utricularia* from Cheshire for *Insectivorous plants*. 1874 CD to P, thanking for sending *Utricularia*—Carroll 445, who identifies P as Bartholomew 1818–1898.

Prichard, James Cowles 1786–1848. Physician & ethnologist. FRS 1827 Physician to Bristol Infirmary. Some hesitant ideas about evolution in *Physical history of mankind*, 1813. Poulton, *Sci.Progress*, 1, Apr.1897, and *Essays on evolution*, 1908, 173–192, stresses importance of 2nd edition, 1826. 1844 CD to Hooker—LLii 29, MLi 43 refer. DNB.

Primula 1862 On the two forms, or dimorphic condition, in the species of *Primula*, and on their remarkable sexual relations, *J.Proc.Linn.Soc.Lond.(Bot.)*, 6:77–96 (Bii 45, F1717); French translation of this paper with CD's on *Catasetum* and on *Linum, Ann.Sci.nat.Bot.*, 19:204–295 (F1723). 1868 On the specific differences between *Primula veris*, Brit.Fl. (var. *officinalis* of Linn.), *P.vulgaris* Brit.Fl. (var. *acaulis*, Linn.) and *P.elatier* Jacq.; and on the hybrid nature of the common oxslip. With supplementary remarks on naturally produced hybrids in the genus *Verbascum, J.Linn.Soc.Lond.(Bot.)*, 10:437–454 (F1744). 1874 Flowers of the primrose destroyed by birds, *Nature*, Lond., 9:482, 10:24–25 (Bii 183, 184, F1770, 1771).

Pringsheim, Nathanael 1823–1894. German botanist. 1878 P seconded CD's election to Koenlich-Preussische Akademie as Corresponding Member—LLiii 224.

Pritchard Rev. Charles 1808–1893. Astronomer & educationalist. FRS 1840. Founder & Headmaster of Clapham Grammar School 1834–1862. Savilian Prof. Astronomy Oxford 1870. All CD's sons, except William Erasmus D, went to this school, but only George & Francis were taught by P. DNB.

Pritchard, George Missionary at Papiete, Tahiti. British Consul in Tahiti 1837–1844, in Samoa 1844–157. 1835 Nov. CD met and attended his church on Nov.22.

Prothero, Sir George Walter 1848–1922. Historian. KBE 1920

FBA. Fellow of King's College Cambridge 1872–1896. Cambridge friend of CD's sons. 1882 P was on 'Personal Friends invited' list for CD's funeral. 1903 P drew Francis D's attention to Baden Powell's article in favour of natural selection in *Essays and reviews*, 7th edition, 1861, 138–139; quotation from it—MLi 174. DNB.

Pryor, Marlborough Robert 1848–1920. Man of business. Cambridge friend of CD's sons. 1882 P was on 'Personal Friends invited' list for CD's funeral.

Public natural history collections 1858 *Public natural history collections. Copy of a memorial addressed to the Right Honourable the Chancellor of the Exchequer* [Benjamin Disraeli], no place, no publisher; signed by CD & eight others (F371).

Pucklands, Great & Little Two fields to W of Down House, bought by Buckston Browne 1931, 19½ acres together. Royal College of Surgeons research station built on Little P; B gave £100,000, of which £83,000 was invested after purchase and building. Great Pucklands was known as 'Stoney field' by the Ds.

Pugh, Miss Governess at Down House for about a year 1856–1857. P later went mad and was in an asylum, paid for by *Sir* John Hawkshaw whose children she had taught. CD paid £30 a year for her to have a holiday. 1866 ED visited P—EDii 185. P was alive in 1885.

Pumilio argyrolepis 1861 Notes on the achenia of *Pumilio argyrolepis* [an orchid], *Gdnr's Chronicle*, No.1:4–5 (Bii 36, F1709).

Punch, Mr Nickname for Powell, curate at Downe 1869–1870.

Puy *see* Du Puy.

Pyt House Wiltshire. Home of Charles Langton in 1866.

Q

Quatrefages de Bréau, Jean Louis Armand de 1810–1892. French naturalist. Foreign Fellow RS 1879. 1859 CD sent 1st edition *Origin* to Q. 1867 CD to Q, about French translation of *Origin*—MLi 201. 1868 CD to Stainton, CD had written to Q about silk moths—FUL 109. 1869 Q to CD, opposes CD on evolution, but hopes that their differences of opinion will never alter their good relationship—Carroll 368, 379, 382. 1870 *Charles Darwin et ses précurseurs Français: étude sur la transformisme*, Paris.

Queen Anne Street Cavendish Square, London. N.14 *Miss* G. Tollet there in 1859 Apr. No.31 Hensleigh Wedgwood's house. No.57, later No.6, house of CD's brother Erasmus Alvey D, 1852– .

Queries about expression These queries were distributed by CD, probably originally in mss to people in contact with primitive races, to discover what expressions were used in different circumstances. They were printed as follows: 1. 1867 [No copy known], title probably *Queries about expression for anthropological enquiry*, Cambridge or Boston, Mass., printed for Asa Gray before Mar.26, fifty copies (F871); this was the first edition anywhere, *see* No.4. 2. 1867 Signs of emotion among the Chinese, *Notes & Records for China & Japan*, 1:105, Aug.31, anonymous, submitted by Robert Swinhoe from mss received from CD (F872). 3. 1867 *Queries about expression*, single sheet, [?London], printed for CD late in the year (F873). 4. 1868 Queries about expression for anthropological enquiry, *Rep.Smithson.Instn*, for 1867; [324], text perhaps that of No.1 and perhaps printed from a copy (F874). No.3 is printed in all editions of *Expression*, 1873– , in which the answers are analysed. *See also* 1972 *Bull.Brit.Mus.* (*nat.Hist.*), hist.Ser., 4:205–219: 1975 *J.Soc.Biblphy nat.Hist.*, 7:259–263.

Query to Army Surgeons 1862 CD circulated a questionnaire to army surgeons about health of troops in the tropics. No copy known (F799), but text is printed in *Descent*, i:244–245.

Questions about the Breeding of Animals [1839] 8 pp, [London], probably late Apr., certainly before May 5 (F262); facsimile 1968, wrongly dated [1840] (F263). *See also J.Soc.Bibl-phy nat.Hist.*, 5220–225, 1969.

Questions for Mr Wynne An earlier set of questions in mss about the breeding of animals. Transcribed by Paul H. Barrett in Howard E. Gruber, *Darwin on man*, 423–425, 1974 (F1582).

Quiz A dog belonging to John Innes. 1862 Jan taken over by Down House. 1862 May Q was shot for biting.

R

Rade, Emil of Münster. 1877 R sent CD a photographic album of 154 German scientists for his 68th birthday. R originated the idea. The album is finely bound and t.p. decorated by A. Fitger who also contributed a dedicatory poem. Feb.16 CD thanks R and writes to Haeckel on the subject—LLiii 225–226.

Rain 1863 Yellow rain, *Gdnr's Chronicle*, No.28:675 (Bii 81, F1727).

Rájon, Paul Adolph 1842/1843–1888. 1875 R engraved on copper the Ouless portrait of CD.

Raleigh, Sir Walter 1861–1922. English scholar. Kt 1911. 1881 Oct. CD & ED took tea with R in Cambridge. DNB.

Ralfs, John 1807–1890. Surgeon & botanist. R lived at Penzance, Cornwall and sent CD *Pinguicula* for *Insectivorous plants* from there. DNB.

Ram, Miss 1927 Headmistress of an unsuccessful girls school at Down House for a brief period; the British Association bought out the remainder of her lease.

Ramsay, Sir Andrew Crombie 1814–1891. Geologist. Kt 1881 FRS 1862. Director General Geological Survey 1871–. 1846 CD to Lyell, R was in favour of sudden elevations; CD scoffs—MLii 120. c1850 R visited Down House for weekend—Carroll 69. 1856 CD 'talking with Ramsay about subsidence and the origin of continents and oceans'—LLii 77. 1859 CD sent R copy of 1st edition of *Origin*. 1859 CD to Lyell, 'I infer from a letter from Huxley that Ramsay is a convert'—Mli 137. Biography: A. Giekie 1895. DNB.

Ramsay, Marmaduke ?–1831. Cambridge friend of CD and tutor at Jesus. 5s of *Sir* Alexander R, b of *Sir* Andrew R. R intended to go on a projected trip to Canaries with CD when he died.

Ramsgate Kent. 1850 Oct.18 CD visited for the day from Hartfield, Sussex.

Ransome, George Agricultural instrument maker of Ipswich. 1849 or 1850 R commissioned set of 60 Ipswich Museum portraits for British Association meeting there in 1851. CD to R, happy to promote R's project and subscribes £1 towards portrait of 'the Bishop'. There are 2 bishops in the set, both of Norwich, Edward Stanley, died Sep.1849, and Samuel Hinds, appointed Oct.1849—Carroll 81. 1850 R gave CD a set which includes CD by T. H. Maguire.

Ras Family nickname for Erasmus Alvey D; also for Erasmus D [III].

Rats 1879 [Letter] Rats and water casks, *Nature*, Lond., 19:481 (Bii 218, F1785), supporting a letter from Arthur Nichols, *ibid.*, 19:433.

Raverat, Gwendolen Mary *see* Darwin.

Raverat, Jacques ?–1925. Artist. m 1911 Gwendolen Mary Darwin, d.s.p.

Ray Club *see* Cambridge Ray Club.

Ray Society Instituted 1844, for the publication of biological monographs. 1851, 1854 published CD's *Monograph of the sub-class Cirripedia*, two vols. 1856 CD to Hooker, 'I profited so enormously by its publishing my Cirripedia, that I cannot quite agree with you on confining it to translations'—MLi 94.

Rayleigh, Baron *see* Strutt.

Reader, Thomas Mellard 1832–1909. Geologist. 1881 R wrote to CD about the success of *Worms*—LLiii 217. 1881 CD to Hooker, about R's views on permanence of continents—LLiii 247.

Reade, William Winwood 1838–1875. Traveller & controversialist. ?1869 R gave CD information on Africa for *Expression*. CD sent *Queries about expression* to—Carroll 371. 1872 *The martyrdom of man*, London.

Real Accademia dei Lincei CD Foreign Member 1875.

Reale Accademia della Scienze Turin. CD received their Bressa Prize of 12,000 francs 1879.

Recife *see* Pernambuco.

Recollections of my mind and character *see* Autobiography.

Reed, Rev. George Varenne 1816–1886. Anglican clergyman. Rector of Hayes, Kent, 1854–1886. R was tutor to George, Francis, Leonard & Horace D before they went to Clapham Grammar School. 1859 R gave CD a cutting of 'carrion-smelling Arum'—J. R. Moore, *Notes & Records Roy.Soc.*, 32:51–70, 1977. 1882 R was on 'Personal Friends invited' list for CD's funeral.

Reeve, Mrs 1849 CD travelled by coach to British Association meeting at Birmingham with—LLi 378.

Reeves The family ran the blacksmith's forge at Downe, grandfather, father and, in 1951, son. ?Successors to 'Old M' q.v.

Regent Street London, No.24 1833 home of Erasmus Alvey D.

Reinwald, C. Publishers of Paris; published 1st French editions of eleven of CD's books, as well as editions of *Origin* from 1873 onwards, also *Life and letters*, 1888.

Rejlander, O. G. Professional photographer of London. R photographed CD c1870. 1882 steel engraving of R's photograph by C. H. Jeens is fpce to *Charles Darwin: memorial notices*, London, which had appeared in *Nature*, Lond., Jun.4, 1874.

Religious Views 1871 Letter from Mr. Darwin [on religious views], *Index*, 2:404 (Bii 167, F1753). The letter addressed to *Dr* F. E. Abbott.

3Rendel, Emily m 1866 Clement Wedgwood.

Reviews The best list of reviews of CD's works is that of J. P. Anderson, 1887 q.v. A. Ellegård 1958, surveys reviews in the press, in relation to popular rather than scientific opinion, in great detail with full reference. No collection of reviews has yet been published.

Rhadamanthus Minor 1863 Nickname for Henrietta Emma D, given by Huxley. 'Mr. Huxley used to laugh at for the severity of her criticisms'—MLi 238. R son of Zeus and Europa, one of the judges of the underworld.

Rhea 1837 [Notes on *Rhea americana* and *Rhea darwini*], *Proc.zool.Soc.Lond.*, Part V, No.51:35–36, follows John Gould's original description of *R.darwini* (Bi 38, F1643).

Rhinoceros Tree *see* Elephant tree.

Rhodes, Francis, later Darwin 1825–1920. m 1849 Charlotte Maria Cooper D. R inherited Elston under will of his brother-in-law, Robert Alvey D, and changed his name in 1850. 1882 R was present at CD's funeral as head of the senior branch of D family.

Rice, Thomas Spring [I] 1790–1866. Statesman. 1st *Baron* Monteagle of Brandon 1839. Chancellor of the Exchequer 1835–1839. 1837 Aug. R authorized £1000 grant for publishing scientific results of *Beagle* voyage. DNB.

Rice, Thomas Spring [II] 1849–1926. 3rd *Baron* Monteagle 1909. Cambridge friend of CD's sons. Irish resident landlord, of Foynes, Co. Limerick. 1882 R was on 'Family Friends invited' list for CD's funeral. WWH.

Rich, Anthony ?1804–1891. Chapel Croft, Heene, Worthing,

Sussex. Honorary Fellow of Caius College, Cambridge. 1878 Dec. R made a will leaving nearly all his property to CD, on death of himself, then 74, and his sister; at that time it included some property in Cornhill, London, with income above £1000. 1879 May 6 and 1881 Sep.8 CD visited R at Worthing. 1882 CD to R about success of *Worms*. 1882 After CD's death R left his estate to the children, except house and contents which went to Huxley who immediately sold it. Final value of estate c£3000. R was no relation and the gift was in recognition of CD's contribution to science.

Rich, Claudius ?–1831. m Mary Mackintosh.

Rich, Mary *see* Mackintosh.

Richardson, Sir Benjamin Ward 1828–1896. Physician. Kt 1893 FRS 1867. 1876 CD to Romanes, R's letter to *Nature* is capital. Experimentation on animals for the advancement of practical medicine, *Nature*, Lond., 14:148–152. DNB.

Richmond, George 1809–1896. Artist. RA. Especially portrait painter in water colour. 1839 Mar. water colour by R, unsigned, of CD, painted in London, note on back says 1840 Mar. Pencil sketch for this found in Botany School Cambridge 1929. 1839 Water colour of ED—EDii 31,33 refer.

Richmond, Sir William Blake 1842–1921 Artist. KCB 1897 RA 1895. s of George R. 1879 Jun. CD sat for him in LL.D. robes, exhibited RA 1881. £400 subscribed by members of Cambridge Philosophical Society, in whose rooms it now is. 1881 CD & ED went to see it in the Society's Library, 'the red picture, and I thought it quite horrid, so fierce and so dirty'—EDii 248. Francis D 'according to my own view, neither the attitude nor the expression are characteristic of my father'—LLiii 222. DNB.

Richter, Hans 1843–1914. Hungarian pianist & conductor. 1881 May R visited Down House—LLiii 223. R wrote of his visit in *Neue Tagblatt*, Wien, republished in O. Zacharias, *Charles R. Darwin*, Berlin 1882.

Ridge, The House at Hartfield, nr Tunbridge Wells, Sussex, on border of Ashdown Forest. Home of Sarah Elizabeth Wedgwood [II] 1849–1868. Quarter of a mile from Hartfield Grove, home of Charles Langton.

Ridgemount House at Bassett, N. Stoneham, Southampton, Hampshire. Home of William Erasmus D 1862–1892.

Ridley, C. 1878 CD to R, about *Dr* E. B. Pusey and evolution, a stern letter 'Dr. Pusey's attack will be as powerless to retard by a day the belief in evolution'—LLiii 235.

Riley, Charles Valentine 1843–1895. Entomologist. State Entomologist to Missouri 1868. Entomologist to US Department of Agriculture 1878–1894. 1875 CD to Weismann, R supports Weir's views on caterpillars—MLi 357. 1871 CD to R, 'our Parliament would think any man mad who should propose to appoint a State Entomologist'—MLii 385.

Ring ?1862 R's wife ill, ?a villager at Downe—Darwin-Innes 212.

Rio de Janeiro Brazil. 1832 Apr.4 *Beagle* arrived at. Apr.8–23 CD travelled inland. Jul.5 *Beagle* Left.

Rio Negro [I] Patagonia, Argentina. 1833 Aug.11 *Beagle* at. CD travelled from there overland, c850 km, to Buenos Aires, arriving Sep.20.

Rio Negro [II] Entre Rios, Uraguay. 1833 Nov.22–26 CD stayed with *Mr* Keen at his estancia on rio Beguelo, a tributary, and collected fossils nearby.

Ritchie, Mrs *see* Ann Isabella Thackeray.

Ritchie, Sir Richmond Thackeray Willoughby 1854–1912. Civil Servant. KCB 1907. m Ann Isabella Thackeray, his father's 1st cousin. 1882 R was on 'Personal Friends invited' list for CD's funeral. DNB.

Rivers, Thomas 1798–1877. Nurseryman, of Sawbridgeworth, Herts. ?1866 CD to R, on bud variation—MLi 275. ?1866 CD to R, on plant variation in general—LLiii 57. 1874 CD to Newton, R had reported great increase in number of birds in his garden—N&R 47. R is repeatedly referred to in *Variation*. DNB.

Riviere, Briton 1840–1920. Painter. RA. 1870 CD sent copy of *J.Researches* to R.

Robertson, George Croom 1842–1892. Philosopher. Prof. Mental Philosophy University College London 1866– . 1877 Apr. CD sent R his mss Biographical sketch of an infant, as editor of *Mind*, with explanatory letter—LLiii 234. 1882 Jan. CD to Romanes, indicating that R was involved in helping Grant Allen in his financial difficulties—Carroll 612.

Robinson 1868 Curate at Downe, unsatisfactory and walking with village girls at night. 1870 R was Curate at Bearstead, Kent—Darwin-Innes 223, 226.

Robinson, Harold & Samuel Picture framers and restorers of St John's Wood, London; worked for *Sir* George Buxton Browne. 1929 Rs moved into Down House as assistants.

Harry returned to Wimpole St, to look after B and to Hayes, Middlesex on B's death. Samuel became custodian of Down House 1955 until death in 1958.

Robinson, Sydney s of Samuel R. Custodian of Down House from his father's death 1958 to 1975.

Robinson, Rev. Thomas Romney 1792–1882. Astronomer. FRS 1856. Director of Armagh observatory. 1846 CD met R at British Association meeting, Southampton. 1849 CD met R at British Association meeting, Birmingham, where R was President. DNB.

Rock seen on an iceberg 1839 Note on a rock seen on an iceberg in 61° South latitude, *J.geogr.Soc.*, 9:528–529 (Bi 137, F1652).

Rodwell, John Meadows 1808–1900. Orientalist. Rector of St Ethelburga's Bishopsgate, London 1843. R was nephew of William Kirby, entomologist. Cambridge contemporary of CD. 1860 R to CD, about *Origin*. Francis D footnote 'My father remembers him saying "It strikes me that all our knowledge about the structure of our earth is very much like what an old hen would know about a hundred acre field, in a corner of which she is scratching"'—LLii 348. DNB.

Rogers, Henry Darwin 1809–1866. Geologist. FRS 1858. Born in USA. Prof. Geology Glasgow. 1860 CD to Lyell, 'He goes very far with us'—LLii 291.

Rolfe, Robert Monsey 1790–1868. Judge & statesman. 1st *Baron* Cranworth 1850. Lord Chancellor 1852. 1865 R lived at Holwood, nr Downe. DNB.

Rolleston, George 1829–1881. Comparative anatomist. FRS 1862. Prof. Anatomy & Physiology Oxford 1860–1881. 1861 CD had heard R speak at Linnean Society. 1871 CD to Busk, R had pointed out error about supracondyloid foramen in 1st issue of *Descent*—Carroll 387. 1875 R to CD, on primitive man—MLii 46.

Romanes, George John 1848–1894. Biologist. FRS 1879. m 1879 Ethel Duncan 5s 1d. R worked at University College London and later at Oxford. R was the most important of CD's younger biological friends, frequent correspondent and more than once at Down House. Francis D records a conversation with R telling of a discussion with CD about recognition of natural beauty and its relation to natural selection—LLiii 54. 1873 Dec.7 CD would like to meet R and asks to lunch—Carroll 453, 454 (dated ?1874). 1874 CD first met R in London this year—*Life of Romanes* 13. 1874 CD to R, 'How glad I am that you are so young'—*Life of Romanes* 14. 1874 CD introduces R to Hooker—Carroll 456, 457. 1874 R to CD, on disuse of organs—MLi 352. 1877 CD to R, pleased to propose R for Royal Society—Carroll 503. 1877 CD to R, astonished that R has not been elected—Carroll 509. 1878 CD to R, 'Frank says you ought to keep an idiot, a deaf mute, a monkey, and a baby in your house'—MLii 49. 1880 Dec.17 'I have now got a monkey. Sclater let me choose one from the Zoo'—*Life of Romanes* 105. 1881 Apr. CD to R, about letter from Frances Cobbe on vivisection in *The Times*—LLiii 206. 1882 R was on 'Personal Friends invited' list for CD's funeral. 1882 *Animal intelligence*, London (F1416), contains many extracts from CD's notes; 1883 *Mental evolution in animals*, London (F1434), contains CD's essay on instinct, 355–384; 1892–1897 *Darwin and after Darwin*, 3 vols, London; 1893 *An examination of Weismannism*, London. Biography: Ethel Romanes (wife) 1896. DNB. Most R letters are at American Philosophical Society and printed in Carroll.

Romanian First editions in: *Journal of researches* (F225) 1958; *Origin of species* (F746) 1950; *Fertilisation of orchids* (F824) 1964; *Climbing plants* (F864) 1970; *Variation under domestication* (F924) 1963; *Descent of man* (F1106) 1967; *Expression of the emotions* (F1205) 1967; *Insectivorous plants* (F1243) 1965; *Cross and self fertilisation* (F1271) 1964; *Different forms of flowers* (F1361) 1965; *Movement in plants* (F1348) 1970; *Autobiography* (F1532) 1962.

Römer, Ferdinand 1818–1891. Prof. Mineralogy & Geology Breslau. 1851 R sent fossil cirripedes to CD. CD sent R *Fossil cirripedes*—*Lychnos*, 1948–1949:206–210.

Romilly, Caroline ?–1830. m 1870 Lancelot Baugh Allen as 1st wife.

Roots 1882 The action of carbonate of ammonia on the roots of certain plants, *J.Linn.Soc.Lond.(Bot.)*,19:239–261 (Bii 236, F1800).

Rorison, Gilbert 1821–1861. Episcopalian clergyman of Peterhead, Aberdeenshire. Anonymous author of *The three barriers: notes on Mr. Darwin's 'Origin of species'*, Aberdeen 1861, preface signed G.R., anti-evolution. The barriers are the breast, the backbone and the brain. 1862 CD to Huxley, '(a theological hash of the old abuse of me), Owen gives the author a new resumé of his brain doctrine'—MLii 341.

Rosas, Juan Manuel 1793–1877. Cattle rancher & Dictator of

Argentine. 1833 R helped CD with horses and safe conducts on inland journeys—*J.Researches*. 1834 CD to E. Lumb 'The Caesar-like Rosas'—J. H. Winslow, *J.hist.Geogr.*, 1:347–360, 1975. 1852 R was overthrown and retired to Swaythling, Hants. CD met at Southampton.

Rose, Sibyl m 1917 C. J. Wharton Darwin.

Ross, Captain John Clunies Merchant navy captain. Proprietor of Cocos Keeling Islands, arrived 1827, living on Direction Island. 1833 Apr.3 CD met there. Clunies Ross V is present proprietor under Australian Government.

Rothenstein, Sir William 1872–1945. Artist. Kt 1931. 1909 Bronze medallion of CD by R shown at Christ's College Cambridge anniversary exhibition.

Rothrock, Joseph Trimble 1839–1922. American botanist. R answered CD's queries for *Expression* on American Indians. 1862 CD to Gray, refers to R's work on *Houstonia*—Darwin-Gray 43.

Roux, Wilhelm 1850–1934. German embryologist. 1881 R sent CD a copy of his *Der Kampf der Thiele*, 1881. CD to Romanes, thought the book important, especially on the struggle of cell against cell within the body—LLiii 244.

Rowlands, Moelwyn Jones *see Darwin's notebooks*.

Rowlett, George ?–1834. Purser on 2nd voyage of *Beagle*; he was, in his late 30s, the oldest man aboard. 1834 Jun. R died at sea.

Royal Botanic Garden Kew, Surrey. Developed as a personal estate around Kew Palace by George III, was taken over as the National botanic garden, research centre and herbarium in 1840. First Director *Sir* William Jackson Hooker; 2nd *Sir* Joseph Dalton Hooker, his son; 3rd *Sir* William Turner Thiselton-Dyer, J. D. H.'s son-in-law. CD visited and received much plant material from, for his botanical work.

Royal College of Physicians of England CD awarded Baly Medal 1879.

Royal College of Surgeons of England 1953 took over Down House and have administered it since. Their research station, on Little Pucklands field, marches with the Down House estate to the south. 1974 published, under Phillimore imprint, Atkins, *Down, The home of the Darwins*.

Royal Geographical Society CD Fellow 1838.

Royal Institution Albemarle St, London. 1880 Apr.9 Huxley gave address to on 'The coming of age of The origin of species', published in *Nature*, Lond., 22:1-4, and in *Science & culture*, 310. 'In the above-mentioned lecture Mr Huxley made a strong point of the accumulation of palaeontological evidence which the years 1859 to 1880 have given us in favour of evolution'—LLiii 240.

Royal Irish Academy Dublin. CD Honorary Member 1866.

Royal Medical Society of Edinburgh CD Member 1826–1827 whilst a medical student. Honorary Member 1866.

Royal Society The D family is the only one in the history of the Society to have had a continuous succession from father to son of Fellows, with no year without at least one fellow, from Erasmus D [I], elected 1761, to *Sir* Charles Galton D, died 1962. The succession continues, through the female line, to Richard Darwin Keynes, elected 1959. There were three living Fellows briefly in the spring of 1882 and again 1903–1912. CD was elected Fellow 1839 Jan.24; member of Council 1849–1850, 1855–1856; Royal Medal 1853; Copley Medal 1864. 1877 CD to Romanes, who had failed to be elected in that year; Hooker (then President) had implied that age and position in scientific society weighed heavily, as did having been proposed many times; youth is a disqualification—Carroll 509. 1890 Darwin Medal instituted, with residual funds from Darwin Memorial appeal; the effigy of CD is reduced from medallion by Allen Wyon. *see also* Philosophical Club, X Club.

Royal Society of Edinburgh CD Fellow 1865.

Royal Society of New South Wales Sydney. CD Honorary Member 1879.

Royer, Mlle Clémence-August 1830–1902. 1862 R translated *Origin* into French, adding her own footnotes. 1862 CD to Gray, R 'must be one of the cleverest and oddest women in Europe' LLii 387. 1862 CD to Quatrefages, 'I wish the translator had known more natural history'—MLi 202. 1867 CD to Lyell, about the translation, 'Nevertheless with all its bad judgement & taste it shows, I think, that the woman is uncommonly clever'—LLiii 73, Carroll 332.

Royle, John Forbes 1799–1858. Surgeon & naturalist. FRS 1837. Originally in Medical Service in India. Prof. Materia Medica & Therapeutics King's College London 1836–1858. Secretary of Geological Society before CD. ?1840 CD to R, thanking for a book, perhaps *Illustrations of the botany . . . of the Himalayan mountains*, [1833–]1839[–1840]; 'Long may our rule flourish in India'—MLi 67. DNB.

Ruck, Amy Richenda 1850–1876. d of Lawrence R. m 1874 *Sir* Francis D as 1st wife. Died in childbed. CD's daughter-in-law. 1876 Sep.15 CD to G. W. Norman, 'she was sweet and gentle'; Francis D had gone to N. Wales for the funeral—Carroll 497. Some *Mrs* Ruck, perhaps her mother, was visiting ED in Cambridge 'once a year' in 1890; she taught ED solo whist.

Ruck, Lawrence of Pantlludw, nr Machynlleth, Wales. f of Amy Richenda R.

Rucker, Sigismund Orchid grower of West Hill, Wandsworth, Surrey. R lent CD *Mormodes ignea*, goblin orchid—Allan 205.

Rüdinger, Nicolaus 1832–1896. Anatomist. 1876 CD to Lawson Tait, R had written to CD about regeneration of digits—MLi 363.

Rugby Warwickshire. 1852 CD & ED visited William Erasmus D at Rugby School. 1858 CD & ED stopped there on return from British Association meeting at Glasgow.

Ruskin, John 1819–1900. Poet & social reformer. 1879 CD met and made friends with in the Lake District; visited his home, Brantwood, Coniston, but could not understand the Turner's in R's bedroom. CD considered R's mind clouded—EDii 238. 1879 CD to Romanes, 'We saw Ruskin several times, and he was uncommonly pleasant'—*Life of Romanes* 98. DNB.

Russian First editions in *Letters on geology* (F7) 1959; *Journal of researches* (F226) 1870–1871; Bar of sandstone off Pernambuco (F270) 1936; *Coral reefs* (summary only, F320) 1846; *Coral reefs* (complete, F321) 1936; *Volcanic islands & South America* (F323) 1936; *Manual of scientific enquiry* (CD's article only, F336) 1860; *Memoir of Professor Henslow* (CD's recollections only, F832) 1959; On the tendency of species to form varieties (F370) 1939; *Origin of species* (F748) 1864; *Fertilisation of orchids* (F825) 1900; *Climbing plants* (F865) 1900; *Variation under domestication* (F925) 1867–1868; *Descent of man* (F1107) 1871; *Expression of the emotions* (F1206) 1872; *Insectivorous plants* (F1244) 1876; *Cross and self fertilisation* (F1272) 1938; *Different forms of flowers* (F1302) 1948; Biographical sketch of an infant (F1314) 1877; *Erasmus Darwin* (CD's notice only, F1324) 1959; *Movement in plants* (F1349) 1896; *Vegetable mould and worms* (F1408) 1882; *Autobiography* (F1533) 1896. 'The Collected Works, edited by S. L. Sobol', 1935–1959, is by far the most comprehensive in any language.

Ruthin Denbigh, Wales. 1831 Aug. CD visited with Sedgwick on geology trip.

Rütimeyer, Carl Ludwig 1825–1895. Swiss palaeontologist. Prof. Comparative Anatomy Basel. 1867 CD to Lyell, R had sent him his pamphlet *Über die Herkunft unserer Thierwelt*, Basel 1867, but CD had not read it or opened the pages—Carroll 331. 1868 R author of *Die Grenzen der Thierwelt: eine Betrachtung zu Darwin's lehre*, Basel. CD had this pamphlet translated by Camilla Ludwig.

Ryan, Mary Julia Margaret Cameron's pretty maid who often sat for her, known as The Madonna. 1868 CD & family met R—EDii 191.

Ryde, Jane Harriet 1794–1866. m *Sir* Francis Sacheveral D.

S

Sabine, Sir Edward 1788–1883. Astronomer & physicist. KCB 1869 FRS 1818 PRS 1861–1871. *General* R.A., saw little action, but went on several expeditions as scientist. S was antidarwinian. 1849 CD to Hooker, CD had travelled with S to British Association meeting at Birmingham, comments about *Mrs* S 'A very nice woman she is, and so is her sharp and sagacious mother'—LLi 378. 1864 S to CD, asking him to attend Royal Society to receive Copley Medal; CD did not go—MLi 257. 1864 S's Presidential address to Royal Society about CD's Copley Medal, 'Speaking generally and collectively, we have expressly omitted it [*Origin*] from the grounds of our award': a remark which caused much offence—MLiii 28. DNB.

Sagitta 1844 Observations on the structure and propagation of the genus *Sagitta, Ann.Mag.nat.Hist.*, 13:1–6 (Bi 177, F1664) French, *Ann.Sci.nat.Zool.*, 1:360–365.

St Andrews Fife, Scotland. 1827 CD visited on spring tour.

St Croix, Elizabeth 1790–1868. m 1817 William Brown D.

St Helena Atlantic Ocean. 1836 Jul.7–14 *Beagle* at. CD stayed ashore 4 days 'within a stone's throw of Napoleon's tomb'.

St Paul's Rocks Atlantic Ocean, uninhabited island, with St Peter, belonging to Brazil. 1832 Feb.16–17 *Beagle* at and CD landed.

Sales, Sydney Landowner at Downe, W & N of Down House. 1843 CD bought an acre and a bit from him. 1872 'Mr.Sales would be sure to build some more ugly houses on it if he got the land'. 1881 CD bought a strip of field on W side of Down House, beyond orchard, for a hard tennis court.

Saliferous Deposits 1838 Origin of saliferous deposits: salt lakes of Patagonia and La Plata, *J.geol.Soc.*, 2:127–128 (F1651), an extract from *Geological observations on South America*, 73–75, before publication. 1846 Origin of saliferous deposits, *Quart.J.geol.Soc.(Proc.)*, 2:127–128 (Bi 212, F1673).

Salin, Vernon 1868 Acting Curate at Downe, spelling is

doubtful—Darwin-Innes 220.

Salisbury, Marchioness of *see* Alderson.

Salisbury, Marquis of *see* Robert Arthur Talbot Gascoyne Cecil.

Salt 1847 Salt, *Gndr's Chronicle*, No.10:157–158 (Bii 14, F1676).

Salt on Carbonate of Lime 1844 What is the action of common salt on carbonate of lime?, *Gdnr's Chronicle*, No.37:628–629 (Bi 198, F1668).

Salt-Water and Seeds *see* Seeds.

Salter, John William 1820–1869. Palaeontologist to Geological Survey 1846–1863. 1861 S showed CD some evolutionary series of brachiopods at Museum of Practical Geology, Jermyn St, London—LLii 367.

Salter, Thomas Bell 1814–1858. Physician & botanist of Ryde, Isle of Wight. Nephew of Prof. Thomas Bell. 1855 S was sending seeds to CD for hybrid studies—Darwin-Henslow 175, as I.B.S.

Salvador Brazil, also called Bahia. 1832 Feb.22–Mar.18 *Beagle* at and CD ashore. 1836 Aug.1–17 *Beagle* returned and CD ashore.

Sanderson, Sir John Scott Burdon, Bart 1828–1905. Physician & physiologist. 1st *Bart* 1899 FRS 1867. Prof. Physiology University College London 1874–1882; Oxford 1882–1895. Regius Prof. Medicine Oxford 1895–1904. 1875 S saw and agreed to Litchfield's sketch for vivisection bill. 1881 CD attended lecture by S at Royal Institution on plant movement; audience applauded on CD's entrance—EDi 245. S helped CD with experiments for *Insectivorous plants*. 1882 S was on 'Personal Friends invited' list for CD's funeral. After CD's death, S was much involved in controversies on vivisection. DNB.

Sandown Isle of Wight. 1858 Jul.–Aug. CD & family visited.

Sandys, John Edwin 1844–1928. Classical scholar. Public Orator Cambridge 1876–1919. 1877 Nov.17 S gave oration on CD's Honorary LL.D. DNB WWH. 'Tu vero, qui leges naturae tam docte illustraveris, legum Doctor nobis esto'—LLiii 222.

Sandwalk Path in grounds of Down House, used regularly by CD for constitutional walk. 1846 S was laid down around woodland planted from pasture rented from *Sir* John William Lubbock. 1874 It was bought from *Sir* John L. Sandpit at S end was used for dressing the path; there was a summer-house at far SE end—EDii 76.

Santa Fé Argentine. 1833 Oct.2–15 CD was at.

Santiago Chile. 1835 Mar.13 CD visited on his way from Valparaiso to cross the cordilleras to Mendoza; Apr.10 returned through.

Santo Jago Cape Verde Islands, Atlantic Ocean. 1832 Jan.17–Feb.8 *Beagle* at Porto Praya and CD landed. 1836 Aug.31–Sep.5 *Beagle* again at and CD landed.

Saporta, Louis Charles Joseph Gaston, Marquis de 1823–1995. French palaeobotanist. 1863 CD to Lyell, S was pro-*Origin*—LLiii 17. 1868 CD to S, about the growth of belief in evolution in France—LLiii 103. 1878 CD to S, about his election to Académie des Sciences—MLi 376. S was a fairly frequent correspondent on botanical matters.

Sara 1881 Nurse to Bernard Richard Meirion D—EDii 246, 247.

Sarcey, Francisque 1827–1899. French dramatic critic. 1880 S lunched at Down House in summer with Édmond Barbier.

Schaaffhausen, Hermann Joseph 1816–1893. German anthropologist. 1853 Über Beständigkeit und Unwandlung der Arten, *Verhandl.Naturhist.Vereins*, Bonn, which is an evolutionary forerunner. 1860 S sent a copy to Lyell.

Scherzer, Carl Heinrich, Ritter von 1821–1903. Austrian ethnologist. S edited *Reise der . . . Fregatte Novara*, 1861–1862. 1868 CD to S, addressing him as Ministerial Rath, thanking for translating *Queries about expression*, 'and inserting'—Carroll 356. 1879 CD to S, 'What a foolish idea seems to prevail in Germany on the connection between socialism and evolution through natural selection'—LLiii 237.

Schimmelpeninck, Lambert of Bristol. m 1806 Mary Ann Galton. Moravian.

Schimmelpeninck, Mary Ann *see* Galton.

Schlagintweit-Sakünlünski, Hermann Alfred Rudolph von 1826–1882. German botanist & geologist. 1857 CD to Hooker, 'I believe he is returned to England, and he has poultry skins from W. Elliot of Madras'—MLi 99. CD spells, with doubt, 'Schlagenheit'. 1860 CD to Lyell, 'Do not trust Sclagenweit [sic]', about yak-cattle crosses; paper with his brother Robert von S-S., *Rep.Brit.Assoc.Adv.Sci.*, 27:106–108, 1857—Carroll 230, Stauffer 438.

Schleiden, Matthias Jakob 1804–1881. German botanist and, with Schwann, founder of the cell theory. 1864 CD to Welsh, S was, with other Germans, coming round to belief in natural selection—MLi 259.

Schlesische Gesellschaft für Vaterlandische Cultur Breslau. CD Honorary Member 1878.

Schmerling, Philippe Charles 1791–1836. French geologist. 1863 CD to Hooker, concerning antiquity of man, 'Falconer . . . does not do justice to . . . Schmerling'—LLiii 19.

Schomburk, Sir Robert Hermann 1804–1865. Kt 1844. Naturalist in West Indies. c1850 S visited Down House for weekend—Carroll 69. c1862 S told CD about the three forms of *Catasetum tridentatum* which had been described as belonging to three different genera—*J.Linn.Soc.(Bot.)*, 6:151–157. DNB.

Schulze, Karl August Julius Fritz 1846–1908. Prof. Technische Hochschüle Dresden. 1875 CD to S, thanking him for copy of *Kant und Darwin*, Jena 1875—Carroll 470.

Schweizerbart'sche Verlag Publisher of Stuttgart, Germany. 1860–1882 S published 1st German editions of eleven of CD's books, as well as 2nd edition of *Journal of researches* 1875 and *Life and letters* 1887–1888.

Science Defence Association 1881 was formed as a result of prosecution of David Ferrier. CD's name was put forward as President, but he declined—MLii 439.

Scientifics 1880 fifty members visited Down House and were entertained with claret-cup, wine and biscuits. Francis D talked to them, but CD did not appear. Perhaps a working mens' club—Atkins 85.

Sclater, Philip Lutley 1829–1913. Orinithologist & animal geographer. FRS 1861. Secretary to Zoological Society of London 1859–1902. 1860 CD to S, thanking for list and notes on Galápagos Islands birds—Carroll 195, 197. DNB.

Scoresby, Rev. William 1789–1857. Anglican clergyman, whaler & arctic scientist. FRS 1824 DD 1839. 1855 CD corresponded with S on seed transport—LLii 56. DNB.

Scotland Apart from his time at Edinburgh University, 1825 Oct.22–1827 Apr.c24, CD made 2 tours in Scotland. 1827 Apr.–May, on leaving University, Dundee, St Andrews, Stirling, Glasgow and from there to Belfast. 1838 Jun. by boat from London to Leith, Edinburgh. Loch Leven, Glen Roy, Glasgow on a geological trip. 1855 CD & ED went to British Association meeting at Glasgow.

Scott, John 1838–1880. Botanist. On staff at Royal Botanic Garden Edinburgh 1859–1864. Curator Botanic Garden Calcutta 1864– . 'The only naturalist who can be described as a

pupil of Darwin's' [sic]—Poulton, *Darwin and the Origin* 53.
1861 CD to Hooker, 'I have been corresponding largely with
him; he is no common man'—LLiii 300. 1867 Brief biography
by *Sir* George King, 'shy and modest almost to being apologe-
tic', 'almost morbidly modest'—MLi 217. 1863 CD to S, 'I
cannot help doubting . . . whether you fully comprehend
what is meant by natural selection'—MLi 239. 1864 CD to
Hooker, 'I have paid the poor fellow's passage out to India';
CD had thought of employing him at Down House, and
suggested that Hooker take him on at Kew. He left Edinburgh
'at what . . . he considered discouragement and slight'. CD
met S once, between Mar. and May 1864. 1867 CD to Hooker,
he had had a nice letter from S on acclimatization—MLii 3.
1871 S offers to repay his fare; CD replies strongly that he 'a
rich man' had given it as a present, not as a loan—MLii 331.
1873 S helped with *Expression*, p.21 'The habit of accurate
observation, gained by his botanical studies, has been brought
to bear on our present subject'.

Sea-Water and Seeds 1855 Does sea-water kill seeds?, *Gdnr's
Chronicle*, No.15:242 (Bi 255, F1682); 1855 [same title], *ibid.*,
No.21:356–357 (Bi255, F1683); 1855 Effect of salt-water on
the germination of seeds, *ibid.*, No.48:789 (Bi 262, F1688);
1857 On the action of sea-water on the germination of seeds,
J.Proc.Linn.Soc.Lond. (Bot.), 1:130–140 (Bi 264, F1694).

Sedgwick, Rev. Adam 1785–1873. Geologist. FRS 1830. Fellow of Trinity College & Woodwardian Prof. Geology Cambridge 1818–1873. 1831 Aug. CD made geological tour in N.
Wales with S. 1859 CD sent S 1st edition of *Origin*. 1859 S to
CD, 'I have read your book with more pain than pleasure . . .
You have *deserted*—after a start in that tram-road of all solid
physical truth—the true method of induction, and started us in
machinery as wild, I think, as Bishop Wilkin's locomotive that
was to sail with us to the moon'—LLii 248. 1859 CD to
Huxley, S 'has laughed till his sides ached at by book'—MLi
130. 1860 S spoke to Cambridge Philosophical Society,
reported in *Cambridge Chronicle*, May 19, 'Darwin's theory
may help to simplify our classifications . . . but he has not
undermined any grand truth in the constancy of natural laws,
and the continuity of true species'—MLi 149. 1870 CD &
family called on S at Cambridge in May. Fine friendly letter
from S, 'I was overflowing with joy when I saw you'—MLii
236. Biography: Clark & Hughes 1890. DNB.

Sedgwick, Sara 1839–1902. of Cambridge, Mass. sister of Theodora S. m 1877 William Erasmus D. CD's daughter-in-law. Friend of Chauncey Wright—LLiii 165, *Letters of Chauncey Wright*, 246–248.

Sedgwick, Theodora of Cambridge, Mass. sister of Sara S. m Charles Naughton. 1878 S visited Down House and Bassett. 1884 S visited The Grove, Cambridge.

Seeds, Vitality of 1855 Vitality of seeds, *Gdnr's Chronicle*, No.46:758 (Bi 260, F1686); 1855 Effect of salt-water on the germination of seeds, *ibid*., No.47:773 (Bi 761, F1687); 1855 [same title], *ibid*.,No. 48:789 (Bi 262, F1688); 1855 Longevity of seeds, *ibid*., No.52:854 (Bi 263, F1689); 1857 On the action of sea-water on the germination of seeds, *J.Proc. Linn.Soc.Lond.(Bot.)*, 1:130–140 (Bi 264, F1694); 1857 Productiveness of foreign seed, *Gdnr's Chronicle*, No.46:779 (Bi 264, F1698). CD's collections of seeds are in the Botany School, Cambridge.

Seedling Fruit Trees 1855 Seedling fruit trees, *Gdnr's Chronicle*, No.52:854 (Bi 263, F1690).

Self-Fertilisation 1865 Self-fertilisation, *Hardwicke's Science Gossip*, 1:114 (Bii 132, F1734). see also *Cross and self fertilisation*, 1876.

Semper, Carl Gottfried 1832–1893. German zoologist. Prof. Zoology Würzburg. 1874 CD to S on Coral formations in Pellew Islands—LLiii 182. 1878 CD to S, on speciation in relation to isolation, 'I should think nearly perfect separation would greatly aid in their "specification" to coin a new word'—LLiii 160. 1878 CD to S, on variation; S was strongly in favour of direct action of environment—LLiii 344. 1879 S sent CD proof sheets of *Die natürlichen Existenzbedingungen der Thiere*, 1880. 1881 CD to S, on variation, 'the even still kinder manner in which you disagree with me'—MLi 391. *Der Haeckelismus in der Zoologie*, Hamburg 1876.

Senkenbergische Naturforschende Gesellschaft, Frankfurt-am-Main CD Corresponding Member 1873.

Serbian First editions in: *Origin of species* (F766) 1878; *autobiography* (F1542) 1937.

Serbo-Croat First edition in: *Journal of researches* (F244) 1949.

Settegast, Hermann Gustav 1819–1908. 1870 H sent CD a copy of his book *Die Thierzucht*, Breslau 1868—MLi 324. Boschetti, Francesco, *Darwin-Settegast transformisti, Linneo-Sanson non transformisti, e le Leggi dell'Ereditarieta*, Turin 1890.

Sevenoaks Kent. 1877 Oct.5–26 CD had family holiday in a rented house.

Seward, Sir Albert Charles 1863–1941. Palaeobotanist. Kt 1936 FRS 1898. Prof. Botany Cambridge 1906–1936. Master of Downing College 1915–1936. 1903 S edited, with Francis D, *More letters of Charles Darwin*; 1909 edited, in CD centenary year, *Darwin and modern science*. DNB.

Seward, Anna 1747–1809. Poet & author. The Swan of Lichfield; lived there 1754–1809. S was author of *Memoirs of the life of Dr. Darwin*, London 1804. 1879 CD to Reginald D, he had written his introduction to Krause's biography of Erasmus D [I] 'to contradict flatly some calumnies by Miss Seward' —LLiii 219. Generally considered that S wanted to marry Erasmus D after death of his 1st wife and was chagrined when he married Elizabeth Chandos Pole. DNB.

Sex Ratios 1868 [Inquiry about sex ratios in domestic animals], *Gdnr's Chronicle*, No.7:160 (Bii 135, F1743).

Sexual Selection 1876 Sexual selection in relation to monkeys, *Nature*, Lond.,15:18–19 (Bii 207, F1773); 1880 The sexual colours of certain butterflies, *ibid*.,21:237 (Bii 220, F1787); 1882 On the modification of a race of Syrian street dogs by means of sexual selection, by Dr. [W.] Van Dyck, with a preliminary notice by Charles Darwin, *Proc.zool.Soc.Lond.*, No.25: 367–370 (Bii 278, F1803); this was CD's last publication. Sexual selection forms Part II of *Descent*, chs VIII–XXI, more than half the book.

Seymour, Edward Adolphus, Duke of Somerset 1775–1855. 11th *Duke* FRS 1797. President of the Linnean Society 1834–1837. S was influential in obtaining money from the Exchequer for publication of scientific results of *Beagle* voyage. DNB.

Seymour, Gertrude ?–1825. m 1812 John Hensleigh Allen [I].

Shaen, Emily *see* Winkworth.

Shaen, Margaret J. d of William S. Family friend and continued to visit ED. 1887 ED to S, 'My dear one felt you completely one of the family and not "company" '—EDii 280.

Shaen, William 1870–1887. Solicitor & educationalist. m 1851 Emily Winkworth, 2s are mentioned, John & Godfrey, 1d Margaret. 1882 S was on 'Family Friends invited' list for CD's funeral. 1888 ED to Henrietta Emma Litchfield, 'Now I must write declining to subscribe to Shaen memorial at Bedford College'. 'I do not care about the higher education of women, though I ought to do so'—EDii 172. 'After all I did send £10 to the Shaen Memorial'.

Shanklin Isle of Wight. 1858 Jul.–Aug. CD & family visited.

Sharpe, Daniel 1806–1856. Geologist. FRS 1850. S was in Portuguese mercantile business. 1846 CD to S on cleavage and foliation—FUL 104. 1849 CD to Lyell, CD had been discussing mica schist with S—MLii 131. 1846–1851 CD to S, on cleavage and foliation—MLii 199–204.

Sharples, Rolinda ?–1838. 1816 Pastel of CD with sister Emily Catherine is always said to be by 'Sharples'. Rolinda d of James S (?1750–1811) is the only S who fits for date. The earliest portrait of CD.

Shaw 1829 Taxidermist of Shrewsbury—LLi 175.

Shaw, Joseph 1786–1859. Fellow of Christ's College Cambridge 1807–1859. Senior Tutor in CD's time. 1827 Oct. 'Admissus est pensionarius minor sub Magistro Shaw', but CD did not go up until Lent term. S liked hunting and the Newmarket races.

Sheep 1880 [Letter] Black sheep, *Nature*, Lond.,23:93 (Bii 224, F1790), containing extracts from a letter from 'Mr. Sanderson', about selective value of black sheep in Australian flocks.

Shell Rain 1855 Shell rain in the Isle of Wight, *Gdnr's Chronicle*, No.44:726–727 (Bi 259, F1685).

Shells 1878 Transplantation of shells, *Nature*, Lond.,18:120–121, introducing a letter from Arthur H. Gray, *ibid.*, 120 (Bii 214, F1783); 1880 The Omori shell mounds, *Nature*, Lond., 21:561, introducing one from Edward S. Morse, *ibid.*, 561–562 (Bii 222, F1788); 1882 On the dispersal of freshwater bivalves, *Nature*, Lond., 25:529–530 (Bii 276, F1802).

Sheppard, Nathan 1834–1888. 1884 *Darwinism stated by Darwin himself*, New York; selected by S, the first book of selections.

Sherbrooke, Viscount *see* Robert Lowe.

Shipley, Sir Arthur Everett 1861–1927. Zoologist. GBE 1920 FRS 1904 Master of Christ's College Cambridge 1910–1927. S, with J. C. Simpson, organised the exhibition of Darwiniana at Christ's 1909 and initialed its catalogue. DNB.

Shrewsbury newspaper *see* Eddowe's newspaper.

Shrewsbury School 1818 Summer term—1825 Jun.17 CD there; he boarded even though the school was hardly more than a mile from The Mount, his home. Samuel Butler [I] was Headmaster 1798–1836. The old school, which CD attended, is now the borough library, with the large seated statue of CD,

by Horace Mountford, in front. The new school was first
occupied in 1882. The school owns *Sir* Richard Owen's copy
of 1st edition of *Origin*.

Shuttleworth, Sir James Phillips Kay-, Bart 1804–1877.
Physician & educationalist. 1st *Bart* 1849. CD knew him (then
J. P. Kay) at Royal Medical Society Edinburgh. DNB.

Siebenbürgische Verein für Naturwissenschaft Hermann-
stadt. CD Honorary Member 1877.

Simcox S is mentioned as someone CD rode with at Cambridge—LLi 176. S is not in Venn; perhaps a livery stable.

Simon, Sir John 1816–1904. Surgeon. KCB 1887 FRS 1845
PRS 1879–1880.Medical Officer to Privy Council. 1875 S saw
and agreed to Litchfield's draft sketch for a vivisection
bill—LLiii 204. 1881 CD praises his address on vivisection to
International Medical Congress—LLiii 210. DNB.

Simon's Bay Cape of Good Hope, South Africa. 1836 May 31
Beagle anchored at. *see also* Cape Town.

Simonde de Sismondi, Jean Charles Léonard 1773–1842.
Swiss historian. m 1816 Jessie Allen d.s.p. Home Chêne, nr
Vevey. Switzerland. 1837 Emma Allen to Elizabeth Wedgwood, 'I feel it is hard on him to see so much of people he could
never get a taste for, no more than they could for him'; 'Not
even infant schools and savings banks escape his condemna-
tion, while beggary meets with his strenuous support'—EDi
280. 1840 Jun. S & *Mrs* S stayed at 12 Upper Gower St, CD &
ED away most of the time—EDii 54. 1887 ED 'I should not
have patience with his foibles, he would always go against my
taste as wanting manliness'—EDi 279.

Simonde de Sismondi, Jessie *see* Allen.

Simpson, James Crawford 1876–1944. 1909 S, with A. E. Shipley, prepared the Christ's College exhibition of Darwiniana
and initialed the catalogue. 1907–1909 S was at Emmanuel
College as an advanced student; a Canadian from McGill
University, Montreal, Professor of Embryology.

Sismondi, Jean Charles Léonard *see* Simonde de Sismondi. S
de S is always referred to as S in family letters.

Skertchly, Sydney Barber Josiah 1850–1926. Naturalist. 1878
CD may have sent S some of his works 'with my auto-
graph'—MLii 240.

Sketches of 1842 and 1844 CD's earliest drafts of his evolutio-

nary views. Neither was published in his lifetime. Sketch of
1842 was not known to Francis D when he edited *Life and
letters*, 1887; it was found in a staircase cupboard after his
mother's death, 1896. 1. 1909 Francis D, editor, *The foundations
of The origin of species, a sketch written in 1842*, Cambridge
University Press, not published, issued to delegates to the
anniversary celebrations at Cambridge (F1555); facsimile 1969
(1559); 2. 1909 Francis D, editor, *The foundations of The origin of
species, two essays written in 1842 and 1844*, Cambridge, University Press, pp.1–53 from same setting of type as No.1 (F1556);
1958 G. R. de Beer, editor, *Evolution by natural selection*, Cambridge, University Press, contains both drafts (F1557), issued
for the XVth International Congress of Zoology (Darwin
Centenary); facsimile 1871 (F1560). First foreign editions:
German (F1561) 1911; French 1925 (not in F); Italian (F1562)
1960; Russian (F1564) 1932.

Skim, Mrs *see* Mary Ann Galton.

Skinner Schoolmaster at Downe, a flogger.

Skinner, Mrs Wife of Downe schoolmaster. 1884 taught Bernard Richard Meirion D.

Skramovsky, B. Maria *see* Darwin's Notebooks.

Slavery CD, like his grandfather Erasmus D [I] and all educated
whigs, was against slavery; CD especially so from his experience of it in S. America. 1791 Josiah Wedgwood's cameo of a
kneeling slave in chains, with inscription 'Am I not a man and
a brother' is illustrated in Erasmus D [I], *The botanic garden*,
Pt.1, facing p 87, with note 'a Slave in chains, of which he
distributed many hundreds, to excite the humane to attend to
and to assist in the abolition of the detestable traffic in human
creatures'. 1826 Anti-slavery agitation by Josiah Wedgwood
[II] and his family detailed—EDi 181. 1833 CD to his sister
Caroline Sarah, 'What a proud thing for England if she is the
first European nation which utterly abolishes it'—LLi 246.
1833 CD to Herbert, 'Hurrah for the honest Whigs! I trust they
will soon attack that monstrous stain on our boasted liberty,
Colonial Slavery'—LLi 248. 1833 CD at Rio de Janeiro, 'On
such fazêndas as these, I have no doubt the slaves pass happy
and contented lives'—*J. Researches* 1845 24. 'This man had been
trained to a degradation lower than the slavery of the most
helpless animal'—*ibid*. 'I thank God, I shall never again visit a
slave country', followed by two pages of description of its
horrors—*ibid*. 499. 1845 CD to Lyell, 'this odious deadly

subject'—LLi 342. Many of CD's letters to Gray refer to slavery in relation to the American civil war, e.g. 1861 'If abolition does follow with your victory the whole world will look brighter in my eyes and in many eyes'—LLii 169, Darwin-Gray letters 37.

Sleeper, George Washington 1826–1903. Teashop proprietor of Boston, Mass. Putative author of *Shall we have common sense: some recent lectures*, Boston 1849. This purports to precede CD's views on the origin of man. The work is a forgery, probably by his son John F. Sleeper, and probably printed between 1903 and 1912. *see* Poulton, *Proc.Linn.Soc.Lond.*, 1912–1913:26–45, 1913 and *ibid.*, 1913–1914:23–44, 1914, with full facsimile of text. These 2 presidential addresses appeared together, as an offprint, 1914.

Slingsby, Monica m 1894 William Robert Darwin.

Slip-slop, Little Miss Nickname of Emma Wedgwood (ED) in childhood.

Slovene First editions in: *Journal of researches* (F245) 1950; *Origin of species* (F768) 1951; *Autobiography* (F1543) 1959.

Smith Resident at Downe—Darwin-Innes 227.

Smith 1831 CD to Henslow, asking for an introduction to, perhaps Andrew S—Darwin-Henslow 42.

Smith, Albert George Dew, né Dew 1848–1903. Physiologist of Trinity College Cambridge. Skilled photographer and collector of jewels. Friend of Horace D and Director of Cambridge Instrument Company. ?1874 CD to S, about physiology of *Dionaea*; CD had given all his best specimens to J. S. B. Sanderson—Carroll 434. 1882 S was on 'Personal Friends invited' list for CD's funeral.

Smith, Sir Andrew 1797–1872. Physician, naturalist & explorer. KCB 1859 FRS 1857. Director General Army Medical Department, Cape & Natal. 1849 CD to Strickland, about use of author's names in nomenclature which others, including S in conversation, were against—LLi 371. DNB.

Smith, Beatrice Ann Shore m 1865 Godfrey Lushington.

Smith, Edgar Albert 1847–1916. Zoologist at British Museum (Natural History). 1869 CD thanks for proofs of excellent woodcuts for *Descent*.

Smith Elder & Co. Publishers of London. 1838–1843 S published *Zoology of the Beagle*, edited by CD. 1842–1844–1846 S published the three parts of CD's *Geology of the voyage of the Beagle*, and later editions.

Smith, Frederick H. 1805–1879. Hymenopterist at British Museum. Friendly correspondent of CD. 1872 S gave CD information on copulation of bumble-bees—*Bull.Brit.Mus. (nat.Hist.)*. hist.Ser., 3:179, 1969.

Smith, Goldwin 1823–1910. Historian & journalist. 1868 S had lunched at Down House with the Nortons. S was of the opinion that an article in *Pall Mall Gazette*, Aug.22, on science and religion was a mistake—MLi 309. WWH.

Smith, James 1782–1867. Geologist & sailor. FRS 1830. Of Jordanhill, Glasgow. 1848 CD says S had a poor opinion of Chambers' *Ancient sea margins*, 1848. DNB.

Smith, John 1798–1888. Curator, Royal Botanical Gardens, Kew. 1873 CD to Hooker, to ask S about watering plants during sunshine—MLii 410.

Smith, Rev. Sydney [I] 1771–1845. Writer, anglican clergyman & wit. Canon of St Paul's Cathedral, London. Member of Holland House set and friend of Wedgwoods, Allens and Erasmus Alvey D. Many references to in ED. CD 'I once met Sydney Smith at Dean Milman's house'—LLi 75. DNB.

Smith, Sydney [II] Fellow of St Catherine's College Cambridge. Darwinian scholar. 1960 S edited type facsimile of *Letters on geology* (F4).

Smyth, Robert Brough 1830–1889. Australian mining engineer. 1867 S answered CD's *Queries about expression*.

Snelgar, Margaretta m c1840 John Hensleigh Allen [II].

Snow Nickname for Frances Julia Wedgwood.

Snow, Mrs A *Mrs* Snow is listed 1882 amongst 'Personal Friends invited' to CD's funeral.

Snow, George Carrier from London to Downe, from Nag's head public house, Borough, at least from 1849–1855.

Snow, W. 1893 Jun. S was allowed by ED to keep five cows in Down House field.

Snowdon Mountain, N. Wales. 1826 Jan. CD climbed on walking tour.

Soapy Sam Nickname of *Rev.* Samuel Wilberforce.

Sociedad Cientifica Argentina Buenos Aires. CD Honorary Member 1877.

Sociedad de Naturalistas Neo-Granadinos CD Honorary Member 1860.

Sociedad Zoológica Argentina Cordova. CD Honorary Member 1874.

Sociedade de Geographia de Lisboa CD Corresponding Member 1877.

Società dei Naturalisti in Modena CD Honorary Member 1875.

Società Geographica Italiana Florence. CD Honorary Member 1875.

Società Italiana di Antropologia e di Etnologia Florence. CD Honorary Member 1872.

Società La Scuola Italica, Academia Pitagorica Rome. CD Presidente Onorario degli Anziani Pitagorici 1880.

Societas Caesarea Naturae Curiosorum (Société Imperiale des Naturalistes) Moscow. 1870 CD Honorary Member.

Société d' Anthropologie Paris. CD Foreign Member 1871.

Société des Sciences Naturelles Neuchatel. CD Corresponding Member 1863.

Société Entomologique de France CD Honorary Member 1874.

Société Géologique de France CD Life Member 1837.

Société Hollandaise des Sciences à Haarlem, Hollandische Maatschappij der Wetenschappen Haarlem. CD Foreign Member 1877.

Société Royale de Botanique de Belgique Brussels. CD Associate Member 1881.

Société Royale des Sciences Médicales et Naturelles Brussels. CD Honorary Member 1872.

Society of Naturalists of the Imperial Kazan University, [Obshchestvo Estestvoispuitatelei pri Imperatorskom Kazanskom Universitetye] CD Honorary Member 1875.

Somerset, 11th Duke of *see* Edward Adolphus Seymour.

Sorby, Dr Henry Clifton 1826–1908. Geologist. FRS 1857. 1880 S presented address to CD from Yorkshire Naturalists' Union—LLiii 227.

Sorrell, Thomas Acting Boatswain on 2nd voyage of *Beagle*.

South America, Part 3 of Geology of the Voyage of the Beagle 1846 *Geological observations on South America. Being the third part of the geology of the voyage of the Beagle, under the command of Capt. Fitz-Roy, R.N., during the years 1832–1836*, London (F273); contains descriptions of tertiary fossil shells by G. B. Sowerby, and descriptions of secondary fossil shells by Edward Forbes. 1851 combined edition with the two other parts from unsold sheets (F274). 1876 2nd edition, combined with *Volcanic islands* (F276). 1891 3rd edition (F282), only a reprint of 2nd edition; facsimile 1972 from USA edition of 1896 (F307). First foreign editions: German (F312) 1878; USA

(F283) 1891; Spanish (F324) 1906; Russian (F323) 1936.

South American Missionary Society 1885 Apr.24 *Admiral* Sulivan, to *Daily News*, CD subscribed to their orphanage at the Mission Station, Tierra del Fuego, 1867–1881 and saw the Missionary Journal for 1867, although he had at first regarded the task as hopeless. The mission stems from the station on Keppel Island, W Falkland Is.—LLiii 127. *see also* Thomas Bridges.

South Cliff House *see* Tenby.

South Kensington Museum *see* British Museum (Natural History).

Southampton Hampshire. 1846 Sep.9–16 CD & ED attended British Association meeting at. 1868–1880 CD & ED visited their son William Erasmus D at Bassett, outside Southampton, in most years.

Southey, Robert 1774–1843. Poet. 1839 CD met S with Thomas Butler on a stage coach from Birmingham to Shrewsbury, after British Association meeting—Jones, *Life of Samuel Butler*, i, 13. DNB.

Sowerby, George Brettingham [I] 1778–1854. Biological artist & author. s of James S, the first of the S dynasty. 1836 CD to Henslow, 'Also about fossil shells. Is Sowerby a good man? I understand his assistance can be purchased'—Darwin-Henslow 120. 1844 S wrote appendix to CD's *Volcanic islands*. 1846 S wrote appendix to CD's *South America*.

Sowerby, George Brettingham [II] 1812–1844. s of George Brettingham S [I]. 1851–1854 S drew illustrations for all CD's work on cirripedes. 1861 Oct.5–6 S was at Down House drawing orchids for *Fertilisation of orchids* 1862.

Spanish First editions in: *Journal of researches* (F249) 1902; *South America* (F324) 1906; *Origin of species* (F770) 1877, contains 2 letters from CD not printed elsewhere; *Descent of man* (F1124) ?1902; *Expression of the emotions* (F1214) ?1902; *Autobiography* (F1544) 1907.

Spencer, Herbert 1820–1903. Engineer & philosopher. 1c of William George S & Harriet Homes, eight other children all died in infancy. unm. 1860 CD to Lyell, CD had read S's essay on population, *Westminster Rev.*, 57:468–501, 'such dreadful hypothetical rubbish'—Carroll 201. 1865 CD to Lyell, 'somehow I never feel any wiser after reading him, but often feel mistified [sic.]'—Carroll 307. 1866 CD to Hooker, 'If he had trained himself to observe more, even at the expense . . . of some loss of thinking power he would have been a wonderful man'—LLiii 56. 1870 CD to Lankester, 'I suspect that hereafter he will be looked at as by far the greatest living philosopher in England'—LLiii 120. 1873 CD to S, on receiving S's *The study of sociology*, 1873, 'Those were splendid hits about the Prince of Wales and Gladstone. I never before read a good defence of Toryism'—MLi 351. 1874 CD to Romanes, 'I have so poor a metaphysical head that Mr. Spencer's terms of equilibration &c. always bother me and make everything less clear'—Carroll 446. 1874 CD to Fiske, 'with the exception of special points I did not even understand H. Spencer's general doctrine; for his style is too hard for me'—LLiii 193. 1882 S was on 'Personal Friends invited' list for CD's funeral. Works: 1862 *First principles*, London; 1864 *The principles of biology*, London; the whole body of his work in *The synthetic philosophy*, 9 vols, London 1862–1893. Autobiography: 1889 (privately printed), 1894 (published). Biography: Duncan 1908; Medawar 1964, *Encounter*, 21:35–43. DNB.

Spencer, John Poyntz 1835–1910. Whig statesman. 5th *Earl* Spencer of Althorp. 1882 S, as Lord President of the Council, represented the Queen in Council at CD's funeral. DNB.

Spengle CD's family name for *Dr* S. P. Engleheart.

Spiders 1839 Über der Luftschifferei der Spinnen, *Neue Notizen aus dem Gebiete der Natur- und Heilkunde*, (*Froriep's Notizen*), 11: cols 505–509 (F1654), translated from pp 187–188 of *Journal of researches*, 1839. 1873 Aeronaut spiders, *Gdnr's Chronicle*, No.40:1437 (F1765).

Spottiswoode, William 1825–1883. Physicist. FRS 1853. PRS 1878–1883. 1882 S was, as PRS, a Pall-bearer at CD's funeral. DNB. S was Chairman, Darwin Memorial Fund 1882–1883.

Sprengel, Christian Konrad 1750–1816. Botanist. Rector of Spandau, but dismissed for neglecting his duties; *see* J. C. Willis, *Nat. Sci.*, 2, 1893. S's book, *Das entdeckte Geheimniss der Natur im Bau und in der Befruchtung der Blumen*, Berlin 1793, although neglected at the time, was seen by CD as being most important. 1841 CD read the book on Robert Brown's recommendation; 'full of truth' although 'with some little nonsense'; 'It may be doubted whether Robert Brown ever planted a more fruitful seed than in putting such a book into such hands'—LLiii 258. 1873 CD to H. Müller, 'it is a great satisfaction to me to believe that I have aided in making his excellent book more generally known'—LLiii 281. 'Wonderful book'—Barlow, *Autobiography* 127.

Spring Gardens London, No.17. 1831 Sep. CD lodged there whilst preparing for *Beagle* voyage.

Springfield House in Cambridge, home of *Sir* Richard Jebb. 1883 Feb. ED writes from there—EDii 261.

Squirrels The story of young red squirrels mistaking CD for a tree on one of his rounds of the sandwalk is given in Francis D's reminiscences of his father, 'their mother barked at them in agony from a tree'—LLi 115. An American illustration for the episode, entirely imaginary, is reproduced in Atkins, pl.4, 41.

Stafford Staffordshire. 1869 Jun.30 CD stopped at on way back from Barmouth holiday.

Stainton, Henry Tibbats 1822–1892. Entomologist, especially of the micro-lepidoptera. FRS 1867. 1855–1881 CD to and from S, a series of letters on entomological subjects—FUL 106–109. DNB.

Stanford, Sir Charles Villiers 1852–1924. Composer. Kt 1902. 1880 ED had organ of Trinity College Cambridge chapel played for her by S—EDii 240. DNB.

Stanley, Edward Henry 1826–1893. Statesman. 15th Earl of *Derby*, Knowsley Hall. 1882 S was a Pall-bearer at CD's funeral.

Stanley, Edward Smith 1775–1851. 13th *Earl* of Derby. S kept a large private menagerie at Knowsley Hall. President of Linnean Society 1828–1833. 1837 S supported CD's application for a Treasury grant for publishing zoological results of *Beagle* voyage—LLi 283.

Stanhope, Philip Henry [I] 1781–1855. 4th *Earl*. Eccentric, chiefly known for his involvement with the psychotic youth Kaspar Hauser. 1849 'Long ago I dined occasionally with the old Earl. He said one day to me "Why don't you give up your fiddle-faddle of geology and zoology, and turn to the occult sciences"'—LLi 283. DNB.

Stanhope, Philip Henry [II] 1805–1875. Historian. 5th Earl, better known by his courtesy title of *Viscount* Mahon. c1842 CD dined with S in London and met Macaulay. 1849 CD dined with S at his seat, Chevening, Kent. 1856 CD & Lyell dined with S in London—MLi 94. DNB.

Star Hotel Princes St, Edinburgh. 1825 Oct. CD & Erasmus Alvey D stayed there briefly before moving into lodgings in Lothian St.

Stauffer, Robert Clinton Zoologist of University of Wisconsin, Madison. 1975 S edited and transcribed CD's *Charles Darwin's Natural Selection, being the second part of his big species book written from 1856 to 1858,* Cambridge (F1583).

Stebbing, George James Instrument maker, eldest son of an instrument maker of Portsmouth. S was a supernumerary, at Fitz-Roy's expense, on second voyage of *Beagle*.   .

Stebbing, Rev. Thomas Roscoe Rede 1835–1925. Anglican clergyman & naturalist. FRS 1896. S was one of the most distinguished of Victorian marine naturalists. Schoolmaster at Wellington College. 1869 Feb.1 S lectured on Darwinism to Torquay Natural History Society. Mar.3 CD wrote to thank S, 'but a clergyman in delivering such an address does . . . much more good by his power to shake ignorant prejudices'—LLiii 111. 1870 S lectured to same society on Darwinism and the noachian flood. 1870 CD to S, thanking him for a copy of *Essays on darwinism*, London—Carroll 338. 1881 CD to S, thanking him for a letter on S. Butler affair, *Nature*, Lond., 23:336.

Stecher, Robert M. American physician of Cleveland, Ohio. 1961 S transcribed CD's letters to and from Innes, *Ann.Sci.*, 17:201–258. 1969 S transcribed CD's letters to Bates, *Ann.Sci.*, 25:1–47, 95–175. These letters then in S's possession.

Stephen, Sir Leslie 1832–1904. Biographer & critic. KCB 1902. Editor of DNB. Founder of Sunday Walking Club, nicknamed the Sunday Tramps. 1880 S was amongst the friends who advised CD to ignore Samuel Butler's attack on him. 1882 Jan.8 S came to Down House on a Sunday tramp. 1882 S was on 'Personal Friends invited' list for CD's funeral. DNB.

Stephens, Catherine, Countess of Essex 1794–1882. Vocalist & actress. Retired 1835. m 1838 5th *Earl* of Essex. 1825 CD heard her in Edinburgh—MLi 6.

Stephens, James Francis 1792–1852. Entomologist. Author of *Illustrations of British entomology*, [1827–]1828–1835[–1845], *supplement* 1846, London, which contains a number of beetle records, and one of a moth, bearing CD's name, mostly from Cambridge and N Wales. 1829 Feb.23, CD took tea with S, 'he appears to be a very good-humoured pleasant little man'—LLi 175. 1832 S sued James Rennie for infringement of copyright; his legal costs of £400 were raised by friends—Darwin-Henslow 79. 1880 CD to Sarah Haliburton (née Owen), 'I remember the pride which I felt when I saw in a book about beetles the impressive words "Captured by C. Darwin"—LLiii 335.

Stephens, Thomas Selwood Curate at Downe 1859–1867. Innes to CD mentions him in relation to Tegetmeier's design for beehives—Darwin-Innes 210. 1865 S is mentioned about children beating their parents at billiards—EDii 182.

Stereoscopic Company c1881 This company photographed CD, *see* H. & M. S. J. Engel, *Janus*, 49:53–66. A copy of one of the pair is in Arten-Bibliothek, University of Amsterdam.

Stevens, Thomas 1809–1888. Warden & founder of Bradfield College, Berks. m1, 1839, Caroline Tollet. 1839 Josiah Wedgwood [II] gave a piano to ED, as a wedding present which had been his property. 1839 Feb.4 Mrs Josiah W to ED, 'Mr. Stevens is now below strumming upon our old affair'—EDi 30. 1863 Innes to CD mentions S—Darwin-Innes 216.

Stirling Scotland. 1827 CD visited on a spring tour.

Stoddart, D. R. 1962 S transcribed CD's mss notes on coral islands, *Atoll Research Bull.,* No. 88, 20 pp.

Stoke d'Abernon Upcott, Surrey. Home of Josiah Wedgwood [II] 1795–1800.

Stokes, Francis Griffin Historian & bibliographer of Windsor, Berkshire. 1878 CD to S, on intonations of young children—Carroll 541.

Stokes, John Lort 1812–1885. Naval Officer. Admiral 1877. S served on all three voyages of *Beagle*; was mate & Assistant Surveyor on 2nd voyage and commanded at end of 3rd. 1838 CD saw in London. 1882 Apr.27 S letter in *The Times,* printed immediately after report on CD's funeral, about CD's seasickness. CD would say 'Old fellow I must take the horizontal for it'. 'It was distressing to witness this early sacrifice of Mr. Darwin's health, who ever afterwards seriously felt the ill-effects of the *Beagle's* voyage'. 1883 Apr.25 S letter in *The Times* on CD—LLi 224. Author of *Discoveries in Australia,* 1846. DNB.

Stonehenge Wiltshire. 1877 Jun. CD visited from Southampton.

Stoney field Great Pucklands was so-called by the Ds because of the large number of surface flints, due to recent ploughing. *see* Pucklands.

Strawberries 1862 Cross-breeds of strawberries, *J.Hort.,* 3:672 (Bii 70, F1720).

Strickland, Hugh Edwin 1811–1853. Naturalist. FRS 1852. Author of *Strickland code of zoological nomenclature*, 1863, published by British Association. 1849 CD to S, on difficulties in nomenclature in relation to his barnacle work—LLi 372, MLi 68. S was killed by a train. DNB.

Strickland, Sefton West 1839–1910. Barrister. Cambridge friend of William Erasmus D. S was often at Down House. 1882 S was on 'Personal Friends invited' list for CD's funeral.

Struggle for Existence 1859 'We will now discuss in a little more detail the struggle for existence'—*Origin*, ch.3. The phrase was used by Malthus in relation to social competition.

Struggle for Life 1859 Phrase first used in title of *Origin*.

Strutt, John William, Baron Rayleigh 1843–1919. Physicist. 3rd *Baron* 1873 FRS 1873 Nobel Prize 1910. Cambridge friend of CD's sons. Cavendish Professor of Experimental Physic 1879–1884. Chancellor 1908–1919. 1882 S was on 'Personal Friends invited' list for CD's funeral.

Strzelecki, Count Paul Edmund 1796–1873. Australian explorer. KCMG 1869. The title was from his Polish ancestry. 1856 CD to Hooker, S was on election committee of Athenæum, and CD proposed to speak to him about election of Huxley—MLi 89 (misspelt Strezlecki). DNB.

Stuart, Catherine ?–1797. m as 1st wife *Sir* James Mackintosh.

Sudbrooke Park Petersham, Surrey. Water cure establishment run by *Dr* Richard James Lane with Edward Wickstead Lane as physician; ?moved from Moor Park. 1860 Jun. CD at—LLii 256, 324. Now a golf clubhouse.

Suess, Eduard 1831–1914. Austrian palaeontologist. 1871 CD to S, on his election as Foreign Corresponding Member of Kaiserliche Akademie der Wissenschaften, Vienna—Carroll 397.

Sulivan, Sir Bartholemew James 1810–1890. Naval Officer. KCB 1869. *Admiral* 1877. 2nd Lieutenant on 2nd voyage of *Beagle*. 1849 S ranched and traded in Falkland Is. S made enquiries for CD on feral cattle and horses—*J.Researches* 1845 ch.ix. 1850 S was visited in Falkland Is by Huxley. 1867 S persuaded CD to subscribe to South American Missionary Society's orphanage in Tierra del Fuego—LLiii 127. 1885 Jun.9 S was present at unveiling of statue of CD in British Museum (Natural History). Biography: H. N. Sulivan (son) 1896. DNB.

Sunday Tramps An intellectual walking club, technically called the Sunday Walking Club organized by Leslie Stephen. 1882 They dined at Down House, and perhaps other occasions.

Surman, F. W. 1881 Secretary to Erasmus Alvey D. After EAD's death, Aug.26, CD wrote to about some post at British Museum (Natural History)—Carroll 607, 608.

Surtees, Harriet *see* Allen.

Surtees, Rev. Matthew ?–1877. m 1799 Harriet Allen d.s.p. Rector of North Cerney, Wilts. 'The family greatly disliked Mr. Surtees, and he appears to have been jealous, ill-tempered, and tyrannical'—EDi 4. 1816 *Mrs* Josiah Wedgwood to her sister Frances Allen 'the most incomparably disagreeable man I ever saw'—EDi 86. 1824 *Mrs* Josiah Wedgwood to her sister *Mdme* Sismondi, 'Harriet is positively very much attached to him incredible as it may seem, . . . he is a dying man'—EDi 158.

Survival of the Fittest 1859 'The expression often used by Mr. Herbert Spencer of the survival of the fittest is more accurate and is sometimes equally convenient'—*Origin*, ch.3.

Sutton ?1871 CD to A. D. Bartlett, S was a keeper at the Zoological Society of London's Gardens, Regent's Park, who made many observations on monkeys for *Expression*.

Swainson, William 1789–1855. Cabinet naturalist. FRS 1820. S was a proponent of the quinary system of Macleay in classification. 1844 CD to Hooker, 'I feel a laudable doubt and disinclination to believe any statement of Swainson'—MLi 403. DNB.

Swanage Dorset. 1847 Jul. CD had family holiday at.

Swedish First editions in: *Journal of researches* (F259) 1872; *Origin of species* (F793) 1869; *Descent of man* (F1136) 1872; *Autobiography* (F1546) 1959.

Swift, Rev. Benjamin 1819–?1833. m Georgiana Elizabeth Darwin. f of Francis Darwin S. Vicar of Birkdale, Lancashire 1857–1874.

Swift, Francis Darwin 1864–? 2s of Benjamin S & Georgiana Elizabeth Darwin. CD's half cousin. c1920 S compiled and had printed as a broadsheet *Some collateral ancestors of Erasmus Darwin*; this takes the ancestry back to Isaac II, Angelus, Eastern Emperor 1185–1204, in skeleton form; the male D line only goes back to 1644.

Swift, Georgiana Elizabeth *see* Darwin.

Swinhoe, Robert 1836–1877. Ornithologist & consular official in China. FRS 1876. 1866 CD to P. L. Sclater, S had written to

CD about common domestic duck of China. 1867 CD sent S *Queries about expression*, which S had printed in *Notes & Queries for China & Japan,* 1:105. 1871 Feb. S visited Down House.

Sydney New South Wales. 1836 Jan.12 *Beagle* arrived at Port Jackson and anchored in Sydney Cove. CD made short expedition to Bathurst. Jan.30 *Beagle* left for Tasmania.

Sykes, William Henry 1790–1872. Soldier & naturalist. FRS 1834. 1849 CD travelled with S to British Association meeting at Birmingham. 1859 CD to S, recommending Edward Blyth for position as naturalist on China expedition.

Symonds, Hyacinth d of William Samuel S. m1 *Sir* William Jardine *Bart.* m2 *Sir* Joseph Dalton Hooker.

Symonds, Sir William 1782–1856. Naval Officer. Kt 1837 FRS 1835. Rear-Admiral 1854. Surveyor of the Navy 1832–1847. 1848 Jul. CD went in S's yacht from Swanage to Poole—Journal. DNB.

Symonds, Rev. William Samuel 1818–1887. Anglican clergyman & geologist. FRS 1835. f of Hyacinth S. Rector of Pendock, Worcestershire. 1860 CD to Lyell, refers to letter from S on imperfections of geological record—MLi 170. DNB.

T

Tahiti Society Islands, British Colony, later French. 1835
Nov.15/16 *Beagle* arrived, having crossed the date line as it was
then and lost a day; anchored in Matuvai Bay. Nov.18 CD
landed at Papeete and had a short inland expedition, returned
Nov.20. Missionaries were most hospitable. Nov.25 *Queen
Pomare IV* entertained on board. Nov.26 *Beagle* sailed for
New Zealand. 1836 A letter containing remarks on the moral
state of Tahiti, New Zealand &c., *S.Afr.Christian Recorder*,
2:221–238 (F1640); CD's first publication, except for beetle
records in Stephens.

Tait, Robert Lawson 1845–1899. Surgeon & gynaecologist at
Hospital for diseases of women, Birmingham 1871–1893.
1875 CD to T, about use of tails for sensory purposes by
mice—MLi 358. 1875 Apr.18 T stayed at Down House—Carroll 465. 1876 T reviewed 2nd edition of *Variation* in *Spectator*,
Mar.4—MLi 363. 1880 Jul.19 CD sent T £25 'for your scientific fund in Birmingham'—N&R 82. 1881 T to CD, T had
spoken strongly in favour of *Origin* in his physiology lectures
at Midland Institute, and inviting CD to visit Birmingham—unpublished letter. There are eight letters from CD to T
at Shrewsbury School—N&R 79–82.

Tait, William Chaster 1844–1921. Botanist. T was resident at
Oporto; he provided CD with specimens of *Drosophylum* for
Insectivorous plants, after Hooker had been unable to get them.
CD wrote to thank T—MLii 381.

Talandier, Pierre Theodore Alfred Prof. French Royal Military Academy Sandhurst. 1860 CD to Quatrefages, T wanted
to translate *Origin* into French—Carroll 193.

Tara A cob at Down House, used for the coach. T died when ED
was 87. The coachman pronounced him 'tearer'.

Tasker, Mrs 1873 T let lodgings in Downe.

Tasmania 1836 Feb.5–17 *Beagle* at Storm Bay; CD made short
inland journeys.

Tearle, W. of St Neot's, Cambridgeshire. 1880 CD to T, cannot help with his religious doubts.

Teasel 1877 Note to Mr Francis Darwin's paper, *Quart. J.micr.Sci.*, 17:272 (F1777). Francis D, On the protrusion of protoplasmic filaments from the glandular hairs on the leaves of the common teasel (*Dipsacus sylvestris*), *ibid.*, 17:245–277. 1877 [Letter] The contractile filaments of the teasel, *Nature, Lond.*, 16:339 (Bii 205, F1778).

Teesdale, Mr 1880 T took Down Hall—Darwin-Innes 248. 1880 Romanes to CD mentions him twice in relation to death of Sarah Elizabeth Wedgwood—*Life of Romanes* 99, 100. 1881 Jul.23 Romanes spent day with T at Down Hall and called on CD, the last time they met. 1887 T was on 'Personal Friends invited' list for CD's funeral.

Tegetmeier, William Bernhard 1816–1917. Ornithologist & poultry fancier. T helped CD extensively with information for *Variation*. 'Correspondence began in 1855, and lasted to 1881'—LLii 57. 1887 T called on ED at Down House.

Tenby S Wales. South Cliff House; home of Harriet Surtees after death of husband 1827; also of Jessie Sismondi after death of husband 1842, and of Emma and Frances Allen after death of John Hensleigh Allen 1843, four sisters.

Tendency of Species to Form varieties 1858 On the tendency of species to form varieties, and on the perpetuation of varieties and species by natural means of selection, by Charles Darwin . . . and Alfred Wallace, *J.Proc.Linn. Soc. Lond.*, 3, No.9:1–62 (Bii 3, F1699). Communicated by Lyell and Hooker, Tuesday Jul.1. The details of the preparation and publication of this fundamental paper are given in LLi 115–138. First foreign editions: German (F365) 1870; Russian (F370) 1939; Italian (F368) 1960. *see also Zoologist*, 16:6263–6308 (F349).

Teneriffe Canary Islands. 1832 Jan.7 *Beagle* anchored there, but CD could not land there because of quarantine regulations. *see also* Canary Islands.

Tennyson, Alfred, Baron 1809–1892. Poet. 1st *Baron* 1884. 1868 Summer T called on CD several times at Freshwater, I.O.W. T 'did not greatly charm or interest either my father or mother'—EDii 190. c1885 T to *Dr* Grove, 'I don't want you to go away with a wrong impression. The fact is that long before Darwin's work appeared these ideas were known and talked about'—Poulton, *Darwin & the Origin* 9. In memoriam, 1849, contains the idea of a struggle for existence. EB DNB.

Termites 1874 Recent researches on termites and honey bees, *Nature*, Lond., 9:308–309 (Bii 182, F1768), introducing a letter from Fritz Müller.

Terrestrial Planariae 1844 Brief descriptions of several terrestrial planariae and of some remarkable marine species, with an account of their habits, *Ann.Mag.nat.Hist.*, 14:241–251 (Bi 182, F1669).

Thackeray, Anne Isabella 1837–1919. Novelist. d of William Makepeace T. m 1877 Richmond Ritchie, her 1st cousin. 1881 or 1882 T visited Down House, 'a most amusing and pleasant person'—MLii 448. 1882 T was on 'Personal Friends invited' list for CD's funeral.

Theory of Descent 1882 August Weismann, *Studies in the theory of descent*, 2 vols, London; prefatory notice by CD v–vi (F1414); translated from German by Raphael Meldola, with notes and additions by the author, the original, *Studien zur Descendenz-Theorie*, Leipzig 1875–1876, does not contain CD's notice. Foreign edition, of CD's notice only: Russian (F1415) 1939.

Thiel, Dr Hugo 1839–1918. 1869 CD to T, thanking for pamphlet *Über einige Formen der Landwirtschaftlichen Genossenschaften*. T was at Agricultural Station, Poppelsdorf. 'You apply to moral and social questions analogous views to those which I have used in regard to modification of species'—LLiii 112.

Thierry, Charles Philip Hippolytus, Baron de 1793–1864. French refugee & colonist. 1845 CD to Henslow on T's death, 'King of Nukahiva and Sovereign Chief of New Zealand. I wonder what has become of his wretched wife'—Darwin-Henslow 154. The date of the letter is correct but DNB states that T died in 1864.

This is the Question 1838 CD's notes on whether or not to marry. Mss at Cambridge University Library is so headed. Written at 36 Great Marlborough St. Text printed in Barlow, *Autobiography*, 231–234. Sydney Smith [II] has suggested that they were scribbled down in ED's presence, whilst flirting; if so, before Nov.12, when they became engaged.

Thompson 1858 'Thompson of Calcutta'—LLii 113 *see* Thomas Thomson.

Thompson, Mr 1880 A resident at Downe, 'affected by the creeping palsy'—Darwin-Innes 248.

Thompson, Mr 1881 CD to Thiselton-Dyer, on plants with different coloured anthers. CD had written to T for seed of

Clarkia elegans. ?A nurseryman—MLii 301.

Thompson, Sir Harry Stephen Meysey, Bart 1809–1874. Agriculturalist. b of Thomas Charles T. 1st *Bart* 1874. MP for Whitby 1859–1865. 1834 'The two Thompsons of Trinity', Cambridge friend of CD—LLi 256. DNB.

Thompson, James D'Arcy Wentworth 1860–1948. Zoologist. FRS 1916. Prof. Natural History Dundee 1884–1917. 1883 T translated Hermann Müller, *Die Befruchtung der Blumen durch Insekten*, Leipzig 1873, as *The fertilisation of flowers*, London, with preface by CD vii–x (F1883); see LLiii 275. Foreign translation, CD's preface only: Russian (F1433) 1950. DNB.

Thompson, Thomas Charles 1811–1885. b of H. S. M. Thompson. Rector of Ripley, Surrey, 1848–1885. 1834 'The two Thompsons of Trinity', Cambridge friend of CD—LLi 256.

Thompson William 1805–1852. Naturalist & linen draper of Belfast. 1849 CD to H. Strickland, T 'who is fierce for the law of priority'—LLi 370. 1851 CD in introduction to *Living Cirripedia*, 'The distinguished Natural Historian of Ireland'. DNB.

Thomson, Sir Charles Wyville 1830–1882. Biologist. Kt 1876 FRS 1869. T held several chairs in Ireland and Prof. Natural History Edinburgh 1870→. 1872 Director of scientific staff on the Challenger and edited results. 1880 T wrote anti–evolution introduction to them, 'The character of the abyssal fauna refuses to give the least support to the theory which refers the evolution of species to extreme variation guided only by Natural Selection'—MLi 388. 1880 Letter by CD, Sir Wyville Thomson and natural selection, *Nature*, Lond., 23:32 (Bii 223, F1789), in which CD severely castigates T, 'standard of criticism not uncommonly reached by theologians and metaphysicians', *see also* MLi 388. CD omitted, on advice from Huxley, 'for, as Prof. Sedgwick remarked many years ago, in reference to the poor old Dean of York, who was never weary of enveighing against geologists, a man who talks about what he does not in the least understand is invulnerable'. DNB.

Thomson, Thomas 1817–1878. Physician & botanist in India. FRS 1855. T held botanical appointments in Calcutta. 1858 T to CD, about 'what heat our temperate plants can endure'—LLii 113, spelt Thompson. 1860 T to CD, anti-*Origin*, but kindly. 1860 May15 'He is evidently a strong opposer to us'. 1863 CD to Hooker, about T's views on inheritance of acquired characters; CD wrote on 'foreign paper' for forwarding—MLi 233.

Thomson, Sir William, Baron Kelvin 1824–1907. Physicist. Kt 1866 1st *Baron* Kelvin of Largs 1892 FRS 1851 PRS 1890 OM 1902. Prof. Natural Philosophy Glasgow 1846–1899. K was amongst the most distinguished astronomical physicists of his day, but was quite wrong about the age of the earth. 1869 CD to Hooker, 'I feel a conviction that the world will be found rather older than Thomson makes it'—MLi 314. EB DNB.

Thorley, Miss Governess at Down House 'for many years', certainly from 1850–1856, when she was replaced by *Miss* Pugh. 1851 T was present at Malvern when Anne Elizabeth D died. 1855 T helped CD with studies of wild plants—Allan 154. 1882 T was on 'Personal Friends invited' list for CD's funeral.

Thwaites, George Henry Kendrick 1811–1882. Botanist & microscopist. FRS 1865. Director of Botanic Garden Peradeniya, Ceylon 1849→. 1847 CD met at British Association meeting in Oxford—Carroll 118. T was a frequent correspondent, especially on dimorphic flowers—Carroll 293, 295, 297. 1860 T was originally anti-*Origin*, but was coming round—LLii 347, MLi 144, Darwin-Gray 90. 1867 Oct.26 CD sent T printed *Queries about expression*; T provided information about elephants for *Expression*—Carroll 325, 342, 358. *See also Bull.Brit.Mus.(nat.Hist.)*, hist Ser., 4:4:205–219, 1972. DNB.

Tierra del Fuego Argentine/Chile, group of islands at S tip of S. America. 1834 Feb.12–Mar.12, Jun.9–12 *Beagle* surveyed there, CD several times ashore. *See also* Boat Memory, York Minster, Jemmy Button, Fuegia Basket, Richard Matthews, Thomas Bridges.

Times, The London Newspaper, founded 1785 Jan.1 as *Daily Universal Register*. 1859 CD to Lyell, 'the greatest newspaper in the world'—Carroll 182. 1863 CD to Gray, 'The *Times* is getting more detestable (but that is too weak a word) than ever [on slavery]. My good wife wishes to give it up, but I tell her that is a pitch of heroism to which only a woman is equal. To give up the 'Bloody Old *Times*', as Cobbett used to call it, would be to give up meat, drink and air'—LLiii 11.

Times Mail coach from London to Cambridge. 1829 CD to W. D. Fox, CD had travelled by—LLi 174.

Timirazev, Kliment Arkadeevich Botanist. Prof. Botany Moscow. 1877 T visited Down House and had a two hour talk with CD. 1878 CD to Dyer, suggesting that D should get in touch with T about equipping physiological laboratories 'who seemed so good a fellow'—MLii 417. T wrote several books on darwinism and published memories of his visit, 1920 U. Darvina v Daune, *Nauka demokratiia*, 105, *see* J. A. Rogers, *Isis*, 64:498–501, 1973.

Tineina 1860 Do the Tineina or other small moths suck flowers, and if so what flowers?, *Ent.weekly Intelligencer*, 8:103 (Bii 35, F1708).

Tollet, Caroline ?–1840. d of George T. m 1839 Thomas Stevens.

Tollet, Charles s of George T. T changed his name to Wicksted on inheriting Shakenhurst, Worcestershire. Sporting and family friend of CD.

Tollet, Ellen ?1890 Jan. d of George T. 1883 ED visited. She was a life-long friend, 'this death cuts off my last link with past life'—EDii 287.

Tollet, George, né Embury 1767–1855. Agricultural reformer of Betley Hall, Staffs, close friend of Josiah Wedgwood [II]. T assumed the surname on inheriting Betley from his cousin Charles T. T's wife was a very strict calvinist, 3 or more ds 1s. The children were personal friends of ED & CD from childhood. 1816 John Wedgwood lost his fortune in a crisis at Davison's Bank, of which he was a partner. T let him have a house on his estate at a low rate 'for the pleasure of their society'—EDi 102. 1839 T answered *Questions about the breeding of animals*—*J.Soc.Biblphy.nat.Hist.*, 5:220–225, 1969.

Tollet, Georgine d of George T. 1859 CD asked John Murray to send mss of chs 1–3 of *Origin* for her to read; she finally read whole mss. T was then of 14 Queen Anne St, London. 'The lady, being an excellent judge of style, is going to look out for errors for me'—LLii 156. 'One lady who has read all my MS, has found only two or three obscure sentences'—LLii 157. 1881 T wrote *Country conversations*, London privately printed.

Tommy A quiet cob which CD rode for his health on Bence Jones's recommendation. 1868 CD took T to Isle of Wight by train—*Nature*, Lond., 7:360, 1873. 1869 Apr. T stumbled and rolled on CD on Keston Common, bruising him badly. CD never rode again—EDii 195, Carroll 369.

Tony A male dog owned by Sarah Elizabeth Wedgwood [II]. 1880, when she died, he was taken over by CD.

Torbitt, James Agriculturalist of Belfast. 1876–1878 CD, with

Farrer & Caird, subscribed to keep his work on potato blight going. CD to Farrer on the matter—LLiii 348. 1878 CD to T, pessimistic on same subject—MLi 373.

Torquay Devon. 1861 Jul.1–Aug.26 CD had family holiday at. CD made observations on flight paths of male humble bees there.

Tower House *see* Trowmers.

Treat, Mrs of New Jersey, USA, provided information on *Dionaea* for *Insectivorous plants—Amer.Nat.*, Dec.1873:715.

Trimen, Roland 1840–1916. Entomologist. FRS 1883. Civil servant in S. Africa. 1859 T's reminiscences of CD, 'I . . . saw Darwin in the Bird Galleries . . . A clerical friend with me, also a naturalist . . . echoed White's warning by indicating Darwin as "the most dangerous man in England"'. 1863 On the fertilisation of *Disa grandiflora*, *J.Proc.Linn.Soc.Lond.(Bot.)*, 7:144, written by CD from T's notes. 1863–1871 eighteen letters from CD to T, on orchids and on evolutionary problems in the Lepidoptera. 1867 Dec. T stayed at Down House. 1868 Mar. T lunched with CD at 4 Chester Terrace, London house of Sarah Elizabeth Wedgwood [II]—Poulton, *Darwin and the Origin*, 213–246, which prints the letters. WWH.

Tristram, Henry Baker 1822–1906. Anglican clergyman & ornithologist. FRS 1868. 1859 T at first accepted *Origin*, but was later against. 1860 T to Newton, 'The infallibility of the God Darwin and prophet Huxley'—*Life of Newton* 122. DNB.

Trowmers House at Downe, N of Down House, earlier known as Trowmer or Trowmer Lodge, and later as Tower House, named after original family who owned it. 1868 taken by Sarah Elizabeth Wedgwood [II] and where she died in 1880.

Trotty, or Trotty Veck Childhood nickname of Henrietta Emma D.

Truelove, Edward 1809–1899. Publisher & socialist. 1878 T was convicted in High Court for publishing R. D. Owen's *Moral physiology*, London ? edition of 1871, on contraception. 1878 CD to a son of T, unable to sign a memorial against the conviction because he had not heard of T before the trial—Carroll 539.

Truttles 1833 A London bookseller. Henslow to CD, 'I will ask your brother to enquire at Truttles' for Cuvier, *Anatomie des mollusques*, Paris 1817—Darwin-Henslow 67.

Tuamotu Archipelago Pacific Island group, also known as Dangerous or Low Archipelago. 1835 Nov.9–13 *Beagle* sailed through on way to Tahiti, charting two new islands, but did not stop. Fitz-Roy spells Tuaamotu, with chart in appendix to Vol.2 of *Narrative*.

Tuckwell, W. 1829–1919. Anglican clergyman & schoolmaster. 1860 T was present at Oxford British Association meeting and wrote it up in *Reminiscences of Oxford*, 50, 1900—MLi 157.

Turkish First editions in: *Origin of species* (F796) 1970; *Descent of man* (F1137) 1968.

Turnbull, Catherine *see* Mackintosh.

Turnbull, G. H. m Catherine Mackintosh [III] as 2nd husband.

Turner 1829 A Cambridge friend of CD. Not traced.

Turner, Dawson 1775–1858. Banker & botanist. FRS 1803. f of Maria Sarah D.

Turner, Edward Francis T was for many years solicitor to D family. *see* W. M. Hacon.

Turner, Maria Sarah 1797–1850. eldest d of Dawson Turner. m 1815 *Sir* William Jackson Hooker.

Turner, Sir William 1832–1916. Physician. KCB 1901 FRS 1877. Prof. Anatomy Edinburgh 1867–1903; Principal 1903–1916. 1866 T supplied much information for *Descent*. CD met at Royal Society. CD sent T 4th edition of *Origin*—MLii 37. 1871 T to CD, pointed out CD's confusion of intercondyloid foramen in the humerus with the supracondyloid, in *Descent*, i 28—MLii 105. DNB.

Tyke 1881 A male family dog at Down House.

Tyler, Anne m 1836 Thomas Josiah Wedgwood.

Tyler, Helen Mary m 1866 John Darwin Wedgwood.

Tylor, Sir Edward Burnett 1832–1917. Anthropologist. Kt 1912 FRS 1871. Reader in Anthropology Oxford 1884– , Prof. 1896. 1871 CD to T, on receiving a copy of T's book *Primitive culture*—LLiii 151. DNB.

Tyndall, John 1820–1893. Physicist. FRS 1852. Superintendent of Royal Institution 1867–1887. T was a distinguished scientific popularizer. 1864 CD to Hooker, 'I am sorry to hear that Tyndall has grown dogmatic. H. Wedgwood was saying the other day that T's writing and speaking gave him the idea of intense conceit. I hope it is not so for he is a grand man of science'—MLii 155. 1868 Oct.24 T stayed the night at Down House with Gray and the Hookers. 1874 Lyell to CD, congratulating him of T's Presidential Address to British Association at Belfast, 'you and your theory of evolution may be fairly said to have had an ovation'—LLii 455. The Address with

additions published London 1874, also in *Fragments of science*, 2
vols, 6 edition 1879. 1882 T was on ' Personal Friends invited'
list for CD's funeral. DNB.

U

Ukrainian First editions in: *Origin of species* (F797) 1936; *Autobiography* (F1547) 1949.

Unione Publisher of Turin. 1871–1888 published eleven first Italian editions of CD's works, as well as 2nd Italian edition of *Origin of species*, 1875.

United States of America First editions published in: *Zoology of the voyage of the Beagle, Part V, Reptiles* only (F9a) 1975; *Journal of researches* (F16) 1846; *Coral reefs* (F278) 1889; *Volcanic islands & South America* (F283) 1891; *Origin of Species* (F377) 1860; *Fertilisation of orchids* (F802) 1877; *Climbing plants* (F838) 1876; *Variation under domestication* (F879) 1868; *Descent of man* (F941) 1871; *Expression of the emotions* (F1143) 1872; *Insectivorous plants* (F1220) 1875; *Cross and self fertilisation* (F1250) 1877; *Different forms of flowers* (F1278) 1877; *Biographical sketch of an infant* (F1306) 1956; *Erasmus Darwin* (F1320) 1880; *Movement in plants* (F1327) 1881; *Vegetable mould and worms* (F1363) 1882; *Life and letters* (F1456) 1887; *More letters* (F1549) 1903.

Upper Gower Street London. No. 12, later 110 Gower St., first home of CD & ED on marriage. 1838 Dec. 31 CD moved in. 1839 Jan. 29 ED moved in. They called it Macaw Cottage from the gaudy curtains. It was rented furnished, with a long thin garden backing on to Gower Mews North, later Malet Place. 1842 Sep. 14 ED left for Down House; Sep. 16 CD left. William Erasmus D and Anne Elizabeth D were born there. For many years the house was part of Messrs Schoolbred's warehouse system. It was bombed 1941 and not repaired. Site now part of Biological Sciences building of University College London, which bears the London County Council blue plaque to 'Charles Darwin Naturalist', which was originally on the house. Garden now part of Foster Court car park. Staff: Gardener, Williams; Menservants, Edward, Jordan, Parslow.

Ur-hund *see* Polly.

Usborne, Alexander Burns Master's Assistant on 2nd voyage of *Beagle*. 1835 U took command of a small schooner and surveyed the whole coast of Peru, after *Beagle* had left for Galápagos Islands. The boat was then sold and U returned to England via Cape Horn, before 1836 Nov.—Fitz-Roy, *J.R. Geogr.Soc.*, 6:311–343, 1836. *Captain* 1867. 1887 U was alive—LLi 221.

V

Valdivia Chile. 1835 Feb.8–20 *Beagle* at. Feb.20 earthquake; CD was on board and Fitz-Roy in the town.

Vale Cottage 1835 CD to W. D. Fox, from Lima, mentions it; perhaps F's family home at Osmaston nr Derby.

Valparaiso Chile. 1834 Jul.23 *Beagle* arrived at. CD stayed ashore and made expedition inland Aug.14–Sep.27; CD then ill until end Oct., when *Beagle* returned and set out for Chiloe. 1835 Mar.11 *Beagle* at again.

Van John 1829 CD to W. D. Fox, from Cambridge, 'A little of Gibbon's History in the morning, and a good deal of *Van John* in the evening'—LLi 176. 1880 CD to J. M. Herbert mentions V, again in italic—*Notes & Records*, 23:73. University slang for vingt-et-un, a card game.

Variation Under Domestication 1867–1869. Title in Russian [*On the origin of species. Section I. The variation of animals and plants under domestication. The domestication of animals and the cultivation of plants*], St Petersburg, translated from English corrected proofs by V. O. Kovalevskïi; issued in 7 parts, of which 1–4 appeared in 1867, preceeding the 1st English edition (F925). 1868 *The variation of animals and plants under domestication*, 2 vols, London (F877), 1st issue Jan., 4 lines errata in Vol.1, 7 in Vol.2; 2nd issue with corrections (F878), 1 line erratum in Vol.1; 1875 2nd edition (F880). First foreign editions: French (F912), German (F914), USA (F879) 1868; Italian (F920) 1876; Dutch (F912) 1889; Hungarian (F919) 1959; Romanian (F924) 1963. Facsimile of 2nd issue (F908) 1969.

Variations 1862 Variations affected by cultivation, *J.Hort.*, 3:696 (Bii 71, F1721); 1873 George H. D. Variations in organs, *Nature*, Lond., 8:505 (Bii 292, F1763), by G. H. D. but gives his father's views.

Variegated Leaves 1844 Variegated leaves, *Gdnr's Chronicle*, No.37:621 (Bi 198, F1667).

Vaux, Henry Sandys Wright 1818–1885. Antiquary & ancient geographer. FRS 1868. Department of Antiquities British

Museum 1841– . 1856 CD consulted V about *Variation*—Carroll 128. DNB.

Vaynol N Wales. 1826 CD visited on riding tour with Caroline Sarah D—*Journal*.

Vegetable Mould and Worms 1881 *The formation of vegetable mould through the action of worms, with observations on their habits*, London (F1357); facsimile of 2nd thousand (F1410) 1969; 3rd–6th thousands (F1359–1362) 1881–1882, contain small corrections by CD; 7th thousand (F1364) 1882 & 11th thousand (F1373) 1888, contain small changes by Francis D. First foreign editions: French (F1403), German (F1404), Italian (F1407), Russian (F1408), USA (F1363) 1882; Armenian (F1402) 1896. *See Sir* Arthur Keith, *Nature*, Lond., 149:716, 1942.

Veitch, James 1792–1863 & his son James 1815–1869. Nurserymen of Royal Exotic Nursery, King's Road, Chelsea, London. 1861 V supplied orchids for CD's work, 'Mr James Veitch has been most generous'—LLiii 768, MLii 276. J. H. Veitch, *Hortus Veitchii*, London 1906.

Verbascum *see Primula* 1868.

Vermin and Traps 1863 Vermin and traps, *Gdnr's Chronicle*, No.35:821–822 (Bii 83, F1728).

Vestiges 1844 *Vestiges of the natural history of creation*, London. An anonymous work on evolution, by Robert Chambers q.v. c1850 CD to Hooker, calls the author 'Mr Vestiges', although he had identified the author correctly.

Vierweg, Friedrich, und Sohn Publisher of Brunswick, Germany. 1844 published *Journal of researches*, the 1st translation or printing abroad of any of CD's books, and the only translation of the 1st edition.

Villa Franca, Baron de 1881 CD to Romanes, V 'wrote to me from Brazil about two years ago' on sugar-cane varieties—MLi 390. 1887 CD to Romanes, R would prepare paper on sugar-cane hybrids for the press, *see* V & Glass, *Proc.Linn.Soc.Lond.*,80–81—Carroll 611.

Vincas 1861 Fertilisation of Vincas, *Gdnr's Chronicle*, No.24:552 (Bii 40, F1711). 1861 Vincas, *ibid.*, No.37:831–832 (Bii 41, F1716).

Vines, Sydney Howard 1849–1934. Botanist. FRS 1885. Reader in Botany Cambridge. 1881 Oct. CD & ED took tea with in Cambridge. Nov. CD to V on plant chemistry—LLiii 346. DNB.

Virchow, Rudolf Ludwig Carl 1821–1902. Pathologist & politician. For.Mem. RS 1884 Copley Medal 1892. Prof. Pathological Anatomy Berlin 1856– . 1877 V gave an address at Münich connecting evolution with socialism, published as *Die Freiheit der Wissenschaft im modernen Staat*, Berlin, translated into English 1878. Haeckel replied to it. 1878 V seconded CD's election to Koeniglich-Preussische Akademie der Wissenschaften, Berlin.

Vivisection CD's part in the agitation and Commission on this subject are considered in LLiii 199–221 & MLii 435–441. 1875 CD to Romanes, warns R not to discuss experiments on animals in front of Darwin women, since it would horrify them—Carroll 465. 1881 CD letter to Frithiof Holmgren, *The Times*, Apr.18, *Brit.med.J.*, 1:660, *Nature*, Lond., 23:583 (F1792); also in anti–Vivisection pamphlet by George Jesse (F1356), all 1881, also in LLiii 205–206, and in Sweden. 1881 Darwin on vivisection, *The Times*, Apr.22 (F1793). 1881 CD to Romanes, about *The Times* letter, 'I thought it fair to bear my share of the abuse poured in so atrocious a manner on all physiologists'—*Life of Romanes* 116. *see also* David Ferrier.

Vivisection Commission 1875. CD gave evidence before it in London Nov.8; *Viscount* Cardwell, the Chairman, came to the door to receive him. Members: *Baron* Winmarleigh, W. E. Forster, *Sir* J. B. Karslake, T. H. Huxley, Prof. Erichssen, R. H. Hutton, with Nathaniel Baker, Secretary. 1876 *Report of the Royal Commission on the practice of subjecting live animals to experiments for scientific purposes; with the minutes of evidence and appendix*, London, HMSO Command 1397; CD's evidence 234, paras 4662–4672 (F1275). 1876 *Digest of evidence* etc., Command 1397.1, CD's evidence 34 (F1270).

Volcanic Islands 1844 *Geological observations on the volcanic islands visited during the voyage of H.M.S. Beagle, together with some brief notices of the geology of Australia and the Cape of Good Hope. Being the second part of the geology of the voyage of the Beagle, under the command of Capt. Fitz-Roy, R.N. during the years 1832 to 1836*, London (F272), appendices by G. B. Sowerby [I] and W. Lonsdale. 1851 combined edition of the 3 parts from unsold sheets, with new preliminaries (F274). 1876 2nd edition, combined with Part 3 *South America* (F276). 1891 3rd edition, combined as 2nd edition (F282). 1972 facsimile of an 1896 issue (F307). First foreign editions: German (F312) 1877; USA (F283) 1891; French (F310) 1902; Russian (F323) 1936.

Volcanic Phaenomena and Mountain Chains 1838 On the connexion of certain volcanic phaenomena, and on the formation of mountain chains and volcanoes as the effect of continental elevations, *Proc.geol.Soc.*, 2:654–660 (Bi 53, F1649). 1840 On the connection of certain volcanic phaenomena in South America; and on the formation of mountain chains and volcanoes as the effect of the same powers by which continents are elevated, *Trans.geol.Soc.*, 5:601–631 (Bi 54, F1656).

Volcanic Rocks and Glaciers 1845 Extracts from letters to the General Secretary, on the analogy of the structure of some volcanic rocks with that of glaciers, *Proc.Roy.Soc.Edinb.*, 2:17–18 (Bi 193, F1670); letters from CD to E. Forbes.

Voyage of the Beagle *see Journal of researches*. This title was first used in Harmsworth Library edition, 1905 (F106).

Voyage of the Beagle, Charles Darwin and *see Charles Darwin and* etc.

Voyage of the Beagle, diary *see Diary of the voyage* etc.

W

Waddington, Mrs *see* Marianne Port.

Wagner, Johann Andreas 1797–1861. German geologist. 1863 CD to Falconer, 'Poor old Wagner always attacking me in a proper spirit' . . . 'sent me two or three little brochures, and I thanked him cordially'—MLi 229. Author of Zur Feststellung der Artbegriffen, *München Situngb.*, 301, 1861.

Wagner, Moritz Friedrich 1813–1887. German traveller & naturalist. 1868 CD to Weismann on W's views about evolution in his pamphlet *Die Darwin'sche Theorie und das Migrationsgesetz*, Munich, English translation London 1873—LLiii 157, MLi 311. 1872 CD to Weismann refers to W's views—LLii 156. 1876 CD to W, about his evolutionary essay in *Das Ausland*, May 31, 1875—LLiii 158.

Wagner, Rudolph 1805–1864. German anatomist & physiologist. Prof. Zoology Göttingen. 1860 CD to Huxley, W had sent CD a copy of his abstract of L. Agassiz, *Essay on classification*, 1857, Louis Agassiz's Principien der Classification . . . mit Rücksicht auf Darwins, *Göttingischen Gelehrten*, 1860—LLii 330.

Wales CD visited Wales on ten occasions. 1813 Summer, family holiday at Gros, Abergele. 1819 Jul. family holiday, Plas Edwards, Towyn. 1820 Jul. riding tour with Erasmus Alvey D, Pistyll Rhayader. 1822 Jul. holiday with Susan Elizabeth D, Montgomery. 1828 Summer, reading party under G. A. Butterton, Barmouth. 1829 Jun. beetle collecting with F. W. Hope, Barmouth. 1830 Aug. beetle collecting N. Wales. 1831 Aug. geology trip with A. Sedgwick, Llangollen, Ruthin, Conway, Bangor, Capel Curig, then Barmouth alone. 1842 Jun. for geology, Capel Curig, Bangor, Caernarvon. 1869 Jun. family holiday, Caerdeon, Barmouth.

Walker, Francis 1809–1874. Entomologist. Assistant at British Museum. 1839 W described CD's chalcid material from *Beagle* in Vol.2 of *Monographia Chalciditum*, 2 vols, London, and elsewhere.

Wallace, Alexander 1830–1899. Physician & lepidopterist of Colchester. 1868 CD to J. Weir, giving W's views on sexual selection in *Bombyx mori*—MLii 66. 1868 CD to H. T. Stainton, giving W's views on sex ratio in *Bombyx cynthia*—FUL 108. W is often referred to in *Descent* as an expert on various species of silk moth.

Wallace, Alfred Russel 1823 Jan.8–1913 Nov.7. Traveller & naturalist. FRS 1905 (he refused it in 1892) OM 1908. Royal Medal 1868, Darwin Medal 1890 (first recipient), Copley Medal 1908. Linnean Society Darwin-Wallace Medal 1908 (first recipient), DCL Oxford 1889. 8th c (of 9) of Thomas Vere W & Mary Ann Greenell. m 1866 Annie Mitten 1s William G, 1d Violet. Hooker called W 'Darwin's true knight'. W's first employment was, by his b John, as a land surveyor. The most important periods of his life were, as a collector of natural history specimens, in the Amazons 1848–1852, and in the Malay Archipelago 1854–1862.

On his return to England, his only income until 1881 was from sale of specimens and from authorship. In 1881 he was granted a civil list pension of £200 p.a., Jan.7. 1879 Dec.17 CD & Hooker first raised the matter—LLiii 228. Although CD and Ẇ were always on friendly terms and W often visited Down House, there was never the intimacy that there was with Hooker, Falconer or Huxley; nor did they fully understand each other's scientific views. 1855 On the law which has regulated the introduction of new species, *Ann.Mag.nat.Hist.*, 16:184–196.

1857 CD to W, 'You say that you have been somewhat surprised at no notice having been taken of your paper in the Annals. I cannot say that I am, for so very few naturalists care for anything beyond the mere description of species'—LLii 108. 1858 Jun.18 Fri. CD received letter from W, written at Ternate, Mollucas, enclosing his paper 'On the tendency of varieties to depart indefinitely from the original type' in mss. CD wrote to Lyell the same day 'Your words have come true with a vengeance—that I should be forestalled'—LLii 116.

1858 Jul.1 Tues. Hooker and Lyell communicated CD & W's joint paper to Linnean Society, On the tendency of species to form varieties and species by natural means of selection, *J.Proc.Linn.Soc.Lond.,Zool.*, 3:45–62 (F346), W's paper 54–62. 1858 Jul.25 CD sent 'Some half dozen copies' of the offprint to W and 'I have may other copies at your disposal'. Oct.12 CD to Hooker, 'I have sent eight copies by post to Wallace, and will keep others for him'—LLii 138. The whole episode is considered in detail in LLii 115–140. 1860 Dec.24 W to Bates, 'I do honestly believe that with however much patience I had worked and experimented on the subject, I could never have approached the completeness of his book—its vast accumulation of evidence, its overwhelming argument, and its admirable tone and spirit'. 1870 CD to W, 'I fear we shall never quite understand each other'—LLiii 125. 1871 'I then applied to Mr Wallace, who has an innate genius for solving difficulties'—*Descent* i 416. W was Pall Bearer at CD's funeral. W moved house often and had four houses built to his own design, the last at Wimborne, Dorset, where he died. Main works: 1853 *Palm trees of the Amazons* [50 copies]; 1853 *Travels on the Amazons;* 1869 *Malay Archipelago*; 1870 *Contributions to the theory of natural selection*; 1876 *Geographical distribution of animals*; 1882 *Island life*; 1889 *Darwinism*. Autobiography: *My life*, 2 vols, 1908. Biography: Marchant 1916; George 1964. Bibliography: in Marchant 1916. 1966 H. L. MacKinney, Alfred Russel Wallace and the discovery of natural selection, *J.Hist.Med.*, 21:333–357, discusses the development of W's views and its relationship to those of CD. DNB.

Wallich, George Charles 1815–1899. Physician & marine biologist. Naturalist on H.M.S *Bulldog* 1859–1860. Army surgeon and botanist in India. 1860 W sent CD a copy of his pamphlet *Notes on the presence of animal life at vast depths in the sea*, London, for private circulation. CD thanks W for—N&R 58. 1861 CD met W at Linnean Society—MLi 184. 1882 Mar.28 CD to W, on deep water organisms and asking for a copy of his lecture on Protista; CD's last recorded letter—N&R 59. DNB.

Walpole, Lady Dorothy Frances 1826–1913. Elder daughter of Horatio W, 3rd *Earl* of Orford. m 1848 Reginald Henry Nevill. W was an enthusiastic gardener at Dangstein, Rogate, Hants, 1851–1878. 1861 W helped CD with *Orchids*, 'responded in a wonderfully kind manner, and has sent a lot of treasures'—MLii 278. 1874 CD to W, thanking her for providing plants for *Insectivorous plants*, especially *Utricularia montana*, which lives in moss on trees, unlike the usual species which are aquatic—LLiii 327, Carroll 449. W called on CD at Down House but he was ill. CD called on W several times in London. Autobiography: *Under five reigns*, London 1910, 106–112, has reminiscences of CD and five letters from. Biography: R. Nevill (son), London 1919, 56–58, has reminiscences and one letter. CD signed W's birthday book, which was illustrated by Kate Greenaway.

Walsh, Benjamin Dann 1808–1869. Entomologist. W was contemporary with CD at Cambridge; Fellow of Trinity 1838. W emigrated to USA and was State Entomologist of Illinois 1868–1869, when he was killed in a railway accident. b of J. H. Walsh. 1864 W to CD, reintroducing himself; they had met in CD's rooms at Cambridge. W comments on *Origin*, 'The first perusal staggered me, the second convinced me, and the oftener I read it the more convinced I am of the general soundness of your theory'—MLi 249. C. V. Riley described W as 'one of the ablest and most thorough entomologists of our time'—MLi 248. 1868 CD to W, on 13 and 17 year cycles in cicadas—MLii 89. 1868 W to CD, he could not answer CD's *Queries about expression.*

Walsh, John Henry 1810–1888. Naturalist. b of Benjamin Dann W. W wrote under pseudonym of 'Stonehenge'.

Walton Hall nr Pontefract, Yorkshire. Home of Charles Waterton. 1845 Sep. CD visited and stayed the night—LLi 343.

Ward, William George 1812–1882. Catholic theologian & philosopher. 1861 CD sent W Gray's pamphlet *Natural selection not inconsistent with natural theology*—Darwin-Gray 76, where Henshaw Ward is suggested.

Wareham Dorset. 1847 Jul. CD & family visited on way to holiday at Swanage.

Waring, Anne 1662–1722. d of Robert W. m 1680 William Darwin [II]. CD's great great grandmother. W inherited manor and hall of Elston, nr Newark, Staffs, from George Lassels or Lascelles, her mother's 2nd husband. *See also* Brass Close.

Waring, Robert ?–1662. f of Anne W and origin of the forename Waring in the Darwin family. CD's great great great grandfather.

Warren, Mr 1853 CD to Henslow. W had written to CD from Brighton; the matter concerned some speculative investment, but Barlow was unable to trace further—Darwin-Henslow 169.

Warrington, Robert 1807–1867. Chemist and one of the earliest popularizers of the marine aquarium. 1867 CD to Wallace, 'Mr Warrington has lately read an excellent and spirited abstract of the '"Origin" before the Victoria Institute, and as this is a most orthodox body, he has gained the name of the Devil's Advocate. The discussion which followed . . . is very rich from the nonsense talked'—LLiii 69. Identification uncertain.

Waterhouse, Alfred 1830–1905. Architect. 1865 W designed British Museum (Natural History). Atkins 89 suggests that W visited Down House, but in error for George Robert W. q.v.

Waterhouse, George Robert 1810–1888. Mammalogist & entomologist. Keeper of Mineralogy & Geology at British Museum (Natural History). A friend of CD and often at Down House. 1838–1839 W wrote *Zoology of the voyage of the Beagle*, Part II, *Living Mammalia*. 1843 CD to Lyell, 'if Waterhouse is hired he will enjoy his seven shillings a day from the British Museum, as much as most men would ten times the sum!'—LLi 344. 1843 CD to W, 'I believe . . . that if every organism which ever had lived or does live were collected together . . . a perfect series would be presented, linking all . . . into one great quite indivisible group'—*Memorials of Charles Darwin*, 8, 1909. 1847 CD reviewed W's *A natural history of the Mammalia* Vol. 1, *Marsupialia*, 1846, in *Ann.Mag. nat.Hist.*, 19:53–56, unsigned, (Bi 214, F1675); CD's only book review. DNB.

Waterton, Charles 1782–1865. Naturalist & traveller, of Walton Hall, nr Pontefract, Yorkshire. ?1826 CD met W in Edinburgh with J. Edmonston who had been trained as a bird skinner by W. 1845 CD visited W at Walton Hall. 1845 CD to Lyell, 'He is an amusing strange fellow; at our early dinner, our party consisted of two catholic priests and two Mulatresses' [W's sisters-in-law]—LLi 344. W was author of *Wanderings in South America*, London 1825. EB, DNB.

Watford Natural History Society, later Hertfordshire. CD Honorary Member 1877.

Watkins, Frederick 1808–1888. Archdeacon of York 1874–1888. Cambridge friend of CD, member of the Gourmet Club. 1860 CD to W on evolution, 'I think the arguments are valid, showing that all animals have descended from four or five primordial forms; and that analogy and weak reasons go to show that all have descended from some single prototype'—LLii 328. 1887 W gives memories of CD collecting beetles and talking of the beauty of the Brazilian forests—LLi 168.

Watson, Hewett Cottrell 1804–1881. Botanist & phrenologist, specialist in distribution of British plants. 1857 CD to Hooker, W had marked up a Flora for CD to show which he considered to be good species. 1859 CD sent W 1st edition of *Origin*. W accepted evolution by natural selection. 1861 CD to Hooker, W accuses CD of egotism, 'In the first four paragraphs of the introduction, the words "I", "me", "my", occur forty-three times'—LLii 362.

Way, Albert 1805–1874. Antiquary. Cambridge friend of CD; they collected beetles together. 1827 'Became acquainted with Fox & Way & so commenced Entomology'—Journal. 1860 Apr. CD to W about antiquarian information on breeds of horses, 'Eheu, Eheu, the old Crux Major days are long past' [*Panagaeus crux-major*, a beetle collected by CD and Way at Cambridge]—Carroll 205. W edited *Promptorium parvulorum*, 1843–1865. DNB.

Weale, James Philip Mansel South African naturalist. 1867 CD to Hooker, W had sent seeds from locust dung from Natal—MLii 4. 1868 CD to Hooker, the grasses from the seeds had flowered—MLi 303. *see Origin*, 5th edition, 439, 1869.

Webb, Mr 1855 CD to Henslow, CD was sending cirripedes to care of W. ?Curator of Ipswich Museum—Darwin-Henslow 173.

Webster, Mary m 1887 Ernest Hensleigh Wedgwood.

Wedgwood, Agnes *see* Harley.

Wedgwood, Alfred Allen 1842–1892. 5c of Hensleigh W. m 1873 Margaret Rosina Ingall, and had offspring. Known as Tiny Tim. CD's 1st cousin once removed.

Wedgwood, Allen *see* John Allen W.

Wedgwood, Amy 1835–? 2c of Francis W. unm. CD's 1st cousin once removed.

Wedgwood, Anne *see* Tyler.

Wedgwood, Anne Jane 1841–1877. 4c of Henry Allen W. m 1864 Ralph Edward Carr. CD's 1st cousin once removed.

Wedgwood, Arthur 1843–1900. 5c of Henry Allen W. unm. CD's 1st cousin once removed.

Wedgwood, Bessy [I] *see* Elizabeth Allen.

Wedgwood, Bessy [II] *see* Sarah Elizabeth W [II].

Wedgwood, Caroline 1836–? 2c of Henry Allen W. unm. CD's 1st cousin once removed.

Wedgwood, Caroline Louisa Jane 1799–1825. 4c of John Wedgwood. unm. CD's 1st cousin.

Wedgwood, Caroline Sarah *see* Darwin.

Wedgwood, Catherine 1774–1823. 6c of Josiah W [I]. unm. Known as Kitty. CD's aunt. Lived at Parkfield, Cardiganshire until her death.

Wedgwood, Major Cecil ?–1916. s of Godfrey W & Mary Hawkshaw. CD's 1st cousin twice removed. Partner Josiah W & Sons Ltd, 1884–1916. WWH.

Wedgwood, Charles 1800–1820. 5c of John W. unm. CD's 1st cousin.

Wedgwood, Charlotte 1797–1862. d of Josiah W [II]. m 1822 Charles Langton as 1st wife. CD's 1st cousin & sister-in-law. Known as Lotty. W died at St Leonard's, Sussex. 1824 'Her fair hair reached to her knees'—EDi 155.

Wedgwood, Cicely Mary 1837–? 3c of Francis W. m Clarke Henshaw. CD's 1st cousin once removed. 1867 W was in Cambridge.

Wedgwood, Clement 1840–1889. 4c of Francis W. m 1866 Emily Rendel and had offspring. CD's 1st cousin once removed.

Wedgwood, Constance Rose 1846–1902. 6c of Francis W. m 1880 Hermann Franke. CD's 1st cousin once removed.

Wedgwood, Edith Louisa d of Robert W & Mary Halsey. m 1877 Clement Frederick Romilly Allen. CD's 1st cousin once removed.

Wedgwood, Effie *see* Katherine Euphemia W.

Wedgwood, Eliza *see* Sarah Elizabeth W [III].

Wedgwood, Elizabeth [I] *see* Allen.

Wedgwood, Elizabeth [II] *see* Sarah Elizabeth W [II].

Wedgwood, Emily *see* Rendel.

Wedgwood, Emma [I] 1808 May 2 at Maer Hall—1896 Oct.2 at The Grove, Cambridge. 9th and last c of Josiah W [II], named after her aunt Emma Allen. m 1839 Jan.29, by *Rev.* John Allen W, Charles Robert Darwin, at St Peter's Church, Maer. CD's 1st cousin & wife. 1822–1823 ED was at school at Greville House, Paddington Green, London. Before marriage, ED travelled on the continent with her family, 1818 Apr. visited Paris; 1824–1825 Paris, Geneva, Florence, Sorrento, Rome, Milan; 1826 Geneva; 1827 Cologne; 1838 Paris.
She also made a number of visits in British Isles, sometimes to relatives; 1823 Scarborough; 1828 Clifton; 1837 Edinburgh. 1836 Oct. 'We are getting impatient for Charles's arrival' [on return of *Beagle*]—EDi 272. Nov. 'We enjoyed Charles's visit

uncommonly'—EDi 273. 1838 Nov.11 CD proposed, at
Maer, and was accepted. After marriage ED devoted her life to
CD and to bringing up the children. After CD's death she
spent the summers at Down House and the winters at The
Grove, Huntingdon Rd, Cambridge. ED is buried in Downe
churchyard. 'A beautiful needlewoman, a good archer, and she
rode, danced and skated'. 'She played delightfully on the
piano'. 'She had lessons from Maschelas and a few from Cho-
pin'—LLi 62. She read French, German and Italian. 'Her
brown hair kept its warm tint almost to the end of her life with
hardly a grey hair in it.' 'In 1824 she could sit on her hair'—EDi
155. ED was sometimes known as Mammy by the children.
CD's opinion of ED is omitted from LLi 69, which was
published whilst she was alive. 'You all well know your
mother, and what a good mother she has ever been to all of
you. She has been my greatest blessing, and I can declare that
in my whole life I have never heard her utter one word which I
had rather had been unsaid. She has never failed in the kindest
sympathy towards me, and has borne with the utmost patience my frequent complaints from ill-health and discomfort. I
do not believe she has ever missed an opportunity of doing a
kind action to anyone near her. I marvel at my good fortune
that she, so infinitely my superior in every single moral quality, consented to be my wife. She has been my wise adviser and
cheerful comforter throughout life, which without her would
have been during a very long period a miserable one from
ill-health. She has earned the love and admiration of every soul
near her'—MLi 30, Barlow, Autobiography 96.
On her religious views, 'In our childhood and youth she was
not only sincerely religious—this she always was in the true
sense of the word—but definite in her beliefs. She went regularly to Church and took the Sacrament. She read the Bible
with us and taught us a simple Unitarian Creed, though we
were baptised and confirmed in the Church of England'—EDii 173, Barlow, Autobiography 238. ED's religious
views are stated in 2 letters to CD. 1. ?1839, soon after marriage. CD appended a note 'When I am dead, know that many
times, I have kissed and cryed over this C.D.'—EDii 173
omitting note, Barlow, Autobiography 237. 2. 1861 Jun., CD
appends a note 'God bless you'—EDii 175, Barlow, Autobiography 238.

ICONOGRAPHY 1 1839 Water colour by George Richmond, done at the same time as that of CD, now in the family. 2 c1853 Photograph by Maull & Fox, with Leonard D at Down House. 3 1881 Photograph by Barrand. 4 Pastel by Fairfax Murray, now in the family. 5 1895 Photograph by *Miss* M. J. Shaen at Down House.

PRINTED WORKS c1825 ED wrote a reading book for her Sunday School class at Maer; the class was taught by the family and held in the laundry; 'these she had printed in large type; the book contained four little stories, one about a "plumb pie" [sic]. We, her own children were taught to read out of this little book, and were fond of these stories'—EDi 142. 1887 ED wrote a 4 line preface to the 1st edition in book form of Henry Allen W's *The bird talisman*, which she had printed for the benefit of her grandchildren. Biography: 1904 Henrietta Litchfield (daughter), privately printed, Cambridge; the same, published edition, 1915 London. 1952 Gwen Raverat (granddaughter), *Period piece*, ch.8.

Wedgwood, Emma [II] *see* Houseman.

Wedgwood, Ernest Hensleigh 1838–1898. 3c of Hensleigh W. m 1887 Mary Webster, 1s. Known as Erny. CD's 1st cousin once removed.

Wedgwood, Fanny *see* Frances W [II].

Wedgwood, Frances [I] *see* Crewe.

Wedgwood, Frances [II] 1806–1832 Aug.20. 8c of Josiah W [II]. unm. 'Freckled plain-faced faithful Fanny'. CD's 1st cousin & sister-in-law.

Wedgwood, Frances [III] *see* Mosley.

Wedgwood, Frances [IV] *see* Mackintosh.

Wedgwood, Frances Julia 1833–1913. 1c Hensleigh W. unm. CD's 1st cousin once removed. Known as Snow. 1861 The boundaries of science, a dialogue, *Macmillan's Mag.*, Jul. CD's comments on, 'I could not clearly follow you in some parts, which is in main part due to my not being at all accustomed to metaphysical trains of thought'—LLi 313. 1867 'I do find myself so wicked for finding Snow such a dreadful bore . . . begging to discuss fate and free will . . . so tactless a woman I never came near and gets worse'—E. M. Forster, *Marianne Thornton*, 223.

Wedgwood, Francis 1800–1888 Oct.1. Potter. 6c of Josiah W [I]. m 1832 Apr.26 Frances Mosley, 3s 4d: 1. Godfrey, 2. Amy,

3. Cicely Mary, 4. Clement, 5. Lawrence, 6. Constance Rose, 7. Mabel Frances. CD's 1st cousin and brother-in-law. Senior Partner in Josiah Wedgwood & Sons Ltd 1844–1875. Of Barlaston, Staffs. 1878 Jun. CD & ED visited. 1879 W visited Down House and again in 1885. 1884 W visited The Grove, Cambridge.

Wedgwood, Godfrey 1833–1905. 1c of Francis W. m1 Mary Hawkshaw 1s Cecil. m2 Hope Elizabeth Wedgwood 1d Mary Euphrazia. CD's 1st cousin once removed. Senior partner Josiah Wedgwood & Sons Ltd, 1875–1905. Lived Idlerocks.

Wedgwood, Harry *see* Henry Allen W.

Wedgwood, Helen Mary *see* Tyler.

Wedgwood, Henry Allen 1799–1885 Oct. 5c of Josiah W [II]. m 1830 his 1st cousin Jessie W. 3s 3d; 1. Louisa Frances, 2. Caroline, 3. John Darwin, 4. Anne Jane, 5. Arthur, 6. Rowland. CD's 1st cousin and brother-in-law. Known as Hal or Harry. Barrister. Author of *The bird talisman* q.v. 1827 Essex Court, Temple; 1837 Seabridge nr Maer, Staffs; c1847 The Hermitage, nr Woking, Surrey.

Wedgwood, Hensleigh 1803–1891 Jun.1. 7c of Josiah W [II]. m 1832 Frances Mackintosh 3s 3d: 1. Frances Julia, 2. James Mackintosh, 3. Ernest Hensleigh, 4. Katherine Euphemia, 5. Alfred Allen, 6. Hope Elizabeth. CD's 1st cousin and brother-in-law. Known as Hen and with wife as the Hens. Barrister & philologist. 1831–1837 Police Magistrate. 1839– Registrar of Hackney Cabs. Author of *A dictionary of English etymology*, 3 vols, London, 1859–1865. In CD's London years he saw much of W, but later apparently seldom. 1880 CD to W, about an essay on religion and science by W which no good scientific journal would publish, 'there have been too many attempts to reconcile Genesis and science'—Carroll 573. 1885 W visited Down House. ?1840 16 Upper Gower St, ?1849 42 Chester Terrace, 1868 4 Cumberland Place, 1879 31 Queen Anne St, all London. 1876 Hopedene, Surrey, a house lent to him.

Wedgwood, Hope Elizabeth 1844–? 6c of Hensleigh W. m Godfrey W as 2nd wife. CD's 1st cousin once removed.

Wedgwood, James Mackintosh 1834–1864. 2c of Hensleigh W. unm. Known as Bro. CD's 1st cousin once removed.

Wedgwood, Jane *see* Louisa Jane W.

Wedgwood, Jessie 1804–1872. 6c of John W. m 1830 Henry Allen W. CD's 1st cousin.

Wedgwood, John 1766–1844. 2c of Josiah W [I]. m Louisa Jane

Allen 4s 3d: 1. Sarah Elizabeth, 2. John Allen, 3. Thomas Josiah, 4. Caroline Louisa Jane, 5. Charles, 6. Jessie, 7. Robert. CD's uncle. Evangelical and became rigid after death of d Caroline in 1825. The Hill, Abergavenny.

Wedgwood, Rev. John Allen 1796–1882. 2c of John W unm. CD's 1st cousin. Vicar of St Peter's Maer 1825– . 1839 Jan.29 W married CD and ED there.

Wedgwood, John Darwin 1840–1870. 3c of Henry Allen W. m 1866 Helen Mary Tyler d.s.p. CD's 1st cousin once removed.

Wedgwood, Josiah [I] 1730–1795 Jan. Potter. 13c of Thomas W. m 1764 Sarah W (a cousin) 4s 3d: 1. Susannah, 2. John, 3. Richard, 4. Josiah [II], 5. Thomas, 6. Catherine, 7. Sarah Elizabeth. Founder of the firm of Josiah Wedgwood & Sons Ltd. CD's maternal grandfather. Close friend of Erasmus D [I]. Etruria Hall, Staffs. Biography: Meteyard 1865.

Wedgwood, Josiah [II] 1769–1843 Jul.12. Potter. 4c of Josiah W [I]. m 1792 Sarah Elizabeth Allen 4s 5d: 1. Sarah Elizabeth, 2. Josiah [III], 3. Mary Anne, 4. Charlotte, 5. Henry Allen, 6. Francis, 7. Hensleigh, 8. Frances, 9. Emma. Known as Jos. CD's uncle and father-in-law. Maer Hall, Staffs 1819– . Senior partner of Josiah Wedgwood & Sons Ltd 1795–1841. CD was on close terms with and it was he who persuaded CD's father to let him go on the *Beagle* voyage. Sydney Smith of W, 'Wedgwood's an excellent man—it is a pity he hates his friends'—EDi 74. CD 'I used to apply to him . . . the well known ode of Horace, now forgotten by me, in which the words "nec vultus tyranni" etc come in'—LLi 44. [Justum et tenacem propositi virum/Non civium ardor prava juben-tium/Non vultus instantis tyranni/Mente quatit solida. The just man and firm of purpose not the heat of fellow citizens clamouring for what is wrong, nor presence of threatening tyrant can shake his rocklike soul—*Odes* III,iii,1.]

Wedgwood, Josiah [III] 1795–1880 Mar.11. Potter. 2c of Josiah W [II]. m 1837 Caroline Sarah Darwin 4d: 1. Sophiah Marianne 1838–1839, 2. Katherine Elizabeth Sophia 1842–1911, 3. Margaret Susan 1843–1875, 4. Lucy Caroline 1846–? Known as Joe. CD's 1st cousin. Senior partner Josiah Wedgwood & Sons Ltd 1841–1844. Leith Hill Place, Surrey. 1880 CD to Hensleigh W, condoling on his death, 'there never existed a man with a sweeter disposition'—Carroll 573.

Wedgwood, Julia *see* Frances Julia W.

Wedgwood, Katherine Elizabeth Sophia 1842–1911. 2c of

Josiah W [III]. unm. Known as Sophy. CD's 1st cousin once removed.

Wedgwood, Katherine Euphemia 1839–? 4c of Hensleigh W. m 1873 *Sir* Thomas Farrer, *Baron* Farrer, as 2nd wife. Known as Effie or E. CD's 1st cousin once removed. 1870 Spring, W stayed at Down House.

Wedgwood, Kitty *see* Catherine W.

Wedgwood, Lawrence 1844–1913. 5c of Francis W. m 1871 Emma Houseman and had offspring. CD's 1st cousin once removed.

Wedgwood, Lotty *see* Charlotte W.

Wedgwood, Louisa Frances 1834–1903. 1c of Henry Allen W. m 1864 William John Kempson. CD's 1st cousin once removed.

Wedgwood, Louisa Jane *see* Allen.

Wedgwood, Lucy Caroline 1846–? 4c of Josiah W [III] m 1874 Matthew James Harrison. CD's 1st cousin once removed.

Wedgwood, Mabel Frances 1857–? 7c of Francis W. m 1880 Arthur Parson. CD's 1st cousin once removed.

Wedgwood, Margaret Rosina *see* Ingall.

Wedgwood, Margaret Susan 1843–? 3c of Josiah W [III]. m 1869 Arthur Charles Vaughan Williams. CD's 1st cousin once removed. Mother of Ralph Vaughan Williams, 1877–1968, musician. 1885 W gave ED her dog Dicky.

Wedgwood, Mary [I] *see* Halsey.

Wedgwood, Mary [II] *see* Hawkshaw.

Wedgwood, Mary [III] *see* Webster.

Wedgwood, Mary Ann 1796–1798. 3c of Josiah W [II]. CD's 1st cousin.

Wedgwood, Mary Euphrazia Only c of Godfrey W & Hope Elizabeth W. CD's 1st cousin twice removed.

Wedgwood, Richard 1767–1768. 3c of Josiah W [I]. CD's uncle.

Wedgwood, Robert 1806–1880. 7c of John W. m1 1834 Frances Crewe s.p. m2 Mary Halsey and had issue. CD's 1st cousin once removed.

Wedgwood, Rowland 1847–? 6c of Henry Allen W. m1 Sophia Helen Rudd. m2 Agnes Harley. CD's 1st cousin once removed.

Wedgwood, Sally *see* Sarah Elizabeth W [III].

Wedgwood, Sarah 1734–1815. m 1764 Josiah W [I] (a cousin). CD's maternal grandmother. ED's paternal grandmother. The only grandparent alive in their lifetimes.

Wedgwood, Sarah Elizabeth [I] 1778–1856 Nov.6. 7c of
Josiah W [I]. unm. Known as Sarah. CD's aunt. 1823, on death
of her sister Catherine, W moved from Parkfields to Camp
Hill on Maer Heath. 1847 W moved to Petleys, Downe, and
died at Down House. W was popular with CD's children and
at Down House almost every day.

Wedgwood, Sarah Elizabeth [II] 1793–1880 Nov.7. 1c of
Josiah W [II]. unm. Known as Elizabeth or Bessy; often called
Miss Wedgwood, as eldest unmarried daughter. CD's 1st
cousin. c1847 W moved from Staffordshire and built The
Ridge, Hartfield, on borders of Ashdown forest and near the
Langtons. Earlier in her life she had built a school on Caldy
Island, nr Tenby and she also built one at Hartfield. 1868 W
moved to Trowmer Lodge, Downe. 1860 CD to Lyell, 'I
showed the case [of orchids] to Elizabeth Wedgwood, and her
remark was 'Now you have upset your own book, for you
won't persuade me that this could be effected by Natural
Selection'—MLi 156. 'The last twelve years of her life, happy
with her garden, her little dog Tony, her devoted servants'—EDii 106. 1880 CD to Romanes, 'As good and generous a woman as ever walked this earth'—*Life of Romanes* 101. 'I
think none of us felt quite at ease with our aunt'. Description of
this awesome woman—EDii 105.

Wedgwood, Sarah Elizabeth [III] 1795–1857. 1c of John W.
unm. Known as Sally in youth, Eliza later. CD's 1st cousin
once removed.

Wedgwood, Snow *see* Frances Julia W.

Wedgwood, Sophia Helena *see* Rudd.

Wedgwood, Sophiah Marianne 1838–1839. 1c of Josiah W
[III]. CD's 1st cousin once removed.

Wedgwood, Susannah 1765 Jan.3–1817 Jul.15. 1c of Josiah W
[I]. m 1796 Apr.18 Robert Waring Darwin. Known as Sukey.
CD's mother, ED's aunt. 'My mother died in July 1817, when
I was a little over eight years old, and it is odd that I can hardly
remember anything about her except her deathbed, her black
velvet gown, and her curiously constructed work-table'—LLi
27. 1807 W to her brother Josiah W [II], 'Everyone seems
young but me'. 'She seems never to have been very
strong'—Meteyard 357. W buried St Chad, Montford, Shropshire, in chancel; called Susan on husband's tombstone.

Wedgwood, Thomas [I] ?–1739. Potter. W had 13 children of
which Josiah W [I] was the last. CD's maternal great-

grandfather. Although there were many W potters before T.W., he was amongst the best of them.

Wedgwood, Thomas [II] 1771–1805. 5c of Josiah [I]. unm. CD's uncle. W was an invalid. Has been described as the first photographer. EB—'To England belongs the honour of first producing a photograph'. *see* T.W., An account of the method of copying paintings upon glass and of making profiles by the agency of light upon nitrate of silver, with observations by H. Davy, *J.Roy.Instn.*, Jun., 1807.

Wedgwood, Thomas Josiah 1797–1862. 3c of John W. m 1836 Anne Tyler d.s.p. Known as Tom. CD's 1st cousin. Colonel in Scots Fusiliers. W fought as an Ensign at Waterloo—EDi 68. St Mary's nr Tenby.

Wedgwood, Tom *see* Thomas Josiah W.

Weir, John Jenner 1822–1894. Naturalist & accountant. Controller General H.M. Customs. 1868 Sep.12 Sat. W stayed at Down House, with Wallace and *Mrs* W, and Blyth; Bates was hoped for but probably not; Hookers came for Sunday lunch; 'A very good man'—MLi 309. 1868 CD to W, 'I read over your last ten (!) letters this morning, and made an index of their contents for easy reference; and what a mine of wealth you have bestowed on me' [the letters on selection especially in caterpillars]—MLii 71. 1875 CD to Weismann, on W's work on selection in caterpillars—MLi 357.

Weismann, Friedrich Leopold August 1834–1914. Entomologist & student of inheritance. Prof. Zoology Freiburg. 1868 CD to on selection—MLi 357. 1872 CD to W, W was having trouble with his eyes, 'eyesight is somewhat better'—MLii 95. CD to W, having read *Über der Einfluss der Isolirung auf der Artbildung*, Leipzig 1872—LLiii 155. 1879 W sent CD his work on *Daphnia*, CD thanks for and refers to Meldola's slow progress of translation of *Studien*—N&R 83. ?1881 CD to W, praising *Studien*, 'excited my interest and admiration in the highest degree'—LLiii 231. 1875–1876 *Studien zur Descendenz-Theorie*, Leipzig; translated by R. Meldola as *Studies in the theory of descent*, London 1882, with prefatory notice by CD v–vi (F1414). 1868 *Ueber die Berechtigung der Darwin'schen Theorie*. Leipzig.

Wells 1852 Bucket ropes for wells, *Gdnr's Chronicle*, No.2:22 (Bi 252, F1680), giving the depth of the Down House well as 325 ft. The subject of deep wells, *Gdnr's Chronicle*, No.30:518 (Bi 274, F1696).

Wells, Leonard Henry ?–1903. W drew pictures of fowls for CD through Tegetmeier—de Beer, *Introduction* vii to facsimile of *Questions about the breeding of animals*, 1968.

Wells, William Charles 1757–1817. Physician & scientist. FRS 1793. Born Charleston, S. Carolina, settled in London 1785. Author of *Two essays*, 1818, a posthumous work which contains reprints of his two previously published and fundamental papers on dew and on binocular vision, with an appendix about a black and white woman, Harriet Trets, which contains the rudiments of the idea of natural selection. There is an excellent summary by Thomas Thomson, *Ann.Philosophy*, 1:383, May 1813, of the paper as read to the Royal Society, Apr.1 & 8, 1813. The matter is referred to in historical sketch in 3rd edition *Origin*, 1861. 1865 CD to Hooker, 'a Yankee has called my attention to a paper attached to Dr. Wells' famous "Essay on Dew", which was read in 1813 to the Royal Soc., but not [then] printed, in which he applies most distinctly the principle of Natural Selection to the Races of Man. So poor old Patrick Matthew is not the first'. *see* K. W. Wells, *Isis*, 64:215–225, 1973.

Welsh, Jane Baillie 1801–1826. m 1826 Thomas Carlyle. CD met the Carlyles on several occasions in London. 1838 CD to ED, 'I cannot think that Jenny is either quite natural or quite lady-like'—MLii 13. DNB.

Werner, Abraham Gottlob 1749–1817. German geologist. Proponent of the neptunian theory that all rocks were deposited as precipitation from water.

Wernerian Natural History Society Edinburgh. 1808–1839. The Society was active during CD's time at Edinburgh University and published *Memoirs*, Vols I–VIII, 1811–[1839]. CD does not seem to have been a member.

West Hackhurst House at Abinger, Surrey. 1879 Jul. CD & ED were lent the house from Saturday to Tuesday.

West, Lady [Mary Catherine] 2d of 5th *Earl* de la Warr. m1 2nd *Marquis* of Salisbury . m2 1870 15th *Earl* of Derby. Holwood House, nr Downe. Her son by 1st marriage, R. A. T. G. Cecil, m 1857 Georgiana Alderson. ?1874 CD to W, cautioning about spiritualism—MLii 443. 1882 Jul. W called on ED at Down House from London and straight back again—EDii 260

Westcroft A house in Kent which CD considered buying before he saw Down House—MLi 33.

Westwood, John Obadiah 1805–1893. Solicitor & entomolog-

ist. 1st Hope Prof. Zoology (Entomology) Oxford
1861–1891. 1855 CD proposed W for Royal Medal of Royal
Society—N&R 65. 1860 W's anti-evolutionary views discussed—LLii 267. W 'proposed to the last University Commission the permanent endowment of a lecturer to combat the
errors of Darwinism'—*Darwin and the 'Origin'* 15. *DNB*.

Whale–Bear Story Occurs in its full form at p.184 of 1st edition
of *Origin* 1859; also in 1st 4 USA printings 1860, and in J.
Lamont, *Seasons with the sea-horses* 1861. 'In North America the
black bear was seen by Hearne swimming for hours with
widely open mouth, thus catching, like a whale, insects in the
water. Even in so extreme a case as this, if the supply of insects
were constant, but if better adapted competitors did not
already exist in the country, I can see no difficulty in a race of
bears being rendered, by natural selection, more and more
aquatic in their structure and habits, with larger and larger
mouths, till a creature was produced as monstrous as a whale'.
The reference is to Samuel Hearne, *A journey from Prince of
Wales Fort in Hudson's Bay, to the Northern Ocean . . . 1769–72*,
London 1795. 1860 edition reads '. . . swimming for hours
with widely open mouth, thus catching, almost like a whale,
insects in the water.' The rest is omitted. 1881 CD to R. G.
Whiteman, 'This sentence was omitted in the subsequent editions, owing to the advice of Prof. Owen, as it was liable to be
misinterpreted; but I have always regretted that I followed this
advice, for I still think the view quite reasonable'—MLi 393.
1860 CD to W. H. Harvey, 'As it offended persons, I struck it
out in the second edition; but I still maintain that there is no
special difficulty in a bear's mouth being enlarged to any
degree useful to its changing habits'—MLi 162.

Wharton, Mr Headmaster of William Erasmus D's preparatory
school. 1852 CD to W.E.D., telling him to write to W—EDii
145.

Wharton, Mary Dorothea d of Rt Hon. J. Lloyd Wharton. m
1894 *Colonel* Charles Waring Darwin.

Whewell, William 1794–1866. Astronomer & philosopher.
FRS 1820. Master of Trinity College Cambridge 1841–1866.
1860 W to CD, 'I cannot, yet at least, become a convert. But
there is so much of thought and of fact in what you have
written that it is not to be contradicted without careful selection of the ground and manner of the dissent'. W refused, for
some years, to allow a copy of the *Origin* into the Library of

Trinity College—LLii 261. DNB.

Whitby, Mrs Breeder of silkworms. 1846 Sep. CD met W at meeting of British Association, Southampton.

White, Adam 1817–1879. Assistant in the Zoology Department of British Museum 1835–1863. Copious writer on natural history topics, including popular books. 1854 W applied for Chair of Natural History Edinburgh with printed testimonials, one by CD, but withdrew them on hearing that E. Forbes had applied. 1863 W retired from British Museum with mental illness. 1864 W reprinted testimonials, including CD's, with additions, to obtain paid lecturing in Edinburgh, his native town to which he had retired. 1859 R. Trimen's reminiscences to Poulton, 'I was at work in the next compartment to that in which Adam White sat, and heard someone come in and a cheery mellow voice say "Good-morning Mr. White;—I am afraid you won't speak to me any more". . . Ah, Sir! if ye had only stopped with the *Voyage of the Beagle!'*—Poulton, *Darwin and the Origin*, 214. 1877 CD to Günther, 'that poor mad creature'—FUL 96.

Whitehead, Mr The first tenant of Down House after ED's death, leasing it 1900–1906. W owned the first motor car in Downe. 'Shadowy figure'—Atkins 102.

Whiteman, R. G. 1881 CD to W, explaining why he omitted the whale-bear story from 2nd and subsequent editions of *Origin*—MLi 392.

Whitley, Rev. Charles 1808–1895. Cousin of J. M. Herbert. Vicar of Bedlington, Northumberland. Reader in Natural Philosophy Durham. Hon.Canon of Durham. Intimate friend of CD at Cambridge and had been at Shrewsbury School. Member of Gourmet Club. 1838 W invited CD to Durham—N&R 85.

Whymper, Edward 1840–1911. Artist & alpinist. 1886 W made wood engraving of Boehm statue of CD, fpce of *Rep.Darwin Memorial Fund*, 1888.

Wibury Wiltshire. A house taken by Charles Langton, 1865.

Wickham, John Clements 1798–1864. Naval Officer. W was on all three voyages of *Beagle*. 1st Lieutenant on 2nd voyage. Captain commanding on 3rd voyage. W was first Government Resident at Moreton Bay (now Brisbane), Queensland 1853–1860. CD got on better with W than with any other officer. 1832 'Wickham is a glorious fine fellow'. 1834 'Although Wickham always was growling at my bringing more dirt on board than any ten men, he is a great loss to me in the *Beagle*. He is by far the most conversible being on board'—Barlow, *CD and the voyage of the Beagle*, 59, 103.

Wickstead, Charles *see* Tollet.

Wien 1856 There is a tradition that CD once asked Hooker where 'this place Wien is, where they publish so many books'; it is substantiated by CD to Hooker, 'to write to "Wien" (that unknown place)'—MLi 93.

Wiesner, Julius 1838–1916. Prof. Botany Vienna 1873–1916. 1881 CD to W, about movement in plants and thanking him for sending *Das Bewegungsvermögen der Pflanzen*, Vienna 1881—LLiii 335.

Wilberforce, Rev. Samuel 1805–1873. 3rd s of William Wilberforce. Known as Soapy Sam from his habit of 'washing his hands', whilst preaching or talking. Bishop of Oxford 1845–1869, Winchester 1869–1873. FRS 1845. 1860 Jun.30 Sat. W spoke anti-*Origin* at British Association meeting Oxford. 1860 Jul. W reviewed *Origin* in *Quart.Rev.*, primed by Owen. Jul.20 CD to Huxley, 'I would give five shillings to know what tremendous blunder the Bishop made; for I see that a page has been cancelled and a new page gummed in' [pp.251–252]—MLi 156. W of *Origin*, 'the most unphilosophical work he ever read'—LLii 285; another version 'the most illogical book ever written'—Lyell, *Life* ii, 358. 1860 CD to Innes, 'Did you see the Quarterly Review, the B. of Oxford made really splendid fun of me and my grandfather'—Darwin-Innes 207. 1874 *Essays contributed to the Quarterly Review*, 2 vols, London, review of *Origin*, i, 23–85. DNB.

Wilkes, Lieut. Charles 1798–1877. USA Naval Officer. 1836 W was in London fitting out US Exploration Expedition of 1838–1842; CD called on W—Carroll 6.

Wilkinson, Rev. Henry Marlow 1828–?1906. W examined *Utricularia* for CD for *Insectivorous plants*.

Williams 1839 a gardener, employed by CD at 12 Upper Gower St, mentioned in CD's personal mss accounts.

Williams A spiritualist medium. 1877 CD to Romanes, 'a very clever rogue'—Carroll 513, 514. 1878 CD to Romanes, about W's exposure in *Spiritualist Newspaper*, 13, Sep.2.—Carroll 548.

Williams, Arthur Charles Vaughan 1835–1875. m 1869 Margaret Susan Wedgwood. Father of Ralph Vaughan W, 1872–1958, musician.

Williams, Henry 1792–1867. Missionary in New Zealand, formerly a Naval Officer. W arrived at Waimate, Bay of Islands, N. Island in 1822. 1835 Dec. CD stayed at his house, 'He is considered the leading person among the missionary body'—*S.Afr.Christian Recorder*, 231, *J.Researches*, 1845, 426. DNB.

Williams, Margaret Susan *see* Wedgwood.

Willis, Olive Margaret 1877–1964. Founder & Headmistress of Downe House School, which was at Down House 1907–1922; at Cold Ash, Newbury, Berks 1922– . *see* Anne Ridler, *Olive Willis and Downe House*, London 1967.

Willis, Robert 1800–1875. Engineer & historian. FRS 1830. Prof. Mechanism Cambridge, 1837–1875.

Wills, William Petty Officer Armourer on 2nd voyage of *Beagle*, on *Adventure* on 1st voyage.

Wilmot, Rev. Darwin 1845–1935. W's mother was 2nd d of *Sir* Francis Sacheveral D, CD's half 2nd cousin. W was Headmaster of Macclesfield Grammar School. 1930 W had Erasmus D's [I] commonplace book which he lent to Hesketh Pearson for *Doctor Darwin*, 225, 1930. It is now at Down House.

Wilson A missionary in Tahiti for more than 30 years, except for a short period when the missionaries had to flee to New South Wales. W arrived on mission ship *Duff* in 1797. 1835 Nov. CD met at Matavi.

Wilson, Alexander Stephen 1827–1893. Agricultural botanist of Edinburgh. 1878–1880 CD to W, on races of Russian wheat—MLii 419.

Wilson, Edmund Beecher 1856–1939. Cytologist. Prof. Zoology Columbia 1909–1928. 1881 CD to W, thanking him for information of *Scyllaea*, a nudibranch mollusc found on *Sargassum* which it closely mimics. W to Poulton, 'His extraordinary kindness and friendliness towards an obscure youngster who had of course absolutely no claim on his time or attention'—Poulton, *Darwin and the Origin*, 107–108.

Wilson, Edward 1814–1878. Australian politician. W first went to Australia in 1842; later of Hayes Place, Kent. 1873 'Owing to the great kindness and powerful influence of Mr Wilson . . . I have received from Australia no less than thirteen sets of answers to my queries'. This refers to CD's leaflet *Queries about expression*, 1867. These included one from Dyson Lacy in Queensland, who was a relative of W—*Expression* 19. DNB.

Winchester Hampshire. 1846 Sep.13 CD & ED visited and St

Cross on day trip from British Association meeting at Southampton.

Winmarleigh, Baron *see* Patten.

Winkworth, Emily m 1851 William Shaen.

Winter-flowering plants 1869 Fertilisation of winter-
flowering plants, *Nature*, Lond., 1:85 (Bii 160).

Wiseman, Lady Catherine *see* Mackintosh.

Wiseman, Sir William 1st husband of Catherine Mackintosh.

Wollaston, Thomas Vernon 1822–1878. Naturalist. W wintered in Madeira and other Atlantic islands, due to ill–health,
and was a specialist in their invertebrate fauna, especially
beetles. 1855 CD to Hooker, 'Wollaston's "Insecta Maderen-
sia": it is an *admirable* work'—LLii 44. 1860 W wrote hostile
review of *Origin* in *Ann.Mag.nat.Hist.*, 5:132. 1868 CD to
Stainton, 'I have been sincerely grieved to hear about poor
Wollaston's affairs, in which, I am told, you have taken so kind
an interest'—N&R 57. DNB.

Wood, Searles Valentine 1798–1880. Palaeontologist &
banker. 1860 W was pro-*Origin*—LLii 293. DNB.

Wood, T. W. 1870 W drew figs 9, 10 & 14, of cats and a snarling
dog for *Expression*, 1872. 1870 CD to A. D. Bartlett, CD knew
W personally in London and asks Bartlett to give him facilities
at Zoological Gardens—MLii 101.

Wood, Sir William Page, Baron Hatherley 1801–1881. Barrister. 1st *Baron* 1868 KT 1852. Fellow of Trinity Cambridge
1824–1879. Judge, Lord Chancellor 1868–1877. 1831 CD to
Henslow 'Captain Fitzroy (probably owing to Wood's letter)
seems determined to make me [as] comfortable as he possibly
can'—LLi 203. 1831 CD to Susan D, 'Wood (as might be
expected from a Londonderry) solemnly warned Fitz-Roy
that I was a whig'—LLi 208. 1832 'Wood and I had intended
writing by the Decr packet'—Darwin-Henslow 65. 1831 CD
to Henslow, 'If you see Mr Wood remember me very kindly
to him'—LLi 204. DNB.

Woodhouse Shropshire. Home of W. M. Owen and his children. CD was often there for shooting and social occasions,
both before *Beagle* voyage and on his return.

Woodward, Samuel Pickworth 1821–1865. Malacologist.
Assistant Department of Geology & Mineralogy British
Museum 1848–1865. 1856 Jun. CD to W, had read his *Manual
of the Mollusca*, 1851–1856, with 'much solid instruction &
interest'. CD hoped to see him in London in about a fort-

night—Carroll 129. 1856 Jun. CD to Lyell and to Hooker, on W's views on extended continents—LLii 72–74. 1856 Jul. CD to W, on species—MLi 96. 1860 CD to W, on volcanoes—FUL 112. DNB.

Woodyeare, John Fountain (né Fountain) 1809–1880. Cambridge friend of CD. Domestic Chaplain to Dowager *Countess* of Cavan 1851–1880.

Wonder Coach from London to Shrewsbury. 1835 CD to Susan D mentions it—LLi 261.

Woollya Settlement at Tierra del Fuego. 1833 Jan.27 R. Matthews, missionary, landed there from *Beagle*; Feb.6 M taken off again.

Woolner, Thomas 1825–1892. Sculptor. 1868 CD sat to W for bust which was finished in 1869; now in Botany School Cambridge. 'It has a certain air of pomposity, which seems to me foreign to my father's expression'—Francis D LLiii 106. Carroll 194, says that the Wedgwood relief in CD's set at Christ's College Cambridge is by W; another copy, which C illustrates, is at American Philosophical Society, Philadelphia. 1871 CD to W, 'One reviewer ("Nature") says that they ought to be called, as I suggested in joke, *Angulus Woolnerianus*'—LLiii 140. *Nature,* Lond., Apr. has Angulus Woolnerii. W had discovered this small cartilaginous lobe in the human pinna, which is more usually called Darwin's peak; it is referred to in *Descent* i 22, with woodcut. 1877 May, W visited Down House. 1882 W was on 'Personal Friends invited' list for CD's funeral. DNB.

Working Men's College London, later Birkbeck College. R. B. Litchfield was one of the founders. 1873 Henrietta Litchfield—'Several times after my marriage, my father and mother invited the party to Down. The first time was in the summer of 1873 . . . often as many as sixty or seventy'—EDii 213.

Worms 1869 The formation of mould by worms, *Gdnr's Chronicle*, No.20:530 (Bii 137, F1745). 1880 CD to H. Johnson, 'My heart & soul care for worms & nothing else in the world just at present'—N&R 74. 'Darwin had none but kindly feelings for worms'—L. Stephen, *Biography of Swift see also Vegetable mould and worms*.

Wormstone The original stone was used by CD to measure the movement of soil due to earthworms. The stone now at Down House was reconstructed by the Cambridge Instrument Company, Horace D's firm, in 1929—Atkins 118.

Worthing Sussex. 1879 May 6–7 CD visited to see Anthony Rich. 1881 Aug. 8–10 the same.

Wray, Leonard Hume 1816–1901. Fruit grower. CD corresponded with on trimorphic flowers of strawberries.

Wright, Chauncey 1830–1875. Computor in National Almanac Office, Cambridge, Mass. c1860 CD corresponded with on phyllotaxy after he had read W's papers in *Astronomical J.*, No. 99, 1856 and *Math.Monthly*, 1859—LLiii 52. 1871 W reviewed Mivart's *The genesis of species* in *N.Amer.Rev.*, Jul. Oct.23, CD arranged to have it published as a pamphlet, with additions, *Darwinism: being an examination of Mr St George Mivart's Genesis of species*, London. 1871 Sep. CD to Hooker, describes W's review as 'a very clever, but ill-written review'—MLi 332. 1872 W wrote in *N.Amer.Rev.* in reply to an article by Mivart in *ibid.*, Apr. 1872 Sep. W stayed at Down House. W to Sarah Sedgwick, 'I was never so worked up in my life, and did not sleep many hours under the hospitable roof'—LLiii 165, also in *Letters of Chauncey Wright,* 246–248.

Wrigley, Alfred 1818–1898. Headmaster of Clapham Grammar School after C. Pritchard, 1861–1882. Leonard & Horace D were educated by W.

Wychfield Huntingdon Rd, Cambridge. Home of *Sir* Francis D.

Wyman, Jeffries 1814–1874. American palaeontologist. Hervey Prof. Anatomy Harvard. W was a friend of Asa Gray. 1860 CD to Lyell, W had written to CD about brains of rodents—MLi 169.

Wymonsold, Frances m in 17c William Alvey. CD's ancestor in 6th generation.

Wynne, Mr Before 1839 CD addressed some questions on animal breeding to W. A rough copy in CD's hand was transcribed by P. H. Barrett in H. E. Gruber, *Darwin on man*, 423–426, 1974 (F265). W was a friend of CD's father and bred Malay fowl, otherwise not traced.

Wyon, Allan 1843–1907. Sculptor and medallist. Chief engraver of H.M. seals. 1882 W made bronze medallion of CD. Royal Society Darwin Medal was reduced from this. An electrotype from original wax is at British Museum (Natural History).

XYZ

X Club A small scientific dining club in London. Founded 1864 and met regularly until 1892, then sporadically until 1911 on Hooker's death; last surviving member was Lubbock, died 1913. Members were Busk, Hooker, Spencer, E. Frankland, Huxley, Spottiswoode, T. A. Hirst & Lubbock. All, except Spencer, were FRS and they dined before RS meetings, discussing its business affairs. CD was not a member and appears never to have dined with them, but he was on intimate terms with several. *see* J. V. Jensen, *Brit.J.Hist.Sci.*, 5:63–72, 1970.

Yahgan Indian tribe of eastern Tierra del Fuego, to which the four Indians taken to England by Fitz-Roy on 1st voyage of *Beagle* belonged. Full name Yahgashagalumoala (the people from the mountain channel), shortened by T. Bridges.

Yarrell, William 1784–1856. London stationer & naturalist. 1831 CD to Susan D, Y had helped with buying equipment for *Beagle* voyage. 'But one friend is quite invaluable . . . he goes to the shops with me and bullies about prices'—LLi 208.

Yiddish First edition in : *Descent of man* (F1138), 1921.

York Minster Fuegian man, taken to England by Fitz-Roy on 1st voyage of *Beagle*; returned on 2nd voyage. Named after an islet near Cape Horn Island. Name in Alikhoolip language Elleparu. Y was aged c26 in 1830; he was killed in a quarrel before 1872.

York Place No.27, Baker St, London. 1855 CD rented this house for Jan. & Feb.; returned to Down House Feb.15—MLii 205, 207.

Young, George 1819–1907. Lord Advocate of Scotland. Judge of the Court of Session, with title *Lord* Young, 1874–1905. 1875 Y lunched at Down House—Darwin-Innes 242. DNB.

Z *see* **Edward Blyth.**

Zacharias, Emil Otto 1846–1916. German freshwater biologist of Geestemünde. 1877 CD to Z, had sent him a pig's foot with an extra digit, which W. H. Flower examined—Carroll 511, 512. 1877 CD to Z, on the development of his belief in evolution, 'When I was on board the *Beagle* I believed in the permanence of species'—MLi 367. 1876 *Zur Entwicklungstheorie,* Jena. 1882 *Charles R. Darwin und die Culturhistorische Bedeutung seiner Theorie vom Ursprung der Arten,* Berlin.

Zeeuwsch Genootschap der Wetenschappen te Middleburg CD Foreign Member 1877.

Zoological Society of London Regent's Park, founded 1826. CD Corresponding Member 1831, Fellow 1839. 1882 Apr. CD to W. Van Dyck, 'the Zoological Society which is much addicted to mere systematic work'—LLiii 253.

Zoology of the Beagle 1838–1843 *The zoology of the voyage of H.M.S. Beagle, under the command of Captain Fitzroy, during the years 1832 to 1836,* edited and with notes by CD; 19 numbers making up 5 parts. Part I, *Fossil Mammalia,* 4 numbers 1838–1840, by Richard Owen. Part II, *Mammalia,* 4 numbers 1838–1839, by G. R. Waterhouse. Part III, *Birds,* 4 numbers 1838–1841, by John Gould [& G. R. Gray]. Part IV, *Fish,* 4 numbers 1840–1842, by Leonard Jenyns. Part V, *Reptiles* [and Amphibia], 2 numbers 1842–1843, by Thomas Bell. (F8–9). Facsimile Part V only (F9a) 1975.

Zoophilus *see* Edward Blyth.